# FORM-ING WEL-FARE

Ed.
Katrine Lotz
Deane Simpson
Kirsten Marie Raahauge
Kjeld Vindum
Mette Jerl Jensen
Jannie Rosenberg Bendsen

# FORMING WELFARE

The Danish Architectural Press

# Contents

Katrine Lotz

# Introduction

Since 2008, two issues have increasingly attracted the interest of a wide range of architects, designers, urban planners and architectural historians in Northern Europe. One of these is the basic question of how architecture, design and urban planning contribute toward positive developments in society. The other concerns the part that these same disciplines have played historically in the implementation and transformation of the Danish welfare state.

There are many reasons for this upsurge in interest. It is a well-known fact that there is a need for efficient, stable and, above all, safe social structures in many places around the world. This has brought the North European welfare models into focus, as these are apparently able to sustain relatively strong economies while responding and adapting to changes in the economic and demographic patterns. The American political scientist Francis Fukuyama has analysed these needs and summarized them with the term 'Getting to Denmark'.[1] It is therefore reasonable to assume that the long haul against poverty, sickness, unemployment, illiteracy and housing shortage which China, India and Africa are faced with may be inspired by the Scandinavian models and welfare systems. It is equally obvious, however, that there are plenty of challenges to the European welfare states: ageing populations, heavy demands on welfare benefits, massive healthcare expenditures, growing social inequality and a political climate that is not conducive to major reforms, to name just a few. There are thus several good reasons why we need to take a closer look at both the background for the welfare state and its current challenges, as indeed done by a growing number of political scientists, economists, sociologists and historians, and in recent years by architects and architectural researchers as well.

In the welfare state's heyday, lasting from the mid-1950s to the late 1970s, most of Northern Europe experienced a construction boom, during which more square metres were built than in all the preceding centuries combined, and the bulk of these are still standing. Given the present resource and climate crisis, there is reason to believe that reuse and transformation of existing buildings in the future will account for an increasing part of the construction activity. However, to be able to assess and optimize the existing, one

must prove its value in relation to future requirements and suggest a possible course of action. Moreover, it is important not just to focus on the building's architectural qualities and potentials, but also to consider its architecture and spatial layout with reference to its original context and its present communal and societal applications.
As architects and designers, we are often asked what values our work contributes to the processes it forms part of, and what are the tangible effects of architecture and design?[2] It is therefore hardly surprising that there is a growing interest in reconnecting with our profession's social origins. This is not a question of reverting to the role of a socio-engineer, or of dispensing with the artistic dimension, but rather a wish to evaluate and explore the existing interrelations between architecture, society and architects. The resulting debate, which involves both the architectural organizations, the educational institutions and the research community, reaches beyond matters of economy, competition from other professions or time-consuming control measures that do nothing to further the quality of the product. Instead, it focuses on the important question of how architecture, planning and design can help solving social problems. What part does architecture and spatiality play in the development of concrete welfare systems? How can we investigate and conceive architecture so that the tangible effects and contributions to a better everyday life for the many remain an articulate part of both the works and their underlying basis?
The first thing that strikes anyone who takes an interest in the linkage between the rise of the welfare state and the architecture of the day, is that the subject has been more or less absent from the past 25 years' debate on and research into the Danish welfare model and, furthermore, that architectural history has little to say about architecture's association with the state that – whether directly or indirectly, through lending or other forms of financing – acted as the main client during the entire second half of the 20th century. Architecture and welfare state are two separate domains, to be sure, but they are based on the same fundamental idea of a good life for the individual as well as the community. Therefore, it seems natural to look for a correlation between the considerable success that architecture and architects enjoyed throughout most of the 20th century, on the one hand, and the forming and rapid expansion of the democratic European welfare states, on the other. Had architecture and physical planning played no part in the development of the welfare state, it might have been justifiable to trivialize them in our historiography but, in fact, construction of all kinds of housing, institutions, cities and landscapes took place on an unprecedented scale. The quality of much of this has been disputed, but the housing shortage that had been a pressing problem since the end of the Second World War was solved, and a number of projects, among them many institutions, were of a high architectural standard. In addition to this, huge investments were made in energy- and transport infrastructure, making the lack of interest and research into this issue even more extraordinary.
Those analyses and descriptions of the welfare state that are rooted in economic and social science do not devote much space to architecture, design or spatial planning. The five-volume encyclopedia on the development of the Danish welfare model does not specify either the green plan from 1936, the Finger Plan from 1947, the regional development laws from 1958 or the 1960s' national planning framework even though their influence on housing, city and landscape policies, as we know them, cannot be overrated. However, a precursor of the 2004-work does include a single chapter on housing.[3] Here, Erik Ib Schmidt,

author of several important debate books on the welfare state, actually claims that 'Neither village society, industrial society nor urban society, neither "service society", "information society" nor "nanny state", or whatever we call it, is the result of pre-planning and subsequent efforts to implement the plans. The same goes for cities and suburbs […].'[4]

Architecture's public dimension has, to varying degrees, been part of the Danish architectural discourse since the mid-1800s, but when it comes to the interrelation between architecture and the development of the Danish welfare model, architects and architectural theorists have been remarkably uncommunicative. A few remarks have found their way into the literature, though. One of these appears in the anthology *Arkitekturens Praksis* where the theorist Jørgen Sestoft observes that 'The governmental bodies of the Western "welfare societies" […] are probably the most accommodating client group that architects have collaborated with in recent years."[5] He furthermore writes that '[…] the official "welfare society" has assumed some of the same cultural obligations as the historic patronages, thereby providing architects with extraordinary work opportunities in the form of publicly-funded, but privately designed and realized institutions for education and social welfare, administration, technology etc.'[6] In his preface to the 1993-edition of *Nordic Architecture*, the architect Nils-Ole Lund says that 'In Scandinavia, international modernism was translated into a pragmatic, socially aware architecture, which was also nuanced and "humane" in its formal expression. One can speak of an architecture for the welfare state.'[7] Other prominent architectural voices such as Kay Fisker, Tobias Faber and Poul Erik Skriver do not seem to have given the subject much thought either. Not even the large three-volume work on Danish planning from 1830 to 2015 offers a systematic appraisal of the rise of the welfare state.[8]

However, a more systematic, and specifically architectural, perspective was offered by the now-defunct journal *Arkitektur DK*, the last two issues of which were devoted to an affectionate and critical reappraisal of the journal's entire back catalogue from 1956 to 2012. But Jesper Pagh, who edited the two volumes, did not find any manifest indications that the architects of the day were guided by a deliberate attitude towards the welfare state either.[9]

When it comes to the more recent debate, the majority of architects and architecture's responses to social challenges have fallen into two discourses, more or less: on the one hand, represented by the conceptual architecture of the pragmatic turn from the 1990s and 2000s, whose narratives chiefly rely on the functional programme, and whose overriding ideas and communication thereof often seem to preclude a more elaborate and distinctive interaction with the surroundings. On the other, phenomenologically inspired discourses that possess a certain force of expression, but often appear overly empathic and esoteric to those who participate in the development of architecture and, moreover, rarely contribute with overriding analyses, critique or reflections on the relations with architecture's fundamental conditions and the necessary interdisciplinarity. As Jesper Pagh writes in his article 'From the Common Good to the Common Market?', you can say that as long as architectural theory exclusively understands and reads architecture as motifs and metaphors – and thus focuses on image formations rather that what the aggregate architecture contributes to the lived life – we will never learn anything new about the interrelation between architecture and society.

## The anthology

The starting point for the original working group 'Forming Welfare', which was set up 2010-11 at the Royal Danish Academy of Fine Arts, School of Architecture,[10] was a wish to qualify the interplay between design, architecture and planning, on the one hand, and the historic and current development of the open and equal welfare societies in Denmark and the rest of Scandinavia, on the other. Similar studies have been made in other North European countries, most notably with the anthology *Architecture and the Welfare State*, published in 2015.[11] Here one can learn about the general relationship between the development of the various European welfare models and, more specifically, about the part that architecture and planning have played, as exemplified by a number of cases. The anthology *Swedish Modernism: Architecture, Consumption and the Welfare State* from 2010 has a similar aim.[12]

In 2013, the conference 'Forming Welfare' took place at the School of Architecture, and two years later the research journal *Nordic* published a special issue with the same title, both of which featured contributions from the same circle of writers as the present anthology.[13] In 2016, the research project 'Spaces of Danish Welfare', which originates from the same research community, qualified for support from the Danish Council for Independent Research.

An important purpose with this anthology, other than contributing to the existing debate and research within the field, is to introduce new readers – whether architectural students, students from the humanities or social sciences, architects or other interested parties – to the correlation between the design professions and the core values of the society that is the basis for their practice. The anthology focuses primarily on the Danish scene, with a few digressions to Sweden and Greenland. Its organizational structure does not reflect an ambition to provide a proper historiography or a complete revision of conventional beliefs. Instead it offers a number of keys to the understanding of the relationship between spatial and physical planning, architecture and design, and the way in which space, form and materiality are brought into play whenever social and economic welfare systems are established.

A possible explanation for the lack of interest in the correlation between architecture and the rise of the welfare state is the inconsistency of our individual perceptions. Ever since its emergence immediately before and during the Second World War, 'welfare state' – as a political agenda and concept – has been defined and analysed by a growing number of political scientists, economists, sociologists, and in recent years historians as well. Meanwhile, architecture and design have primarily been defined by architects and art historians, who have focused on the Danish translation of the international Modern Movement's various currents. It is therefore quite challenging to devise analytical models that are able to embrace both of these as well as analyse their interrelations. The obvious risk, here, is to explain one with the other, and thus not explain any of them. The anthology identifies a need for the development of new interdisciplinary analytical tools that, based on a wider knowledge, can articulate how architecture and society actually interrelate

Skolen ved Sundet from 1936 by Kaj Gottlob. The school was originally a school for weak children. With the aula's top lights and large open glass facades, the classrooms got light from both sides. Danmarks Kunstbibliotek, Samlingen af Arkitekturtegninger.

Ø
NØ
N
NV
V
SV
S
SØ

and interact. To dismiss both 'architecture' and 'welfare state' as mere 'constructs' in order to focus on how 'reality' is continually created and negotiated by a wide range of actors is, of course, an option, but that would entail that you had to spurn a lot of studies and concepts that themselves have had, and still have, an effective history. This has therefore not been employed as an analytical strategy.[14]

## The rise of the Danish welfare state

First of all, it is important to distinguish between a number of terms. 'Welfare' is a generic and rather vague term that covers both concrete help to those that need it and notions of 'a good life' for the individual or the community.[15] 'Welfare society' is an idealized notion of the good society that allows every one of its citizens to realize his/her full potential in safety, freedom, relative prosperity and – according to the common understanding also – political freedom. The term 'welfare state' is introduced in the 1950s, first as a political and then an analytical concept, primarily applied to the fields of economy, political science and sociology, which focus on concrete and long-established balances between the state, the civil society and the market, and various modes of economic regulation.[16] Researchers generally agree that the first to carry out a comprehensive analysis was sociologist and demographer Gøsta Esping-Andersen, who identified three different types of welfare states: the liberal state, as in the US and the UK; the conservative state, as in Germany; and the social democratic state, as exemplified by Sweden.[17]

The welfare state's conceptual framework has its origin in the Enlightenment's ideas of a humane society and the European civil revolutions. As the industrialization gathered speed, the great migrations from country to town and the extensive social redistribution lead to widespread poverty among farm labourers and the working class, making it politically imperative to address 'the social issue'.[18] This development was catalyzed by the labour movement's demands for improved conditions, but the welfare systems were essentially developed in consensus with the land and capital owners who recognized the necessity of bridling the market forces in order to avoid a situation where the labour force, in Marx's words, would no longer be able to reproduce itself.[19] Another important purpose was to stem the extensive emigration to the US, South America and Australia.

Welfare historians agree that the old-age pension that was introduced in various forms all over Northern Europe[20] during the 1880s and 1890s, including in Denmark in 1891, was the first step along the path that eventually lead to the rise of the proper welfare state in the 20th century. The first laws about old-age provision were a direct response to the humiliating poverty that was a fact of life for a substantial part of the population, but these early laws did not entail any privileges. The allocation depended on local assessment and was subject to conditions which were often moral in nature. The universal retirement pension, as we know it, was only introduced in 1956.

Building on government-appointed commissions such as the housing commission from 1916 and the population commission from 1935, a range of social reforms were then introduced, with the Liberal Party's 'Minor Social Reform' as a starting point, and thus social benefits gradually became based on principles of justice rather than personal assessment.[21] The Social Democrat K.K. Steincke is known for his untiring efforts to reform and improve throughout the 1910s and 1920s. In 1933, the Social Democratic Party, the Liberal Party and the Social Liberal Party reached a comprehensive and momentous agreement on social policy issues, known as the Kanslergade agreement, which went a step further towards principles of justice and universality. The new social benefits lead to the construction of many new town halls and enlargements of old ones.[22]

The UK, in particular, was hard hit by the Great Depression of the 1930s, and the British government therefore appointed a commission that came up with the report *Social Insurance and Allied Services*, also known as the *Beveridge Report* after its author. Here we find one of the most resilient and conclusive definitions of the purpose of the welfare state, namely to fight society's five 'Giant Evils': 'Want, Disease, Ignorance, Squalor and Idleness.'[23]

The report became an important source of inspiration for the politico-economic foundations laid before, during and after the Second World War. Other influences were the Swedish couple Gunnar and Alva Myrdal's ideas of an active family policy and the British economist John Maynard Keynes' notion of an active fiscal policy where the state would use publicly-financed infrastructure and construction to revive the ailing economy. These ideas strongly affected how the predominantly social democratic governments handled the post-war period's massive increase in population and the resulting demand for all kinds of institutions and housing, and later the hefty infrastructural needs of a fast-growing industrialization. So when the Marshall Aid jump-started the economy in 1948-52, and thereby the development of the welfare state, it was the culmination of more than 60 years of ongoing reform work.

The Social Democratic parties have traditionally been credited as a kind of authors, but one must keep in mind that these were essentially consensus projects that were backed by parties from across the political spectrum.[24] Many reforms were simply ad-hoc solutions to specific challenges.[25] And here lies the key to the important insight that none of the North European welfare models are based on a coherent political project, or driven by a single set of ideas or values, and that the definitions therefore have to be relatively open in order to allow for their complexity. The political development's contribution to the forming of public welfare systems is important, but it is just as important to understand the Danish model's historical links between civil society, state and market, just as both the labour market parties and many of the popular movements that arose in the aftermath of the 1864-defeat in the Danish-Prussian War at times have exerted a considerable influence. The co-operative movement and the housing movement, for instance, frequently liaised with the governing bodies. The labour movement and women's lib were essentially a fight for civil rights, but other influential movements were not as fundamentally universalistic. The folk high school movement's aim was to liberate the individual through education, but it was initiated by and for church people and affluent farmers, high schools for working-class youth being a later invention. The co-op movement's dairies likewise optimized the agricultural export, just as co-operative consumer societies brought financial benefits to their members. The housing movement's first pioneering schemes – such as *Arbejdernes Byggeforening* [The workers' building society], known for Kartoffelrækkerne in Copenhagen and other residential developments – looked after their own members, which were minor public servants or the more affluent working-class, who thus generated both jobs and accommodation for themselves.[26] But regardless of the different starting points, the movements all sprang from the belief that a strong community, based on participation and co-determination, can accomplish more than any of us can do separately.[27]

If we apply a historical perspective that reaches right back to the granting of the Constitution in the mid-1800s, it is evident that both the so-called Danish utopia[28] and the universal social state – a social structure that guarantees a basic standard of living for all citizens and equal access to social benefits, regardless of income – have had their fair share of critics all along. The main conflicts and issues of the current political debate have essentially been there since the introduction of the old-age pension in 1891: universal or income-dependent welfare benefits? Rights or handouts? What is the definition of poverty? Are the welfare systems being abused? Collective solutions or freedom of choice? Public or private welfare suppliers? Centralization or decentralization?[29]

## The struggles

Although the energy crisis in 1973 hit the welfare state hard after more than 20 years of uninterrupted economic growth, the welfare programme continued to be expanded. However, the political balance shifted and the protests, primarily against the so-called 'nanny state' and the pressure of taxation, intensified. By the late 1970s, people had begun talking about 'the impending financial deroute,'[30] and successive governments therefore chose to rewind parts of the active fiscal policy and instead began to stimulate the market economy.[31]
Given the many welfare rights and matching welfare schemes, the extensive infrastructure and all the new housing and institutions that were developed in the period from the early 1950s and well into the 1990s, it is tempting to describe the time after 2001 as a period of decline. The political centre of gravity shifted away from the Social Democratic Party and centre-left towards coalitions of neoliberalism and national conservativism, and many of the functions that used to be part of the public domain were now put out to competitive tendering between private suppliers on market terms. In spite of the ambitious planning legislation that was passed between 1969 and 1974 (and which is still effective), the basic conditions for spatial planning changed and urban development became increasingly driven by market mechanisms rather than value-based visions of a connected whole.[32] No wonder that the architects, who had contributed as planners, landscape architects and designers of institutions and housing, and thus exerted a professional influence that reached far into the political engine room, perceived this development as a kind of degradation. With their professional know-how and impartial consultancy, they had seen themselves as not only serving the client but also the community and the public good, making the shift towards a much more market-driven construction industry hard to swallow.

## Landscapes, Planning, Institutions and Housing

The present articles are grouped under four thematical headlines: Landscapes, Planning, Institutions and Housing. In between these weave four narratives, each of which discusses and analyses a particular feature of the relationship between architecture, welfare state and architects.

## The narratives

*Jesper Pagh* opens the anthology with 'From the Common Best to the Common Market?', a familiar story of decline and how architects from the glory of using their artistic talent to build an equal, open and better society for the many have surrendered more or less uncritically to individualism, consumerism and the market forces. Pagh asks what we can learn from this interpretation and how it can help us develop a professional practice that is able to embrace the sociological tendencies and translate them into a critical architecture that addresses the challenges of our present society. This spawns a critical revisit to an architectural history that, on perhaps somewhat flimsy grounds, has defined architecture as being rooted in a shared, humanistic, national and Nordic tradition – an interpretation that became associated with the construction of the welfare state. As for the observation that architects nowadays find it harder to claim a value-based position for themselves, since the profession is no longer tied up with either tradition or a 'grand societal project', Jesper Pagh suggests that architects should reclaim the role as active co-creators of society by figuring out how architecture kan address some of the greatest challenges of our time.

*Kirsten Birk Hansen*'s article 'The Danish Project. Developing Greenland into a Modern Welfare Society' explains how the planning programme that was supposed to turn Greenland into a modern, industrialized welfare society largely relied on the rational ideological framework that was developed in Denmark during the welfare state's golden years. Some of the welfare project's basic dilemmas unfolded here in the clash between a vulnerable indigeneous culture with difficult living conditions and the firm belief in a progress based on rational solutions imposed by the Danish welfare state; between development and marginalization, between paternalism and self-determination, with special emphasis on industrialized prefab housing. Accounts of the decisions made by Greenland Technical Organization (GTO), which was responsible for the development, reveals an at times quite ruthless paternalism and a lack of understanding for the Greenlandic civil society and culture and the arctic way of life. Centralization, as such, was not one of the welfare state's objectives. A regional development act that was introduced in 1958 thus operated with one central and several regional development councils. But the councils were abolished in 1990 and their duties reassigned to the Ministry of Business and Industry. After that, the law was primarily used as a means of promoting trade, and the two structural reforms in 1970 and 2005, which reduced 1388 municipalities and 24 counties by 1970 to 98 municipalities and five counties by 2007, further added to the extensive centralization.[33]

With her narrative 'Towards the Outskirts – Welfare Spaces in Tønder', *Kirsten Marie Raahauge* describes how the visible and tangible effects of the increasing centralization alter our perception of the provincial town. When care-giving, educational and legislative institutions such as the hospital, the high school and the courthouse are robbed of their purpose and meaning, it cannot help impacting the spatial and material structures. The commercial life changes, as does the urban life, and this happens in much the same way all around the world. The local mirrors the global and the idiosyncrasies and characteristics that have been eroded by regions and provincial towns. Particularities and dissimilarities dissolve so that everything becomes more alike, with the changes resembling the changes that take place anywhere else.

An important key to the period's architecture is provided by the journal *Arkitektur DK* which, from 1957 through 2012, regularly documented the latest additions to the Danish architectural landscape. Basing their article 'Welfare's Spaces as Architecture-Historical Construction' on a rereading and summarizing of the journal's entire back catalogue, with particular focus on its

coverage of school architecture, *Jesper Pagh and Maja de Neergaard* discuss how architectural history not only chronicles the achievements of the past but also conditions the current potentials, and how this affects our whole perception of what is possible.
*Jannie Rosenberg Bendsen* demonstrates, with her article 'A Tale of Danish Architecture – Nils-Ole Lunds Interpretation of Danish Architecture', how a prominent architectural historian has contributed to a strong self-image and sense of belonging among Danish architects. One of Nils-Ole Lund's most important messages was that Danish architecture is more than just aesthetics; it is also, and just as much, a question of ethics. In the second half of the 20th century, architects took on great social responsibilities, an aspect which is first of all reflected in the period's housing.

## Landscapes

The civil society's strong communities and organizations and the political emphasis on solidarity and the common good – moral issues that concern the individual citizen as well – have been key elements in the development of the Danish welfare society throughout most of the 20th century, and have often formed the basis for the welfare state's official policies.[34] The idea of the collective and the universal has similarly served as a guiding principle for the planning and design of public spaces, notably landscapes and urban spaces. Here, the basic values remain more or less intact and just as relevant, as reflected by the current debate on urban spaces for all. Parallel to this, and corresponding with the prevailing view on architecture, the trendsetting landscape architectural discourse adopted an analytical approach which was based on ideals inherited from modernist architecture and art, rather than the development of the welfare state or the goals and values of its public clients.[35]
*Ellen Braae* explains in her article 'Welfare Landscapes and Communities' how collectivity and solidarity found expression in the welfare landscapes that emerged around new development, infrastructure and housing, and how we need to understand the characteristics, values, practices and discourses embedded in these welfare landscapes in order to appreciate and articulate their ethical function as a setting for the many. The design of the landscape conveys a moral message that concerns the relationship between the individual and the collective and thus reflects the architect's idea of collectivity and hope of – one may even say naive faith in – the potential of social engineering or 'nudging' by means of the design. After that follows the article 'Infrastructure as Landscape', in which *Rosalina Wenningsted-Torgard* describes the public spaces and landscapes that contain the welfare city's infrastructural waterways. By carefully examining these waterscapes, and by bringing concepts like scale, exposure and porosity into play, Torgard demonstrates the untapped potential in seeing technical service installations as elements that are relevant from an architectural and landscape architectural perspective. If the underlying resource basis is articulated in the design and planning of the good city, it may lead to interesting new spaces for social interaction. *Tomas Wikström*, on the other hand, lends a voice to a special kind of self-organization that complements the physical layout of the welfare city, so to speak, namely the shortcuts created by people living in the Stockholm suburbs in their attempt to compensate for the rigidity of the development plan. A joint effort that manifests itself as a kind of civil disobedience, but nevertheless a shared experience that leaves a distinct mark on the public space.

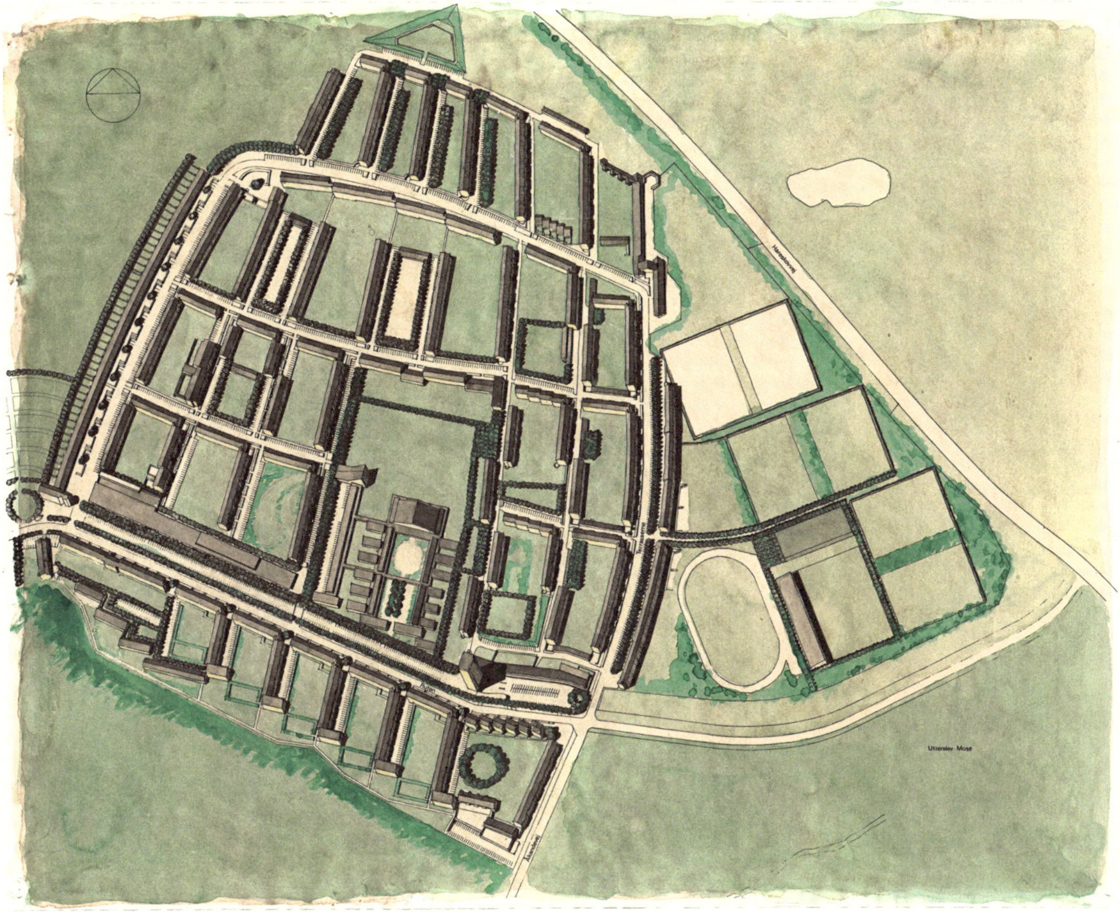


Tingbjerg, residential housing, by Steen Eiler Rasmussen and C. Th. Sørensen, from 1956-1970. An example on a 'pattern city', with a relatively low settlement that fits into the landscape. Danmarks Kunstbibliotek, Samlingen af Arkitekturtegninger.

## Planning

With the increasing industrialization, the continuous migration from country to town and the gradual expansion of the welfare systems came a need for longer-term planning, and the extensive legislation that came into existence in 1969-74 had several forerunners. The first attempt at law-making took place in 1925, but the first proper planning act did not see the light of day until 1938. One of the best known plans under this act is the so-called Copenhagen Finger Plan from 1947-49, which laid down guidelines for the future development of the Greater Copenhagen Area. However, these early initiatives were surpassed in 1974 by a new act that was a full, coordinated palette of planning tools for use on all levels, and moreover driven by a few well-defined goals.[36] These planning goals were basically the same fundamental ideals that drove the developing welfare project in the second half of the 20th century: implementation of an equal and fair society, as the overriding objective; master planning, as the chosen MO; and public involvement, as the basic planning principle for the new regional municipalities and county council districts. Parts of the legislation replaced the regional development grants as a means of balancing the development in rural and urban areas. Today, a liberal real estate market and inter-city competition for investment and business have taken over as the basic parameters for any attempt at making inclusive urban planning.

In the article 'The Welfare Institution as Urban Point of Concentration', *Jens Kvorning* discusses the important function that public institutions, such as the school, the kindergarten, the nursing home, the library and the swimming bath, have as structuring factors for the spatial development of the welfare city. The article identifies Danish planning's main influences as being the European modernist visions of the 1920s and 1930s, but just as important are the British New Towns' and Garden Cities and their separate enclaves, whose distribution of institutions result in distinct hierarchies – a model that became a major inspiration for the extensive urban development of the 1960s and 1970s. With reference to past and present planning theories, Kvorning calls for a reevaluation of the part that welfare institutions can play in an urban planning that is increasingly conditioned by the market and therefore compelled to be much more dynamic. Here, the institutions, if properly reviewed and redefined, can hold the key to the forming of spatial and social focal points for the further development of our welfare cities.

*Jørgen Møller* explains in his article 'Planning and the Welfare Society' how the public sector's physical planning may be perceived as a kind of large-scale welfare design. Citing a number of examples, Møller demonstrates how the changes and paradigm shifts that have conditioned the planning practice in the period from the mid-20th century to the present each in their own way have affected the ability to influence the development/dismantling of towns and villages – and thereby the so-called 'rural marginalization'. These are the aims and tools that often disappear from, or are written out of, the subsequent revisions of the legislation in favour of a strong focus on economic growth in the cities, with a resulting tendency to geographical centralization of welfare institutions such as police and jurisdiction, hospitals, schools, teacher-training colleges and other middle-range educational institutions, eldercare, libraries etc. Møller argues that, although the planning act and the structural reforms have been blamed for standing in the way of progress in villages and rural areas, they still provide scope for development and adaptation of small local communities, as long as this happens as a collaboration between the municipality and the active village community. *Deane Simpson* describes in his article how contemporary notions of the liveable city and the sustainable city, as promoted and quantified by various rankings, are deeply rooted in a more comprehensive, neoliberal restructuring and redefinition of our cities. In recent years, Copenhagen has become known to the rest of the world as a Nordic welfare/design utopia, partly thanks to various city rankings that paint a picture of a much more attractive, affluent and both environmentally and financially competitive city compared to the Copenhagen of the 1980s and 1990s. There are nevertheless indications that the city has become a much more unequal place; a place where residents are increasingly segregated according to income. The idea of 'the good life' appears to be targeted the more resourceful part of the population and the associated aspiration towards a collective and environmentally responsible future more or less confined to the area within the historical and compact city. The article demonstrates how a number of actors and dynamics interact to create this situation.

## Institutions

The many town hall extensions and annexes that were built in the 1930s were a direct result of the new and comprehensive social legislation. They provided the space that was needed for new kinds of employees and new kinds of meetings between citizen and munipality. This is a good example of the direct impact that legislation has had on the built environment.[37] Another example is the development of new school building typologies, which has often happened as a natural consequence of new legislation within the field. A recent case in point is Ørestad High School, where class space and shared space are two among a number of elements within a large hall that spans the entire height and length of the building. The direct cause of this typological innovation was the passing of a new high school reform. The same causal relationship applies to the construction of kindergartens, universities, hospitals, nursing homes, prisons, mental hospitals and, not least, culture facilities where architecture has been, and still is, a determining factor when it comes to orchestrating the citizen's meeting with the State.[38] The extensive evolution of the public institutions can, in many ways, be seen as the most obvious spatial and material manifestation of the burgeoning welfare state and its basic values.[39]

The article 'A Coherent Whole: Gottlieb Bindesbølls Mental Hospitals Regarded in a Welfare-Historical Perspective' by *Peter Thule Kristensen* looks at the Danish historicist architect Michael Gottlieb Bindesbøll's mental institutions and their welfare-historical significance. Bindesbøll designed three so-called asylums in the mid-19th century. These not only show that the State was increasingly taking responsibility for the treatment of the mentally sick, they also speak of a general faith in architecture's healing powers. So, if we want to understand the later welfare state, for which public health is a top priority, it makes perfect sense to study Bindesbøll's hospital architecture. His work furthermore represents a romantic view of the world that may have influenced the welfare society more than we are aware of. *Loa Kristine Teglgaard Christensen*'s article 'When the Institution Steps in over the Threshold' explores the gap and intersection that appear between home and institution when the home enjoys an undisputed position as the preferred spatial setting for care of the impaired and vulnerable elderly, as is the case today. This uncontested status is supported by normative perceptions of the home as an autonomous base where the elderly resident, however impaired and dependent, is allowed to retain his/her dignity.

What actually happens, however, is that the autonomy and control are challenged when treatment and care are administered within the parameter of the home. In other words, the home does not remain intact. *Camilla Hedegaard Møller*'s article 'Colours for Welfare? The Controversy around Gernes's Decoration of Herlev Hospital' looks at the dispute about Poul Gernes' decorations at Herlev Hospital and the ensuing discussion about whether art can contribute to welfare for the patients. This dispute broke out after the controversial 2012-renovation of one of the floors in the public hospital that the artist Poul Gernes decorated in the 1970s. His multi-storey installation has over time acquired the status of an artwork that benefits the patients. However, the hospital's cardiac unit were of a different opinion. With Actor-Network Theory (ANT) as her narrative approach, Camilla Hedegaard Møller describes the events that preceded the renovation, how power was mobilized and how the decoration itself contributed as an active player. *Mette Jerl Jensen and Kjeld Vindum*'s article 'The Waiting Room as Welfare Design' explores the fundamental question: what is welfare design? The answer, according to Jerl and Vindum, is that welfare design is architecture and form which promote togetherness. Focusing on social, institutional spaces, and with the waiting room as their specific point of reference, the authors furthermore reflect on what concrete manifestations this so-called welfare design may have.

## Housing

By the early 20th century, the severe housing shortage that was a consequence of the industrialization's migration from country to town, and which had the urban working class living under miserable conditions, was already regarded as a political responsibility. It was therefore a cardinal point for the recently formed Social Democratic Party, and consequently the first Danish housing committee was set up in 1916, with the dual purpose of surveying the housing shortage, on the one hand, and paving the way for the introduction of social housing, on the other.[40] While most other European nations developed publicly subsidized and initiated housing until the financial collapse in 1929, the Danish housing industry evolved as a symbiosis between the State and various self-organized housing associations, thanks to a well-developed subsidy regime – a system that is still in operation today.[41] When the housing boom finally arrived, it was therefore thanks to cooperations, municipalities and housing corporations, rather than private developers with the State as lender and lawmaker, as was the case in Sweden. The building societies had already been responsible for a substantial part of the workers' housing that had been necessitated by the massive migration from country to town, just as there were many of the same parties involved, including a large number of architects, building trusts and planners, as well as a contingent of sociologists and economists that reached deep into the political engine rooms.

*Marie Stender* has conducted an anthropological investigation of two contemporary housing estates. In her article 'Islands of Shared Identity. An Anthropological Portrait of Lange Eng & 8 House', she calls attention to the fact that these close-knit communities have a social drawback as well: being largely based on shared interests and identities, they serve their purpose inwardly by creating a good environment for the residents, but they also put up a shield against the surrounding world, thereby contributing to the architectural and social segmentation. The article discusses the societal implications of this, drawing parallels to the welfare society where extensive redistribution and solidarity in the current discourse seem

Kildeskovshallen in Gentofte by Karen and Ebbe Clemmensen from 1966-1969 and 1970-1972 and expanded in 2001-2002. An example of one of the countless sports facilities that was built in the second half of the 20th century. Danmarks Kunstbibliotek, Samlingen af Arkitekturtegninger.

to depend on internal homogeneity and external delimitation. *Masashi Kajita*'s article 'Re-addressing the Social Dimension of Accessibility: Towards an Inclusive Society' disposes of the common perception that accessibility solely is a question of liberating disabled people from disabling environments. The concept of accessibility actually has much more to offer, being a decisive factor for the realization and improvement of every individual's social presence in the built environment where it promotes independence, participation and enjoyment. The article reconsiders accessibility's social dimension, while offering an alternative insight into the ways that difference, vulnerability and sensitivity can lead to environments with greater potential for all – which raises the question whether accessibility can become a more central factor when we discuss the design of spaces and buildings. *Heidi Jacobsgaard Schøbel*'s article 'Meetings between Generations: A Rethinking of Welfare's Institutions for Children and the Elderly' is an elaboration of her master project from the Royal Danish Academy of Fine Arts, School of Architecture where she reimagined the concept of welfare institutions and -housing for children and the elderly. Basing her observations on real-life meetings between children and elderly people, she makes a number of concrete suggestions for how the institution, by facilitating four different kinds of meetings, can serve as a social catalyst for contact between generations. This idea is further expanded through a diagrammatical section that shows how architects can instigate inter-generational meetings in welfare institutions via the building's design and organization. Finally, the article 'Use Matters in Architectural Production' by *Heidi Svenningsen Kajita* studies how architects interrelate with other actors when producing welfare architecture, where the architect's role is to design via media such as drawing, product specification and material description. The standards and conventions of the construction industry primarily see architectural drawing and specification as media that communicate the measurable and tangible, but these are also capable of embracing the immeasurable and intangible. The article thus stresses the expedience of including *use* in the architectural media.

## Notes

1 F. Fukuyama (2014). Fukuyama, a former visiting professor at Aarhus University, claims that 'not even the Danes necessarily know how they "got to Denmark".'

2 The Danish Association of Architectural Firms have compiled a list of different architectural works and described their respective effects: www.danskeark.dk/taxonomy/term/3

3 H. Vestergaard: 'Boligpolitik i Velfærdsstaten' in N. Ploug, I. Henriksen & N. Kærgaard (eds.): *Den Danske Velfærdsstats Historie* (2004), p. 260.

4 E.I. Schmidt: *Red velfærdsstaten – et debatoplæg* (1997), p. 27.

5 J. Sestoft: 'Arkitekturens sociale historie' in Brandt et al. (1974), pp. 151-52.

6 Op.cit.

7 N.-O. Lund: *Nordisk Architecture* (1993 (2008)), p. 5.

8 A. Gaardmand, D. Lund & H.-H. Madsen, *Dansk Planlægning I-III* (2016).

9 J. Pagh (ed.): *Arkitektur DK* No. 2 and 3. Special issue on the welfare society's architecture (2013).

10 The working group 'Form til Velfærd/Forming Welfare' was set up in 2011. Since then, its members have organized an international conference on the subject in 2012, a special issue of the research journal *Nordic* (*Nordic* #4: 'Forming Welfare') and the Inter-Scandinavian Research-Network for Welfare and Architecture, with the participation of researchers from the Scandinavian countries, who have met 3-4 times a year between 2013 and 2016. The core members of 'Form til Velfærd/Forming Welfare' were Mette Jerl Jensen, Kjeld Vindum, Kirsten Marie Raahauge, Jesper Pagh, Peter Thule Kristensen and Katrine Lotz.

11 T. Avermaete, D. van den Heuvel & M. Swenarton: *Architecture and the welfare state* (2015).

12 H. Mattsson & S.-O. Wallenstein (eds.): *Swedish Modernism; Architecture, Consumption and the Welfare State* (2010).

13 *Nordic Journal of Architecture* 2015 Vol. 5 No. 4.

14 See, for instance, A. Yaneva: *Mapping Controversies in Architecture* (2012), which is a good example of this kind of analytic approach to the interplay between architecture and society.

15 See, for instance, O.F. Kirkeby: *Om Velfærd* (2011).

16 J.H. Petersen, K. Petersen & N.F. Christiansen (eds.): *Dansk Velfærdshistorie* 1-6 (2010-14), Vol. 3, p. 117.

17 G. Esping-Andersen (1990). There does not exist an exhaustive list of literature and criticism with relevance to the present subject area, but J.K. Galbraith: *The affluent society* (1958) (primarily the US) and Anthony Giddens: *The Third Way* (1998) have both been major political influences. Giddens opens the discussion about the future of the welfare states with reference to the increasing globalization. Among Danish welfare researchers, the team behind 'Forming Welfare' has first of all been inspired by Professor of Sociology L.B. Kaspersen (2008), Professor of Economics and Public Administration B. Greve and Political Scientist and Head of Department E.I. Schmidt (1997), as well as debate books by, among others, O.F. Kirkeby (2011), C. Bjørn (1998) and H. Fonsmark (1990). The reports from the government-appointed welfare commission of 2003 are also worth reading; these can be accessed online. Hans-Christian Jensen has, with his PhD thesis from 2005, investigated how the Danish design culture and practice relate to the wider concept of welfare. Professor of History Per H. Hansen's book *Da danske møbler blev moderne* (2006) describes in detail how the success was due to the collaboration between architects, joiners, manufacturers and a benevolent state.

18 Petersen, Petersen & Christiansen (2010-14), op.cit., Vol. 1.

19 C. Jensen: *Velfærdsstaten – en introduktion,* p. 14.

20 Petersen, Petersen & Christiansen (2010-14), op.cit., Vol. 1.

21 Petersen, Petersen & Christiansen (2010-14), op.cit., Vol. 3, p. 103.

22 N. Dahlkild: *Huse der har formet os – arkitekturhistorien bag danskernes institutioner og offentlige rum* (2015).

23 Petersen, Petersen & Christiansen (2010-14), op.cit., Vol. 3, pp. 108-10.

24 H. Fonsmark: *Historien om den danske utopi* (1990), pp. 83-86.

25 E.I. Schmidt: *Red velfærdsstaten – et debatoplæg* (1997), p. 27.

26 Nygaard (1984), op.cit.

27 Ibid.

28 Fonsmark (1990), op.cit., and C. Bjørn: *Dengang Danmark blev moderne – eller historien om den virkelige danske utopi* (1998), p. 45.

29 Schmidt, (1997), op.cit., pp. 43-58.

30 http://denstoredanske.dk/Danmarkshistorien/Lavv%C3%A6kst_og_frontdannelser/Polarisering_indadtil_og_udadtil/Oliekrise_og_hegnsp%C3%A6le/Mod_afgrundens_rand

31 Fonsmark (1990), op.cit.

32 A. Gaardmand, D. Lund, H-H. Madsen: *Dansk Planlægning I-III* (2016).

33 Ibid., Vol. 2 and 3.

34 At least until 2001, when the mantra about collective solutions for the many was challenged by a growing individualization and the demand for optional welfare solutions, such as open enrolment and free choice of hospital.

35 See, for instance, Malene Hauxner: *Fantasiens Have* (2002), Sven-Ingvar Andersson (ed.): *Havekunst i Danmark* (1990), Annemarie Lund: *Danmarks Havekunst III* (2002).

36 Gaardmand, Lund & Madsen (2016), op.cit., Vol. 2 and 3.

37 Dahlkild (2015), op.cit., p. 128

**38** See also the 6-volume work on Danish architecture from 1979, edited by Hakon Lund (who does not take a systematic approach to the architecture of the welfare state either, though) and special issues of the journal *Arkitektur DK* Vol. 2 and 3 from 2013 about the architecture of the welfare state.
**39** Schmidt (1997), op.cit., p. 40.
**40** For a comprehensive description of post-war housing, see Nygaard (1984), op.cit. Also Henning Bro's article 'Boligen mellem natvægterstat og velfærdsstat' (2006), pp. 33-58, contains a survey of the correlation between the rise of the welfare state and the housing boom. The article is based on Bro's PhD thesis from 2008 by the same name.
**41** The development of the Norwegian housing industry featured many of the same elements as in Denmark, but here all social housing units were sold as owner-occupied flats in 1984-85.

**Literature**


- Andersson, S.-I. (ed.): *Havekunst i Danmark.* The Danish Architectural Press, Copenhagen 1990.
- Avermaete, T., van den Heuvel, D., & Swenarton, M.: *Architecture and the Welfare State.* Routledge, London 2015.
- Bjørn, C.: *Dengang Danmark blev moderne – eller historien om den virkelige danske utopi.* Fremad, Copenhagen 1998.
- Brandt, P.Å.: Marcussen, L., Sestoft, J., & de Waal, A. (ed.): *Arkitekturens Prakis – bidrag til en teori.* Borgen, Copenhagen 1974.
- Bro, H.: 'Boligen mellem natvægterstat og velfærdsstat', *Arbejderhistorie* nr. 4, Taastrup 2006, pp. 33-58.
- Dahlkild N.: *Huse der har formet os – arkitekturhistorien bag danskernes institutioner og offentlige rum.* Museum Tusculanums Forlag, Copenhagen 2015.
- Esping-Andersen, G.: *Three Worlds of Welfare Capitalism.* Polity Press/Blackwell, Cambridge 1990.
- Fonsmark, H.: *Historien om den danske utopi.* Gyldendal, Copenhagen 1990.
- Fukuyama, F.: *Political Order and Political Decay.* Farrar, Straus and Giroux, New York 2014.
- Gaardmand, A., Lund D. & Madsen, H.-H.: *Dansk Planlægning bd. I-III.* Bogværket, Copenhagen 2016.
- Hansen, P.H.: *Da danske møbler blev moderne: historien om dansk møbeldesigns storhedstid.* University Press of Southern Denmark and Lindhardt & Ringhof, Copenhagen 2006.
- Hauxner, M.: *Fantasiens have: Det moderne gennembrud i havekunsten og sporene i byens landskab.* The Danish Architectural Press, Copenhagen 1993.
- Jensen, C.: *Velfærdsstaten – en introduktion.* Hans Reitzels Forlag, Copenhagen 2011.
- Jensen, H.C.: *Fra velfærd til designkultur: Velfærdsengagement i dansk designteori og designpraksis i det 20. århundrede.* PhD thesis, University Press of Southern Denmark, 2005.
- Kaspersen, L.B.: *Danmark i Verden,* Hans Reitzels Forlag, Copenhagen 2008.
- Kirkeby, O.F.: *Om Velfærd.* Gyldendal Public, Copenhagen 2011.
- Lund, A.: *Danmarks Havekunst* III. The Danish Architectural Press, Copenhagen 2002.
- Lund, H. (ed.): *Danmarks Arkitektur* 1-6. Gyldendal, Copenhagen 1985.
- Lund, N.-O.: *Nordic Architecture.* The Danish Architectural Press, Copenhagen 1993 (2008).
- Mattsson, H. & Wallenstein, S.-O. (eds.): *Swedish Modernism; Architecture, Consumption and the Welfare State.* Blackdog Publishing, London 2010.
- Nygaard, E.: *Tag over hovedet – Dansk boligbyggeri fra 1945 til 1982.* The Danish Architectural Press, Copenhagen 1984.
- Pagh, J. (ed.): *Arkitektur DK* nr. 2 og 3. Special issue on *Velfærdssamfundets Arkitektur* [The welfare society's architecture]. The Danish Architectural Press, Copenhagen 2013.
- Petersen, J.H., Petersen, K. & Christiansen, N.F. (eds.): *Dansk Velfærdshistorie* 1-6. University Press of Southern Denmark, Odense 2010-2014.
- Schmidt, E.I.: *Red velfærdsstaten – et debatoplæg.* Munksgaard, Copenhagen 1997.
- Søberg, M. (ed.): *Nordic Journal of Architecture* 2015, Vol. 5 No. 4.
- Vestergaard, H.: 'Boligpolitik i Velfærdsstaten' in Ploug N., Henriksen, I. & Kærgaard N. (eds.): *Den Danske Velfærdsstats Historie,* The Danish National Centre for Social Research, Copenhagen 2004.
- Yaneva, A.: *Mapping Controversies in Architecture.* Ashgate, London 2012.

Jesper Pagh

# From the Common Best to the Common Market?

**In continuation of Danish architecture's Golden Age as it unfolded in the welfare state's formative decades after the Second World War, a story is often told about how the architects eventually came to orient their efforts around the market more than they did around the community. What is taken up in this article are the questions of how this story came to be created and what we can learn from it if we want to develop a professional practice that will succeed in meshing with society's development and manage to transform this into a critical architecture, targeted towards the societal challenges we are facing today.**

*The desire to do something has to come from being able to see the merits of the assignment. (...) handling an assignment properly also requires elevating society at large. You can't just tug at a single toft of hair in one single location.*

(Tyge Arnfred (born 1919), architect and former partner in Fællestegnestuen, in *Arkitektur DK* 2-2013)

*The 8 House is not some kind of important prestige building. It's pretty much a matter of dirt-cheap apartments out there in unpretentious Copenhagen South, on Amager.*

(Bjarke Ingels (born 1974), architect and founder of BIG, in *Euroman* 9-2012)

*That which I regard as the identity's development: well, that's, you could say, an identity that moves from a social, community- and project-oriented identity towards a market-oriented, adaptable identity with global horizons. And this is a movement that could maybe also be described as a movement from profession to business.*

(Kjeld Vindum (born 1950), architect and lecturer at the Royal Danish Academy of Fine Arts, School of Architecture, in a lecture delivered December 9, 2010, at the Danish Architecture Centre)

The first decades after the Second World War are often highlighted as the heyday of Danish architecture: a period when social engagement and a pronounced interest in everyday life's organization converged with massive public investments and a craftsmanship- and material-related understanding at an absolute high-water mark. *The Architectural Review* categorized the period's Nordic architecture as 'New Empiricism', which Nils-Ole Lund, according to Fisker[1] and Faber,[2] construed as an expression of acknowledgement of the Nordic welfare state's excellences, which could already be spotted immediately after the end of the war. In continuation of this edification towards a common good, what is often told is a story of decline, which takes its origins in the course of the 1970s, the decade things started to go downhill when it came to social commitment, craftsmanship and architectonic quality. Modernism's universalism and the scale and quality that are salient characteristics of the 1960s' industrialized buildings now met with increasing resistance. Globalization, commercialization and a critique of modernism led to what Erik Nygaard (1995) describes as *Arkitektur i en forvirret tid*

[Architecture during a time of confusion] and what Kim Dirckinck-Holmfeld (2007) refers to as *Modernismens sammenbrud* [The collapse of modernism].

It's not difficult to find support for this story of decline if you take a look around, as Kjeld Vindum also does in his lecture, but it's hard to get through to practising architects with this 'normative twofold critique', which rests on the implicit assumption that not only are they lesser architects but that they are also lesser people than the individuals in their parents' and their grandparents' generation. And when this wins the day, it's very hard – keeping this assumption in mind – to come up with an answer about what today's practising architects should be doing instead.

Vindum's description of the market-oriented, adaptable identity is followed up by a discussion of whether such an identity is really an identity at all. Vindum examines an assortment of the 00s' buildings and concludes that there has not been any kind of development whatsoever, on the formal and organizational level, in the past 50 years. While the surrounding society has changed decisively in the same period, the architects' houses are standing perfectly still, Vindum claims, and goes on to suggest that the reason for this is that the architects do not know what they are doing. There is no longer a direct link between the values that underlie society's development and the values that the majority of architects carry along with them. Thus they are not managing to be active co-creators in society's development, as they were doing successfully in the period spanning from the end of the Second World War to some time in the early 1960s. This is one of Vindum's central points. The complexity in society is growing, and the architects have not figured out how to embrace this complexity, says Vindum, and suggests that '(...) a formal understanding be developed which is in accord with its time, and which is fuelled by a clear sense about what's going on in other disciplines.'[13]

It is the intention with the present article to contribute to the discussion of how such an under-

standing can be brought about. How can we understand the structural conditions under which architecture comes forth, so that a practice can be developed that manages to grab hold of society's development and transpose it into an architecture which is genuinely in tune with its time, which is critical, and which possesses the potential for change and does not merely manifest itself in motives and metaphors?

In order to do this, however, I believe that it is also necessary to revisit and critically inquire about the understanding we have when it comes to the architects' contribution to the development of the welfare society. In the third section of this article I will outline, first, how this narrative has been constructed through architecture history. Then I will attempt to destabilize the narrative by calling a number of social science perspectives into play. In the closing discussion, I will be taking a closer look at how we, as architects, can understand society's development today, and how this understanding can contribute to creating the formal understanding in concord with its own time, which Vindum is looking for. One basic premise of the article's analysis and discussions is that there exists a necessary interdependence between developments in the profession and developments in the social sciences. And it is a second premise, that it is necessary to maintain this perspective in order to be able to say anything meaningful about both aspects in this situational context.

## Cities, buildings, landscape and society – the architect as builder of society

Kay Fisker's notion of *the functional tradition* articulates an understanding of the architecture's development and purpose, which builds further on an ideological and culture historical reading of *the specifically Danish* in architecture as something that runs across art history's respective period divisions and manifests itself, instead, through a continuous focus on undemonstrative anonymity and unobtrusive harmony while avoiding the spectacular in favour of the thoroughly cultivated and harmonious, buttressed by ideals like order and unpretentiousness.[4]

As Jannie Rosenberg Bendsen astutely points out,[5] this understanding, that certain specifically Danish values and a specifically Danish mentality manifest themselves through architecture, has exerted a great deal of influence on the architects' self-understanding, and has concomitantly generated a conception about solidarity. These stand as an understanding and a conception that have largely been created through the very *writing* of architecture history. Although still today, there are discussions being carried on, and on a wide scale, about whether it makes sense anymore in a globalized world to keep on talking about anything being *specifically* Danish,[6] the

8-House, BIG 2009.
Photo: Adrian Täckman.

functional tradition, through its ability to continuously absorb a wide range of other and changing views on architecture in context and to continuously assimilate these, has evolved into an extremely robust framework for the architects' self-understanding, which is still applicable to a considerable extent.[7]

The understanding of a being part of a historically and culturally conditioned tradition, which has largely been written up in Knud Millech and Kay Fisker's *Danske Arkitekturstrømninger 1850-1950* (1951), is closely linked to an emphasis of the landscape's importance with respect to the architectural understanding; this is something on which both Tobias Faber, in *Dansk arkitektur* ([1963] 1977), and Steen Eiler Rasmussen, in *København* (1969), also place special emphasis. The significance that the physical environment has to bear on everyday life's qualities and experiences, which Steen Eiler Rasmussen unfolded in *Om at opleve arkitektur* (Eng., *Experiencing Architecture*) (1957), and which Jan Gehl subsequently dealt with in *Livet mellem husene* (Eng, *Life Between Buildings*) (1971), underscores the consequence of the architect as *social engineer* with a concomitantly ensuing responsibility to those people for whom one is designing. Finally, an underlining of the connection between cities and buildings that (again) Steen Eiler Rasmussen describes in, for example, *København* [Copenhagen] (1969) and *London* (1973) is linked up with physical planning, which, in the first decades after the Second World War, was a discipline process on which the architects still had even greater influence;[8] with this, there was, at that time, a more substantial social importance associated with the profession. With this as background, an exegesis of history is delineated about how the architects that were active during the period between the two world wars and immediately after the Second World War, planned and designed, by the unfurling of their own social commitment and their artistic talents, the welfare society's most important building blocks and, in so doing, contributed to bring-

ing about the situation that we, today, are one of the world's most equal and prosperous societies. At the same time, they brought forth some of history's best and most beautiful houses. It is within this comprehensive understanding that the subsequent story of decay takes its source.

It's not hard to see all the connections among the post-war period's urgent need for homes, schools, hospitals, institutions, etc.; the emerging welfare society's notions of the good life and a common good; and the results that have now come to be canonized as some of the best that have ever been created in Danish architecture. What we can spot, forthwith, is a coincidence between the architecture's (and the welfare society's) 'Heyday', 'Epoch' and the topical question, 'Where are we going?', which, respectively, happen to be the titles of the three volumes of *Dansk Velfærdshistorie* [Danish Welfare History], which cover the period 1956-2014.[9]

Whether the one would have led *directly* to the other does seem difficult to determine, though.

## State, form, market and civil society

The coupling between architecture and welfare in the post-war period is, to a great extent, supported and sustained – for better or worse – in quite a bit of the recent literature,[10] and is also applicable outside the narrow academic discussion. In the introduction to the government's architectural policy – *Mennesker i centrum* [Putting People First] – the situation is illuminated in such a way that Danish architecture and Danish design have been playing roles, on all scales, in giving our welfare society a form that is characterized by humanism, and which reflects our democratic and transparent society.[11]

This is a perspective that is elevating in relation to a profession which has experienced major upheavals, in the course of recent decades, in the form of an ever increasing globalization of the markets in which it operates and a rampant commodification of its services – and which, moreover, is (and always has been) undergoing constant negotiation, within its own ranks, about its own societal justification.[12]

So much the worse it is, then, that in that portion of the literature about society's and particularly the Danish welfare state's development which is *not* being written by architects,[13] architecture plays only a marginal role – if any role at all. The socio-economic aspects surrounding the housing movement; new institutional- and organizational forms; and especially the construction sector are all important elements. In this correlation, the spatial aspects and architecture as such appear chiefly to be of interest for the architects themselves.

However, just because this topic has apparently been overlooked in research on the welfare society, one cannot conclude that the notion of the architects' contribution to the development of the welfare state is something that was merely construed by and for the architects themselves. It is rather the case that we can point out that when one, in welfare research, gives precedence to the social and economic policies, then the importance of *how* these are being materialized in our cities and our buildings is being overlooked. Then again, I could argue, conversely, that in architecture history, where it is, of course, materiality that has priority, we have been giving too *little* space to the importance of the political, economic and social structures, within which the architecture comes into being, and thereby we, all too often, wind up presenting the matter as if architecture *in itself* has a society-changing force. It is necessary to maintain an overview of *the connection* and *interdependency* between the social and the material, and it is crucial that we not fall into

Courtyard house, Albertslund Syd,
Fællestegnestuen 1963-68.
Photo: Strüwing.

making the fallacy of attributing to either the one or the other the sole power of agency.

The sociologist Gøsta Esping-Andersen has described how the Scandinavian 'social democratic' welfare model differentiates itself from other welfare models by being characterized by a universal (and high) service level, primarily organized, financed and controlled by the government, with a relatively low degree of commodification of the services to follow.[14]

This model involves an inordinately high degree of state-run institutionalization of the relationship between society's primary agents – government, market and civil society – and the delivery of welfare services.[15] For the sociologist, institutionalization in this context refers to the process of embedding social relation within society as a whole, and, institutions as such constitute an organizational form, through which the state – as well as the districts and the regions – distribute their organization, their financing and their management. However, as far as architects are concerned, it is buildings that have to be designed and that have to be built. To this end, they accordingly contrib-

ute, with their professional expertise, to giving *form to welfare* – through a practice whose performance, in this context, can hardly be considered in isolation from the relationship between state, market and civil society.

In the welfare state's formative years, following the Second World War, the institutionalization that Esping-Andersen is speaking about was undergoing an enormous degree of development. What concomitantly ensued were a large number of (public) construction assignments, which the architects naturally pounced on. That things proceeded so very well with the welfare architecture, for so many years, is not necessarily due the fact that the architects were simply enormously adept but maybe just as much because the profession, as such, evolved into a climate where a considerable portion of the assignments were posed by a rapidly evolving welfare state, which was focused on a particular apprehension about an institutionalization of the community, an apprehension that was very closely in tune with the majority of the profession's practitioners' own conceptions about the good life and a common good. Therefore, one might claim, the connection between the social and the material aspects of society's development arose spontaneously. There was – as Kjeld Vindum is prospecting for today – a formal understanding, which was in tune with its time: the architecture profession happened to be in the right place at the right time.

## A formal understanding, in concord with its time

The question remains, then: How do we go about establishing this new kind of understanding if it cannot arise spontaneously, as was the case a few generations back? In *Gode intentioner og uregerlige byer* [Good intentions and Unruly Cities] (2008), Tom Nielsen sets the stage for a discussion of how we can develop the cities of the future when the ideals that served as the point of departure for the development of the modern welfare city are being challenged and emptied of their significance, and he calls perspectives from politics, economics and the social sciences into play, in order to light the way for a possible way forward. Here, I will try to briefly outline three mutually contrasting perspectives from the social sciences that dominate a considerable portion of the discussions going on in the planning field, perspectives that I believe may also have implications to bear on the situational coherence, of which today's architects and today's architecture form constituent parts.

The first of these perspectives spans between *the global and the local*, and is often simply referred to as globalization. Globalization is characterized by dispersion and the disbandment of known structures, but also implies a focus on new, site-specific concentrations of power that arise in synch with the global propagation of the market economy.[16] Zygmunt Bauman describes how the importance of space in globalization becomes, at one and the same time, less important and more significant, *pari passu* with the fact that we, on the one hand, can go wherever we want to while, at the very same time, we don't feel entirely safe where we are.[17] In architecture, this is starting to become especially apparent as we see that the architects, on the one hand, are helping to create uniform and well-designed global corridors and, on the other hand, are designing beautiful place-specific destinations.[18] Hans Ibelings discusses how a *super modernism* manifests itself in the duality between an identity-less *international* style, on the one hand, and *place branding starchitecture*, on the other.[19] Accordingly, globalization also comes to signify an increased focus on the local, and in the discussions about globalization's

Small street, Albertslund Syd,
Fællestegnestuen 1963-68.
Photo: Strüwing.

impact on architecture, there is a great deal of focus on how the architects' role is evolving, specifically in connection with an increased commercialization of urban development.[20]

The second perspective spans between different forms of *regulation and deregulation* of the economy. This perspective is often described as neo-liberalization – a concept that, in many contexts, is utterly predominating in discussions about the development of the global political economy. As is the case with globalization, neo-liberalization is similarly a concept that abounds with contradictions. On the one hand, neo-liberalization brings in its train an extensive privatization of what was formerly public property, and thus immediately implies diminished regulation of the market, with increased competition in mind.[21] On the other hand, this development has transpired through a different type of regulation, which is characterized by the situation that presently, there are other groupings in society whose interests are being looked after, especially through the means of an increase in the financialization of architecture and urban development.[22] This shows itself in revised planning- and control forms and -rationales,[23] which have a direct influence to bear on what importance can be ascribed to architecture, in terms of economic, political and social parameters – in many cases, as a meaningful factor of power in the international competition among the world's metropolises concerning attracting investments and places for the employment of people.[24]

The span between *community and individualization* constitutes the third perspective that I want to point out here. While we generally take our mark in construing 'community' as something good,[25] the sense of belonging to certain groups

in society is undergoing development all the time.[26] Traditional place- and tradition-bound communities are under pressure, with an individualization of risk and responsibility and with challenges posed to our ontological security as consequences.[27] At the same time, though, new forms of communities are arising, which take their origin in other social groupings, in other societal issues, and in a new focus on geographical places, and, to boot, with new communication- and mobility forms as their centres of rotation.[28] This also implies that public space, in a physical sense, takes on a new meaning: it comes to be transformed from being a point of departure for norm-establishing communities to functioning more and more as a commercialized market place – a phenomenon whose reality and consequences are becoming a topic of ongoing discussion.

These three perspectives can be considered dualisms, understood in the sense that the concepts 'spanned' in each of the aforementioned pairings clearly stand in mutual opposition to each other, although they may certainly exist – and must necessarily be acknowledged – at one and the same time. There is accordingly no matter of the paired antitheses in each perspective being regarded unequivocally as articulating a movement from one position to another. To a certain extent, we can see that, in certain periods, the one contrasting pole has taken over in preference to the other. But at the essential core of the matter, it is important to keep in mind that opposites, at all times, co-exist, side by side, and that, to a certain extent, they can only be understood and can only be described in terms of each other.

Neo-liberalization involves not only deregulation, but also brings along new forms of regulation. With globalization follows also a new significance of the local. And while we often focus on a greater degree of individualization in society at large, what is also constantly arising in this movement are new communities, which manifest themselves in other ways than those with which we are familiar. While the first two perspectives –globalization and neo-liberalization – are functioning, in many instances, as such strong structural conditions that most people, in their everyday lives, appear compelled to be subjugated to the consequences they precipitate, the situation is somewhat different with the latter. What can be seen here are several examples of how *urban gardening*, for example, and other grass-root-oriented movements – typically in cities and often focused on impermanence, and concentrated in neighbourhoods that are undergoing transition – take a very concrete approach to counteracting what otherwise appears to be the overwhelmingly dominant trend and succeed in creating new free spaces, where people, taking their point of departure in the establishment of new communities, are trying to create locally-based albeit globally-oriented networks that issue from the basis of a radically different economic reasoning than that which dominates the neo-liberalization of the global political economy.[29]

## Deliberate surrender

It may seem to be a long way off from such a sociologically based conceptualization to a specifically concrete architecture, but I believe that it is necessary to move into depth with the understanding of society that is being developed in the social sciences and which, in geography and in the planning field, can potentially be linked most directly to the spatial and material practice that belongs to the architects if we are all going to be able to say anything meaningful at all about *what we want* with architecture.

The three perspectives discussed above and the consequences of these will quite possibly be regarded, in most contexts, as architecture's



Gullfosshus, Kay Fisker 1928.
Photo: Jonals.

scourge; nonetheless, they adequately describe architecture's frame conditions, and with a sufficient understanding of these, they can also constitute architecture's possibility.
If one seriously wants to go about calling these perspectives into architectural practice, one would do well revisiting the strategy that OMA/ Rem Koolhaas, in the description of their plan for Melun Senart, refers to as 'a deliberate surrender – tactical manoeuvre to reverse a defensive position'.[30] The surrender will then consist of a completely targeted and pragmatic effort to gain knowledge about the surrounding society and to understand it on its own terms – and under the cover of this tactical manoeuvre, the profession's current defensive position, through the development of spatial organizations and design expressions that extend beyond the narrow market-fixated understanding, reverses the metaphor and the compositional motif formation.

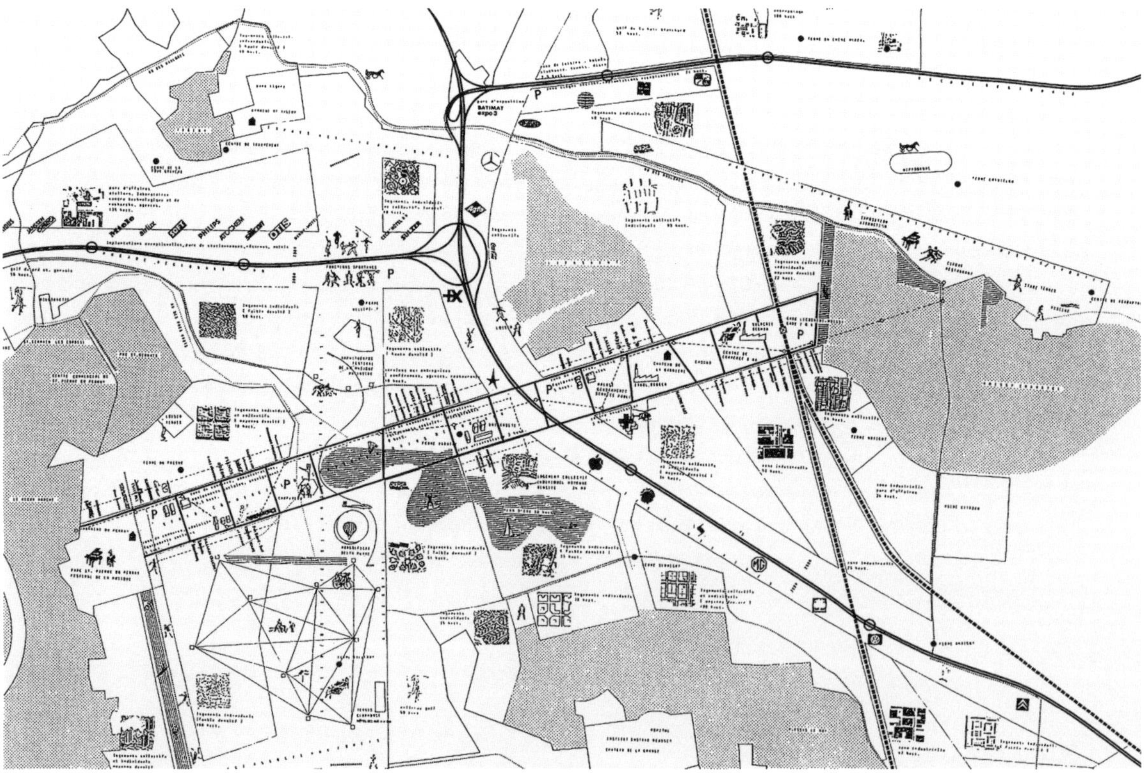

Ville Nouvelle Melun Senart, OMA 1987.

This does not mean to say that the architects are simply going to have to blindly accept the development that is taking place and actively support this through their exertions. Nor does this appear to be imminent. However, with my personal and professional knowledge of the profession's practitioners, I dare to go so far as to agree with Vindum when he says that no longer is there any direct link between the values that underlie the development of society and the values that the majority of architects are carrying with them.[31] Thus, the connection between the social and the material aspects of society's development does not arise spontaneously in the same way as I declared, in the introductory section of this article, was formerly the case. If this connection is going to be re-established, and if the architects are once again going to be active co-creators in society's development, this is accordingly going to have to transpire through critically making up our minds about how architecture can provide solutions to some of our time's greatest challenges by embracing these challenges directly, in the midst of the messy, complex and contradictory context from which they were spawned.

**Notes**

1 K. Millech and K. Fisker: *Danske Arkitekturstrømninger* (1951).
2 T. Faber: *Dansk Arkitektur* (1977).
3 K. Vindum: "Dansk arkitektur under forandring? Dansk arkitektur som identitetsprojekt", 2010.
4 N.-O. Lund: *Nordisk Arkitektur* 3 (2008), p. 18.
5 J.R. Bendsen: *Enkelhed, mådehold og funktionalitet* (2009) and J.R. Bendsen: 'Værdiernes Værdi' in *Arkitektur DK*, (6) 2010, pp. 53–54.
6 M. Keiding: 'Dem og os eksisterer ikke længere – interview med Kent Martinussen' in *Arkitektur DK*, 54(6), 2010, pp. 12-15; J. Pagh: 'Dansk Arkitektur Import-Eksport A/S' in *Arkitekten*, 110(11), 2010, pp. 66-69, K. Vindum & K.L. Weiss (eds.): *Den ny bølge i dansk arkitektur* (2012).
7 J.R. Bendsen (2010) op.cit.; J. Pagh (2010), op.cit. and K. Lotz: 'Dansk Arkitektur som velfærdseksport' in *Arkitekten*, 112(10), 2010, pp. 46-48.
8 A. Gaardmand: *Dansk byplanlægning: 1938-1992* (1993).
9 J.H. Petersen, K. Petersen & N.F. Christiansen (eds.): *Velfærdsstaten i tidehverv. Dansk Velfærdshistorie bind 5: 1973-1993* (2013); J.H. Petersen, K. Petersen & N.F. Christiansen, editors: *Velfærdsstatens storhedstid. Dansk Velfærdshistorie Vol. 4: 1956-1973* (2012); K. Petersen (ed.): *13 historier om den danske velfærdsstat* (2013), and J.H. Petersen, K. Petersen & N.F. Christiansen (eds.): *Hvor glider vi hen? Dansk Velfærdshistorie Vol. 6: 1993-2014* (2014).
10 M. Keiding, M. Amundsen & K. Dirckinck-Holmfeld: *Dansk arkitektur siden 1754* (2007); H.E. Langkilde, K. Dirckinck-Holmfeld & J. Hegner Christiansen: *Arkitekten 100 år.* (1998); N.-O. Lund: *Nordisk Arkitektur* (2008); T. Nielsen: *Gode intentioner og uregerlige byer* (2008) and P.B. Pedersen: *Arkitektur og plan i den danske velfærdsby 1950-1990 – Container og urbant raster* (2005).
11 Danish Ministry of Culture: *Arkitekturpolitik – Mennesker i centrum* (2014).
12 See, for example, M. Grubbauer & S. Steets: 'The Making of Architects: Knowledge Production and Legitimation in Education and Professional Practice'. *Architectural Theory Review*, 19(1), 2014 pp. 4-9; Keiding (2010), op.cit.; K. Lotz (2010), op.cit., and O. Schoch, K. Vindum & S. Bjerring: 'Hvordan designer vi og hvorfor' in *Arkitekten*, 112(6), 2010, pp. 32-75.
13 See, for example, H. Andersen (ed.): *Sociologi – en grundbog til et fag,* 4th edition. (2011); B. Greve: *Velfærdssamfundet – en grundbog* (2008); B. Greve: 'Velfærdsstaten' **in** B. Greve, A. Jørgensen & L.J. Elm (eds.) *Det Danske Samfund* (2014), p. 45-66; J.H. Petersen, K. Petersen & N.F. Christiansen (eds.): *Velfærdsstaten i tidehverv. Dansk Velfærdshistorie Vol. 5: 1973-1993* (2013); J.H. Petersen, K. Petersen & N.F. Christiansen (eds.):

*Velfærdsstatens storhedstid. Dansk Velfærdshistorie Vol. 4: 1956-1973* (2012); K. Petersen (ed.): *13 historier om den danske velfærdsstat* (2013), and J.H. Petersen, K. Petersen & N.F. Christiansen (eds.): *Hvor glider vi hen? Dansk Velfærdshistorie bind 6: 1993-2014* (2014).

**14** G. Esping-Andersen: *The three worlds of welfare capitalism* (1990); B. Greve: *Velfærdssamfundet – en grundbog* (2008), and Greve (2014), op.cit.

**15** Greve (2008), op.cit. and Greve (2014), op.cit.

**16** D. Harvey: *The Condition of Postmodernity* (1990).

**17** Z. Bauman: *Fællesskab* (2002).

**18** J. Kvorning: 'Tourist Urbanism – The Peaceful Path to Real Reform?' in *Arkitektur DK*, 54(2), 2010, pp. 87-89; S. Sassen: *Cities in a World Economy,* 4th edition (2012), and J. Brash: *Bloomberg's New York – Class and Governance in the Luxury City* (2011).

**19** H. Ibelings: *Supermodernism: Architecture in the age of globalization* (1998).

**20** M. Provoost: 'For det fælles bedste' in *Arkitektur DK*, 57(1), 2013, pp. 8-15; Vanstiphout: 'Nothing More Political' in *Volume*, (34), 2012, pp. 10-16; J. Kvorning: 'Tourist Urbanism – The Peaceful Path to Real Reform?' in *Arkitektur DK*, 54(2), 2010, pp. 87-89, and J. Brash (2011) op.cit.

**21** S. Graham & S. Marvin: *Splintering urbanism : networked infrastructures, technological mobilities and the urban condition* (2001), and D. Harvey: *A brief history of neoliberalism* (2007).

**22** Sassen (2012), op.cit. and Harvey (2007), op.cit.

**23** Brash (2011), op.cit.; K. Sehested (ed.): *Bypolitk – mellem hierarki og netværk* (2003) and D. Harvey: 'From Managerialism to Entrepreneurialism: The Transformation' in Urban Governance in Late Capitalism. *Geografiska Annaler. Series B, Human Geography*, 71(1), 1989, p. 3.

**24** Sassen (2012), op.cit.; J. Brash: 'The ghost in the machine: the neoliberal urban visions of Michael Bloomberg', and H. Ibelings: *Shifts. Architecture after the 20th century* (2012).

**25** Bauman (2002), op.cit.

**26** G. Delanty: *Community* (2003).

**27** A. Giddens: *Modernitet og selvidentitet* (1996); Z. Bauman: *Flydende modernitet* (2006); and U. Beck: *Risikosamfundet* (1997).

**28** Bauman (2002), op.cit.; G. Delanty: *Community* (2003); R.D. Putnam: *Bowling Alone* (2008); and M. Freudendal-Pedersen: *Mellem frihed og ufrihed*. Thesis type (2007).

**29** J. Andersen et al. (eds.): *Byen i bevægelse* (2012), and S. Andersen & M. Toft-Jensen (eds.): *Byen bliver til* (2012).

**30** OMA: *Ville Nouvelle Melun Senart* (1997).

**31** Vindum (2010), op.cit.

**Literature**


- Andersen, H. (ed.): *Sociologi – en grundbog til et fag*, 4th edition, Hans Reitzels Forlag, Copenhagen 2011.
- Andersen, J., et al. (eds.): *Byen i bevægelse*, Roskilde Universitetsforlag, Copenhagen 2012.
- Andersen, S. & M. Toft-Jensen (eds.): *Byen bliver til*, Forlaget PB43, Copenhagen 2012.
- Bauman, Z.: *Flydende modernitet*, Hans Reitzels Forlag, Copenhagen 2006.
- Bauman, Z.: *Fællesskab*, Hans Reitzels Forlag, Copenhagen 2002.
- Beck, U.: *Risikosamfundet*, Hans Reitzels Forlag, Copenhagen 1997.
- Bendsen, J.R.: *Enkelhed, mådehold og funktionalitet*. University of Copenhagen, 2009.
- Bendsen, J.R.: 'Værdiernes Værdi' in *Arkitektur DK*, (6), pp. 53-54, 2010.
- Brash, J.: *Bloomberg's New York – Class and Governance in the Luxury City*, the University of Georgia Press, Athens, Georgia 2011.
- Brash, J.: The ghost in the machine: the neoliberal urban visions of Michael Bloomberg. *Journal of Cultural Geography*, 29(2), 2012, pp. 135-153.
- Delanty, G.: *Community*, Routledge, London & New York 2003.
- Dirckinck-Holmfeld, K.: 'Det moderne sammenbrud' in Keiding, M., Amundsen, M., & Dirckinck-Holmfeld, K. (eds.): *Dansk Arkitektur siden 1754*. The Danish Architectural Press, København 2007, pp. 311-95.
- Esping-Andersen, G.: *The three worlds of welfare capitalism*, Polity Press, Cambridge, UK 1990.
- Faber, T.: *Dansk Arkitektur*, The Danish Architectural Press, Copenhagen 1977.
- Freudendal-Pedersen, M.: *Mellem frihed og ufrihed*. Thesis type. Roskilde Universitetscenter, Institut for Miljø, Samfund og Rumlig Forandring, Roskilde 2007.
- Gehl, J.: *Livet mellem husens*, The Danish Architectural Press, Copenhagen 1971.
- Giddens, A.: *Modernitet og selvidentitet*, Hans Reitzels Forlag, Copenhagen 1996.
- Graham, S., & Marvin, S.: *Splintering urbanism: networked infrastructures, technological mobilities and the urban condition*, Routledge, London & New York 2001.
- Greve, B.: *Velfærdssamfundet – en grundbog*, Academica, Aarhus 2008.
- Greve, B.: 'Velfærdsstaten' in Greve, B., Jørgensen, B., & Elm, L.J. (eds.): *Det Danske Samfund*. Hans Reitzels Forlag, Copenhagen 2014, pp. 45-66.
- Grubbauer, M., & Steets, S.: 'The Making of Architects: Knowledge Production and Legitimation in Education and Professional Practice' in *Architectural Theory Review*, 19(1), 2014, pp. 4-9.

- Gaardmand, A.: *Dansk byplanlægning: 1938-1992*, The Danish Architectural Press, Copenhagen 1993.
- Harvey, D.: 'From Managerialism to Entrepreneurialism: The Transformation' in Urban Governance in Late Capitalism. *Geografiska Annaler. Series B, Human Geography*, 71(1), 1989, p. 3.
- Harvey, D.: *The Condition of Postmodernity*, Blackwell, Oxford 1990.
- Harvey, D.: *A brief history of neoliberalism*, Oxford University Press, Oxford & New York 2007.
- Ibelings, H.: *Shifts. Architecture after the 20th century*, The Architecture Observer, Amsterdam 2012.
- Ibelings, H.: *Supermodernism: Architecture in the age of globalization*, NAi, Rotterdam 1998.
- Keiding, M.: 'Dem og os eksisterer ikke længere – interview med Kent Martinussen' in *Arkitektur DK*, 54(6), 2010, pp. 12-15.
- Keiding, M., Amundsen, M., & Dirckinck-Holmfeld, K.: *Dansk arkitektur siden 1754*, The Danish Architectural Press, Copenhagen 2007.
- Kulturministeriet: *Arkitekturpolitik – Mennesker i centrum*, Copenhagen, 2014.
- Kvorning, J.: 'Tourist Urbanism – The Peaceful Path to Real Reform?' in *Arkitektur DK*, 54(2), 2010, pp. 87-89.
- Langkilde, H.E., Dirckinck-Holmfeld, K., & Christiansen, J. Hegner: *Arkitekten 100 år*, The Danish Architectural Press, Copenhagen 1998.
- Lotz, K.: 'Dansk Arkitektur som velfærdseksport' in *Arkitekten*, 112(10), 2010, pp. 46-48.
- Lund, N.-O.: *Nordisk Arkitektur*, The Danish Architectural Press, Copenhagen 2008.
- Millech, K.: *Danske Arkitekturstrømninger* K. Fisker, editor, Østifternes Kreditforening, Copenhagen 1951.
- Nielsen, T.: *Gode intentioner og uregerlige byer*, Arkitektskolens Forlag, Aarhus 2008.
- Nygaard, E.: *Arkitektur i en forvirret tid: internationale strømninger 1968-1994*, Christian Ejlers' Forlag, Copenhagen 1995.
- OMA: *Ville Nouvelle Melun Senart*, 1997.
- Pagh, J.: 'Dansk Arkitektur Import-Eksport A/S' in *Arkitekten*, 110(11), 2010, pp. 66-69.
- Pedersen, P.B.: *Arkitektur og plan i den danske velfærdsby 1950-1990 – Container og urbant raster*, Arkitektskolens Forlag, Aarhus 2005.
- Petersen, J.H., Petersen, K., & Christiansen, N.F. (eds.): *Hvor glider vi hen? Dansk Velfærdshistorie bind 6: 1993-2014*, Syddansk Universitetsforlag, Odense 2014.
- Petersen, J.H., Petersen, K., & Christiansen, N.F. (eds.): *Velfærdsstaten i tidehverv. Dansk Velfærdshistorie bind 5: 1973-1993*, Syddansk Universitetsforlag, Odense 2013.
- Petersen, J.H., Petersen, K., & Christiansen, N.F. (eds.): *Velfærdsstatens storhedstid. Dansk Velfærdshistorie bind 4: 1956-1973*, Syddansk Universitetsforlag, Odense 2012.
- Petersen, K. (ed.): *13 historier om den danske velfærdsstat*, Syddansk Universitetsforlag, Odense 2013.
- Provoost, M.: 'For det fælles bedste' in *Arkitektur DK*, 57(1), 2013, pp. 8-15.
- Putnam, R.D.: *Bowling Alone*, New York, Simon & Schuster Paperbacks, New York 2008.
- Rasmussen, S.E.: *London*, Gyldendal, Copenhagen 1973.
- Rasmussen, S.E.: *Om at opleve arkitektur*, GEC Gads, Copenhagen 1957.
- Rasmussen, S.E.: *Steen Eiler Rasmussens København: Et bysamfunds særpræg og udvikling gennem tiderne*, Gads Forlag, Copenhagen 1969.
- Sassen, S.: *Cities in a World Economy* 4th edition, Sage, London 2012.
- Schoch, O., Vindum, K., & Bjerring, S.: 'Hvordan designer vi og hvorfor' in *Arkitekten*, 112(6), 2010, pp. 32-75.
- Sehested, K. (ed.): *Bypolitk – mellem hierarki og netværk*, Akademisk Forlag, Copenhagen 2003.
- Vanstiphout, Wouter: 'Nothing More Political' in *Volume* (34) 2012, pp. 10-16.
- Vindum, K.: 'Dansk arkitektur under forandring? Dansk arkitektur som identitetsprojekt', 2010.
- Vindum, K., & Weiss, K.L. (eds.): *Den ny bølge i dansk arkitektur*, The Danish Architectural Press, Copenhagen 2012.

# Landscape

Ellen Braae

# Welfare Landscapes and Communities

**Danish housing developments of the post-war era were a cornerstone in the implementation of the welfare vision and the overall urban and landscape planning in the post-war period. The new city was a *horizontal* city and – as it will be my primary ambition to show – a green and landscape-like city. The landscape came, in Denmark, to play a prominent role and became synonymous with 'The Good Life', but it also presented a number of moral imperatives. The article concerns how communities and community feelings found their expression in the Danish 'welfare landscapes'.**

## Introduction

After the Second World War, what we today call The Welfare City emerged. In Denmark, more than half of the current building stock stems from the period after 1945. Yet we can see that the post-war era's urban areas constitute far more than half of the total urban area. The new city was a horizontal city and, in particular, a green and-like city, where the landscape played a prominent role – both in planning and in the design of the many building typologies, where schools, town halls, sports facilities, infrastructure, industrial areas, and especially residential areas, demanded extensive tracts of land. The landscape became synonymous with 'The Good Life', but also presented a number of moral imperatives. The notions of community and of strengthening the democratic spirit are two essential aspects of the post-war era's Welfare City, which to a great extent have been achieved through the green open spaces. Below, I will take a closer look at how communities and a sense of community are expressed in the 'welfare landscapes' which are an integral and constituent aspect of the achievement of the Danish welfare state. My investigation is related to the time when the welfare landscapes took their beginnings, although the perspective is still current, since the question of community is no less relevant today than it was immediately after the Second World War, when Europe, in many respects, lay in ruins. In an international context, recent conventions, which Denmark has also endorsed, emphasize the shared landscape as perhaps the single most important component for the individual's well-being and for a socially stable Europe.[1] My interest is related to the welfare landscape, by which is meant a physical, spatial phenomenon that, in terms of scale, spans from design to planning, from the balcony with a view of the housing project's open park, to the green wedges in the Greater Copenhagen *Finger Plan*. In turn, this is related to how the architects – landscape architects and urban planners – designed the basis for communities in the development of the Danish welfare city, where I consider housing projects within the framework of The Finger Plan.

## What are 'welfare landscapes'?

Post-war urban development far exceeds the urban development in the decades before and after 1900. This applies not only to the number of square metres constructed, but also to the area seized and laid claim to by the city. The new city can be seen as a counter-response to the densely built-up city, with its endless rows of slums, which were mainly the result of private speculation-fuelled construction in the new urban quarters outside the city's original walled fortifications. This was a counter-response in which the landscape played a prominent role as a guarantor for and symbol of The Good Life, and as the antithesis of the industrial city's diseases and social misery. The post-war vision of The Good Life thus concerned daylight, fresh air and good health for everyone, but also democracy as a new (inter)national and local fellowship.

Equal access to green open spaces is a dogma in international Modernist urban planning and architecture,[2] and received special attention in Denmark from an early stage.[3] In addition to offering sunlight and fresh air, green open spaces are considered to be an ideological prerequisite for a healthy life.[4] This is a continuation of a long-standing *leitmotif* in European thinking, whereby green outdoor spaces rank as universal symbols of liberty and equality, and as a collective and humanistic prerequisite for a new and better life,[5] while fashioning the physical framework for Vitalism's concept of a sound mind in a healthy body.[6] This tradition, which was significantly reinforced after the Second World War and which, to some extent, still applies,[7] is expressed particularly in social housing and urban planning. In Denmark, the State is the central protagonist in this development and mediates the market and civil society within the 'social democratic' welfare model that characterizes the Nordic countries.[8] The State thus assumes universal responsibility for all citizens throughout their lives: women and men, from cradle to grave; and also governs geographically, from coast to coast, via public services, zoning, and conservation measures. Even though

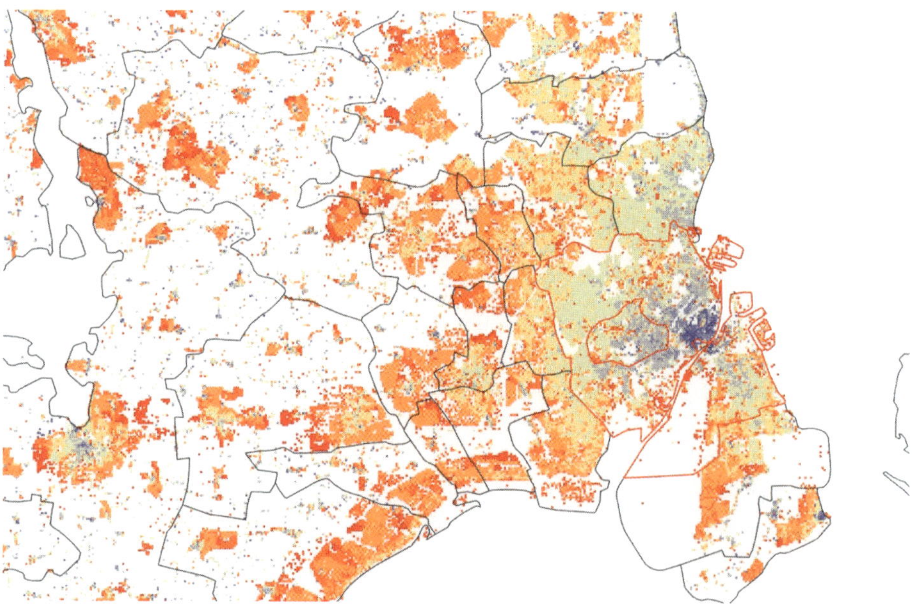

Copenhagen's development.
The areas marked in yellow, orange or red were all built after 1945.
(Courtesy of Dansk Bygningsarv).

residential construction is presented as the cornerstone of the achievement of The Good Life for every citizen, my point is that it is just as much in 'the outdoor spaces', i.e. the housing project's 'common ground' or landscape, and how the planning process treats nature assets and recreational spaces, that the materialization of the ideological mindset upon which the post-war era's ambitions rested really takes place. Furthermore, it is part of the welfare aspect of these local 'outdoor spaces' or residential landscapes that they are connected to the large-scale, recreational aspects of the overall planning, and thereby contribute to an experience of the landscape as a shared concern.

## Danish landscape architecture as an international reference point

In the decades after the Second World War, Denmark was an international model for public housing. The residential construction projects were described as a 'spatial ensemble' which, with its

The Danish landscape architect C.Th. Sørensen's book *Parkpolitik* [Park Policy], which was published in 1931, came to exert a great deal of influence within Denmark and abroad. The cover of the book was embossed with the slogan: "Fremtidens Park er til at røre sig i!' [The future's park is for exercising!] and was embellished with three drawings that signalled, respectively: taking care of the gardening chores, sports activities and little children at play, thus addressing the entire gamut of the age spectrum: from childhood through adulthood and into old age.

This photograph of The Children's Pond next to the new housing development Fredhäll, designed in 1937 by Oswald Almqvist, emblematically renders the notion of The Good Life in 'natural' surroundings.

well-integrated dialogue between structural architecture, landscape architecture and overall planning that was established in Denmark in 1945-75, was a source of great inspiration abroad, in the same way as the specific landscape-architectural aspects.[9] Equivalent and more sustained international attention was paid to the Danish way of handling the balance between the urban and the rural landscape, between built-up and unbuilt areas, which was iconized in the Finger Plan from 1947. This was a continuation of the report *Københavnsegnens Grønne Omraader* [Green Areas in the Copenhagen Region] from 1936, which was aimed at safeguarding areas of particular landscape-related or recreational value, and ensuring that there would be access to them. The need for conservation and for development, as expressed in the two plans in combination, is represented by the pedagogical figure of 'the hand', of which the palm represents the 'old' Copenhagen and 'the fingers' are the new city, determined and defined by arterial thoroughfares such as S-trains and major radial roads, as well as the green wedges that 'separate' the fingers. Both the planning and the design of the public housing projects denote local 'imagined communities',[10] where the landscape both frames and forms the centre of the planned micro-society. The landscape's design contains moral assertions concerning the relationship between the individual and the collective,[11] and thereby reflects the architects' notions about community and their hopes for – some might even say their almost naïve faith in – opportunities for both 'social engineering' and moral

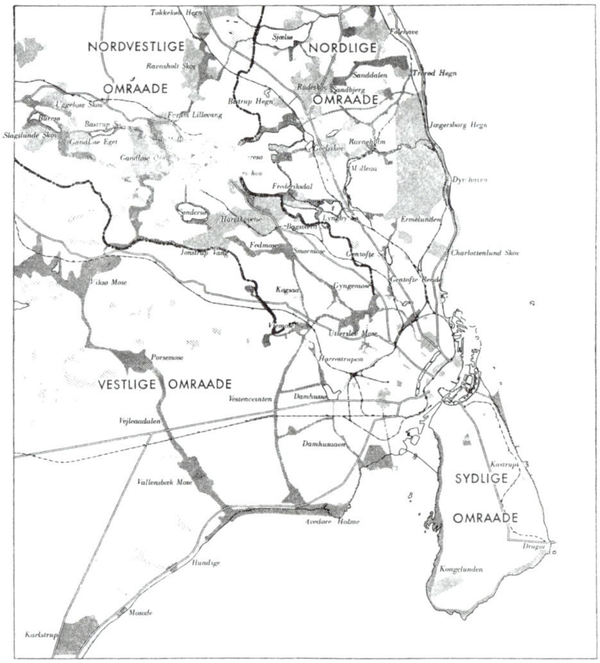


*Den Grønne Betænkning* [The Green Report] functioned as a preliminary plan for Regionplanen for Storkøbenhavn [The Regional Plan for Greater Copenhagen] (1936) and focused on the conservation of interconnected green areas.

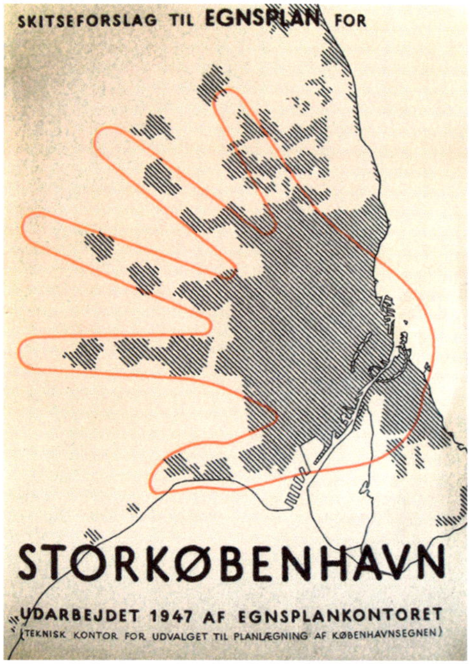


The iconic *Finger Plan* from 1947 indicates Copenhagen's future urban development as it proceeds along 'the fingers'. The Green Report's designated areas appear, indirectly, as green wedges.

influence through design.[12] It is therefore crucial to examine which characteristics, values, practices and discourses are embedded in the welfare landscapes, in order to understand and formulate their spatial ethical function as a shared framework for many people.[13]

## Sense of community

Danish political culture is the result of an especially Danish modernization process, which builds on an accumulated and learned experience that, when they stand together, people of humble means can actually bring about change. This basic narrative descends from smallholders, the folk high school movement and the cooperative movement, via the trade unions, to various social and cultural movements in the 20th century.[14]
Architecture plays a special role in the State's functional mediation of social interaction based on equality, consensus and conformity. The almost institutionalized perception of The Good Life applies to everyone. For some time now, however, this universal understanding has been disintegrating. It is claimed that we currently face a crisis whereby the inherited, persistent truisms related to traditional forms of community no longer have practical validity.[15] The burning question is, of course, what this means for the many 'built communities' which make up the welfare city.
Let us first take a closer look at how former notions of community have been shored up and sustained, both physically and spatially. At the outset, it may be prudent to outline a few positions related to the concept of community. There are two basic notions of community. One is built on the idea of a pre-existing general will, a *volonté générale*, that forms the basis for the social community. This collective 'general' thinking can be found in the writings of Rousseau and, later on, Hegel, that gave the State a monopoly on the pursuit of society's common concerns.[16] We find the other notion of community in the idea of the 'egalitarian aristocracy', which praises individual freedom, independence and awareness of oneself, one's appearance, one's body and one's language.[17] The egalitarian aristocracy characterized the salons of the 1600s – as a thoroughly aestheticized and gestural way of life, where the civilized social conventions adapted to life in the city were referred to as 'urbanitas', and where urbanity was synonymous with gallant conduct. The egalitarian aristocracy fashioned the ideal for the subsequent community way of thinking, where the community establishes the framework for and forms the individual freedom of expression.
The first notion of community refers to a large collective entity and thus concerns the idea of a pre-existing general will. The second is based on the individual, who is civilized *into* a community. These two notions of community are interesting when seen from a philosophical, aesthetic angle, where the German philosopher Kant expounds on the aesthetic as a way of being in the world, and as a faculty of judgment, and sets this in relation to rational thinking; understood as a condition of balance. Schiller goes one step further with the idea of balance between sensibility and reason and introduces the idea of 'aesthetic education' as the path to the goal: 'the aesthetic function'. This condition or function is intended to bring human beings into balance and eliminate divides between those who are ruled by their senses, which, in Schiller's perspective, means the lowest social classes of people, and those who are guided by reason.[18] The aesthetic education thus contributes to the constitution of the human community. Accordingly, we can understand aesthetics as a social and community-generating instrument. The connection between aesthetics and nature has a long and complex antecedent history, but is proximate and intricate. Landscape as

an aesthetic category, by which we mean nature in our image, encounters resistance with the post-war era's increasing industrialization, whereby to a greater and greater extent reality no longer complies with our ideal perceptions of nature.[19] There is therefore an awareness of loss embedded in the post-war era's rapid urban expansion, both on the overall scale and at local level. The central questions are, then, what the landscape gave to the community when the residential areas were created, and which community-promoting role the landscape can still play today.

## The large and the small scale

The intricate balance between conservation and development which is found in the relationship between *Københavnsegnens Grønne Omraader* from 1936 and *Fingerplanen* from 1947, is the welfare state's bedrock. Denmark was, on the one hand – like its Scandinavian siblings – a progressive welfare state, which guaranteed a direction, determined action and legislation. On the other hand, conservation was an important component of the early political advances.[20] At the equilibrium point between conservation and development, the landscape comes to play an important role in the constitution of communities. In the municipalities north of Copenhagen, the 'nature suburbs', were created, where the conservation of nature came to be a particularly active urban development instrument, in the sense that conservation indirectly determined where urban development was to take place. Urban development was thus not formulated on an overall basis, but rather as a series of partial plans, which avoided consideration of the large open areas which, in the meantime, were gradually being conserved and then subsequently amassed into Søllerød Natural Park, a 300-hectare nature conservation area in the centre of the municipality. Most of the conservations were offshoots of the plans in *Københavnsegnens Grønne Omraader,* which focused primarily on historical landscapes. In Søllerød, this focus was widened to also include recreational areas such as parks and forests, although arable land was also included. Conservation became an urban planning tool to determine what was to be built, and where, and to avoid the 'endless rows of brick walls', as one of the key persons, Conservative-party mayor Erik Øigaard, put it.[21] These endless rows of brick walls were, for example, row houses, blocks of flats and, overall, densely-built complexes for average-income and less affluent citizens. In Søllerød, the result was a general provision that land could not be parcelled out in lots of less than 1,000 $m^2$. Community was thus being defined positively as a wish to conserve nature. When regarded as urban areas, the conserved nature areas set the framework for a community. This community is also socially determined by setting the framework for who can be included, in both physical and economic respects. On the one hand, residential construction constituted a joint European post-war task, while on the other hand, it was implemented locally in different ways. In Denmark, residential construction was the cornerstone of the achievement of the welfare state, with special and unique premises for the interaction between a robust housing movement, favourable state loans, effective planning and policy-making, socially committed architects, and skilled craftsmen.

In Copenhagen, Aarhus, Aalborg, Odense and other major Danish cities, the new housing projects were built on greenfield sites on the fringes of the old cities and were conjoined by roads and, in some cases, S-trains, which reflected future expectations. Internationally, requirements concerning light and air resulted in long, detached

The plan shows the town of Søllerød in 1988. The white and the yellow areas indicate the conserved natural areas that constitute Søllerød Naturpark [Søllerød Natural Park]. In 1943, the yellow areas were designated as sites for future urban development and their dimensions were such that nature conservation initiatives were activated. This came, albeit indirectly, to set the tone for urban development. (Courtesy of Jens Johannesen, Rudersdal Museums)

blocks of flats. In Denmark, however, a special type was developed: the 'open large block',[22] where the buildings were 'pushed' out to the site's perimeter, creating an interior open space or landscape. On the one hand, Danish residential construction is, in this way, inscribed directly into the major fundamental narrative and conjoins scale-related relations from the individual home with the large recreational landscapes. On the other hand, close studies reveal several notions of community that challenge the relation between the individual and the 'State'.

## Nærumvænge

Despite the aversion in Søllerød towards 'the endless rows of brick walls', through which one 'could [not] move around and only see villas and surrounding gardens', we do find a few multi-storey blocks of flats here. One of them is Nærumvænge, designed by architect Palle Suenson and landscape architect C.Th. Sørensen, and constructed in several phases between 1949 and 1961. In its overall contours, Nærumvænge establishes the transition from Nærum to Jægersborg Hegn, a conserved green area. In the nexus between the new development and the conserved area, between the existing Nærum and the new highway, we find Nærumvænge Torv [Plaza], with its shops, a post office and a community centre situated around a large parking area with direct view to the nature area. The rest is modulated as a rim development consisting exclusively of homes: two- or three-storey yellowbrick buildings

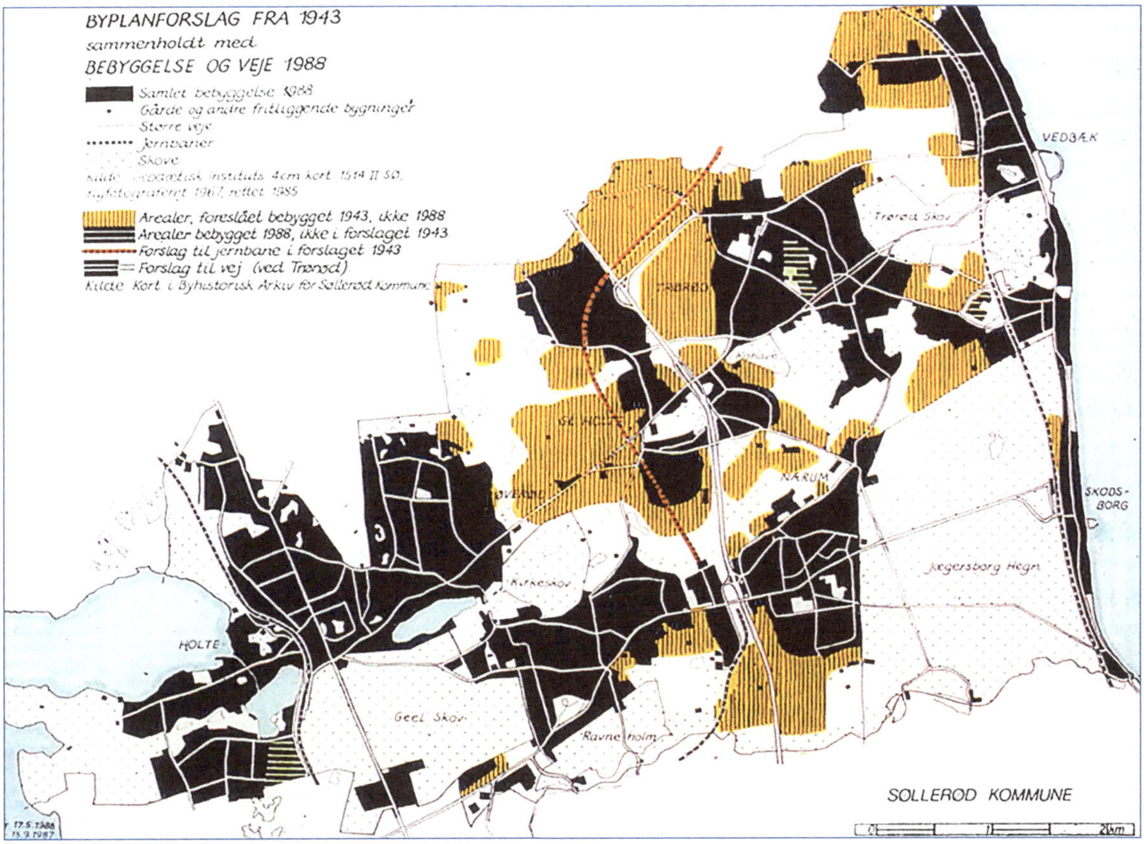

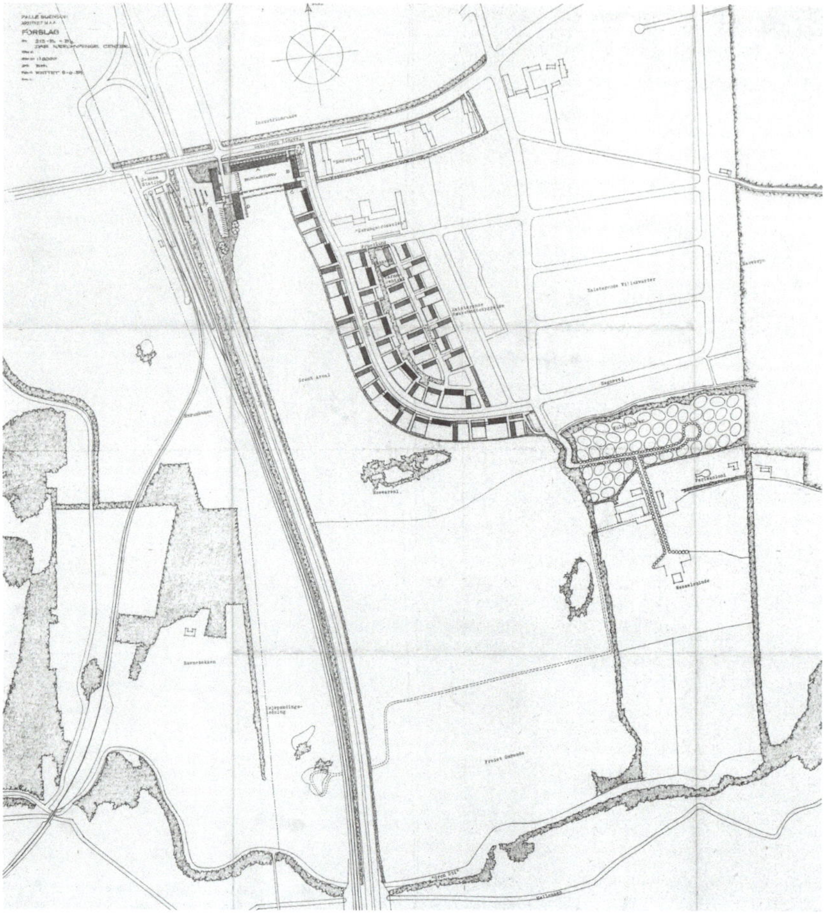


At first glance, Nærumvænge forms a striking transition to the preserved Jægersborg Hegn. As you zoom in, the housing development comes to be delineated in an increasingly varied way – and in spatial dialogue with the open areas.

Facing the preserved terrain, Nærumvænge establishes a modulated transition, where the shorter building volumes are positioned perpendicular to the borderline, while the taller ones are situated so as to be running along its breadth, even though they have been pulled back from the line. The shape of the hipped roof helps to visually draw the housing development 'down' towards the terrain. (Courtesy of Dansk Bygningsarv).

→
Dividing walls, half-high walls and hedges establish a distinctive interplay between building and landscape. These transitions are found again in the facades, where brick has been used, both inside and outside. (Courtesy of Dansk Bygningsarv).

with a distinctive hipped roof, which visually draws the buildings down towards the ground. In their lengthwise direction, the buildings follow a slightly curved course, interrupted rhythmically by transversely-oriented lower buildings which thus give rise to inwardly inflected spatialities running along the outwardly inflected curve. In this way, this structure is recapitulated in a layer inside the rim itself and accordingly duplicates the narrative. The buildings are modular, with panels of lightweight materials between the structurally-determined transverse walls, which are frequently elongated outside the building as sheltering and retaining walls. These wall elements interact reciprocally with hedges, as they also do on the ground's surface, where the lawns interact reciprocally with the yellowbrick surfaces. Overall, this is a display of how the transition between city and landscape can be construed by architecture and landscape architecture. The landscape, in the form of the conserved areas which configure the quarter, exerts a direct effect on the architecture.

The community is bound up, on an individual level, with the relation between the individual home and the large, green nature area. The vertically sectioned and storey-partitioned buildings appear as readable 'single-family cells', which communicate with the extensive landscape space outside the development. There is no middle ground, although a type of allotment gardens are established in connection with a few of the buildings. These are individual gardens, of which some reflect the flats, while others are empty, non-articulated lawns. The sense of community is actualized, in this way, on a pragmatic level, in connection with the shopping centre, and overall, but also more abstractly, in relation to the green area. Yet precisely because the shopping centre provides access to the larger landscape-like spaces and constitutes a meeting point for people outside the housing complex itself, Nærumvænge embodies the possibility that the landscape can indeed constitute the mediating factor with the capacity to provide a common space for others than those who have their homes in the building complex.

## Bredalsparken

An aerial photo from 1954, taken while Bredalsparken was still under construction, shows how the housing development was originally located at the bottom of the Vallensbæk wedge.[23] It can be seen how the new urban quarter spreads out around and outside the existing built-up areas, and on the outer side of the old town centre of Hvidovre. The buildings at Bredalsparken were designed by the architect Svenn Eske Kristensen, while the site plan and the landscape were designed by the landscape architect Axel Andersen. The site plan is a large open block: a mixture of long and detached blocks of flats, where all the buildings are consistently oriented southwest, towards the afternoon sun, and a block housing development, where the blocks give way to a large, central park space. The overall building complex appears as a park with a continuous common green 'floor', with large trees and scattered vegetation. The park-like character is underpinned by several design inventions. First of all, the differences in the site's level are treated as gliding transitions, with the result that the ground's floor appears as one continuous 'cloth', without folds or pleats, underpinning the experience of fluid spatial sequences and of a holistic entity. This green 'floor' extends all the way into the buildings' plinths, with the result that the buildings appear as solid, sharply-cut elements of fired bricks that have been pressed down into the soft, plastic clay-like soil, which in itself underscores the landscape-like character. The pathways meander at the horizontal level, while longitudinally following the course of the site. Apart from along the main

This aerial photograph of Bredalsparken, from 1954, displays the entire housing development as a giant 'solar collector' at the bottom of the Vallensbæk wedge.

→
Today, Bredalsparken is surrounded by more recent suburban sprawl and appears as one large park-like development.

access road, which conjoins the shopping centre with the central commons, there is no use, anywhere, of roadside trees, which might otherwise draw a line. The concept used has far more to do with space and spatial transitions than with lines and delimitations. This also helps to tone down the pathways' presence, for the benefit of the interaction between the buildings' stringent location and the casual and apparently random location of individual trees and groups of trees.

If we step down a level and zoom in on the transition between park and building, we can see that this junction has been articulated in several ways. On the buildings' challenging northeast sides, a variety of means have been put to use. Here we find, among other things, the entrance function, with a need for large paved surfaces; these seem detrimental to the park character. As a response to this daunting situation, the entrance level has been lowered compared to the surrounding terrain, so that it does not seem so dominant. As another response, the trellises suspended across the entrance area elicit associations with gardens and parks, and allow the green aspect to extend, quite literally, all the way into the building. The generous assortment of plants endows the area with a paradise-like character, an Elysium, where selected characteristic species of trees engender local identities within the aggregate building development's faintly defined constituent areas. The parallel displacement of the detached blocks of flats creates outdoor spaces on the buildings' sun-exposed sides, which are shielded from the westerly wind. In this way, a building cluster gives space for a small area in the park, thereby indicating a spirit of community among the people living in the adjacent groups of flats. Both as a totality and in its detail, the development sets a framework for how adult outdoor life can flourish, requiring people to be dressed according to the norms of the day, to meet neighbours' glances from the balconies.

In Bredalsparken, the sense of community is a matter of collective concern, and one could argue

that an indirect goal for the entire development – besides creating contemporary residential dwellings – is an aesthetic education, whereby all of the residents, whatever their origins, are choreographed into a scenography that gives great weight to the sense of community and to the landscape, shaped as stylized nature. The aesthetic dimension can be regarded as an instrumentalization, but also represents values *per se,* by virtue of the experience embedded in this universe. It is an apparently non-designed nature, which is simultaneously the image of a nature that sets people free from their dependence on nature in the form of keeping kitchen gardens and having livestock, and it is a nature formed as almost fractally constructed communities, where a small group of residents share one entrance and the functions that are found here. Furthermore, these residents can meet others from neighbouring stairwells out on the lawn in front of the group of buildings, and in the next stage, they can make use of the commons, together with the rest of the complex. To the east, the development converges with the surrounding town at the shopping centre, and looking towards the west, there is the vast landscape space of The Finger Plan. Here, all kinds of people are gathered together around a new way of living, where the spaces are shaped in order to strengthen a sense of community, but where there is not much room for individual interpretation and appropriation. Today, Bredalsparken's interior landscape is no longer directly connected with the Vallensbæk wedge, but it still appeals to and gathers the development's residents, and continues to establish frameworks around new activities such as playgrounds and cultivated gardens.

The division of the various quarters is articulated in a subtle way and supported by the choice of trees. The location of the housing units ensures both optimum sunlight for the individual flats and large landscape-like spaces that contribute to extensive spatial differentiation, in a way that presents a striking contrast to the more traditional positioning of parallel blocks of flats.

## Conclusion

Even though the Copenhagen area as a metropolis obviously holds a special status in Danish planning, the principles and values in the selected examples recur again and again on a national basis. New residential projects are situated outside the well-established cities and they both create and are oriented towards green open spaces. In the overall layout of the post-war era's city, the landscape, together with the infrastructure, becomes a constituent factor and takes on the role of a continuum, an amalgamating element within the function-segregated city; and simultaneously mediates between the city and the existing landscape, and between development and conservation. The communities, read as spatial structures, are construed and constructed in both their interiors and exteriors, as well as in their multi-scalar relations. Landscape features are used both to demarcate them from others and to create access and availability. Moving down to the local scale, there is both an interior and an exterior, and a chain of relations that range from the living room, the balcony or bay window, to the green commons in front of the building, and through the inner commons and further out to The Finger Plan. The communities, however, are formed on the basis of two different basic models: the collective general thinking; and the 'egalitarian aristocracy', whereby the latter exists within the framework of the former. In Nærumvænge's architecture and plan layout, the individual is in direct opposition to the good, albeit abstract, nature, while all of the differences in Bredalsparken, on the other hand, are collectivized into a common space that is subdivided into elements that appear to be identical. The question of spatially materialized notions of community is naturally challenged by the many communities that we today see unfolded in virtual space, and which are characterized by disregarding and overriding geography. Analogously, the landscape-like elements are challenged by other and more materially-rooted processes of change, such as climate change adaptations and densification, whereby the landscape's identity-creating apparition becomes, in certain contexts, a goal of the change and, in others, a conservation value. Feelings of community are dynamic, however, and must constantly be reformulated *by* those who are involved, so as to be perceived as meaningful *for* those who are involved. In a democratic perspective and in relation to the European Landscape Convention of the Council of Europe's perception of the landscape as shared ground, it is crucial, however, that public landscapes unceasingly continue to be inclusive rather than exclusive. Moreover, these welfare landscapes must necessarily balance between being *exclusively* something for somebody and *inclusively* inviting others inside. Today, however, the development does seem to be polarized, since the residential landscapes tend to enclose themselves exclusively around their own residents, while The Finger Plan's green wedges probably reflect existing support among the general population since, up until now, the wedges have withstood the pressure of urbanization. Nonetheless, by virtue of their static, anaesthetic and anonymous appearance, the wedges do not manage to allure anybody into any kind of community.

I would like to express my thanks to my welfare-landscape interested colleagues at the University of Copenhagen, Associate Professors Svava Riesto, Henriette Steiner, and Anne Tietjen, as well as Professor Tom Avermaete, TU Delft, with whom I have discussed many sub-topics and with whom I have built up the research project *Reconfiguring Welfare Landscapes*, funded by the Danish Council for Independent Research, which has partial overlaps with the present contribution.

**Notes**

1 FARO: *Convention on the Value of Cultural Heritage for Society* (2005); Den Europæiske Landskabskonvention 2000.
2 CIAM – Congress Internationaux d'Architecture Moderne: *La Charte d'Athènes or The Athens Charter* (1933). Translated by J. Tyrwhitt (1946).
3 C.Th. Sørensen: *Parkpolitik i Sogn og Købstad* (1931).
4 C. Wagenaar (ed.): *Happy: Cities and Public Happiness in Post-war Europe* (2004).
5 K. Worpole: *Here Comes the Sun. Architecture and Public Space in Twentieth-Century European Culture* (2000). M. Bolt & J. Lund (eds.): *Fællesskabsfølelser. Kunst, politik, filosofi* (2009).
6 M. Hauxner: *Paradisets have* (1993).
7 J. Barnett: *City Design. Modernist, Traditional, Green and Systems Perspectives* (2016), p. 59.
8 G. Esping-Andersen: *The Three Worlds of Welfare Capitalism*, Princeton University Press (1990, 1993).
9 G. Boye (ed.): 'Gardenmaking in Denmark, International Exhibition of Landscape Architecture, London August 1948'. Special edition of *Havekunst*, Vol. 29, 1948; E. Hiort: *Housing in Denmark since 1930* (1952); J. Woudstra: 'Danish Landscape Design in the Modern Era (1920-1970)', in *Garden History* 2 (1995), pp. 222-241, and M. Treib (ed.): *The Architecture of Landscape 1940-1960* (2002).
10 B. Andersson: *Imagined Communities: Reflections on the Origin and Spread of Nationalism* (1983).
11 G. Setten: 'The habitus, the rule and the moral landscape' in *Cultural Geographies* October 2004, vol. 11 no. 4, p. 392.
12 N. Albertsen and B. Diken: 'Welfare and the City' in *Nordisk Arkitekturforskning* 2, 7-22, 2004.
13 M. Swenarton, T. Avermaete & D. van den Heuvel (eds.): *Architecture and the Welfare State* (2015); T. Avermaete & D. van Heuvel (eds.): 'Otero-Pailos – The European Welfare State Project: Ideals, Politics, Cities and Buildings'. Special edition of *Footprint Journal* 9, Autumn 2011 and K. Worpole: *Here Comes the Sun. Architecture and Public Space in Twentieth-Century European Culture* (2000).
14 H. Kaare Nielsen: 'Fællesskabets posttraditionelle vilkår' in Bolt & Lund (2009), op.cit., pp. 39-62.
15 Ibid., M. Grøtta: Fellesskapets estetikk, eller kunsten å leve i fellesskap, in Bolt & Lund (2009), op.cit., pp. 129-146.
16 Kaare Nielsen (2009), op.cit.
17 Grøtta (2009), op.cit.
18 Ibid.
19 B. Kleimann: *Das ästhetische Weltverhältnis* (2002).
20 T. Arrhenius & J. Otero-Pailos: The Art of Organizing Attention in *Nordic Journal of Architecture*, no. 3, vol. 2, (2012), pp. 73-75.
21 C. Christiansen: 'Naturfredning og byplanlægning' in *Hovedstadsmetropolen efter 1945*, Bro et al. (eds.) (2011), p. 146.
22 S.I. Andersson. & S. Høyer: *C.Th. Sørensen – en havekunstner* (1993), p. 82.
23 www.krak.dk, retrieved March 28, 2016.

**Literature**


- Albertsen, N. & Diken, B.: 'Welfare and the City' in *Nordisk Arkitekturforskning* 2, 2004, pp. 7-22.
- Andersson, B.: *Imagined Communities: Reflections on the Origin and Spread of Nationalism*. Verso, London & New York 1983.
- Andersson, S.I., & Høyer, S.: *C.Th. Sørensen – en havekunstner*, The Danish Architectural Press, Copenhagen 1993.
- Arrhenius, T., & Otero-Pailos, J.: 'The Art of Organizing Attention' in *Nordic Journal of Architecture*, no. 3, vol. 2, Copenhagen 2012, pp. 73-75.
- Avermaete, T., & Heuvel, D. van den (eds.): 'Otero-Pailos – The European Welfare State Project: Ideals, Politics, Cities and Buildings'. Special edition of *Footprint Journal* 9, Autumn 2011.
- Barnett, J.: *City Design. Modernist, Traditional, Green and Systems Perspectives*, Routledge 2016.
- Bendsen, J.R., Engell, H., & Lind, O.: *Danmarks Almene Boliger. Copenhagen*: BL Danmarks Almene Boliger/Danish Social Housing and The Danish Centre for Architecture, Copenhagen 2012.
- Bjørn, N. (ed.): *Arkitektur der forandrer: Fra ghetto til velfungerende byområde*, The Danish Architectural Press, Copenhagen 2008.
- Bolt, M. & Lund, J. (eds.): *Fællesskabsfølelser. Kunst, politik, filosofi*. Klim, Aarhus 2009.
- Boye, Georg (ed.): 'Gardenmaking in Denmark, International Exhibition of Landscape Architecture, London August 1948'. Special issue of *Havekunst*, vol. 29, 1948.
- Bro, H.: 'Naturforstæderne' in *Hovedstadsmetropolen efter 1945*, Bro et al. (eds.), Hovedstadsområdets Kulturhistoriske Arkiver, Copenhagen 2011, pp. 132-35.
- Braae, E.: 'Hvorfor 1940erne og 1950ernes boligbebyggelses-landskaber' in *Landskab* 6, 2016.
- Braae, E., & Riesto, S.: 'Kunst, Natur og Fællesskab. Guldalder for dansk landskabsarkitektur og -planlægning', in *1940'erne og 1950'ernes murede boligbebyggelser. Bygningskultur og Bevaringsværdier*, Dansk Bygningsarv, 2015, pp. 44-47.
- Buus, H.: *Indretning og efterretning. Rockefeller Foundations indflydelse på den danske velfærdsstat 1920-1970*, Museum Tusculanums Forlag, Copenhagen 2008.

- Bøggild, S., & Braae, E.: 'The Green Heritage of the Danish Welfare State' in *Nordic Journal of Architecture* no. 4, vol. 5, Summer 2015, pp. 84-93.
- Christiansen, C.: Naturfredning og byplanlægning, in *Hovedstadsmetropolen efter 1945*, Bro et al. (eds.), Hovedstadsområdets Kulturhistoriske Arkiver, Copenhagen 2011, pp. 137-57.
- CIAM – Congress Internationaux d'Architecture Moderne: *La Charte d'Athènes or The Athens Charter*, 1933. Translated by J. Tyrwhitt. Paris: The Library of the Graduate School of Design, Harvard University, Cambridge MA 1946.
- Council of Europe: 'The Faro Convention', Council of Europe Framework *Convention on the Value of Cultural Heritage for Society*, Treaty No. 199, 01/06/2011 www.coe.int/en/web/conventions/full-list/-/conventions/treaty/199
- Council of Europe: *The European Landscape Convention*, Treaty no 176, 20/10/2000.
- Creagh, L.: 'From Acceptera to Vällingby: The Discourse on Individuality and Community in Sweden (1931-54)' in: *Footprint Journal*, August 1, 2014, vol. 5(2), pp. 5-24.
- Esping-Andersen, G.: *The Three Worlds of Welfare Capitalism*, Princeton University Press, Princeton NJ 1990, 1993.
- Esping-Andersen, G. (ed.): *Why We Need a New Welfare State*, Oxford University Press, 2002.
- Grøtta, M.: 'Fellesskapets estetikk, eller kunsten å leve i fellesskap' in M. Bolt & J. Lund (eds.): *Fællesskabsfølelser. Kunst, politik, filosofi*, Klim, Aarhus 2009, pp. 129-46.
- Gaardmand, A.: *Dansk Byplanlægning 1938-1992*, The Danish Architectural Press, Copenhagen 1993.
- Giedion, S.: *Space, Time and Architecture*, Harvard University Press, Cambridge MA 1967.
- Harwood, E.: 'Post-war Landscape and Public Housing', in *Garden History*, vol. 28, No 1, Summer 2000, pp. 102-116.
- Hauxner, M.: *Paradisets have*, The Danish Architectural Press, Copenhagen, 1993.
- Hauxner, M.: *Open to the Sky,* The Danish Architectural Press, Copenhagen, 2003.
- Hauxner, M.: *Supernatur*, Ikaros Press, Aarhus, 2010.
- Hiort, E.: *Housing in Denmark since 1930*, Julius Gjellerups Forlag, Copenhagen, 1952.
- Lund, A.: *Danmarks Havekunst*, Vol. 3, 1945-2002, The Danish Architectural Press, Copenhagen, 2002.
- Lund, A.: *Guide to Danish Landscape Architecture 1000-2003*, The Danish Arcitectural Press, Copenhagen, 2003.
- Kleimann, B.: *Das ästhetische Weltverhältnis*, Wilhelm Fink Verlag, Munich, 2002.
- Kaare Nielsen, H.: 'Fællesskabets posttraditionelle vilkår' in M. Bolt & Lund, J. (eds.): *Fællesskabsfølelser. Kunst, politik, filosofi*, Klim, Aarhus 2009, pp. 39-62.
- Mattsson, H. & Wallenstein, S.O. (eds.): *Swedish Modernism: Architecture, Consumption and the Welfare State*, Black Dog Publishers, London, 2010.
- Nielsen, T.: *Gode intentioner og uregerlige byer*, Arkitektskolens Forlag, Aarhus, 2008.
- Pedersen, P.B.: *Arkitektur og Plan i Den Danske Velfærdsby 1950-1990: Container og urbant raster.* Arkitektskolens Forlag, Aarhus, 2005.
- Pedersen, P.B.: 'Container and Urban Raster- Elements in the Theory of Urbanism', in *Nordic Journal of Architectural Research*, Welfare City Theory, Vol. 17, no. 2, 2004.
- Pendlebury, Townsend & Gilroy (2009): 'Social housing as heritage: the case of Byker, Newcastle upon Tyne' in *Valuing Historical Environments*, L. Gibson & J. Pendlebury (editors), pp. 179-200. Ashgate, Aldershot, Farnham.
- Rogazcqewska, N.A. et al.: At Huse Alle/How to House, Copenhagen: BL Dannmarks Almene Boliger/ Danish Social Housing, 2014.
- Rørtveit, H.N. & Setten, G.: 'Modernity, Heritage, and Landscape: The Housing Estate as Heritage' in *Landscape Research*, vol. 40 (8), 2015.
- Setten, G.: 'The Habitus, the Rule and the Moral Landscape' in *Cultural Geographies* October 2004, vol. 11 no. 4, pp. 389-415.
- Steiner, H.: 'The Earth does not Move and the Ground of the City – Towards a Phenomenology of the City', in *Journal of Comparative Cultural Studies in Architecture*, 2012, 6, pp. 46-55.
- Stonor Saunders, F.: *The Cultural Cold War. The CIA and the World of Arts and Letters*, The New Press, NY 1999, 2013.
- Sverrild, P.: *Velfærdssamfundets Bygninger*, Bygningskulturens dag, Kulturarvsstyrelsen, Copenhagen 2008.
- Swenarton, M., Avermaee, T., & Heuvel, D. van den (eds.): *Architecture and the Welfare State*, Routledge, New York, 2015.
- Sørensen, C.Th.: *Parkpolitik i Sogn og Købstad*, Gyldendal, Copenhagen, 1931.
- Tietjen, A. (ed.): *Forstadens Bygningskultur 1945-1989: På sporet af velfærdsforstadens bevaringsværdier*, Realdania & Dansk Bygningsarv, Copenhagen, 2010.
- Treib, M. (ed.): *The Architecture of Landscape 1940-1960*, University of Pennsylvania Press, Philadelphia, 2002.
- Wagenaar, C. (ed.): *Happy: Cities and Public Happiness in Post-war Europe*, NAI Press, Rotterdam, 2004.
- Worpole, K.: *Here Comes the Sun. Architecture and Public Space in Twentieth-Century European Culture*, Reaction Books, London 2000.
- Woudstra, J.: 'Danish Landscape Design in the Modern Era (1920-1970)', in *Garden History* 2, 1995, pp. 222-41.

Rosalina Wenningsted-Torgard

# Infrastructure as Landscape

Changing ideas about The Good Life have influenced the planning and the design of urban water infrastructures. Through time, layers of spatial structures have added to and have formed the welfare city as it appears today. In certain periods, the water has been hidden away in subterranean drainage systems, while more recently, there has been a tendency to let the water remain visible on the surface. The technical infrastructures become part of the recreational landscape and the object of spatial interpretation. Brøndby Municipality, in the western region of Copenhagen, is a fine example of how the water, through the times, has brought the landscape into play.

On a rainy summer day, you can experience the water-filled meadows in The Green Wedge in Brøndby as part of a peri-urban landscape surrounded by soccer fields and noise barriers. But it hasn't always been like this around here. In the wake of the spectacular cloudbursts in 2010, the sewerage systems were flooded, and the water had to find place elsewhere. In Brøndby, it was the motorway that got flooded. Since 1956, Rosenåen stream in The Green Wedge has been culverted so that the polluted water would not pose a nuisance to the urban life,[1] but the culverting has also entailed that only a limited amount of water has been able to flow through. At the same time, the increased consolidation of the surface, in synch with the gradual expansion of the suburbs, has entailed that more and more water has been discharged and conducted into the sewer pipes instead of seeping down into the subterranean levels, beneath the fields and meadows. The earliest systematic registrations of the cultivated landscape's catchment systems can be seen in topographical maps from the 1890s. Here Rosenåen's meandering course can be read as a trail running through the terrain, amidst a fine-meshed network of trenches and drainage canals that served to render the flat moraine formation susceptible to cultivation. Today we have changed the practice, with the result that the water is not solely conducted in the fastest possible way to the sewers, as waste. A current tendency, which is linked to climate adaptation, is to let the water remain visible and find its place on the surfaces of the landscape.[2] In the time to come, sustainable infrastructures will also presumably include collection, storage and use of rainwater as a source of supply. This is going to call for the development of general technical solutions, and for knowledge about how the specific urban landscape has been assembled, because the infrastructural decisions have spatial consequences. Through the years, the water infrastructure has, by turns, been visible or has been hidden, in different ways, depending on the geographical

←↓
'The space of the water' depicted in photos and drawing. A natural stream was culverted in 1956. Historical drains was mapped in the 1890's and later on forgotten in the urban development. Water from the modern sewer systems was temporarily visible and disturbs other infrastructures during the cloudburst event in 2010 as can be seen in the image on the previous page. Photos and maps by courtesy of Biofos, 'Forstadsmuseet' and the Danish Geodata Agency.

→
Copenhagen region and suburbs where the Western Rampart forms a curved line across the built 'fingers' and joins Utterslev Bog in the undulating northern areas.
All drawings by the author.

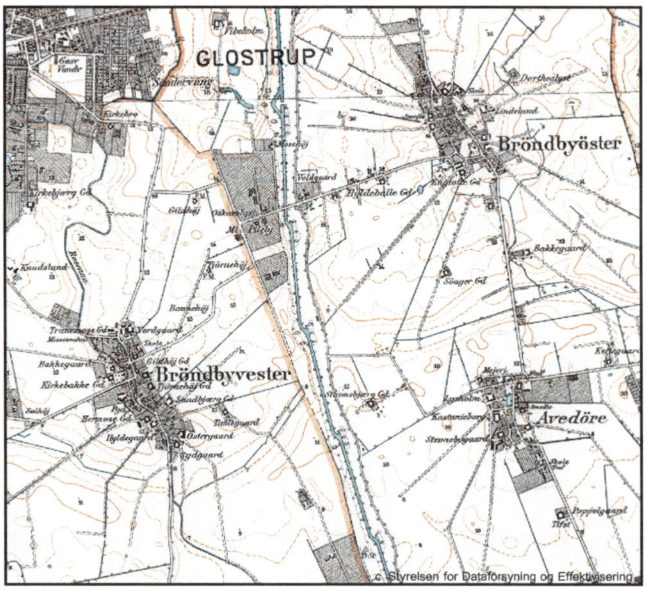

context. However, what landscapes and what common open spaces are linked to the water infrastructure? And how does this manifest itself in the welfare city?

In this article, I will be taking a look at the suburban landscape in the municipality of Brøndby as both a typical and a characteristic example of achieving an architectural understanding of technical service functions as waterscapes. After comparing different cartographic drawings with my observations in the field, I have chosen three water system types that complement each other as spatial phenomena.[3]

In employing the concept, 'the space of the water' I aim to draw attention to how the different types of infrastructural types can be considered spatial, on the basis of the intensities and rhythms that are associated with the dynamics of water. I interpret the water infrastructure as landscape and as urban space, on the basis of visibility and expression, in the form of tones and ambience that are associated with the terrain's layers of interwoven structures and porous textures running transversely to different scales as well as culture-historical origins.

## The space of the water

Various strategies, planning ideas and forms of administration have all influenced the urban water infrastructures and consequently also, albeit to a different degree, the configuration of urban open spaces. In a Danish context, the concept of 'the welfare city' refers to the planned city as it was

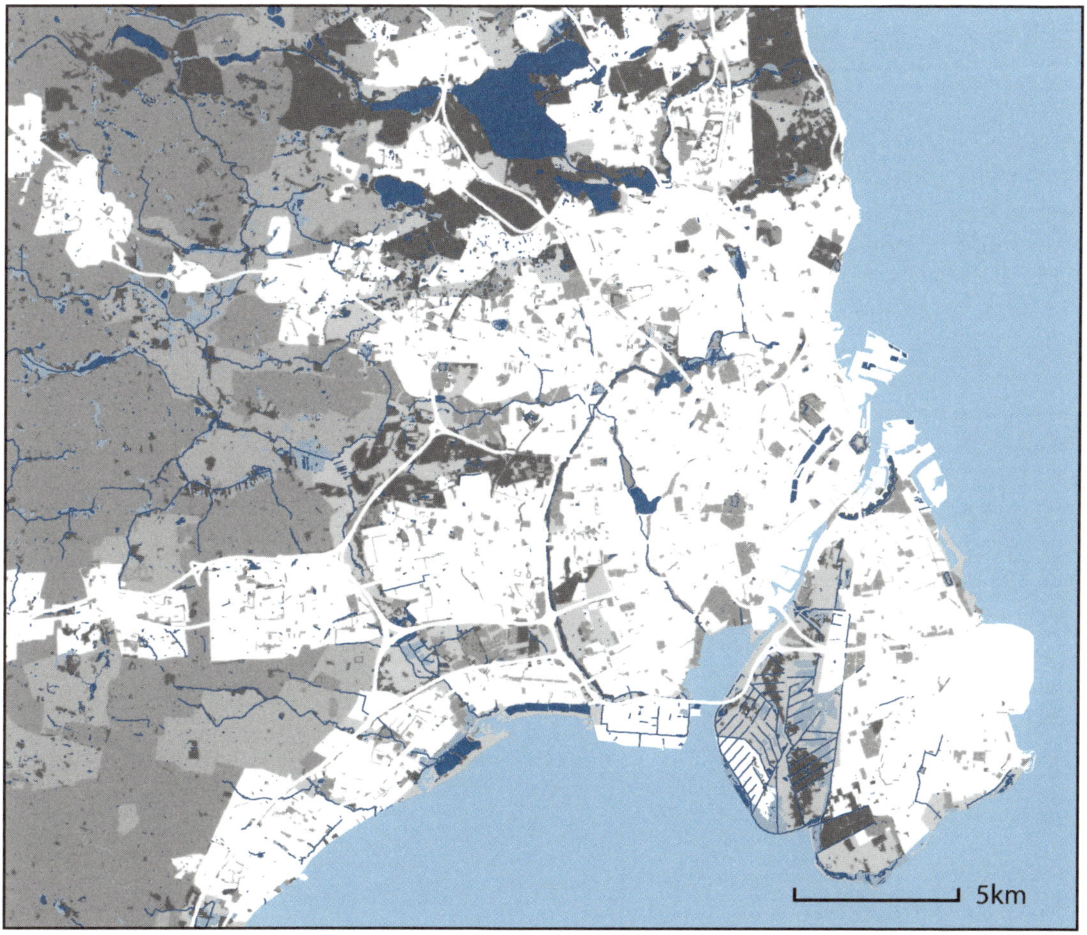

established in the period spanning from the 1950s to the 1990s, and which has been characterized typologically by the architects Poul Bæk Pedersen as *container and urban raster*,[4] and Carsten Juel-Christiansen as *monument and niche.*[5] Modernism's – and accordingly the post-war era's – welfare ideas were motivated by a clear functional division between 'city' and 'rural districts', as can be seen in the concept of The Finger Plan, which was formulated in 1947.[6] In the adjoining plan of green spaces for the Copenhagen region,[7] green wedges extend their way in toward the capital city centre. These 'wedges' where situated in between the developed 'fingers' and programmed with the emerging concept of 'the leisure landscape', as it has been described by Malene Hauxner in her book *Open to the Sky.*[8] If, on the other hand, we take a closer look at the actual realization of The Finger Plan, it is clear to see how preliminary conditions related to the landscape have influenced the demarcation of the boundary between urban and rural terrain in markedly different ways in, respectively, the northern and the south-western regions around Copenhagen. The clear contrasts in the terrain in the northern regions forms the basis for a traditional view of the urban waterscapes as 'blue structures', with a clear outer boundary. The topographic differences between the two regions in question are emphasized by the water-based fortifications that encircle Copenhagen.[9] Whereas the northern part, with Utterslev Bog, consists of an ingenious system of dikes and dams that were set up for the purpose of flooding acreage in the natural terrain, the south-western section consists of the large rampart structure, Vestvolden (1880-1920), where a canal conjoins the bog in the north with Køge Bay in the south.

This chapter sheds light on the urban waterscapes in a geographical situation with more muted nuances in the landscape's topography. In the present analysis, I am making use of the theme of 'water' as a lens through which to view the city. The lens here consists of a process of looking for 'the space of the water' as forms of hollow spaces within the textures that run across different scales. This means to say that I am examining the way in which water can be visible, either directly or indirectly, and I am examining what spaces are connected with the water infrastructure. After interpreting the water courses as 'the space of the water', I have set up an example of how it can be possible, within a designing and planning process, to regard the entire urban landscape as a porous fabric of natural and man-made infrastructures in very different scales, ranging from micro-pores to regional transport structures.

The analysis takes its mark in an understanding of the urban waterscapes as a layered interacting texture and moreover has to do, accordingly, with a way of seeing and describing the landscape. The approach to perceiving the urban landscape in the form of thematic interacting layers of systems has its source in a environmental consciousness that was burgeoning back in the 1970s, when Ian McHarg, with his book *Design with Nature*,[10] established the foundation for what we now designate as 'landscape urbanism',[11] and which also has affected the use of Geographical Information Systems in the municipal planning practice.[12]

In her essay 'Landscapes of Infrastructure', which appeared in *The Landscape Urbanism Reader,* Elizabeth Mossop discusses how a network of open common spaces for urban life can obviously be linked up to open water management systems.[13]

As far back as 1956, Lewis Mumford described the city in terms of human processes that were interwoven with natural processes.[14] In practice, Olmsted's 'Green Necklace', in Boston, stands as a progressive example from the 1860s.[15] In the 1980s and 1990s, there was a great deal of interest in environmental and landscape-based art, which led to considerable attention being paid to natural phenomena and processes in design: a fine example of this can be seen in *The Granite Garden*, a book authored by Anne Whiston Spirn.[16] In her essay, Mossop summarizes how topography and hydrological catchment areas, as underlying structures, can obviously serve as the basis for physical planning and regulation of the urban form. But the question is how this can be accomplished in areas with differences in the terrain that are more vague. To this end, Copenhagen's Western Region fashions a fine example.

The present article contributes to spatial descriptions of the waterscapes as layers of several different materialities and related water dynamics in a nuanced way and in an architectural context. These textures consist of different degrees of permeability or porosity that can contain water in different ways. The saturation influences the ambience by giving off water vapour or by reflecting light, but also by virtue of a certain resonance, as though the entire landscape was comprised of musical instruments that were being activated by the water, the light, the wind and the weather.

The material qualities can be described in terms of porosity or permeability, both horizontally and vertically. A landscape consists of materials that have different degrees of density or hollowness to them. Very small hollow spaces are like pores that allow water to seep through, and are described in terms of the physical principle of 'porosity'.[17] The word 'pore' stems from the Greek *poros*, signifying 'passage', or 'way', and denotes a fine channel or intermediate space within a material. Porosity is, therefore, a given material's degree of hollowness and can be used to also cover a larger scale, so that we can even speak about a given city's *porosity* in the form of those spaces that make the city permeable, in a physical sense, and accessible, in a more figurative social sense.

The societal and social challenges presented by urban areas that have been built up as network, which partly conjoin and partly give rise to barriers, are treated especially thoroughly by Stephen Graham and Simon Marvin in their book *Splintering Urbanism: Networked Infrastructures, Technological Mobilities and the Urban Condition*,[18] and by Paola Vigano in her text about *The Project of a Porous City*.[19] In addition, these hollow spaces can be experienced and sensed in different ways through the rhythm, the tone or the ambience that they bring along. In his essay project from 1967, *A Tour of the Monuments of Passaic, New Jersey*,[20] land artist Robert Smithson presents how technical infrastructures can be contemplated as if they were landscape artworks with special symbolic meaning. Later on in the early 1990's, the French philosopher Henri Lefebvre, in his book Éléments de Rythmanalyse,[21] suggests how buildings can be considered on equal footing with natural phenomena, with the result that the whole city is perceived as a symphony of vibrations and rhythms. This approach relates to an idea first coined in the early 1980's by Bruno Latour of the water and other nonhuman things to be actants in the urban environment, and is recently refined in Jane Bennetts philosophical arguments for *Vibrant Matter – A Political Ecology of Things*.[22]

On the basis of this approach, it is possible that the hidden basins and pipes also manifest themselves indirectly by virtue of their way of affecting the landscape's resonance, fundamental tone and sound – through the materials' porosity and capacity to contain water. That is to say, even though the infrastructures are hidden, it is still relevant to address oneself to the questions of how they should be placed and how they should be elaborated. Their appearance in the landscape is merely more subdued than it is directly visible. In this way, the whole urban landscape has an influence to bear on the water infrastructure. Concrete pipes are in possession of a kind of tone, and the soil water gives the landscape a different kind of sound. It takes longer to establish certain types of waterscapes or they vary more, depending on how much water there is throughout the course of the year.

The city's natural water circuit basically has to do with water from the sky, which then flows along the surface of the ground, and with water from the underground, which presses its way up as spring water and well water. The common meeting ground is the terrain and the landscape's surface, where lakes and streams are filled with rainwater and groundwater. The water in the underground is renewed by rainwater, which seeps down through the various layers of soil rather than flowing onward to the sea.

Stormwater protection is merely one form of water dynamics, which is temporary and transitory. The groundwater balance is a whole different kind of water dynamics, which is slow in its interaction with the porosity. Through the climate-adaptation of discharge systems, there is an infrastructural need for empty basins that can be filled, temporarily. When it comes to water supply, there is an infrastructural need for full reservoirs, even when the weather and the climate vary. The principle of having a hollow space for water is the same, but the purpose and the spatial expression are essentially different when comparing 'the empty' with 'the filled'. In between these extremities are countless variations of forms for and degrees of 'fullness' or 'saturation', in interplay with the urban fabric and the materiality of the landscape.

Because the weather and climate changes cannot be completely predicted, we cannot know the exact volumes of water for which we have to design or when the need is going to be urgent. The amounts will fluctuate between occurrences of intense rainfall and dry periods, with the consequence that it is difficult to dimension the infrastructures precisely.[23] To a certain extent, it is possible to ensure the quality of the infrastructures so that they can contain varying amounts of water. But first and foremost, it is necessary to have an understanding of the water dynamics and thereby a sense of the behaviour of the water, so that the infrastructures can even be over-dimensioned without compromising the spatial qualities of the landscape. By strengthening our sensibility about water's behaviour, we can, as planners and architects, gain a more nuanced spatial and textural repertoire for planning and designing, on a basis that can complement the typical hydrological calculations and quantifications.

## The Brøndby waterscapes

In a Danish context, the natural water dynamics are not constituted by wide rivers or monsoon rains, like elsewhere in the world, but of a much quieter and more unobtrusive character. The extensive coastline is characteristic and it influences the way that the light is diffused. But also, the geologically raised seabed and the fresh ground water are characteristic in a Danish context.[24]

Brøndby is located in the western region of Greater Copenhagen, where the geological firmament is constituted by slightly undulating moraine plains. In synch with the extension of urban areas, i.e. the urban sprawl,[25] of the post-war era, the open spaces changed in function, from having been agricultural fields to being residential and recreational areas for those citizens who, as pioneers, moved away from the closely packed central areas of the capital city – out to the suburbs. Inasmuch as the existing landscape features in the western region have not been as clear and distinct to see as they were, for example, in the undulating and richly-forested regions lying north of Copenhagen, the landscape features there, as things would have it, have not been found to be

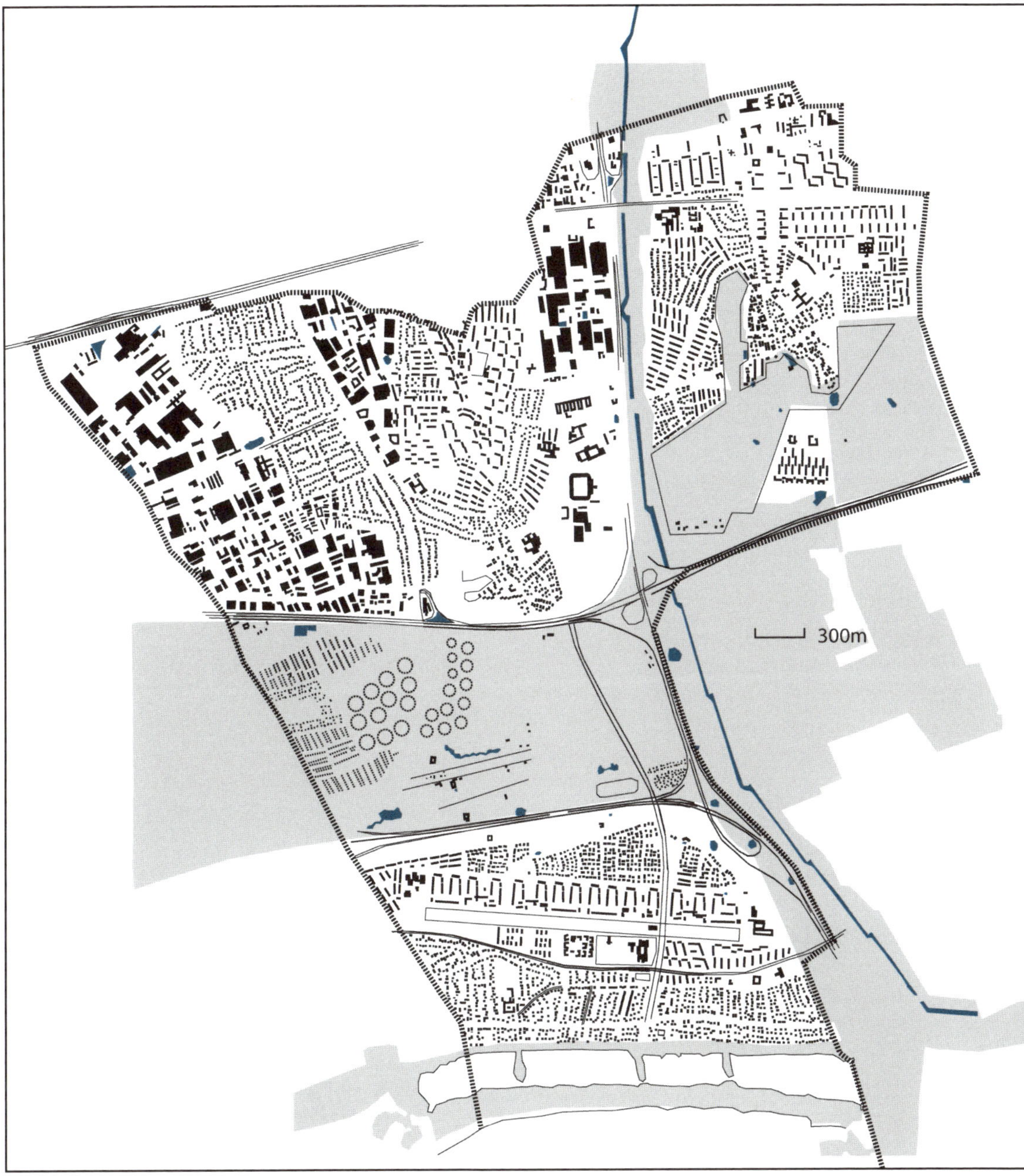


The administrative boundaries of Brøndby Municipality. The canal of the Western Rampart as well as some small ponds appear as clear blue structures. The high-rise buildings in Brøndby Strand and the circular allotment gardens stand out as distinct figures in the typical patchwork of the post-war suburbs of industrial zones, garden streets and common green areas surrounded by regional transportation structures.

particularly worthy of preservation. For this reason, the ambitious modernist planning ideas, such as the designed and constructed regional infrastructures and the green wedges in The Finger Plan, emerge ever so clearly in the demarcation of the developed areas, as can be seen in the ill. p. 65. The suburban landscape of the post-war era is a good place to study the welfare city's infrastructural connections and correlations, especially because there has been sufficient place for adding rather than being limited to having to replace previously existing structures. In the Copenhagen suburbs, old villages are found alongside modern railway stations centres, industrial areas and sports facilities.

The Brøndby suburban landscape is presented here as an interacting, layered waterscape, which has been shaped by changing ideas about supply service and technological development. The mild terrain differences and the thorough cultivation of the surface entail that there have not been clear natural boundaries for how the water would collect. The municipality of Brøndby is the administrative demarcation that contains the two older villages, Brøndbyøster [Brøndby East] and Brøndbyvester [Brøndby West], along with the small modernist suburban centre of Brøndby Strand [Brøndby Beach]. Beneath the surface of the urban landscape, the catchment systems vary in the different areas within Brøndby Municipality, as can be seen in the ill. below. The two most pronounced systems are the combined sewer system and the separate sewer system, which were laid out, respectively, in line with the early urban development that transpired sometime around the 1850s and the modern urbanization that took place after 1960.

The latter two systems were laid out for purposes of servicing urban development and are, in their grid structure, linked to the structural aspects of the urban cultural geography like roads, land registers and buildings. It is from these surfaces that the water is collected. There is an additional third system that has been laid out for purposes of servicing agriculture and the cultivation of fields and is, in its grid structure, linked to structural aspects of the original natural geography like soil conditions and hollows in the terrain. Here, water is collected from the upper soil layers and the wetlands. The blue colour on the maps, p. 69, 70 and 73, marks out the primary water structure in these three systems and also represents three types of waterscapes, each of which is connected with its own physical hydrological principle: respectively, flowing waterways, waterholes and soil water.

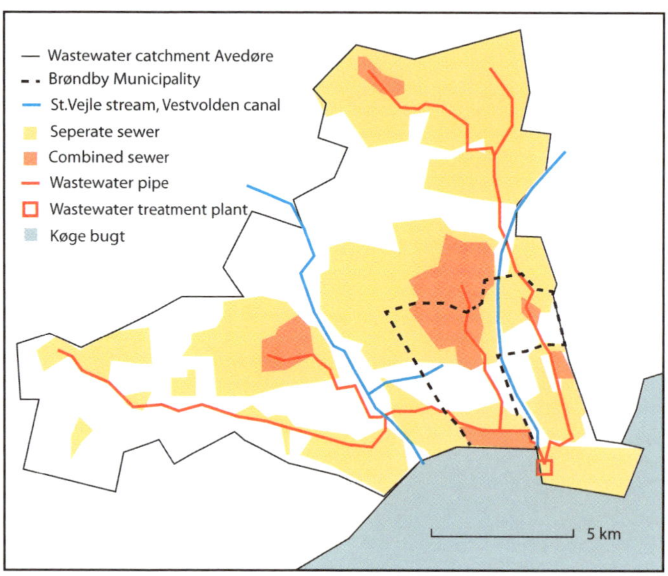


The centralized sewer system covers 10 municipalities and was constructed in the 1960s to efficiently service the new suburbs. The sewer system runs across the 'fingers' towards Køge Bay where an unfortunate bottleneck in Brøndby puts the system under pressure during heavy rain.

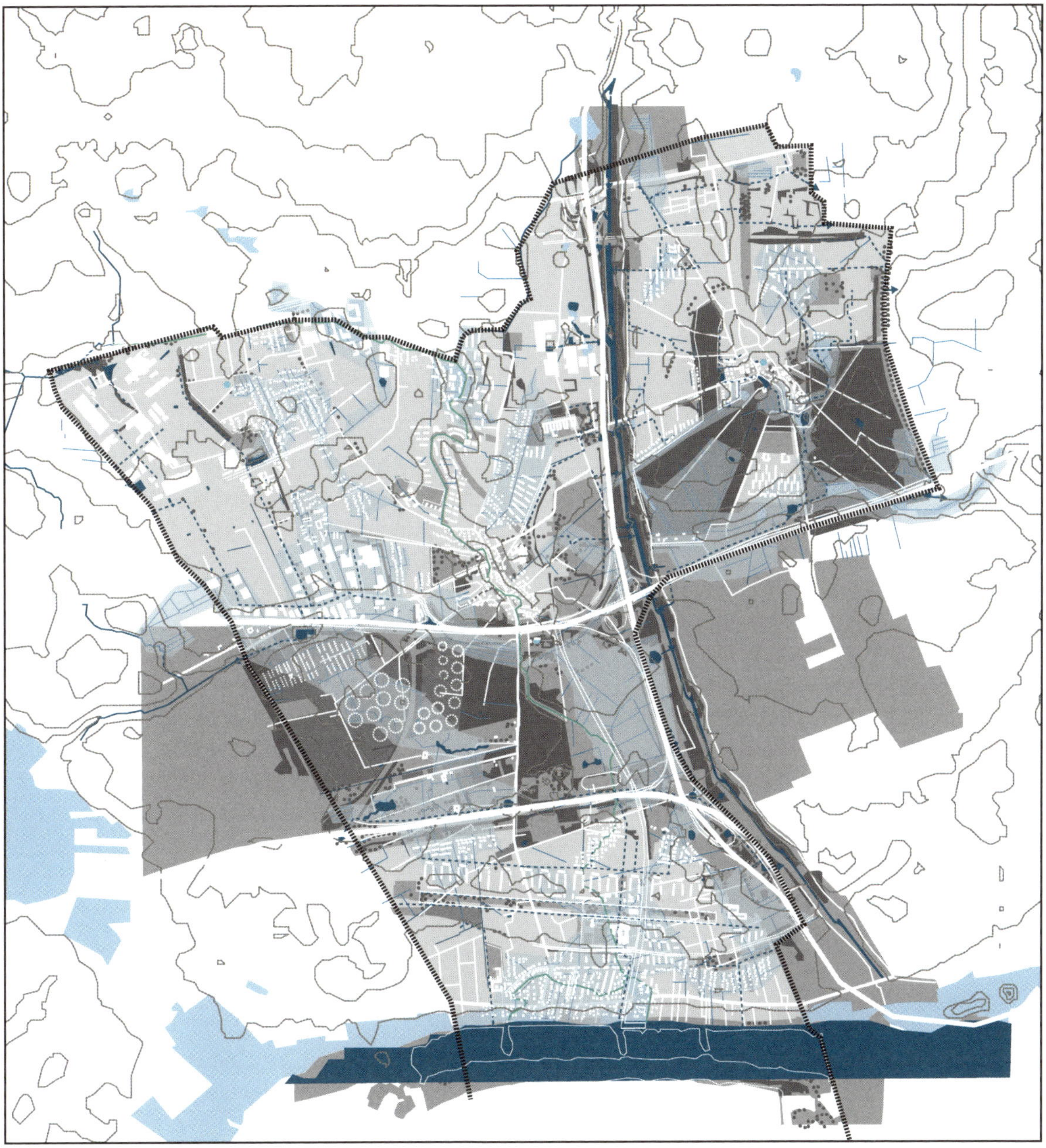

The urban landscape presented as a porous fabric of natural and man-made infrastructures. Included in the drawing are several layers of interacting and overlapping waterscapes in order to describe the topography and hydrological catchments in an area with subtle differences in the terrain.

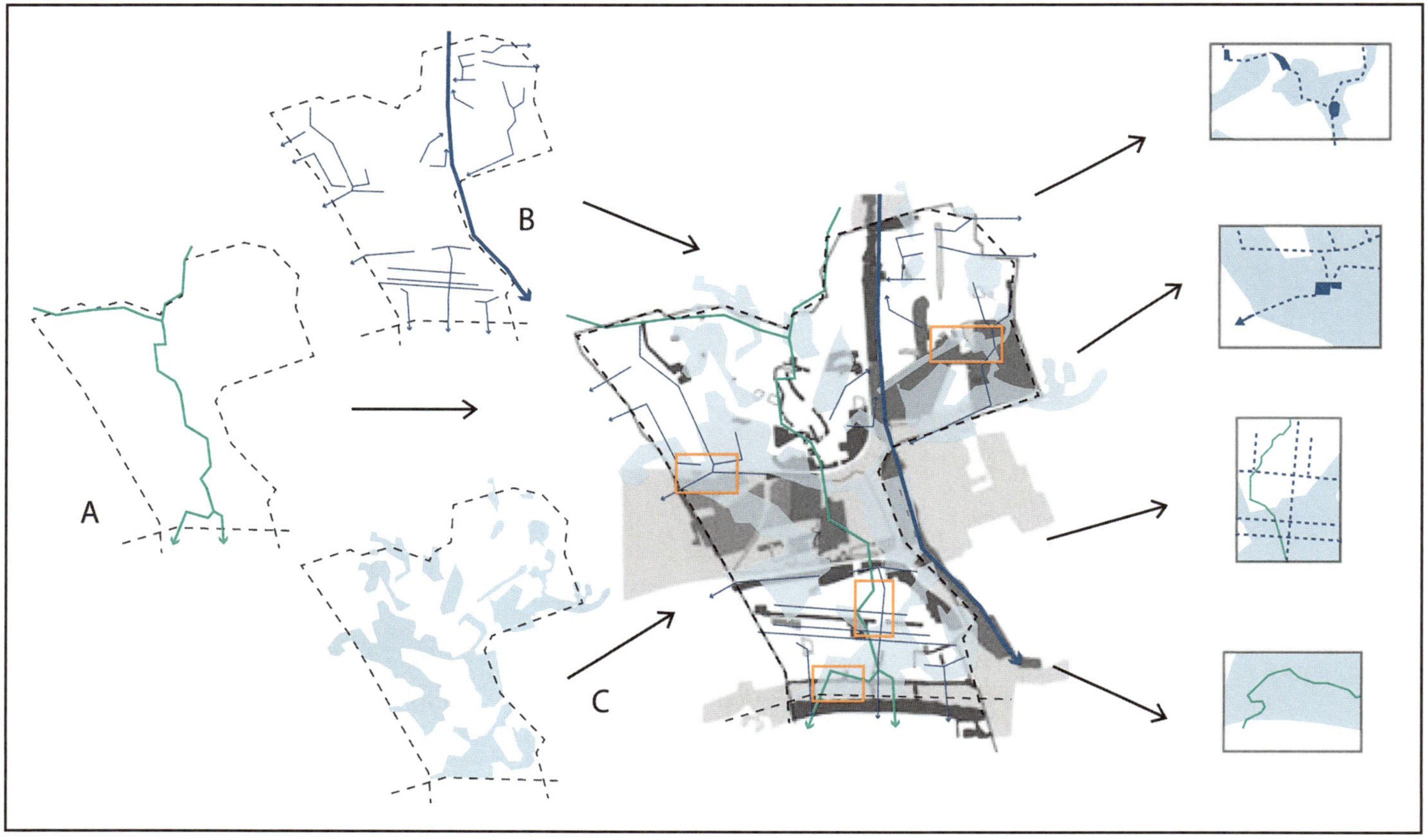


The complexity can be analysed in a nuanced way by thinking across scale for the urban waterscapes. Drawings of the individual system-layers are complemented by examples of 'the space of the water' in smaller sections of combined layers.

In the analysis, I have chosen to put the third of these water systems into play, and accordingly to highlight this as a potential parameter for future planning and design. Whereas each of the two first systems covers its own respective area of the urban landscape, as is made evident in the ill. p. 68, the third system runs transversely to the two areas. It can be found throughout the entire urban area; and it also runs across the administrative municipal boundaries.

I examine whether these three systems can be recognized in today's surface and spatial configuration. The modern urban development has taken place as a marked shift in land use that is based on overall planning ideas, where strategies about efficient regional transport systems have been determinative when it comes to independently placing the landscape characteristics. By contrast, earlier urban development transpired in a far more evolutionary way, by adding to the early villages that were located in relation to the geological terrain and existing water structures, as can be seen in the maps.

## The culverted stream

The first system type relates to the earliest urban areas, from the time before modern separate sewerage. Here, the rainwater is conducted into a sewer, which also takes up waste water from

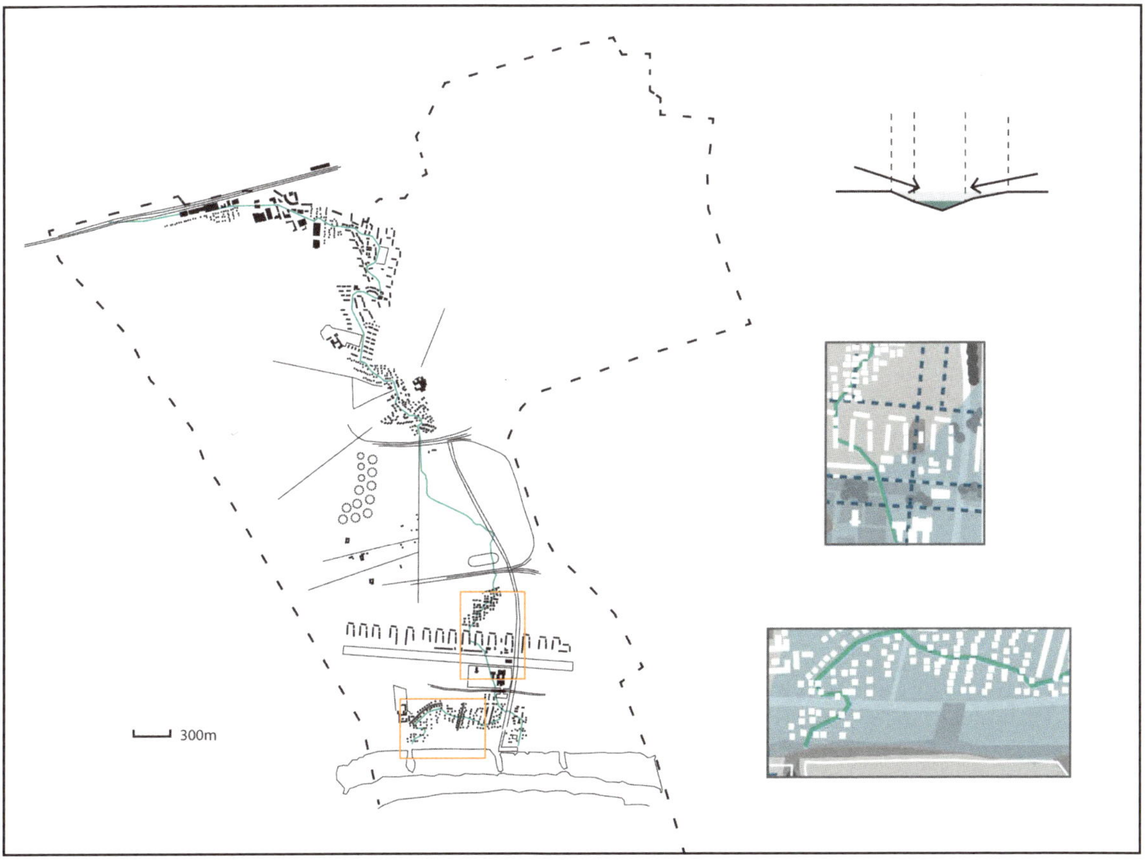


System type A: The culverted stream. The interaction with the surrounding built structures will provide a variation of waterscape experiences if the stream was reopened, varying from dense urban spaces within the 'fingers' to wide open fields in The Green Wedge.

industry and households. From here, all of this water is conducted further to a sewage treatment plant. On the basis of historical maps from The Danish Geodata Agency, I have managed to trace the existing natural stream, Rosenåen [Rose Stream]. What comes to light when comparing my drawing with the technical map is that one segment of the stream is now a part of the sewerage system, which is hidden, as a pipe, under a current urban area.

The map on p. 69, with the first system type (A), is interesting because it tells of a transformation of a natural waterway into being, at least to a certain extent, part of a technical infrastructure. A natural stream changes status and becomes part of the sewer system, for the purpose of handling sewerage overflows during cloudburst situations. In the late 1850s, during the early days of urban development, considerations about hygiene and health provided the reasons for concealing the water infrastructure underneath the ground. Up until that point in time, natural streams and brooks had been functioning as transport systems for waste water from the households and from early industries like slaughterhouses.[26] Only a few visible traces have been left behind by the old buried stream. At certain stretches, the stream still exists, albeit only as a municipal boundary, in the form of simple trenches, hedges and shrubs. At some stretches, a gravel path represents a narrative about former borders or tells a story about what is happening in the subsoil. The stream is situated within the landscape's natural depressions, leading towards the coast, and the water has presumably contributed to the shaping the terrain in such a way that these depressions, over

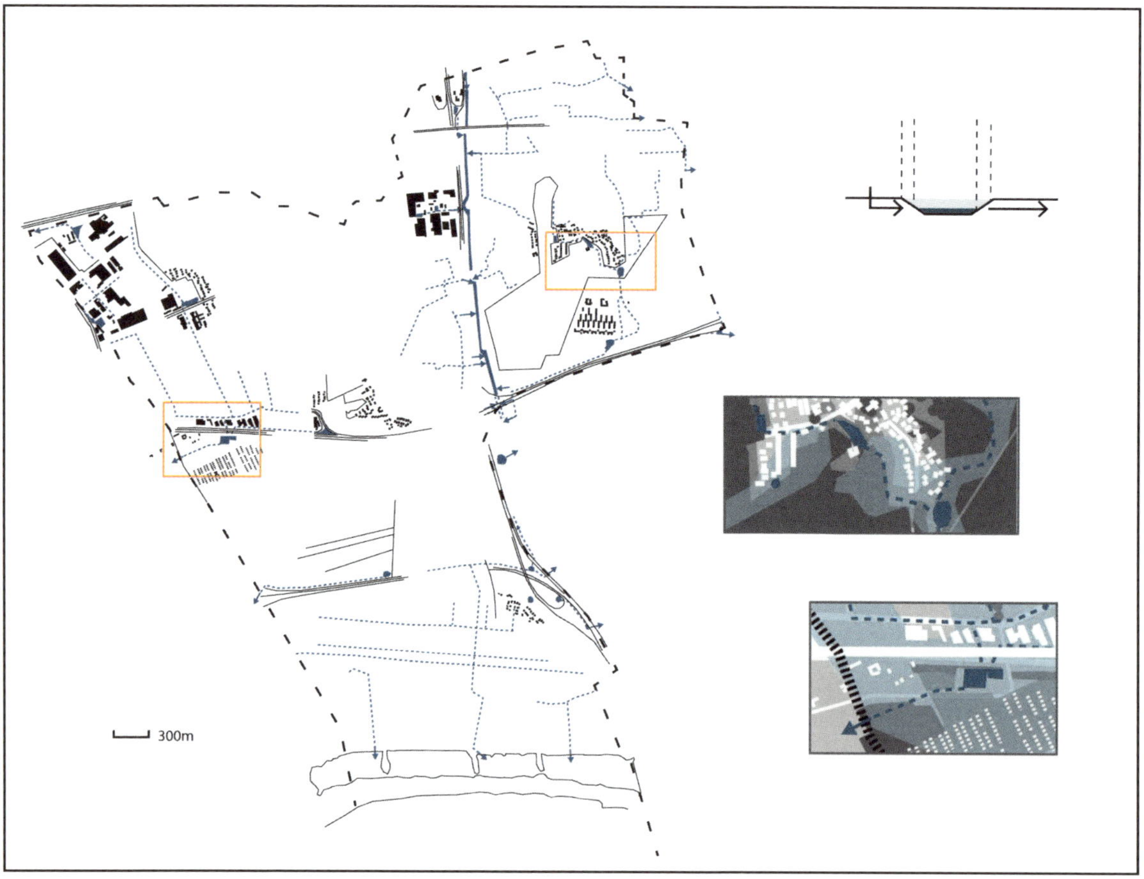

a long period of time, have been intensified by the water that has moved its way here.
Rosenåen has originally ended at the coast in the beach meadows. The area has been inhabited for the past 5000-6000 years. First with Stone Age settlements; while during the Middle Ages, the area was used for grazing and fishing; and in modern times – in the 1900s – what we had here, initially, were greenhouses and, later on, leisure landscapes with summerhouses and seaside hotels. The construction of Avedøre Kloakværk [Avedøre Sewage Plant] in 1965 made it possible once again to go for a swim at the beach, which had otherwise become contaminated by sewage that was flowing directly out into the sea. In the 1980s, a new coastline with bathing beaches and lagoons was constructed.[27] The space of the water at this site has the potential to appear as the swampy coastal region that it has once been. The area is rich in lush gardens. The infrastructural landscape consists of a network of consolidated roads with public access and private garden plots in possession of a soft porosity. The old stream can be detected in the form of certain roads in the western segment, near Silervej, but nothing is revealed in the central segment, near Lindevang, where traces of the old stream run transversely through the gardens. Since the year 2011, rain-beds have been established along the sidewalk on a residential street, Lindevang, and inside the private gardens.[28] The aesthetic expression is a combination of technical details like kerbs with overflow grilles and a wild-like assortment of plants, which changes in character with the seasons.
The high-rise development Brøndby Strand was constructed in the period 1969-74 without taking existing terrain or soil conditions into consideration; instead, the machinery of the time simply paved the way for a traffic separation on several levels that were centred around a 2.5 kilometre long esplanade. The original plan was to build homes for 17,000 people. The plan that was eventually realized, with room for 3,000 people, is still one of the largest housing projects in Denmark.[29]
If a landscape can generally be regarded as a fabric of different porosities, then this particular landscape can be said to be one of hard surfaces, from which the water can flow. The space of the water at this place appears as an efficiently drained surface, from where the water is led away as soon as it falls. The natural stream has been ignored during the planning and has not left behind any visible traces in the current-day urban landscape surrounding the high-rise buildings. The modern rainwater system follows the roads' grid structure, but it is not visible in any way inside the development itself. Upstream of this area, the underground is highly water-soaked because of a closed-down groundwater pump. In the Green Wedge just upstream of the area lies a large empty concrete basin, which was established in the 1960s for the purpose of detaining the rainwater-mixed sewage during heavy downpours. The aesthetic expression here is brutal and technically emphasized. Originally, it has been concealed behind planting, but in connection with a renovation that was undertaken in 2015, the screening was opened visually, with the result that the basin came to be a more prominent part of the cultural landscape.

## The modern rainwater basins

The map on p. 70, with the existing, modern rainwater pipes, has been traced from technical maps of the municipality's water supply. It reveals the pipes that are hidden beneath the consolidated surfaces. The structure in this system type (B) typically follows structural principles that have been operative in modern urban development, which started to take place in Brøndby in the

Systems type B: The modern rainwater basins. Rainwater is conducted below ground and appears only in hollows in the surface. The basins are often placed in the perimeter of built areas as a connection to the larger open spaces forming a waterscape of contrasts.

1960s, when the catchment pipes were laid parallel to the roads and the land register structure. In the 1960s, it was dependable efficiency that was the driving force behind the separation of rainwater from the sewerage system, so as to accordingly minimize the consumption of energy in the sewage treatment process. Since the 1980s, heightened environmental awareness in the planning has turned the focus toward protecting the aquatic environment.[30]

The catchment areas here are primarily building roofs and roads. What this entails is that the attached water dynamics directly reflect precipitation patterns and the condition of the run-off surfaces. The original narrative revolves around the system's construction and tells a tale of modern efficiency. Nowadays, when the climatic conditions have changed and are varying between cloudbursts and everyday precipitation, the basis for a new narrative has been created. The updating of the system consists of coupling several elements to introduce delays before the water meets the natural water environment, which ought to have a certain constant supply/flow of water, so that the fauna and the flora will not die. The system is designed to stand empty and to be ready to handle enormous amounts of water. One possible future narrative could revolve around adjusted fluctuation,[31] in interaction with the subsoil, along with storing and recirculation.

South of Brøndbyvester, in the Green Wedge, there are two basins that are connected to motorways and the industrial area. The basins constitute an example of the modern water system and were designed in order to detain and delay and gradually guide the flowing water away from Brøndby Municipality and towards an old natural stream, 'Bækrenden' [Brook Trench], to the greater stream and valley in Store Vejle Ådal. In 2010, the system became overloaded during a cloudburst, with the result that the water accumulated in a bottleneck created by the narrow creek, and an allotment garden area became flooded. The infrastructural waterscape binds the urban areas together by the water being conducted beneath the motorway, which otherwise constitutes a barrier. In connection with the laying out of a new stretch of train tracks that run along the motorway, a renovation of the basin has been planned. At the same time, the basin is planned to be beautified, so that the technical functions will be hidden for the sake of a more nature-like aesthetic expression, which is thought to be more appealing when it comes to recreational purposes. In large depots like basins, the water level will clearly be disclosed as fluctuating, where the amount of water will be oscillating as a function of changes in the weather. When the basin is open, the water can be seen as a mirroring surface. When, on the other hand, the basin is covered, as is the case in several more recent projects, the surface will – in principle – resound hollowly, depending on how much water happens to be filling the cavernous chamber below.

Further inland and higher up in the terrain lies the village of Brøndbyøster, along with modern building developments from the 1950s, which are close to Brøndbyøster Station and Brøndbyskoven [Brøndby Woods], which was established as a recreational landscape in 1952-60. The village was originally laid out in the 1100s, in the near vicinity of a fresh water source.[32] Here, the water basins in the modern rainwater system come to resemble natural lakes, and it can be only detected that they are parts of a larger system when they are delineated on a map, together with the invisible layers of interconnected pipes, as can be seen on p. 70. The infrastructural water landscape consists of small openings in the surface: like silver mirrors at the fringe of the forest, connected by a concealed network of pipes. As a fabric of different porosities, this is a landscape of

System type C: The drained agricultural land. The drawing shows areas that were once saturated but are now kept dry. With a focused view on 'the space of the water', the vegetation and the upper soil layers of the underground can also be seen as one of the urban waterscapes.

softly undulating terrain, with trees that form part of the water's natural infrastructure, with transport transpiring inside the tree trunk and evaporation emanating from the leaves. The space of the water at this location provides an immersing appearance, inasmuch as all the trees, with their trunks and leaves, are – in principle – water-filled hollow spaces and are consequently both part of the waterscape surrounding the woodland lakes and different forms of waterscapes in themselves. As one element in the climate adaptation of the discharge system that was undertaken in 2015, a few connections between the lakes in the forest were opened up, so that the water could spread out when there are heavy rains. The new aesthetic expression contains a pedagogical value, in which the technical functions are left exposed, so that it will be possible to follow the water's pathways through the forest, even when the trenches are empty.[33]

## The drained agricultural land

The third system (C), shown below, presents a new perspective that I propose to add as a landscape element and as part of the urban waterscape. Knowledge about drains is being employed every now and then in current climate-adaptation projects, but I would suggest to also look at land drains on a larger scale – as a landscape element that runs across municipal borders and as part of a larger historical narrative that brings the western region's cultural landscape all the way back to its geological foundations. Basing my work on historical notations of trenches, which refer to places where there has been a need to drain the ground, I have been able to produce a new layer for the maps of areas with potentially water-saturated soil. This layer is interesting in connection with designing because it indicates where the soil has once been wet and

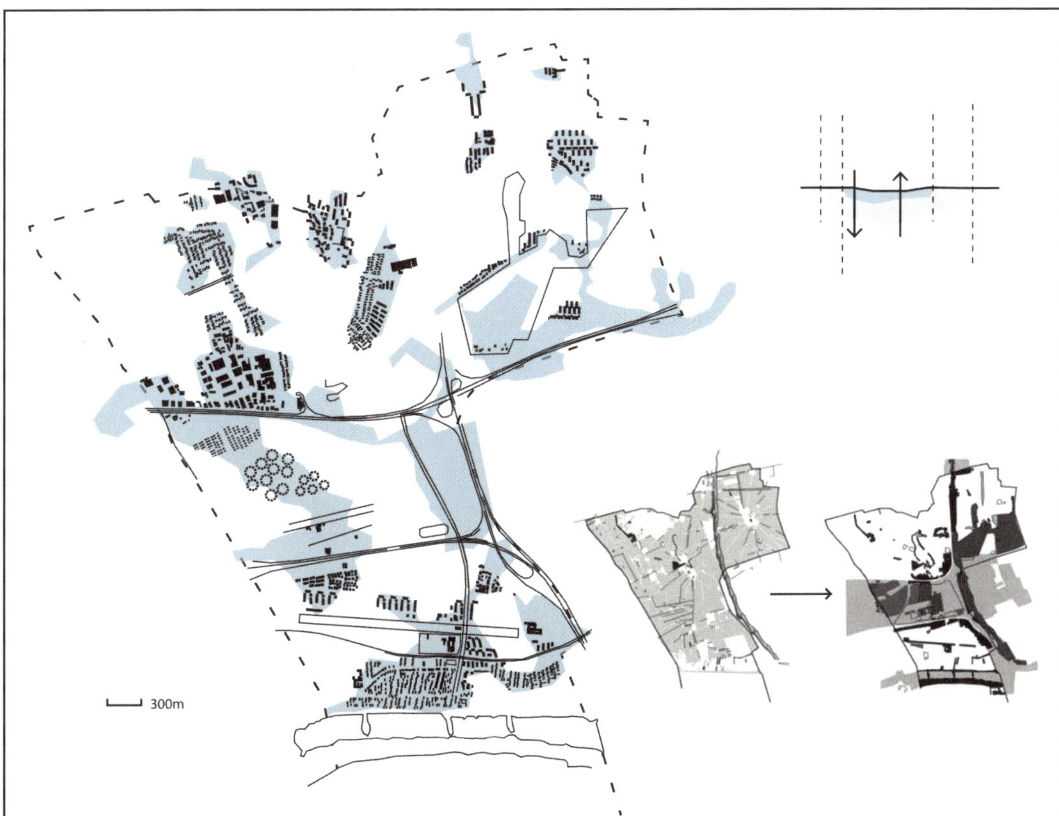

consequently where it is likely to become wet again, if and when the old agricultural land drain eventually breaks down. The original motivation for draining the soil was conjoined with utility-oriented aspirations to, initially, make use of arable land and, subsequently, to undertake an expansion of the city. The rich clayey soil in Brøndby has been suitable for agriculture, and historic maps clearly show the 1800s' star structures around evenly scattered villages, as can be seen on the historical map.[34] The structure follows the principles from the subsurface's soil conditions and original wetlands. System type C is also delineated in the four sectional examples, on p. 69 and 62, with the pale blue coloured surfaces.

## Welfare landscape as liveable place, supply service and resource foundation

Nowadays, on a global level, we are concerned about an increased awareness of resources and we are looking for alternative and renewable forms of supply.[35] In Denmark, we have been basing our water supply on ample amounts of groundwater but it appears likely that we, as a society, are also going to have to be open, in the time to come, for re-use and re-circulation. This is manifesting itself in a tendency where the landscape's technical features are becoming exposed, and where recreational values are included so that the water infrastructures, like open spaces, are coming to be multifunctional. As a point of departure, the existing infrastructures are being supplemented with new landscape-based functions in the form of areas for infiltration and for the temporary delay of rainwater. Our understanding of welfare service is a combination of enormous and controlled separating pipes and basins and alternatives in the form of smaller, local, terrain-based water gardens. This is illustrated in the examples showing the expansion of the large overflow basin in the Green Wedge and the rain-beds on the residential street Lindevang, which, in the interpretation of porosity, represent, respectively, consolidated large-scale hollow spaces for temporary delay and permeable small-scale hollow spaces with increased lushness – on public roads and in private gardens.

Whereas the way of the water has previously been a technical function, to be hidden away and controlled within central systems, with the consequence that there was a clear separation between the spatial configuration on the city's surface and the underground systems, what we have today is a much more dynamic exchange on the surface.

Examples of waterscapes where the water is only visible indirectly or temporarily. Small local plant beds on Lindevang residential street have captured stormwater on its way to the sewer since 2011. The image on the following page shows the large stormwater basin linked to Rosenåen in The Green Wedge, which was constructed in the 1960s and contains 78,000m³ water when the sewers are full. Photos by the author.

The processes are being highlighted as visible aspects of the landscape. By observing the water, we can learn something about how the landscape works.
Whereas the classic mirroring water surfaces create airy space and draws the sky down in the form of reflections, or give rise to streams that point the way and impart a sense of direction to the landscape, and whereas the main attractions are the view and places for sitting beside the water, the new perspective on 'the space of the water' will generate experience-value, which is going to immerse the body, when the water is present, and which is going to free up areas for other activities when the water is not there. What we have here are two fundamental forms of waterscapes. The one is constituted by the open, empty hollow spaces, as consolidated depressions in the surface or porous parts of the surface. They are ready for being temporarily filled during rare and unpredictable events in a rhythm that changes from day to day, with an impetuous and staccato pulse. The other form of waterscape is constituted by surfaces and upper layers of the underground. Here the water is present and ready for use, but is only visible indirectly, through vegetation or through the texture's moisture, surfaces and layers that are present in everyday life. They reflect the course of the year and the seasons in a slow, fluid rhythm, which has the potential to generate new landscape types over time, through changes in vegetation and through the establishment of habitats for plants and wildlife. My analysis accordingly leads to an acknowledgement of the premise that the whole city's materiality, as such, can be regarded in terms of waterscapes and water infrastructures consisting of various forms of hollow spaces, albeit with varying influence on the water's behaviour. The water infrastructures have been designed, to a greater or lesser degree, with the spatial experience in mind. Often, spatial measures have had to do with concealing the infrastructure underneath the ground or behind ramparts and fences. Each one of the three system-type layers displays a technical type that was laid out at a certain time in a historical period. The four sections show an x-ray snapshot of today's condition of overlap and visible traces. The soil water is a frequently overlooked category, which is closely linked to the

landscape's materiality and not merely to the waterway's form as being either stringently piped or meandering 'naturally'. These investigations open up the possibility of letting the moist soil water layer play a role in future strategies and designs. I suggest that we direct our attention toward the draining balance and even toward the porosity of the subsoil and surfaces as a water-bearing landscape materiality, which has the capacity to function in a way that works across the large scale-span and moves within a form that is going to be a combination of natural processes and the urban cultivation of the urban surfaces. Taking part in the elaboration and the planning of these waterscapes is going to be an ongoing architectural task, which will contribute to increasing the population's awareness of the urban resource foundation and supply correlations. What I am suggesting is that by directing our gaze to the spatial interaction between the landscape's materiality and the water's various dynamics, it may prove possible to discover a vital source of inspiration for the design, which will extend beyond the need to know exact dimensionings before a project can commence.

**Notes**

1 Rosenåen [Rose Stream] has reportedly been named in this way because it smelled of anything but roses; this was due to, among other things, industrial waste water coming from Glostrup. In 1911, there were complaints from the primary school that the stench was so unbearable that the children could not concentrate. And in connection with a polio epidemic in the 1950s, a decision was made to cover the stream. Since that time, the stream has had the status of a waste water-technical facility. *Rosenåen,* http://forstadsmuseet.dk/historien-om/rosenaaen/ [2016, 08-09-2016]

2 A progressive trend going on in the sphere of climate adaptation, as an alternative to laying out hidden pipes and basins. Stokman, A.: Water Purificative Landscapes – Constructed Ecologies and Contemporary Urbanism, in *Transforming with water: Proceedings of the IFLA World Congress 2008*, pp. 51-61.

3 The studies have been conducted as part of my PhD-programme: *Reconsidering Urban Waterscapes*, carried out at the University of Copenhagen, in which is a detailed description of the procedure and the methodology.

4 P.B. Pedersen: *Arkitektur og plan i den danske velfærdsby – Container og urbant raster* (2005).

5 C. Juel-Christiansen: *Monument & niche: Den ny bys arkitektur: The architecture of the new city* (1985).

6 P. Bredsdorff: *Fingerplanen* (1947).

7 O. Forchhammer: *Københavnsegnens grønne Områder* (1936).

8 M. Hauxner: *Open to the Sky* (2003).

9 See a more detailed description of the fortification at: http://www.befaestningen.dk/

10 I.L. McHarg: *Design with Nature* (1969).

11 The concept is described in an anthology edited by C. Waldheim: *The Landscape Urbanism Reader* (2006).

12 GIS is an abbreviation for Geographical Information System. T. Balstrøm: *GIS i Danmark* (1999).

13 E. Mossop: 'Landscapes of infrastructure', in *The Landscape Urbanism Reader* (2006), p.. 163.

14 L. Mumford: 'The City, Design for Living', in *Wisdom* 1, no. 11, 1959, pp. 14-22.

15 F.L. Olmsted: Landskabsarkitekt (1822-1903), http://www.emeraldnecklace.org/.

16 A.Sprin: *The Granite Garden: Urban Nature and Human Design* (1984).

17 M.R. Hendricks: *Introduction to Physical Hydrology* (2010).

18 S. Graham & S. Marvin: *Splintering Urbanism: Networked infrastructures, technological mobilities and urban conditions* (2001).

19 P. Vigano: 'The Metropolis of the Twenty-First Century – The Project of a Porous City' in *On Territories – OASE Journal of Architecture* (2009), p. 91. http://www.oasejournal.nl///#091.

20 The article has been published in R. Smithson & J. Flam: *Robert Smithson, The collected Writings* (1996).

21 H. Lefebvre: Éléments de Rythmanalyse (1992).

22 J. Bennet: *Vibrant Matter – A Political Ecology of Things* (2010)

23 An example of the complexity that is associated with climate adaptation can be found in the article: C.F. Frantini et al.: 'Three Points Approach (3PA) for urban flood risk management: A tool to support climate change adaptation through transdisciplinarity and multifunctionality', in *Urban Water Journal*, 2012 (5), pp. 1-15.

24 J. Theilgaard: *Det danske vejr* (2006) and S. Høyer: *Landskabskunst 2* (2007).

25 The urban sprawl in the post-war era was reflected primarily in the form of suburban construction around the larger Danish cities. See Dansk Bygningsarv's book on the suburb's building culture. https://realdania.dk/samlet-projektliste/forstadens-bygningskultur-1945-1989

26 *Brøndbyvesters historie:* http://forstadsmuseet.dk/historien-om/broendbyvesters-historie/
27 *Brøndby Strands historie:* http://forstadsmuseet.dk/historien-om/broendby-strands-historie/, http://arealinformation.miljoeportal.dk/distribution/,
28 http://regnruten.dk/projekter/lindevang-haver/
29 G. Jellicoe: *The Landscape of Man: Shaping the environment from prehistory to the present day* (1995).
30 http://mst.dk/borger/landbruget-miljoeet/baeredygtighed-i-landbruget/vandmiljoeplanerne-et-historisk-overblik
31 'Fluctuation' means that the water will change in intensity, height or speed. M.R. Hendricks: *Introduction to Physical Hydrology* (2010).
32 *Brøndbyøsters historie,* http://forstadsmuseet.dk/historien-om/broendbyoesters-historie/
33 http://regnruten.dk/projekter/ved-lindelund/
34 The star structure stems from 'udskiftningen' as part of the agrarian reforms in the period around 1700-1850, when the fields were re-structured in the form of a star surrounding the villages. Traces of this structure can still be found in the form of planted windbreakers, pathways and trenches. Before that time, the earth was allocated in such a way that all the farmers had many small stripes of both rich and poor soil. Bjørn, C.: *Landboreformerne: forskning og forløb* (1988).
35 F. Pearce: *When the rivers run dry: What happens when our water runs out?* (2006).

### Literature


- Balstrøm, T.: *GIS i Danmark*, Nyt Teknisk Forlag, Copenhagen 1999.
- Bennett, J.: *Vibrant Matter – A Political Ecology of Things*, Duke University Press Durham and London 2010.
- Bjørn, C.: *Landboreformerne: forskning og forløb*, Landbohistorisk Selskab, Odense 1988.
- Bredsdorff, P.: *Fingerplanen*, Egnsplankontoret, Copenhagen 1947.
- Forchhammer, O.: *Københavnsegnens grønne områder*, Egnsudvalget, Copenhagen 1936.
- Fratini, C.F. et al.: 'Three Points Approach (3PA) for urban flood risk management: A tool to support climate change adaptation through transdisciplinarity and multifunctionality', *Urban Water Journal*, 2012 (5), Taylor Francis Group, 2012, pp. 1-15.
- Graham, S., & Marvin, S.: *Splintering Urbanism: Networked Infrastructures, Technological Mobilities and the Urban Condition,* Routledge, London 2001.
- Hauxner, M.: *Open to the Sky,* The Danish Architectural Press, Copenhagen 2003.
- Hendricks, M.R.: *Introduction to Physical Hydrology*, Oxford University Press, New York 2010.
- Høyer, S.: *Landskabskunst 2*, Kunstakademiets Arkitektskoles Forlag, Copenhagen 2008.
- Jellicoe, G.: *The Landscape of Man: Shaping the environment from prehistory to the present day*, Thames & Hudson, London 1995.
- Juel-Christiansen, C.: *Monument & niche: Den ny bys arkitektur: The architecture of the new city*, Rhodos, Copenhagen 1985.
- McHarg, I.L.: *Design with Nature*, Natural History Press, New York 1969.
- Mossop, E.: 'Landscapes of infrastructure', in *The Landscape Urbanism Reader*, ed. Waldheim, Princeton Architectural Press, New York, p. 163, 2006.
- Mumford, L.: 'The City, Design for Living', in *Wisdom* 1, no. 11, 1959, pp. 14-22.
- Lefebvre, H.: Éléments de Rythmanalyse, Éditions Syllepse, Paris 1992.
- Pearce, F.: *When the rivers run dry: What happens when our water runs out?*, Eden Project Books, Transworld Publishers, London 2006.
- Pedersen, P.B.: *Arkitektur og plan i den danske velfærdsby – Container og urbant raster*, The Danish Architectural Press, Copenhagen.
- Web page: arkitekturforskning.net/na/article/download/238/200, [2016, Retrieved on September 8, 2016]
- Spirn, A.W.: *The Granite Garden: Urban Nature and Human Design,* Basic Books, New York 1984.
- Stokman, A.: Water Purificative Landscapes – Constructed Ecologies and Contemporary Urbanism, in *Transforming with water: Proceedings of the IFLA World Congress 2008*, ed. Kuitert, W., Blauwdruk/Techne Press, Wageningen 2008, pp. 51-61.
- Theilgaard, J.: *Det danske vejr*, Gyldendal, Copenhagen 2007.
- Vigano, P.: 'The Metropolis of the Twenty-First Century – The Project of a Porous City', in *On Territories – OASE Journal of Architecture*, eds. T. Avermaete, K. Havik, H. Teerds: #80, NAi Publishers, Rotterdam, p. 91. 2009. www.oasejournal.nl///#091 [2016, 08-09-2016]
- Waldheim, C. (ed.): *The Landscape Urbanism Reader,* Princeton Architectural Press, New York 2006.

Tomas Wikström

# Spontaneous Welfare Design

## Paths and Shortcuts in Modernist Suburbs

**The design and construction of the welfare society were the results of political decision-making, government programmes and planning on a national and municipal level. To combine the term 'welfare design' with 'spontaneous' may therefore seem like a paradox. However, welfare construction had its gaps and loopholes – not only metaphorically but also in a very tangible way. Modernist cities are comprised of separate enclaves for housing, industry and service, surrounded by residual spaces. These residual spaces are criss-crossed by informal paths, forming entire unplanned path systems that 'glue' together the neighbourhoods.**

*Is this what I think it is?*
Bent over the aerial photo in front of us, I point to the thin lines that intersect the grassy areas surrounding the suburb of Rinkeby.

*Yes, those are shortcuts*, says the urban planner we are interviewing. 'We' are the researchers involved in a project about Stockholm's suburbs that explores their public spaces from a broad, interdisciplinary perspective.[1] I intuitively understand the implications of what I am seeing: this is the residents' way of correcting the errors made by modernist traffic planning! My curiosity is roused. From now on, my part of the project will focus on the subject of shortcuts. As my field study I choose Flemingsberg in Huddinge Municipality, south of Stockholm. Flemingsberg is a textbook example of modernist city planning, according to which neighbourhoods were laid out as series of enclaves surrounded by undeveloped land. It is here, within these undeveloped strips of land, that we find the informal paths I wanted to study.

## Modernist urban planning

Modernist cities and neighbourhoods are characterized by well-known and well-chronicled qualities such as light and air, greenery, zoning, traffic segregation, sheltered playgrounds in residential areas etc. Construction is here organized as enclaves: distinct entities with each their own function and often separated by interspaces in the form of grass, shrubbery or leftover forest thickets. A quality which is seldom mentioned, on the other hand, is the existence of spontaneously formed paths that make it possible to take a shortcut through the areas between the enclaves and thereby save time and effort. These overlooked walkways sometimes form entire path systems which are only maintained thanks to the residents' regular use in what can be described as a ongoing 'legwork'. If you look carefully at satellite images of Brasília, for instance, you will find numerous such paths.[2] The planned, rationalistic infrastructure of roads, walkways and bike paths is superimposed by a, from the user's viewpoint, more rational structure of spontaneously formed paths. These paths constitute what may be called 'spontaneous welfare design.' They represent an ongoing investment in the form of human efforts to bridge the gaps created by modernist urban planning. This investment does not figure on municipal budgets and therefore makes no demands on the taxpayers' money. It is this essential, but to the planning profession invisible, work that is the subject of this article. Could it be that the welfare state's residential areas are rendered habitable by the informal and entirely unplanned actions of its citizens?

## Reflections on spatiality

Henri Lefebvre, the philosopher and urban sociologist, is the author of a book with the ambiguous title *The Production of Space* (1991) in which he analyses the urban reality and how this has evolved. In his opinion, this reality is characterized by three spatial aspects: *socio-material* space, *discursive* space and *lived* space. It is important not to imagine these aspects as individual, distinguishable 'spaces', though, they are simply aspects or dimensions of the same complex spatiality. The point is that *discursive space* – the spatial dimensions represented by texts and images, to which architects and planners devote their professional efforts – are not the only relevant aspects. Outside of the discursive space the city is continuously produced and reproduced in an ongoing technical, economic and social process full of contradictions – with people appropriating the city in various ways every day, each of us influencing and changing it with the ways in which we live in it. The creators of the welfare society's cities were driven by a strong ideology that enabled them to carry through extensive housing programmes and radical transformations of historic city centres. However, Lefebvre did not think much of the modernist suburbs; 'these illegitimate hybrids of country and city,' as he called them. His rejection made sense at a time where the construction of modernist suburbs was still in its infancy. Today, these environments constitute a built and lived-in reality – for better or worse – that we have to address in a constructive

manner. The suburbs owe a lot of their good qualities to the active participation of the residents. Another theorist, Michel de Certeau, emphasizes that consumers are by no means just passive recipients, they are also producers. In his book *The Practice of Everyday Life* (1998), de Certeau uses the term 'poaching' as a metaphor for the unauthorized actions that people resort to in order to navigate and appropriate the urban landscape. The taking of shortcuts is a good example of this kind of actions. In a passage that takes its departure in a visit to the World Trade Center in New York,[3] he elaborates his notion of *the voyeur* and *the walker*. While the voyeur's perspective on the city has the clarity of distance and intellect, the walker perceives the city successively, step by step, with new experiences lurking behind every corner. Simply put, this distinction between the voyeur and the walker is echoed in the different positions of the planner and the resident. But in the suburban interspaces – as opposed to the urban jungle of Manhattan – the resident has access to a network of paths. These paths not only make it easier to reach your destination, they also offer information about where you can walk and whether this is a popular and much used route. The path is a product of many people's combined efforts, a product that the walker utilizes with confidence. The path represents what the philosopher Bengt Molander calls 'knowledge in action' (1996). It functions and is used and maintained without specific verbal explanations.

## Flemingsberg

Flemingsberg is a good example of the modernist city planning of the 60s and 70s. Situated just southwest of Stockholm, a 20-minute train ride from the city, Flemingsberg seems designed for commuting. But in fact, the original intention was to provide the staff at the new regional hospital with nearby housing. To the northeast you see the city's distant skyline, with the Globe Arena as the most prominent accent. If you travel in the opposite direction, you will reach Malmoe in just over four hours (by train from Flemingsberg central station), and Copenhagen in another half hour. To the northeast lies Skärholmen, a suburb featuring one of the oldest IKEA stores, and beyond that Lake Mälaren. To the east – beyond forests, lakes and villages – lies the great expanse of the Gulf of Bothnia. Despite the fact that Flemingsberg is surrounded by vast forests, this is not a rural district.[4]

Valleys with fields and meadows between spruce-forested ridges, on land belonging to Flemingsberg manor, made way for the new development in the 60s and 70s. The regional hospital, which covers an area the size of *Gamla stan* in Stockholm, was built first, together with a couple of high-rises for the hospital staff. Then followed several residential developments – all of them situated on high-lying plateaus – an industrial estate and a police station. During the 90s, yet another residential estate, a research centre and Södertörn University followed, and in the 2000s a court centre containing Södertörn lower court was added to the mix.[5] Traffic was planned according to SCAFT, the hierarchical principles for traffic segregation, which stipulate among other things that vehicular traffic should be kept separate from soft traffic.[6] With its zoning and traffic infrastructure, Flemingsberg is in many ways a textbook example of the suburbs built as part of the so-called million programme, but it is also unique thanks to the large number of jobs involved.[7] The densification of Flemingsberg continues here in the 2010s. Right now, the first turf is cut on several large construction projects that build on some of the residual spaces mentioned in this article, including the vast field northeast of Flemingsberg's central station.

The colourful high-rises of Grantorp.
In the distance, we see Stockholm's skyline, with the Globe Arena as the most prominent accent.
All photos by the author.

## Field studies

Shortcuts and other paths are best studied by mapping the area. It is true that some are visible on aerial photos or the satellite images we can access with our smart phones. Others are hidden beneath the foliage of trees, however, and therefore have to be studied on site and then plotted onto a map of the area. Here GPS may be useful, but I preferred[8] to use paper maps and a notebook. Simple images taken with a compact camera have also proved invaluable. The advantage of on-site mapping is that the process also serves as participatory observation: How difficult is it to negotiate this hill? Which traces have people left behind and what do they tell us? Is the shortcut also there in winter when the ground is covered

with snow? Who do you meet on the paths and where are they going?
Mapping, observation and documentation were carried out on a number of occassions, at different times of the year. I visited Flemingsberg a few days at a time and afterwards processed the material back at the office.[9] The observations covered the type of terrain, the quality of the paths (width, wear and tear, passability, etc.), the people traversing the interspaces and the traces left behind. The existence of different kinds of waste (empty beer cans, candy paper, bits of sunflower seeds, processed natural materials such as branches and cones, huts) gives rise to assumptions about the activities that take place in different areas.
I thus had abundant material in the form of maps, photographs and observations on which to base my key interviews about the qualities of the interspaces and the informal paths. 27 interviews were made with residents, club members, employees and students from Flemingsberg. As a basis for this, and to stimulate the conversation, I used my photos of interspaces and paths. During the open interviews, the residents shared their experiences of what they saw as the most significant places. This confirmed or disproved the assumptions I had formed about these places.

## The diverse qualities of interspaces

Flemingsberg is characterized by the diffusion that is typical of the modernist suburbs from the 60s and 70s. From early on, the Swedish million programme were subject to severe criticism because of its vast scale, its lack of complexity and the shortage of attractive meeting places. But these shortcomings are somewhat compensated for by the easy access to outdoor spaces for spontaneous recreation of all kinds, not least in the interspaces that make up 'the sea' in the suburban archipelago. These residual spaces offer a refuge for activities that are 'forbidden' or 'unacceptable' within the planned context. One of the people I interviewed, the head of the tenants' association, told me about a habit she and her daughters had when they were younger: 'After school we went right out into the woods to a large

This steep shortcut leads to the bus stop.
←
Flemingsberg station, Northern rise.

rock, climbed on top of it and screamed at the top of our lungs.'

Flemingsberg's diffusion means that the individual parts or enclaves ar far apart. One of the first things I noticed during my field studies was the legwork that the residents were compelled to do in order to hold together what the modernist planning had fragmented. As a pedestrian in Flemingsberg you are exposed to wind and weather, particularly when crossing the interspaces that are not sheltered by trees. In this respect, the district resembles a rural landscape. The spontaneously trodden paths are the residents' way of reducing the distances and thereby the bother of connecting Flemingsberg's various points of interest. Needless to say, there are footpaths to all the attractions – including the abovementioned rock.

The interspaces are generally what is left when the enclaves have been developed. These spaces are not characterized by formlessness, as Tom Nielsen (2001) suggests with reference to his own studies. On the contrary, they all have distinct forms, being the negative imprint of the enclaves. Even Solá-Morales' term *terrain vague* (1994) seems misleading in this case. In the day-to-day use, they each have very specific attributes. Next to the residential development lies what may be described as *fringe zones*, a wilder expansion of the planned environment and an attractive environment for children to play in. Beyond these are the *intermediate zones* whose grass fields offer a great setting for spontaneous ball games such as soccer or rounders. Sometimes the intermediate zones are strips of forested land, which are so wide that the buildings now and then disappear from sight. Here you can encounter wild animals

A well-used shortcut between commuter train and home.

→

Terrain vague? The interspaces in Flemingsberg turn out to have radically different characteristics. (Yellow: mid-zones. Orange: border zones. Pink and dark blue: infrastructure border zones [Power lines or noise zones]. Light blue: expansion surfaces). Huddinge Municipality.

such as hares, foxes and deers. Power lines, traffic lines and railway lines are surrounded by a safety distance because of electromagnetic radiation, noise nuisance and the risk of accidents: the *infrastructural border zones*. These are not attractive places; nevertheless, the traces found here indicate that both children and adults find them interesting. Illegal rubbish is often dumped here, yet this is also where people go to collect mushrooms or berries. Finally, there are the so-called *expansion areas*, which is land reserved for future expansions, either in the shape of fallow fields or forest. Next to the station, right in the middle of Flemingsberg, is a large area used for commuter parking, a provisional measure of long standing. There is generally a lot of surplus land in Flemingsberg waiting to be developed.

In recent years, urban densification has become increasingly relevant as a means of avoiding construction on farmland, of providing a better basis for local services and of optimizing public transport. However, the widely diverse qualities of the interspaces call for a thorough investigation of the specific properties and the actual use of the different areas. For instance, do these suggest that a nature or adventure park would be more suitable than a series of tower blocks? Residual spaces allow the users to be more than just consumers: they can, in various ways, develop productive relations to these environments.[10]

My findings on the significance of interspaces may be summarized as follows:

• They constitute transitions and linkages – but also boundaries and barriers – between different parts of the urban landscape. To traverse them is literally to cross borders. The spontaneously trodden paths through these are a clear indication of the need to go back and forth between the various enclaves.

• They consist of land that is not subject to specific and detailed programming and therefore offers considerable freedom of action. Being more or less abandoned, they are seldom under the client's control. They provide scope for activities that are not allowed in the well-regulated urban environment. In this particular respect, they are characterized by the vagueness described by Solà-Morales (1994).

• Even in those cases where they are subject to city planning, they are the indirect result of development. They occupy a place on the outer periphery of architects' and planners' awareness and are primarily regarded by these as exploitable land. This is where modernist planning meets ordinary lived space.[11] The desire to make residual spaces 'usable' may conflict with people's spontaneous use of them.

## A network of spontaneously trodden paths

Across the different interspaces run spontaneously trodden paths (see map of paths). Their users – and producers – are described as *wanderers* by Certeau. Since they explore the interspaces for different purposes, the wanderers generate different kinds of paths. Some of these paths are best described as *shortcuts*. Almost anywhere you look for a shortcut, you will find one. The nearest way to the bus: a shortcut. The nearest way to work: a shortcut, etc. No rule without exceptions, though: sometimes you can find a

Spontaneously rampant trailsIn Visratra, Flemingsberg.
→
The shortcut offers a faster and more effective route the goal of the promenade.

well-planned footpath or sidewalk along a street that leads exactly where you want to go. The width and wear of the shortcuts are a rough indication of their popularity. In winter, when the ground is covered with snow, it becomes even more apparent which shortcuts are the most important.

Other paths may be described as *wandering paths*. These meander between trees and rocks and are especially appreciated by dog owners, cross-country bikers and anyone who enjoys walking in nature in close proximity to the development. Here, the main purpose is to commune with nature rather than negotiating it.

Along traffic arteries with no sidewalks people have trodden what may be described as *sidewalk paths*. There may be a planned walkway which you are supposed to follow, but to follow the road seems safer (lighting, passing cars) and is also the most direct route to the goal. The sidewalk paths are therefore a kind of shortcuts.

Interspaces contain significant points of interest that attract different parts of the population. This might be a rock to climb, a hut that a child has built, an abandoned building where you can exercise your personal graffiti style or a clearing which catches the sunlight. Those who want to visit these attractions automatically contribute to the forming of *access paths*.

When I asked the residents if they used the shortcuts, something interesting happened. Some of them reacted as if it were a sin to take a shortcut through a grass field, even though this was already well-trodden by other people. Perhaps in awe of the strict property managers from their childhood. Shortcuts are generally not talked about, it seems. I spoke to two teachers from one of the local schools: *So you are one of those people who take shortcuts*, one of them said surprised when her colleague revealed how she took the shortest route to school.

Nowadays, there are no signs ordering you to keep off the grass. The only sign I found warned me about the risks of taking the shortcut through the woods. *The path is not gravelled in slippery conditions!* It is implied that taking a path or a shortcut is done at one's own risk, just as you do not sue the forest owner if you stumble over a stone in the woods and hurt yourself.

## Conclusion

In order to reach a conclusion on phenomena like paths and interspaces, I will take my point of departure in de Certeau's notion of how ordinary people creatively produce their own living environments. I will also incorporate Molander's concept of practice-based knowledge. This is all about everyday life, about the appropriation of built environments and about the knowledge that is embedded in this production. The implications of architecture and the planned environment are not fully revealed until people start using the buildings and their surroundings, which often happens in ways that are quite different from the ones intended. The result might be described as 'the practices of the wanderer': the wanderer discovers and is confronted with qualities in the environment that are more or less inaccessible to the eye of the voyeur (the architect and the planner). There seems to be a remarkable lack of popular discourse on shortcuts and other spontaneously formed paths.[12] It was difficult to make the residents say anything substantial on this topic. It seems to be a question of *knowledge in action*, which is Molander's term for the things that people do that are not communicated with words but through the actual product – the result of accumulated actions.[13] Continuing Molander's line of thought, we may describe the production of paths as 'knowledge in collective action'. By following the path, a large number of people substantiate its design, while at the same time contributing to its (re)production. This kind of spontaneous welfare design is at once obvious and enigmatic. If the production and use of paths were a practice that it was actually possible to talk about (just like driving, boat building or bricklaying), I believe the people involved would make explicit and detailed evaluations of good or bad paths, paths that satisfy different needs and paths that make different demands on the walker.
Architects and planners need to take another approach: we have to start regarding the actual applications of the built environment as the 'truth'. The buildings or the district may be ever so beautifully designed and empathically conceived, but if the users do not follow the rules prescribed by the planning it means that they have discovered a more efficient way of relating to the houses and the streets. It is the discourse behind the design that is found wanting. The actual application makes the city and the architecture come to life. A constructive dialogue with the people that live in the city is therefore a prerequisite for any realistic planning and design.
The *de facto* application of built environments is still something that very few architects and planners find it worth studying. A notable exception is Jan Gehl and the inspiration provided by his work. However, it is my impression that my younger colleagues take a greater interest in the spontaneous use of the city than my own generation. This is an extremely interesting field that may give rise to a whole new perspective on the design of buildings and urban environments. We live in a time where urban densification is high on the agenda. However, it is important not to rush into things for lack of knowledge and develop open spaces that already have great value as it is, both as venues of leisure and recreation and as canvases for spontaneous welfare design.[14] As my findings suggest, even the construction of entire-

ly new neighbourhoods calls for a questioning of the established planning tradition, which is based on traffic segregation (SCAFT). As the car-based society gradually loses its hegemony, a new field of innovative urban planning emerges in which the inhabitants' day-to-day creativity takes centre stage.

I decided to call this article 'Spontaneous Welfare Design'. We are used to associate the welfare society's configuration and construction with governmental (and municipal) planning. So how can we expect to find anything spontaneous in the residential construction of the 60s and 70s, for instance? My research shows that modernism's thoroughly totalitarian city planning – as represented by Flemingsberg – left unfinished gaps and patches. As already established, these interspaces have two characteristics: they impede the mobility in the area, but they also offer considerable freedom of action. Part of this freedom consists of the possibility of forming shortcuts in order to overcome the inconvenient distances. Thus, independently of the official planning, a network of paths is formed that contributes to the general welfare of people.

**Notes**

1 K. Nylund (ed.): *Periferin i centrum. Gränsöverskridande praktiker I Stockholms offentliga rum* (2007).
2 Try studying Brasília's central axis with Apple's or Google's mapping tools.
3 Needless to say, this was long before that fateful day of September 11th 2001.
4 T. Wikström (a): 'Monumentalitet och mobilitet i Flemingsberg', in *Periferin i centrum* (2007), pp. 87-143.
5 Ibid.
6 Statens planverk: *SCAFT 1968. Riktlinjer för stadsplanering med hänsyn till trafiksäkerhet* (1968) and T. Tägil & F. Werne: 'Förorter i förändring', in *Periferin i centrum* (2007), pp. 23-86.
7 T. Wikström (a) (2007), op.cit.
8 I had access to maps with distinct contour lines from Huddinge Municipality on which to plot the paths.
9 The field studies were carried out during the period 2002-2005. Visits to Flemingsberg were made on 20 or so occasions, each of them lasting 1-4 days.
10 M. de Certeau: *The Practice of Everyday Life* (1988).
11 H. Lefebvre: *The Production of Space* (1991)
12 'Shortcuts are long ways round' runs the old proverb. However, that does not tally with my findings.
13 B. Molander: *Kunskap i handling* (1996).
14 T. Wikström (b): 'Restytor och gränsöverskridande rumsliga praktiker i Flemingsberg', In *Periferin i centrum* (2007), pp 170-78.

**Literature**


- de Certeau, M.: *The Practice of Everyday Life*. University of California Press, Berkeley 1988 (L'invention du quotidien. Vol. 1, Arts de faire, 1980).
- Lefebvre, H.: *The Production of Space*. Blackwell Publishers, Oxford 1991 (La production de l'espace, 1974).
- Molander, B.: *Kunskap i handling*. Daidalos, Gothenburg 1996.
- Nylund, K. (ed.): *Periferin i centrum. Gränsöverskridande praktiker I Stockholms offentliga rum*. Daidalos, Gothenburg 2007.
- Nielsen, T.: *Formløs. Den moderne bys overskudslandskaber*. Arkitektskolens Forlag, Aarhus 2001.
- de Solà-Morales, I.: 'Terrain vague', in *Anyplace*, MIT Press, Cambridge 1994, p. 119.
- Statens planverk: *SCAFT 1968. Riktlinjer för stadsplanering med hänsyn till trafiksäkerhet*. Statens planverk, publication 5, 1968.
- Tägil, T., & Werne, F.: 'Förorter i förändring'. In *Periferin i centrum*, ed. Nylund, K., Daidalos, Gothenburg 2007, pp. 23-86.
- Wikström, T.: 'Residual space and transgressive spatial practices – the uses and meanings of un-formed space', *Nordic Journal of Architectural Research*, no. 1, 2005.
- Wikström, T.: 'Monumentalitet och mobilitet i Flemingsberg'. In *Periferin i centrum*, ed. Nylund, K., Daidalos, Gothenburg 2007a, pp. 87-143.
- Wikström, T.: 'Restytor och gränsöverskridande rumsliga praktiker i Flemingsberg', in *Periferin i centrum*, ed. Nylund, K., Daidalos, Gothenburg 2007b, pp. 145-79.

Kirsten Birk Hansen

# The Danish Project

## Developing Greenland into a Modern Welfare Society

**This article sheds light on the Danish project of transforming and developing Greenland into a modern welfare society. The focus here will be on the built welfare in Greenland, the implementation of which was handled by an organization that was set up specifically for this purpose: GTO, *Grønlands Tekniske Organisation* [Greenland Technical Organization]. This was a grandiose project, with GTO as a kind of 'welfare generator' within a process whose confidence in its own values' validity was striking. The sensitivity to – and the understanding of – the Greenlandic community's specific conditions and values were sometimes flawed; on the other hand, a re-alignment was called for.**

## Greenland as a Danish colony

The first wave of colonization of Greenland took place in the 1700s, when Hans Egede, as a Danish/Norwegian priest, arrived in Nuuk, for the purpose of missionizing the Norsemen who had travelled from Iceland to Greenland around the year 1000. Hans Egede set out to find their descendants, with an eye towards propagating Christianity. Egede did not manage to find any Norsemen; instead, he met an Eskimo community of sealers and whalers that subscribed to an Inuit mythology, a community that he tried to Christianize. It was this missionary activity, combined with trade, which was the starting point for what subsequently became the gradual colonization of Greenland.

After the Second World War, the relationship between Greenland and Denmark was manifested in a remarkable course of development, which could safely be described as one aspect of the second wave of colonization. In 1948, Hans Hedtoft, the Danish Prime Minister, travelled to Greenland and obtained the provincial council's approval for a total change of tack, re-directed toward an opening of the country and its development into a modern society, the living conditions of which would come to stand in reasonable proximity to the rest of Denmark. In 1953, Greenland's status as a colony was phased out; instead, Greenland took on the status of a Danish administrative district. Denmark was at that time in the process of being transformed into a modern welfare state, and as a new 'county', Greenland was now going to be upgraded to a welfare society.

The government set up a *Grønlandskommission* [The Greenland Commission], which was entrusted with the task of hammering out a re-arrangement of Greenland's future; of course, this task included proposals for Greenland's fundamental physical structures. The society of sealers and whalers was going to be replaced by an industrial society, and seal-hunting and sheep-breeding had to be subordinated the development of a mono-industrial commercial way of life based on ocean fishery.[1] A societal development that was going to require an adequate development of housing, urban formation and infrastructure. To bring forth this transformation's physical structures, and in order to remain in charge of the overall strategic planning, the Danes established a new organization: GTO.

In the present article, I will attempt to shed light on the Danish project: developing Greenland into a modern welfare society. It is, in this context, the built welfare, which means to say the construction and planning of urban coherences, on which the focus will be aimed. Here, GTO stands in a central position and the sources that this article draws on are especially GTO's annual reports, which continually tell about the projects and their implementation; the article will also be referring to the ongoing discussions around these architectural projects, which often took on a critical tone in the journal *Arkitekten*.

I will also be comparing GTO's overall and coordinating strategic efforts with the Danish architect studios' contributions to planning, designing and projecting. This mainly revolves around projects where the Danish architects travelled to Greenland and examined the conditions there and subsequently designed projects in Copenhagen, which were then carried out in collaboration with GTO in Greenland.[2]

## From communal dwellings to single-family homes

Seen through the eyes of the Danes, the Greenlanders' own buildings were of a primitive character. At the time that colonization commenced in 1721, the Greenlanders were living in tents in the summer months while during the winter months, they resided in large communal dwellings, in the form of peat huts for several families, where each family lived together in its own bay. Heating inside the homes was fuelled by whale oil lamps, which emitted such a high room temperature that the residents could walk around naked indoors, freed from their heavy skin clothing. For the colonizers, it was this latter custom that occasioned such a powerful incentive for change, because, to put it quite simply, they found both these conditions and this conduct to be objectionable – and,

Wooden house, built by the occupant, in Kanganiut.

→

House, built by the occupant, sometime in the 1960s.

back in 1952 the former Chief Administrative Officer Ph. Rosendahl construed this to have been a direct cause for the demand concerning single-family dwellings for the Greenlanders.[3] Both the fact that several families were living together and the fact that people were moving around inside the home without wearing any clothes were sufficient grounds for promoting the normal Danish residential arrangement, where each and every family had its own abode.

In the 20th century, people started to build houses made only of wood, with peat- or moss-padding insulation material and with roofing felt on the roofs. During the cold winters, it was often the case that several families would move into one and same house, in order to cut down on the costs of fuel, but often the walls were: 'lined with ice, even though the room was crammed.'[4] Tuberculosis flourished, and when the Greenland Commission's medical commission inspected these kinds of often overcrowded houses for ordinary families, the residents were advised about the necessity of light and fresh air. Already in the course of the 1800s, it had become clear to the authorities that the prerequisite conditions for any sweeping improvement in the status of public health inside the overcrowded homes would have to be the development of inexpensive, hygienic types of houses, which could also be made fire-resistant.

## Special circumstances and conditions

Building in Greenland are subject to a number of conditions stamped by a particularly difficult character. This touches especially upon the climate

and to the terrain conditions. There is often a need to blast the rocky ground in order to lay out the roads and the building sites, and the construction season is very short. Up until about 1950, there were only paths between the houses. There were no proper roads, and there were virtually no cars. There are hundreds of kilometres between the small towns and because of the impassable terrain, they are not connected by any roads whatsoever but are one-sidedly oriented towards the sea without any directly attached hinterlands. The consequence is that each of these towns lives out its own autonomous life. The traffic connections transpire either via sea or via planes, and the former kind of traffic is primarily bound to serving the needs of the fishing operations.

Another decisive factor was that most of the materials had to be obtained from outside Greenland: these were often manufactured in Denmark and were shipped and transported via the Atlantic Ocean, where, after reaching their destinations in Greenland, they had to be transported to what were often hard-to-access building sites. In addition, the climate imposed formidable demands on the materials' durability. Moreover, workers who had been dispatched to Greenland from Denmark were often employed to carry out the construction activities, concomitantly giving rise to expenses for their travel costs, for being quartered and for their provisions, as well as to disbursements for other expensive events. 'As a result of these conditions, one needs to reckon on con-

struction in Greenland costing 1½-2 times as much as it would in Denmark.'[5]

## The planners' entry – modern rationality and hygiene

According to The Greenland Commission's report, an expedition with urban planners was dispatched to Greenland in 1950 in order to assess the basis for a modern urban development. The urban planning expedition obtained knowledge about local conditions, registered facts and analysed these, and prepared a report. Here, an image of what was to come was delineated, an image that placed great weight on the proposition that residential construction was supposed to shore up and sustain progress. The developmental possibilities in Nuuk were studied; this was an urban centre that was navigable throughout the whole year. The opportunities for urban development called for high density; and the urban planners recommended a capital-city kind of development in Nuuk.

The urban planning expedition had a forerunner in a doctors' expedition that was working first and foremost with sanitary considerations and looked upon the small do-it-oneself houses as posing the most severe threat of all to the population's health. The urban planners, together with the hygienists, staked out guidelines for the development of Greenlandic housing and urban planning. Guidelines whose horizon was the Danish welfare society with its reformatory program. Especially when it comes to the disciplining of the population and the implementation of rational thinking. Intentions about a necessary regulation of behaviour among the population, which would supposedly be engaged and employed in the fishing industry, called for a corresponding change of attitude towards work.

## Scattered vs. dense residential development

As far as the technical solutions of more overall strategic character were concerned, people were compelled, by and large, to start all over again, and there were not many experiences to be gleaned from the other Arctic areas. When it comes to the building cultures, what supervened in the wake of the peat huts was a tradition of building small wooden houses on the rocky cliffs with views looking out – and without any demarcations in relation to plots. The latter was, of course, similarly a manifestation of the fact that, in Greenland, there are no private property rights. One can only obtain permission to build on a particular site from the community.

Notwithstanding the prevalence of a residential form with many small dwellings made of wood, what there was in Greenland, in the opinion of many Danes, was not really a 'building culture' at all. The architect Hans Erling Langkilde claimed, at some point in the 1970s, that the Greenlanders had not had, 'like we [...] a proper building culture'.[6] This statement has to be regarded as a contribution situated within a residential-social and architectural debate that was being carried on in *Arkitekten* about the wisdom of building concrete blocks of flats, which were supposed to play a part in being able to centralize the population in buildings with running water, heat and toilet facilities and baths. In the period 1964-1981, Langkilde was a member of the supervisory board of GTO, but he represented a critical stance in relation to the organization, and when, in 1974, Langkilde took over the chairman's post, he managed to activate a collaboration where the Greenlanders finally managed to be heard.

In GTOs eagerness to introduce modern blocks of flats, what was being overlooked was that what was actually happening constituted an interven-

View across Sukkertoppen, now Maniitsoq, with three GTO building developments in the background (c. 1968).
Mogens S. Koch / The Danish Architectural Press.

tion into an existing building culture. As a matter of fact, there was a building culture that was based on small single-family houses: these were houses that could be converted and expanded, and these houses provided shelter and enjoyed direct access to outdoor areas, offering possibilities for playing, for making food, for drying and preserving different kinds of reserves and supplies, for storing dog sleds and fishing gear, and they also left ground open in certain spots, where vegetables could be cultivated. This was a building culture that was accordingly addressed to the existing forms of life and to the existing terrain conditions.

One of the fundamental problems that the urban planners were supposed to tackle was infrastructure. The pre-existing residential- and building-culture posed certain problems in relation to modern standards of rationality and hygiene. Because the houses were spread out across the field terrain without roads, it was not possible to introduce a steady arrangement for the removal and disposal of rubbish. There was no sewerage, and residents were compelled to throw away garbage right outside of their houses. If the towns should grow, such conditions could lead to serious health hazards. If, for example, the drinking water, which was being delivered into tanks positioned alongside the individual houses, was now also going to be conveyed via pipes, there would consequently be substantial benefits in having more closely positioned housing forms. Also because what we have here is rocky ground. The same logic could also be applied to the use of other kinds of conduits, such as those conveying central heating. Another advantage of building houses together would be a reduction in the climate-screening surface areas and a reduction in the consumption of heat.

Finally, the often arduous laying out of proper roads presented a problem. The scattered, low construction with a poor coefficient of utilization gave rise to a need for a superfluous, widely branching and costly network of roads.

Another problem was dispersal. Not only were the building developments spread out: the population was also spread out across the towns and village settlements where the dependency on hunting opportunities had led to a scattering of the population at many settlements. Greenland is a vastly expansive and a sparsely populated area. The argument for the envisioned concentration of the population in fewer cities, with the impending dismantling of village settlements as a consequence was actually planned out, primarily, on the basis of commercial concerns, as is evidenced by the so-called 'G60' report: 'Stronger concentration around the most suitable cities. The investments must, in the first instance, be carried into effect in those areas of Greenland that offer the best business-economic opportunities with respect to the improvement of incomes, and these developing cities must be enlarged and organized in such a way that more space can be created for regional movements of workers than has been the norm in the past decade.'[7]

This dispersal, however, also posed certain problems in relation to welfare benefits: in relation to the population's access to schooling, to medical care and to hospitals. This involved enormous difficulties in carrying into effect everybody's equal access to the so-called 'universal welfare benefits'. The equal access that is the hallmark of the Danish welfare society.

Although what was being said was that the goal was exclusively to find the most rational solutions to construction, technically speaking and economically speaking, the rational advantages of denser settlement forms were clear to the urban planners: 'Ordinarily, on a given area that is being planned for single-family homes, twice as many people can live there if, instead, the area is devel-

Illulissat 1 and 2.
Photo: Kjeld Vindum 2012 / The Danish Architectural Press.

oped with non-detached town houses, and four times as many people can live there if this same area is developed with medium-high blocks of flats, and still many more can live there if the constructions are built even higher.'[8]

The urban planners were in agreement about The Greenland Commission's aims when it came to renewing the entire housing stock in Greenland over the course of the ensuing 20 years, but the urban planners could not abide by the commission's proposals that were centred on basing the totality of this grand and impressive housing programme on the erection of nothing other than detached single-family houses made of wood. The wooden houses were generally erected with scanty fire separation distance, so if they were going to be replaced by considerably larger building types, and if the fire separation distances were going to be duly complied with, then, in a good many instances, this would require twice the ground area alone for the existing population. By way of alternative, the urban planners called attention to the idea of constructing semi-detached single-family family homes. At the time, the semi-detached town house happened to be an immensely popular form of housing among Danish architects. One thing was clear: the new form of housing which, according to city planners, stood forth as inevitable in relation to a modern urban development, was the block of flats, that were erected in concrete as pre-cast building constructions.

## Greenland Technical Organization is set up

The Greenland Commission resolved that a technical organization ought to be established that would gather all of the technical facilities and activities under one umbrella. In 1965, GTO was established as a directorate under the Ministry for Greenland. The tasks called for insight into climate-, terrain- and ice-related conditions, and having this knowledge amassed at one central spot appeared to be rational, seeing as it was relevant to all construction going on in Greenland. Greenland was divided into four districts and the organization established and ran contractor- and

building enterprises, with storehouses and different artisan's workshops in all of the Greenlandic settlements. These workshops discharged the smaller-scale, local projects, which people had been figuring would largely be taken over by private building enterprises. GTO's local representatives were also engaged in offering consultancy services, because no other specialized technical expertise was available in Greenland at that time.
In addition to providing Greenland with modern houses, GTO was also entrusted with the responsibility of establishing the appurtenant institutions. There was a need to build schools that ought to be commensurable, approximately, with what was going on in the Danish public schools, and would be offering instruction in both Greenlandic and Danish. And child-care institutions had to be built: among other things, these would serve to potentiate women's equal employment-related opportunities. Also, in connection with young people's higher education, there was a need to establish technical schools that would offer instruction and training to Greenlandic workpersons and artisans, with the appurtenant need for homes.
Also, the establishment of an infrastructure was altogether crucial to a modern societal development, especially in such a sparsely populated, dispersedly built-up, impassable, and geographically extended area of land as Greenland was. Together with the climate, what these conditions entailed, however, was that the establishment of the infrastructure was an arduous enterprise and involved gargantuan costs. Nevertheless, the infrastructure was – and still is – the basis for the requisite business-related development. What was also established were inclusive infrastructures such as port facilities, water-supply installations, electrical power plants and installations for telecommunications.
An equally important growth- and productivity initiative was the improvement of the social, health-related and educational conditions. And it was especially in the health sector that the results were striking. In 1959, GTO's chief engineer, Gunnar P. Rosendahl, could state: 'Population growth is undergoing rampant expansion and is now, in terms of percentage, three times as high as it is in the rest of Denmark. [...] The total population, which in 1950 amounted to 23,000 people, has accordingly risen to 30,500 people in 1958.'[9] At the outset, buildings were built for the people who had been sent to work in Greenland; it was considerations that were paid specifically to these people that were determinative for the buildings' design, whether we are speaking about homes or about institutions. There was nothing new in this, because the Danes, right from the start, had been building primarily for the people who had been sent to work in Greenland and were doing so with all due consideration being paid to their conditions and their needs. Nor was this a state of affairs that appeared to pose any particular problems, inasmuch as the intentions with the whole of GTO's project were to bring Greenlandic circumstances and living conditions on a par with those of the Danish welfare state. This means to say that the Greenlanders were being forced not merely to accept but also to appropriate the ideals and tendencies and the lifestyle that Danish housing symbolized. Accordingly, the building activity stood as an illustration of the colonialist notion that lay behind the Danish efforts in Greenland: the Occidental, technologically advanced civilization was supposed to shape Greenland and the Greenlanders for the coming welfare state.
It was this project around which GTO was supposed to establish the physical frames and when the organization was initiated and activated, what was expected was that its design of the new Greenland would soon be ready. Or as Kaare Hendriksen, of the Technical University of Den-



Workpersons' billeting camp, Nuuk (c. 1966). Architects Jensen & Valeur.

mark, reports: 'People believed that the work could be completed in the course of only ten years. There were, by and large, unlimited funds for carrying out the tasks, and people saw no reason to [...] educate Greenlanders to take part in the process. It was Danish knowledge and know-how that was needed.'[10]

'It is,' as the engineer Poul Lyager writes, 'hard to get around the thought that the whole undertaking, the intensely physical projects and activities [...] were an overprotective violation of a small and vulnerable society [...]. The many specialists who took part were chiefly technicians and administrators [...]. People with proper sociologically related credentials or people with any genuine understanding of – and experience from – corresponding communities and undertakings at other places in the world were simply missing. Evidently, what wasn't even being mulled over was whether or not there might be considerations other than health, education, manufacturing and material improvements, or whether the strategy or the pace could perhaps be unfolded in a different way. But the intentions were for the best.'[11]

## Urban construction

The term 'city' is new in Greenland. Former terms for spots that were settled in Greenland were 'colony' (in the sense of a settlement or outpost outside the kingdom's boundaries), 'trading station' and 'settlement', which, in connection with the Greenland Commission's work, were superseded by the terms 'city' and 'village settlement'. A stated intention with the Greenland town plans was that they were supposed to systemize matters. 'The city must be given a harmonious form and should at all times be characterized by being a laid-out city [...] laid-out with the principal idea of being a manifestation of the life of the community and of the community's culture which people want to have developed at this particular place.' And about the future residential areas, it has been emphasized: 'The task is both to subordinate one-

The black blocks, Ilulissat (1966). Architects Viggo Møller-Jensen and Tyge Arnfred. Kjeld Vindum 2012 / The Danish Architectural Press.

Kitchen in the block of flats, in Frederikshåb, now, Paamiut (c. 1957). Architect Tage Nielsen. Mogens S. Koch / The Danish Architectural Press.

self to the totality's grand lines and to create enclosed, distinctive milieus of surveyable size.'[12] Or, as this was formulated by section architect Vagn Laage, of GTO: 'In the Greenlandic urban construction, we are stressing that the individual buildings are being subordinated to considerations about the totality, with the result that the city or the street scene will not come to be comprised of a string of singular architectural pearls, but rather that they, together, will come to function as one harmoneous whole'.[13] What was being sought was to create a displacement of interest from the individual building to the aggregate building plan, so that each of the houses would, to a more significant extent, be seen as a part of the whole.

The work done during the course of the urban planners' expedition was accomplished almost synchronously with an avid interest in urban planning that arose internationally in the wake of the Second World War, at a moment in history when many cities had to be rebuilt. In its report, the expedition had called attention to the importance of urban planning and had proposed a concentration of the Greenlandic population into urban building developments. The migration from rural to urban areas was viewed as being conditioned by economical and social opportunities – and this pattern was no less valid when it came to the Greenlanders' state of affairs. And the planners were able to console themselves with the thought that the Greenlanders probably ought to follow along with these kinds of migratory trends. On the whole, the GTO refrained from working with the modernization of Greenland in a manner that was attuned to any regional differences and nuances. When the Greenlanders hesitated and balked in response to being asked to leave their places of residence and their homes in order to exchange these for new homes in the town, it was much more a matter of persuading them and getting them to appreciate the new circumstances' qualities; one of the ways this was effectuated was by having the people who had been sent from Denmark move into the new homes. Then, the Greenlanders would certainly soon follow suit – this was the guiding notion on the part of the GTO. However, local conditions were taken into account, such as when urban areas were divided up into separate areas or neighbourhoods, which might be bounded by natural topographical, geological and climatological factors. For example, the snowfall and the formation of snowdrifts are factors that have to be taken into account in relation to the buildings' orientation and in relation to its mutual dispositions. Yet another factor that was crucial to any considerations about residential planning was the size of the Greenlandic family. There were only a few places in the world where the households were as large as in Greenland, where approximately half the population was comprised of children under the age of 14. Through efforts related to 'family planning', however, what was achieved in relatively short order was a 'normalization' – i.e. in comparison to Danish conditions – of the households' size. In 1963, the Ministry for Greenland came to a decision that there would, in principle, no longer be differences between the types of housing designated for people sent to Greenland from Denmark and the types of housing designated for the Greenlandic population.

## The criticism, the phasing out of the GTO and the end of the colonial era

Over the course of the 1970s, in *Arkitekten,* there was a considerable degree of debate about – and a critique of – the functional-rational strategy that GTO's activities were manifesting. Among other things, the debate revolved around the question of whether people would be able to adapt and tailor residential construction to the Greenlanders' needs and way of life. 'We have invested too little imagination and too few new methods in Greenland construction,' summarizes the editor of *Arkitekten*, Poul Erik Skriver, in his criticism of the housing blocks: 'It would have been a more impressive technical feat if, for instance, people in the 1950s had built small and simply equipped homes, which were prepared for expansion and ready for sanitation, at whatever time the requirements in connection with residential standards would become sharpened. And people would have dodged the obvious risk, [...] that a very large number of hefty concrete buildings would become totally outdated in a few years' time [...] This would have been "rational" in a different sense than GTO's perception of the word: it would have been human. What could have been developed instead were forms of industrialized building, where lightweight components [...] could have been used for making new construction and for the expansion of the original small homes. The education and training of Greenlanders to carry out this kind of industrialized construction would have been a more viable task than educating and training them to be participants in the construction of concrete buildings which now dominate the Greenland construction scene.'[14]

The background for the debate that was appearing on the pages of *Arkitekten* was the increasing problematization of GTO's and, on the whole, the Danish project that was geared towards the transformation of the Greenlandic society into a modern welfare society. It is true that infant mortality was declining and it is true that tuberculosis was practically eradicated. Moreover, the level of education had risen and there was certainly improvement in the housing conditions. But at the same time, alcoholism has 'increased colossally, criminality is higher than in Denmark, gonorrhoea is flourishing with alarming proliferation among young people, and a third of the psychiatric patients are under 15 years of age. These are all symptoms of the fact that the Greenlandic people are being placed in a conflict-ridden situation,' as Skriver wrote, as he offered a summary of the conflict-ridden situation: 'Today, 11,000 Danes are helping 40,000 Greenlanders to build a society which, down to the smallest detail, is a copy of the Danish: a society which is, for all intents and purposes, utterly lacking in any preliminary conditions that might be correlated with Greenlandic nature and culture.'[15]

Interior from standard house, Type 67 (circa 1968). Architects Viggo Møller-Jensen and Tyge Arnfred.
Mogens S. Koch / The Danish Architectural Press.

→
Aerial view of Nuuk (c. 1965); on the left: Large Plain with Block 1-10 and the transversely running Block P, under construction.
Mogens S. Koch / GTO.

Originally, GTO's strong suit was that all of the technical development efforts were gathered together into one enterprise that could plan and coordinate the work, and which had ensured continuity and the communication of experiences. With the passage of time, however, this was something of a political drawback. In the 1970s and the 1980s, young Greenlanders were demanding their right to be defining the future development of the Greenlandic society and the rights to the Greenlandic subsoil. In continuation of this, Greenland's Prime Minister, Jonathan Motzfeldt, enunciated, in 1986, his take on the situation: 'The difficult readjustment from being nature people to becoming factory workers – from small houses to high-rise blocks has been accomplished. The worst period is over – and we have, as a people, also arrived at that point that when there is something to criticize, we aim the criticism at ourselves – and we are delighted to be rid of the Danish patronage.'[16]

GTO attained its maximum size in 1968-70. After then, it went downhill. From 1975-78, the Greenlandic municipalities started to establish their own technical administrations, and a number of technical tasks that had previously been handled by the government were now transferred to the municipal field of responsibility. In 1972, Greenland had, along with Denmark, entered the European Common Market but in 1985, Greenland announced that, it was withdrawing from the European Economic Community (EEC); this was done in order to extend its contacts westwards with kinsmen and kinswomen around the Arctic. After the introduction of 'Home Rule', in 1979, GTO was gradually taken over by Greenlanders, up until the time that the organization was placed, in 1987, under the auspices of the Home Rule and eventually had its name changed to NunaTek. In 1991, NunaTek was transformed into Greenland's energy company, Nukissiorfiit. In 2009, three quarters of the Greenlandic population voted

'yes' to the question of self-government, and in June of that same year, the system of self-government took effect.

In 2012, the notorious Block P in Nuuk was torn down. This, the federation's longest concrete block (150 meters), was erected in 1965 and stood as the very emblem of GTO's forming of Greenland. 'Block P was built as a direct consequence of the idea about gathering Greenland's population into larger cities [...]. The good intentions here had to do with giving the people in Greenland the same access to education and the healthcare system, drag and drop, as in the rest of the kingdom,' as the author Jørgen Chemnitz writes.'[17]

## GTO's urban conception vs. the Greenlander's perception of space

It was Block P and the other blocks on Store Slette [The Large Plain] in Nuuk that stood as the most striking manifestations of the urban conception which was GTO's. This conception was commensurate with what was valid and in force, at that point in time, when it came the development of new suburban areas in Denmark. In a global sense, the concrete-element block constituted the expression of the idea surrounding modern habitation; similarly, the orthogonal constellations of blocks constituted the picture of the modern city. In this modern city, the traditional European city's ordered arrangement, with its clearly defined streets and squares, was being replaced by a certain visual order, with open spatialities that were restrained by parallel-situated blocks or by blocks that formed open right angles. Spaces that were never intimate, fully closed or fully open. It was precisely this form of spatiality that, at the closing of the 1960s, i.e. in the years right after Block P was erected, was being exposed to a burgeoning degree of criticism.

And perhaps it was the implementation of this type of urban space, and the associated notion of urbanity, that proved to be especially problematic in relation to Greenlanders and to the Greenlandic landscape. For, as Langkilde stated in *Arkitektur DK* in 1968, 'In this way, the Greenlanders' own building developments do not have space-forming properties of the same character as can be seen in the European building developments. Nor can their landscape be perceived spatially in the same way as what we can measure by European standards, where the landscape is most often culture and not nature. Our conceptions of space and urban space have been handed down through the centuries, but this is simply not the case when it comes to the Greenlanders [...]. The Greenlanders' own building developments are not space-forming, their landscape have wide expanses but cannot be perceived spatially. It is in accordance with this that it has been possible to ascertain that the residents' strongest objection to the Store Slette-construction was not the form of dwelling as such – it was not so much that they were supposed to live in the flats in the housing blocks – but rather the closed 'spaces' in between the buildings. One 'couldn't breathe freely', they were claiming.'[18]

It is possible to discuss, back and forth, Langkilde's perception that the Greenlandic landscape cannot be perceived spatially. But he has certainly grabbed hold of certain differences in the respective perceptions of space. Accordingly, it is not uncommon to hear Greenlanders who have settled in Denmark say that they are 'missing the horizon'. Seen with European eyes, Nuuk can appear fragmentary, as if it consisted of fragments of a city, where the buildings are not related to each other, and with a peculiar traffic pattern, and where one wanders along the sequences that criss-cross the city where the earth is common property.

## Greenland as constructed welfare experiment

Langkilde has stressed that since the late 1700s, Danish-launched construction has been hammered out with an eye towards the needs of the Danes who were stationed in Greenland, especially when it came to residential forms and standards concerning the flats: 'Our present day's Greenlandic residential construction is no harbinger of originality, traditions or regional building customs. It has come from Denmark and is wholly dominated by changing residential-construction ideals. However, it has not been carried into effect without some measure of care and solicitude for the Greenlanders,'[19] he wrote in 1986, the same year that Jonathan Motzfeldt expressed his relief about having gotten rid of the Danes' patronage. The care, or the empathy, that Langkilde is speaking about, was manifest, i.e., in the numerous attempts through the years to design affordable, free-standing house types for the Greenlanders. Much thought was given to the materials, and attempts were made to make adaptations for the climate, for the lifestyle and for the size of the families. One such attempt is described by Ph. Rosendahl, chief administrative officer of Greenland's administration around 1945: 'The price of the building materials turned out to be about the same as it would be for a turf-house of the same size. Additionally, it had an extension with a porch, a storeroom, a woodshed and a room for dog feed; it has now been inhabited for seven years. Its residents praise its warmth and its good lighting conditions. In this way, it is possible to come to the aid of the most disadvantaged sector of the population, especially if, as has been mentioned, private carpentry workshops are set up, from where people can obtain lumber that has been bundled together and that is ready for being set up and ready for building, with the help of instruction manuals and drawings related to how to do this and, if necessary, with expert assistance in performing the manual labour. In designing the house, considerations were paid to the population's practices: for example, there is the plank bed which, in addition to being a sleeping place, is also supposed to be a workstation [...]. But there were also bunk beds that were mounted on the wall so that the children would not need to lie between the parents. [...] Experienced Greenlandic doctors have commended this kind of interior design of a house as being consistent with the population's life habits and as something that symbolizes an improvement in the hygienic conditions for the most disadvantaged.'[20]

Although there were good intentions being voiced here that the Greenlanders were eventually going to live well and although it was eventually possible to effectively reduce the incidence of infectious diseases like tuberculosis, what arose – in synch with the growing population – was a need for more comprehensive solutions and more comprehensive plans: thoughts that were not strangers back at the time of the urban planners' expedition. The solution was blocks of flats in the form of prefabricated concrete blocks. The most signal example of this building type was the Store Slette-building development in Nuuk. The entire scheme called to mind the blueprints representing blocks of flats that were being built at the time in Denmark, but because the construction costs were significantly higher, as mentioned before, and because the amounts subject to adjustments were the same, the flats in Greenland were resultantly designed to be much smaller than those that were built in Denmark. In spite of all the vehement criticism to which these block buildings were subject, in Greenland as well as in Denmark, people just kept right on working with the project. A very important argument for the blocks was the hygienic aspect. The purposive-rational concept made it possible to concentrate the sewerage in relation to the scattered settlements. All the homes could get running water and could have a toilet. The rents were inexpensive; medical visits were less frequent; and the state of people's health was generally better. However, the building developments failed to manifest or express any relationship whatsoever to the Greenlandic way of life, and they played a role in the centralization for which GTO was advocating so strongly in the 1960s.

Something analogous can be said about the concentration of the population and the phasing out of the village settlements. This was, as has been stated, a tremendously difficult process, which could have been handled in a better way, but the concentration was also necessary for creating jobs and for ensuring young people's access to education, and also for ensuring the general population's access to health services.

It was these kinds of ambiguities, within which GTO was actively operating, and if there is a wish to evaluate the development of Greenland in recent times, perhaps it would also be prudent to compare this with the social development that was taking place within other groups of indigenous peoples, in other Inuit societies[21] in Alaska, in Canada and all the way around the Arctic Sea to the Bering Strait, where a critical awareness of global warming and an awareness about the relationship with nature in an impending exploitation of raw materials has been pronounced in recent years.

Here, however, the focus has been on the formation of the new Greenland, with GTO as a 'welfare generator' – a formation that is being perceived as a kind of 'welfare colonialism', based on a specifically Danish understanding of welfare. And in the case of Greenland, the normal Dane was seen as an ideal for the new Greenlander.

**Notes**

1 In 1957, at a series of meetings that were being held for the former Kongelige Grønlandske Handel [The Royal Greenland Trade Department] and the newly established GTO, Permanent Secretary Eske Brun had this to say about the economy: 'We are living a life-lie, about Greenlandic production coming to be self-sufficient [...] This will never come to pass. There is the fishing industry, as far as the Greenlanders' are concerned, and there is only this. In spite of this, the Greenlandic production is, however, a first-rate and reasonable business.' Brun calls attention to the fact, however, that in connection with the discovery of minerals, what could be envisaged are 'exceedingly vast and interesting options that render it so that, for the Danish society, it will be crucially important to hold on tightly to Greenland as our own.' Today, Greenland is, with the Home Rule, oriented in a new way with respect to the surrounding world and is not looking, as was previously the case, negatively upon the situation with regard to the eventual exploitation of the Greenlandic nature's raw materials. P. Lyager: 'Om byplan i Grønland – mellem præstestyre og hjemmestyre', *Byplanhistoriske noter 46*. Dansk Byplanlaboratorium. Copenhagen 2002.

2 GTO's annual reports are available at the University of Copenhagen's Polar Library.

3 Ph. Rosendahl.: 'Grønlænderboliger gennem tiderne', *Arkitekten* 5/1952, p. 82.

4 Ibid., p. 82.

5 A.G. Bak, H. Petersen, E. Staffeldt, E. Nederland & I. Withen: *Bogen om Grønland, FORTID, NUTID, FREMTID* (1978), p. 230.

6 H.E. Langkilde: *GRØNLAND – i går – i dag – i morgen. Booklet accompanying an exhibition about Greenland's technical developments and about Greenland Technical Organization, GTO* (1986), p. 19.

7 G60, hovedsynspunkter bag udviklingsplanen, point # 2. Quoted from: J.C. Kleist: *De grønlandske bygder – hvad skal vi stille op med dem?* Bachelor project 2010, p. 9.

8 'Byens og boligens udformning i det fremtidige Grønland', summary of the commission's report 1950, *Arkitekten* 4-5/1952. p. 95

9 G.P. Rosendahl: 'De seneste års tekniske udvikling i Grønland', *Tidskriftet Grønland* 10/1959, p. 342.

10 From a discussion paper drafted by Kåre Hendriksen, Center for Arktisk Teknologi, DTU, at a workshop centred on GTO's history, University of Greenland 2015, quoted from: http://videnskab.dk/blog/gronlands-tekniske-organisation.

11 P. Lyager: 'Om byplan i Grønland – mellem præstestyre og hjemmestyre' in *Dansk Byplanlaboratorium, Byplanhistoriske noter 46* (2002), p. 16.

12 City planning expedition's report, quoted from: H.E. Langkilde: *Grønlandske byer og boliger*, p. 39.

13 Laage: 'De grønlandske byer', *Arkitekten* 20/1970, p. 471.

14 P.E. Skriver: 'Grønland i Focus', *Arkitekten* 23/1970, pp. 541-42.

15 Ibid., p. 537.

16 G.P. Rosendahl: *Et teknisk udviklet samfund, teksthefte til en udstilling om Grønlands tekniske udvikling og om Grønlands tekniske organisation* (1986), p. 57.

17 And he continues: 'When Blok P was built, Nuuk took its first steps towards transforming itself from a small market town into something that was supposed to resemble an urban landscape.' J. Chemnitz: 'Mikropolis' in *Blok P – en boligblok i Nuuk*, exhibition catalogue, Nordatlantens Brygge (2014), pp. 7-8. See also: B.W. Sørensen og S. Forchhammer: 'Byen og bygden – grønlandske landskaber' in *Dansk Sociologi Nr. 4/25.* Vol. 2014, pp. 24-26.

18 H.E. Langkilde: 'Grønland under Forvandling', *Arkitektur DK* 4/1968.

19 Rosendahl (1986), op.cit., p. 19

20 Ph. Rosendahl: 'Tanker om grønlændernes boliger' in *Det grønlandske Selskabs Årsskrift, c. 1945.* Quoted from: www.gtojvl.dk/83060914

21 Marianne Krogh Andersen writes about Barrow, in Alaska, which is the nightmare scenario, and hereby throws the situation in Greenland into relief: 'Innuteq Olsen, director of Greenland's Foreign Directorate, was educated in the United States and has, at very close range, seen how the Inuit peoples in Alaska are being oppressed. Among other places, he has visited Barrow, where the oil extraction has resulted in giving the Inuit peoples some share of the wealth: Innuteq Olsen describes Barrow as the ugliest city he has ever seen: the buildings are dilapidated, worse than our 'Block P', and worse than the most miserable housing projects in Nuuk. People do not need to work because they are simply rolling in money on account of the shares in oil they have received. What we have here is a mini-Kuwait. Each person has an individual right to spend his own money. However, nothing is being offered to the society and nothing is being offered to beautify the city. People buy insanely expensive cars, and it costs $33,000 just to have one of the cars transported up to the city. It's crazy '. M.K. Andersen: *Grønland mægtig og afmægtig* (2008), p. 286.

**Literature**


- Andersen, H.L., Lyager, P., Boertmann, M., & Teisen, F.: *Kommisionsbetænkning: Byplanforslag i Grønland*, quoted from: 'Byens og boligens udformning i det fremtidige Grønland, referat af kommissionsbetænkningen', 1950, *Arkitekten*, 4-5/52, p. 95.
- Andersen, M.K.: *Grønland mægtig og afmægtig*, Gyldendal, Copenhagen 2008.
- Bak, A.G., Petersen, H., Staffeldt, E., Nederland, E., & Withen, I.: *Bogen om Grønland, FORTID, NUTID, FREMTID*, Politikens Forlag, Copenhagen 1978.
- Birk, K.: 'Danmark i Grønland' i: *Grønland/Greenland revisited*, special issue of: *Arkitektur DK* 04/2012, pp. 6-13.
- Chemnitz, J.: 'Mikropolis' i *Blok P – en boligblok i Nuuk*, exhibition catalogue, Nordatlantens Brygge, Copenhagen 2014.
- GTO's annual reports. Eskimology and Arctic Section's library, University of Copenhagen.
- Hendriksen, K.: Arctic Technology Centre, Technical University of Denmark, workshop about GTO's history, University of Greenland 2015, quoted from: http://videnskab.dk/blog/gronlands-tekniske-organisation
- Kleist, J.C.: *De grønlandske bygder – hvad skal vi stille op med dem?,* bacheloropgave 2010, http://docplayer.dk/333613-De-groenlandske-bygder-hvad-kan-vi-stille-op-med-dem.html
- Langkilde, H.E.: *'Grønlandske byer og boliger. Et forsøg til vejledning – vurdering'* in: Poul Erik Skriver (ed.): *Grønland – i går – i dag – i morgen*, GTO 1986, p. 19.
- Langkilde, H.E.: *GRØNLAND – i går – i dag – i morgen. Teksthefte til en udstilling om Grønland tekniske udvikling og om Grønlands Tekniske Organisation, GTO.* Copenhagen 1986.
- Larsen, J.V.: *Grønlands Tekniske Organisation*, see www.gtojvl.dk/83060912
- Lyager, P.: 'Om byplan i Grønland – mellem præstestyre og hjemmestyre', *Dansk Byplanlaboratorium, Byplanhistoriske noter 46*, Copenhagen 2002. Accessible at www.byplanlab.dk/sites/default/files2/BHU_SKRIFT46.pdf
- Laage, V.: 'De grønlandske byer', *Arkitekten* 20/1970, p. 469.
- Rosendahl, G.P.: 'De seneste års tekniske udvikling i Grønland', in: *Tidsskriftet Grønland* 10/1959.
- Rosendahl, G.P.: 'Et teknisk udviklet samfund' *i teksthefte til en udstilling om Grønlands tekniske udvikling og om Grønlands tekniske organisation*, GTO, Copenhagen 1986.
- Rosendahl, Ph.: 'Grønlænderboliger gennem tiderne', *Arkitekten* 4-5/1952, p. 82.
- Rosendahl, Ph.: 'Tanker om grønlændernes boliger' i *Det grønlandske Selskabs Årsskrift, c. 1945*, see www.gtojvl.dk/83060914
- Skriver, P.E.: 'Grønland i Focus', *Arkitekten* 23/1970, pp. 541-42.
- Sørensen, B.W., & Forchhammer, S.: 'Byen og bygden – grønlandske landskaber' in *Dansk Sociologi* No. 4/25. Vol. 2014, pp. 14-33.

# Planning

Jens Kvorning

# The Welfare Institution as Urban Point of Concentration

**The school, the nursery school, the nursing home, the library, the sports hall and the swimming hall are physical manifestations of the post-war era's welfare policy. At the same time, these institutions are important focal points[1] for everyday life and are accordingly some of the most important structure-providing elements in the welfare city. The present article discusses how these institutions have been conceived and envisioned into the city, and what roles they are going to play in the time to come.**

In this article, I will be discussing the way that institutions like the school, the nursery school, the library and the sports hall have been conceived as elements in the urban fabric and envisioned into the city, and will then be taking a closer look at what roles they, in my opinion, may be assigned in the time to come, for purposes of sustaining and further developing the welfare society's city. It is of vital important that the way of thinking, as such, be scrutinized – this thinking being understood as the thought models and the categories and connections with which the planning profession people are working – since this approach to thinking all too often conceals or fails to bring important issues and correlations up for discussion, and thereby obstructs a relevant discussion about the welfare city's further development. A central contention in this article is that it is important to understand the institution *in a different way* than the way that it was understood, conceived and envisioned in the early post-war era's planning, and that it is important to place the institution in new ways into the planning- and urban discourses.

When the welfare society[2] and the welfare state are being discussed, Denmark is ordinarily categorized within a group that includes the rest of Scandinavian countries, together with Germany and the Netherlands, while England and the United States are regarded as belonging to a different category, and the southern European countries belong to yet a third category.[3] When we train our gaze on the urban-related thinking that has been dominant in the construction of the post-war era's welfare city, it is, however, England that has supplied both the guiding images and the thinking- and planning methodology that have been used in Denmark in the construction of new cities and urban districts. The Anglo-Saxon thinking and tradition can be seen as a pragmatic and acclimatized rendition of the early modernism's urban vision and methodology, coupled[4] with principles drawn from American sociology and urbanism.[5] The Anglo-Saxon way of thinking took up and held the dominant place in the post-war era's urban planning, both because it was related to the triumphant side in the Second World War and because it was developed in synch with the new generation of English New Towns.[6] They appeared in the 1950s and the 1960s as the strongest and most compelling references, because what we had here were new cities built on bare fields, which is why the principles emerged in pure form and corresponded with the atmosphere of 'new beginning',[7] which characterized the Western societies after the war.

What was characteristic of the English New Towns was that they were based on a cell- and hierarchy-way of thinking, which they had inherited from the inter-war period's modernism and from the American concept of the 'neighbourhood-unit'.[8] This approach has to do with identifying and defining the smallest and fundamental elements, and with subsequently viewing the whole as being built up by successive additions of these fundamental cells through clear and simple hierarchical couplings. A group of homes is such a cell, which is collectively organized around a playground, a free space or a recreational area. Several housing groups form the next cell, which is collectively organized around the nursery school. Several nursery schools' surrounding areas are collectively organized around the school and the local shopping centre. Several schools' surrounding areas are collectively organized around the high school and the neighbourhood centre. The traffic system is similarly hierarchical. Automobile traffic is separated from pedestrian and bicycle traffic. The roads for automobiles have a hierarchy that spans from the local, dead-end residential street to more and more specialization-conditioned and faster road categories, and this hierarchy determines who is moving forward, and where, and it divides up the urban landscape into islands with different contents.

This systematics and methodology are something that individuals like Hilberseimer,[9] Hannes Meyer[10] and Le Corbusier,[11] as well as organizations like CIAM,[12] were advocating during the inter-war period. And it became further systematized and operationalized in the planning reports that were drawn up after the Second World War in connection with the English New Towns and in the instructions that issued from many of the newly established research units that were supposed to play a part in modernizing the construction industry and urban planning.[13] It was especially the planning report for the never realized New Town of Hook[14] that took on the status of being some kind of textbook example in modern post-war planning. There is a high degree of similarity between the Hook Report's systematics and the systematics and categorization that were used in the planning reports which were connected with the Køge Bay plan[15] and with many other Danish urban projects of the 1960s and the 1970s. If we look specifically at the villa areas, it is the so-called 'Radburn system' that fashions the paradigmatic model.[16] An important part of this systematics was the quantification of the city's parts and relationships. Large schemes were drawn up which put numbers on the different levels of hierarchical elements in the new city and defined their surrounding catchment areas, their roles and their relationships,[17] and in the next phase, the schematics became determinative for the city's physical structuring and design. The determinative elements were, quite precisely, the welfare institutions.

This thinking and methodology both reflect and produce the image of the welfare city as it was seen and conceived in the early post-war era and up until around 1980. It is a functional and quantitative[18] approach to thinking that dominates, and there is simultaneously a great deal of confidence in planning's capacity to create the modern welfare city, precisely through these hierarchical structuring principles. The early modernism's faith in a form of unity-culture, that there are urban-related solutions which are good for everybody, is also still intact in the post-war way of thinking.

## The Danish welfare city

Since the late 1950s, when there was an upswing in the economy, the women in Denmark have increasingly been working outside the home. From a participation rate in Denmark that was a little under 40% for married women, at the end of the 1950s, the participation rate had risen by the mid-1970s to over 70%.[19] What this signified was that everyday life and rhythms had changed in a radical way. There were few people who were home during the daytime hours in the new residential neighbourhoods, and this alone served to alter the neighbourhood's role and rhythm. The school had always been an organizing point in everyday life, but now, in the new suburbs, the school appeared in a new role and position. And the school was supplemented by the nursery schools, the youth recreation centres and other new institutions, which emerged as organizing points for both the residential areas' flows and the rhythm of everyday life.[20]

The shopping had to be done at other times of the day, depending on the person's working hours and on when the children had to be picked up. Also, new and larger store-types sprang forth; these were localized in clusters and in shopping centres that formed the next hierarchical layer in the new urban areas' organization. In synch with the fact that everyday life was becoming structured, in terms of time considerations, in a way that was essentially different than what had previously been the case, what actually arose were more and more organized offers related to spare time, with new facilities and grounds that could function in relation to these more forcefully partitioned rhythms of everyday life. The sports field and, to a certain extent, also the sports hall and swimming pool, moved from being linked up with organized athletics to being linked up with urban neighbourhoods and quarters.

Urban planning regarded creating the setting for this new reality as its proper task, and the means for doing this was the hierarchical way of structuring. Conversely, it was the new urban areas' hierarchical constructions that maintained this new reality's space-time schemes.[21] Making use of this systematics was perceived as a guarantee that the welfare city could become a reality. It was by these structure-providing facilities that modern daily life could function smoothly, and it was by virtue of the interdependent localization and the hierarchical structure that daily life came to be efficient, comfortable and safe – and therefore modern.

What was carried over from the inter-war period's modernism was an image of the modern urban project as an emancipation project where the effective layout of the city, with its many new institutions, was that which would set the modern person free, and especially the women, to be able to step into a modern world, with its many options and with a richer life as a consequence.[22] In much the same way that the time-studies of the woman in the kitchen[23] could serve to optimize the kitchen's layout and design, to save time and accordingly to liberate the woman, the effective, hierarchical layout of the city would give rise to the effective and emancipating city.

In the post-war methodology, the welfare city's qualities were being manifested and ensured through quantities and hierarchies. However, this planning methodology was also supposed to guarantee equal access to the welfare city's institutions and services through an even apportionment of these layouts. It thus contained a form of thinking along the lines of considerations related to justice and an ambition concerning equal rights to the city for everybody, which proved to be difficult to realize and to secure concurrently with the ongoing development of the welfare society.

The municipal library's content and role have changed significantly in the course of the past 20 years. Opportunities for playing and facilities for holding meetings, and accessibility to computers and all that they connect to, have generated interest from groups that might otherwise not have been users of the library. In this way, the library has become an especially potent institution, when considered in an urban and social context, because it gathers together a wide user group and redeems the ambition of the public space, understood as the place where many people meet and learn, through these meetings, to socialize and to accept each other. In this connection, the new library on Rentemestervej in Copenhagen stands as a successful example. It contains a wide range of possibilities and offers. One can come here to borrow books. One can come here to take a seat, and read, or maybe to do one's homework. One can come here to read newspapers, or to browse through magazines. One can come here to use the computers, for many different purposes. One can come here to play ping-pong or other games that are readily available. One can come here to take part in meetings or to take advantage of courses and lectures that are being offered. One can come here to get a cup of coffee. And people with disabilities are running the café; these individuals are thereby getting new chances and taking on new roles within the local community. One can come here in the summer months to stretch out and relax in the urban garden that surrounds the library. And one can cross back and forth, every which way, among all these possibilities.

This means to say that the library is a place where it is 'easy' to visit: you can have a certain purpose when you visit, or maybe you just feel like going there and seeing what's going on. This openness and this immediate accessibility are also clear to see in the fact that many young women from immigrant families are entering the library and are staying there for long intervals of time, because it is permissible to do so, and because, for some of these young women, this is one of the few public places where, with respect to certain rules prescribed by their families, they are allowed to fare on their own.

The urban quarter in which the new library is situated is one of Danish modernism's high-class urban quarters, with exemplary social housing that was constructed just before the Second World War. However, this is precisely why this is also an urban quarter with very few points of concentration. Whatever concentrations of shops and stores that might originally have been scattered around the area are almost gone now, and for quite some time, there have not been any meeting points that were elevated above the life and the social control that is found in the yard spaces.

## The problematic planning ideology

Today, when one looks at the thinking that guided the development of the welfare city, the relations between the spatial structuring and the social life appear to be either rather unreflective[24] or very mechanical. What lay as an assumption in the concept of the neighbourhood-unit was that the social organization was hierarchized and that social relations radiated from the home as the decisive centre. And early modernism's faith in unity-culture, with the concomitant conviction that there are solutions which are optimal and good for everybody, was also carried over and is living on, to this very day, in much of the planning thinking, in spite of statements about multiplicity, multi-culturalism and network organization.

What was not being sufficiently taken into account in this planning systematics and urban understanding were the temporal displacements in the demand for different forms of service, a demand that is linked up with demographic and structural development. After some time, a few of the nursery schools in the new urban areas became superfluous. Later on, the school capacity had to be reduced; the school's sizes were increased; and schools had to be merged. On the other hand, the frequency of high schools was stepped up, and there was consequently a demand for more. And various new institutions, which might have been linked up with the former institutions, turned up, also. Then these had to be fit into the urban structure. The store structure changed and became more centralized, and local shopping centres disappeared. This entailed that the different hierarchical levels could no longer be sustained, and gradually, the planning placed less weight on these structuring hierarchies and finally wound up completely discontinuing the use of this methodology as the guiding principle. Instead of fixed hierarchies, flexibility in the planning was being regarded as an answer to the city's dynamics and change. Schools and other institutions were now entities in relation to which

people were supposed to take a stance, and school districts were vague and diffluent. One example of the consequence of this approach is the planning and the development of Ørestad, where the public elementary school and the high school were facilities that were actually compelled to buy their way into the new urban quarters, on a par with – and in competition with – private developers' projects. It was and is both sensible and necessary to think in terms of flexibility and dynamics, but doing this moved planning's focus away from the traditional welfare institutions, which now were definitively being left to specialized administrations and, thereby, were no longer being regarded as urban-structural elements with essential significance to bear on daily life's rhythm and on the identity in an urban neighbourhood. Behind this shift in the planning perception and the planning methodology lie experiences with the stringent hierarchies' vulnerability in the face of changed conditions, but there is also the ideological re-orientation that blossomed into a reality, initially with post-modernism's criticism of urban planning's faith in a large order and an aggregate plan, and, later on, concurrently with the influence exerted by a more and more pronounced neo-liberalism and faith in the market as the only reliable registering apparatus and distributor of the city's functions and needs.

However, one can also claim that the quantitative approach and hierarchical thinking that were already afoot in the 1960s served to delimit and isolate the institution as a mechanical element in the urban machine. If only the element was in its proper place, the urban machine could function. In the 1960s' and the 1970s' urban planning, no questions were being asked about what broader social milieus could potentially arise around the school and other institutions, or about what roles such milieus could play with respect to the city's social and cultural life and with respect to the construction of identification points within the urban landscape. It was the service dimension that was the mainstay in the understanding of the welfare institution.

The school has an important function in the city and in the urban quarter as the focal point for the children's everyday life and consequently also for many parents' lives, both because one typically accompanies the children on their way to or from the school and because one takes part in meetings at the school. In addition to whatever has directly to do with the school's everyday operation, most schools also lend out their rooms and their premises to local associations; this further serves to couple the school to the local area. If we limit the welfare city to what we find in the post-war suburbs, then we can safely say that most of the schools have at their disposal large areas of ground for sports and other displays of activity. However, it is only infrequently that the activities and the hustle and bustle that are attached to the school are exposed to view. The school often lies in such a way that it is recessed and is divided off from the surrounding urban quarter by fences, and its sports grounds are typically kept closed and may only be used by the school's students. On this account, whatever potentials the school might possess as a local point of concentration are rendered invisible.

In Amsterdam, and in several other Dutch cities, people have been working – over the course of the past decade – with opening the schools towards the city, especially by letting the playground areas for the older children be part of the city's public areas and by opening up the school's sports grounds for other users. In Denmark, the open-school initiative, which has now become part and parcel of the Primary Education Act, points in the same direction and has already incited several cities to work with opening up the school, both educationally and physically, to the surrounding world.

The school in Copenhagen's Sydhavnen [South Harbour] and the school in Utterslev are examples that can be found in Greater Copenhagen.

Utterslev School is organized around a small street, which offers both a shortcut and a spatial type that does not otherwise exist in areas of this type – situated at a transition between blocks of flats and villas. This street is active during the day, as access and as a series of open spaces for the older children, but it is also active later on, when meetings are being held, or on weekends, when you can see parents and children hanging around on the street, both because their children can make use of the opportunities to play and because the space itself is simply a pleasant and congenial place to stop up and stick around, for a spell.

Sydhavn School, with its amphitheatre and its open play areas, has placed itself as a natural point of concentration in the new Sydhavn quarter, by virtue of offering a spatial opening in the neighbourhood and, at the same time, by constituting an activity-related point of concentration.

In much the same way, the schools in Amsterdam create a point of concentration where there is life and activity going on all day, within a residential quarter that would otherwise be nearly empty during the daytime hours. The school offers to the general public areas that have the character of a garden and, to boot, there are areas and niches that have the character of small urban squares.

This can also be seen in the elaboration of the schools and the other institutions. Many of these institutions turn themselves inwards in much the way that a shopping centre holds onto its customers and evinces no interest whatsoever in making contact with the surrounding city in any other way than through its efficient delivery system. The institution is often organized as a detached, independent building. In the post-war suburbs, there is rarely any ambition that the institutions should or must establish contact with and/or take on any special significance in the neighbourhood, through a public space or through the agency of others of the city's traditional exchange spaces and presentation venues.

## The welfare city today

Nowadays, the post-war era's cities and urban quarters are forming parts of larger regional coherences; these are frames around an everyday life that has acquired new rhythms and has become more differentiated and more spatially divided. At the same time, new dynamics have arisen, both when it comes to changes in the functional and constructed landscapes and when it comes to the way in which we make use of these landscapes. We are moving our way around within the urban region. There are relatively few people who are living a predominantly local life that is centred around the residence. We are working one place, doing our shopping at another place, looking for amusement and entertainment and cultural offers at third places altogether, and cultivating sports at yet a fourth category of places. And we are looking for recreational landscapes everywhere throughout the region. This is true whether we happen to be living in a post-war suburb, in a large urban region, or in a smaller town. The various functions and milieus that we are looking for in our various and sundry dealings within the regional city are subject to a high degree of change and dynamism. New store types turn up at new spots. Public functions are becoming centralized. Cultural milieus and attractions are finding new forms and are being relocated within the urban landscape. Working hours have changed. New leisure- and spare-time cultures are cropping up. What this entails is that many parts of the post-war suburbs have lost their local service supply, and the same thing can be said about the smaller detached cities.

Concurrent with the disappearance of many of the functions that have been operative as local meeting and identification points, what is growing, however, is the attention being paid to the importance of these local meeting points. This suggests that the relationship among the many functions and points of reference concentration that we are looking for in our daily travels within the urban region is not necessarily an equal-valued one. But neither is this relationship an essentially hierarchical one. In the course of any given day or week, the suburban dweller is part of many different milieus that are spread out across the region, but the social and physical milieu that is attached to the residence has a special meaning. However, this meaning has a different import than the hierarchical diagrams were in a position to capture. Although our physical mobility has increased, whether there is a school certainly means a lot for where people will want to settle and for their choice of housing. Whether there is a nursery school also means a lot. Whether there are many leisure time offerings means a lot.[25] These institutions are in demand, in the first place, as entities that are necessary so that everyday life can function. However, concurrently with the gradual disappearance of the functions that were previously the points of origin for meetings and exchanges, what is becoming more and more clear is that these functions and milieus also constitute the very last opportunities to preserve and articulate local meeting places and points of concentration. And it is becoming apparent that these places are the ones that support and crystallize local identities and that structure the mental map's orientation understanding, alongside the world of everyday life in the region. For this reason, one also encounters, in current discussions about the post-war era's urban areas, the 'urban life concept', and most often as something that is absent or missing. The urban life concept is a vague one.[26] It is blurred and can, in this context, primarily be employed as an indicator of an unspecified want or desire. However, precisely in its capacity as indicator, it calls attention to conditions that urban planning and urban policy are going to have to try and deal with if the post-war era's welfare city is going to be able at all to sustain its attractiveness and its ability to function. In diverse studies of preferences related to the choice of dwellings and choice of urban districts buildings, attention is drawn to the importance of meeting places of a more or less binding nature,[27] as an important factor, both when it comes to the choice of dwelling and when it comes to a more general attitude taken towards new urban areas. And in almost all of the architectural competitions about suburban areas that have been held in recent years,[28] the desire for more city life has figured as a central objective, albeit as a very vaguely defined goal.

## Development strategy

What then becomes an important question is which elements, functions and positions within the urban landscape can engender places that redeem this vague wish for 'city life'. My contention is that *a new and expanded understanding of the welfare institutions* constitutes one of the most viable and accessible avenues for drawing nearer to this issue. In what follows, I will be making an argument for this claim. In the first round, as a series of declarations about the possible effect on daily life, on the degree of mobilization and ownership, and on meaning and orientation in the welfare city's landscapes. Thereafter, I will attempt to render these contentions plausible by confronting them with different theoretical positions. Depending entirely on where we happen to find ourselves in the urban landscape, this might involve different institutions with which it is currently possible to work. In the captions to the pictures that accompany this article, I delve more deeply into what the potentials for each of the institutions might be. Here, I will try to advance the argument in a more generalized way.

## Organization of everyday life

Even if most people are moving around a lot, it is the nursery school, the school, the sports hall and perhaps the library which are the important structuring points for daily life. They are important for the children because the institutions, to a great degree, structure their everyday lives, both temporally and socially. They are also important for the parents, both because whether the children are happy and proud of their institution *means something,* and because the institution is also the place for many meetings, both concerning the children's interests and around many other issues that bear on the local community. The institution is one of the places where the local civil society is formed. To the extent that greater approval and meaning can be assigned to such meeting points of concentration upon becoming places where events that are important to the local community are being held, these places take on a new role in the local life and create local points of identification. My contention is, accordingly, that the institution must be understood and has to be used as

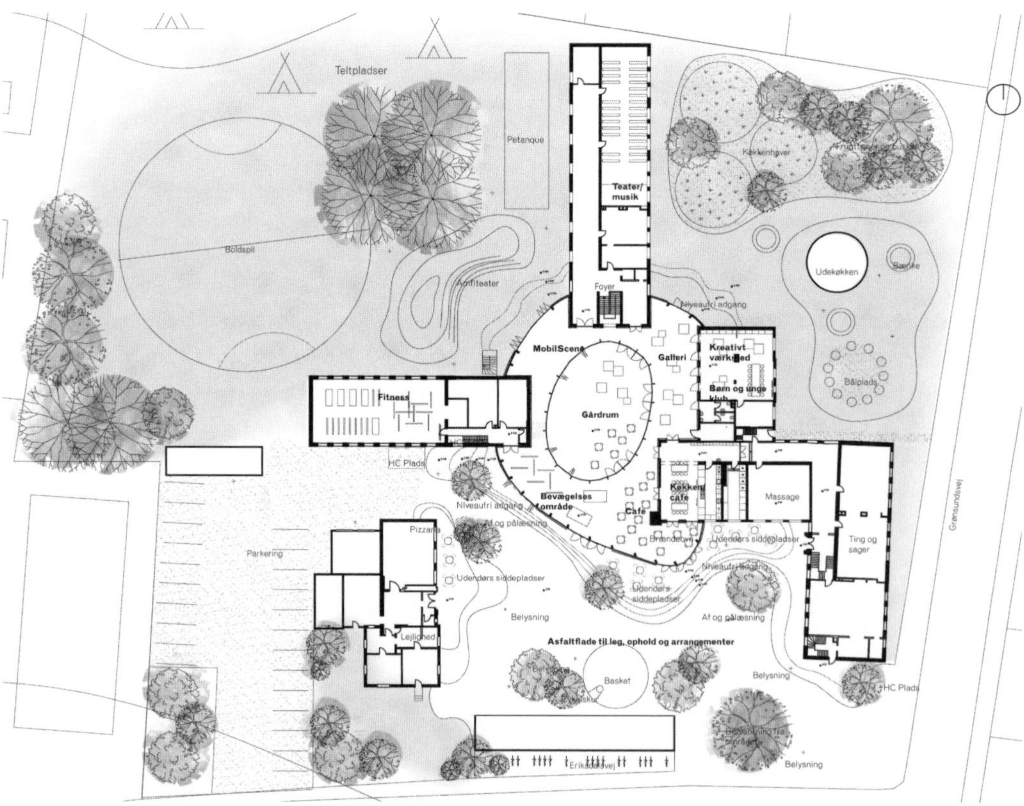

Teltpladser
Petanque
Boldspil
Amfiteater
Teater/ musik
Foyer
Niveaufri adgang
Køkkenhaver
Udekøkken
Bænke
Bålplads
Kreativt værksted
Børn og unge klub
Galleri
MobilScene
Fitness
Gårdrum
HC Plads
Bevægelses område
Café
Køkken/ café
Massage
Ting og sager
Grønsundsvej
Pizzaria
Parkering
Niveaufri adgang
Af og pålæsning
Udendørs siddepladser
Udendørs siddepladser
Belysning
Lejlighed
Asfaltflade til leg, ophold og arrangementer
Af og pålæsning
Basket
Belysning
HC Plads
Belysning

The residents' house is ordinarily perceived as being a specifically local place, which is mostly used for communal meals, for meetings and for parties that all have their source in a particular residential quarter – and it is consequently positioned at the lowest and weakest rung in the hierarchy of activity points and points of concentration. However, the residents' house can also appear as the last bastion for local organization, in keeping with the fact that the other institutions and facilities, which have heretofore been functioning as anchoring points for the local organization, have vanished.
In the town of Balling, on the Salling peninsula in North Jutland, the local sports hall has been expanded, with a building that houses meeting rooms, clinic rooms for various health-related functions, a modest swimming-bathing park and a small café, where the family can go to and have dinner. The facility has been localized in connection with the school and establishes a point of concentration that sustains the village's identity, in keeping with the fact that virtually all the shops and stores have disappeared.
In the town of Horbelev, on the island of Falster, the school was shut down. Then the residents organized themselves and bought the school. They had a project drawn up where they, for a relatively modest budget, could devise a strategy for building into one unit and for converting the old school buildings, so that they would come to fashion the frames around a number of activities which the residents themselves could run: informal child care; a music school; meeting rooms; rooms that can be rented out, as small offices; foyer rooms that can be used for smaller-scale events and for local assemblies of people. And the plaza area in front of the school was spiffed up, so that it has come to appear as the city's square – in an architectural articulation that harmonizes with the town's size and atmosphere.

a potential point of concentration within the local community and that this is one of fewer places where what can transpire is a formulation and an articulation of local values and norms, through exchanges of viewpoints. There is a whole series of different effects and dimensions that are linked up with this role, which I will unfold in what follows.

## Coherence, ownership and mobilization

To the extent that the institutions' functions are opened out from their primary functions, like 'school', to becoming a place where several other kinds of local activities and exchanges are taking place, they actually supervene and crystallize as a potential way of fighting against various forms of segregation's undermining of the institutions and the local community. When the school is the centre for many local meetings and events, then, with a certain degree of probability, it will be able to obtain backing and strength from this very role. And then, reacting to social disparities by putting one's children into a private school will be less of a cut-and-dried move. When the sports hall is the point of origin for types of organization other than the performance of sports activities, as such, and is linked up with other features that are important to everyday life, then the opportunities for creating places along these lines, which can handle and ward off conflicts and can counter segregation, will become enhanced. When there is strong activity around the institutions, then the possibility to oppose budget cutbacks and reductions with creative counterproposals and new couplings becomes greater. When there are local concentrations of activity around the institutions, then the chances of preserving or building the supply of staple goods and other forms of commercial services become greater. When there are local gathering- and activity points, both within and outside the institutions, then the daily life and the movements around and through the suburbs and the small towns will become more eventful and alluring.

## Meaning and orientation in the urban landscape

Many of the welfare city's residential areas are characterized by a high degree of uniformity.[29] In this landscape, the types of institutions that are being discussed make their appearance with a particular potential for differentiation and for designating meaning. Whether we are speaking about the school, the youth club or the sports hall, what the institution contains, both as a building volume and by virtue of its function and its role, is the potential to designate and to give character to a specific place and to mark out a special meaning in this otherwise uniform landscape. The same kind of potential is contained in the city square and the park, even though they have not traditionally formed part of the post-war suburbs' spatial hierarchy.

Anne Mette Kirkeby writes: 'The school is a public institution, and depending on how impressive or humble this building is, the child forms different pictures of the community that the school is part of.'[30] One can expand this statement to declare that the manner in which the school or other institutions and public spaces make their respective marks in the midst of the urban landscape correspondingly establishes images of the local community within which the institution appears. If the school opens towards the street or the road, if it offers a spatial condensation to the town, if it makes its outdoor areas accessible and available to the town, if it provides space to the town for many other activities, then it becomes inscribed in the understanding of the urban area and the local community in many ways and on many different levels. It then creates not only a *visual* reference- and orientation point, but also a *social* reference- and orientation point. If the school closes around itself and withdraws from the public space, then it defines itself as a specialized function, which does not want to take part in the local life, and this tells of a fragmented or 'cellular' community,[31] where we, in the course of the day, find ourselves within isolated and isolating social spaces.

## Gathering the threads

The post-war era's welfare cities were constructed as open cities, with low density, and consequently with few points of concentration that could fashion the basis for ways of organizing the social life. In the past 20 years, this open urban structure has been further challenged through concentrations in both the commercial and the public services, which have resulted in the removal of many of the original points of concentration. The contention in the present article is that the welfare institutions, for a variety of reasons, can and may be conceived and envisioned in other ways, and can be used in novel ways in urban planning, in relation to the thinking and methodology that were developed in the early post-war period. The welfare institutions constitute one of the only opportunities for adding to the suburbs and to other open urban formations; they are organizing points that have the potential to counter the centralization of commercial functions and several public functions. If we are to going to obtain more sustainable suburbs, in both the environmental and the social respects, there is a need to ensure better local services and more local meeting places,[32] because doing this will serve to encourage walking and bicycling and making use of public transport instead of, or supplemental to, getting around by car. If we are going to adapt the suburbs to the demographic changes, then we are going to have to ensure better local service and a more differentiated offering of public spaces and housing types. Therefore, the institutions are going to have to be thought out and elaborated as dynamic, urban elements, both because the regular hierarchies, in which they have traditionally been placed, cannot be sustained, and because these hierarchies do not correspond to the forms of everyday life that are being lived out in the regional welfare city.

They may be conceived and envisioned as parts of the network that brings them into new and changing reciprocal relationships. They may be conceived and envisioned as social organizing points and as spatial organizing points, which set up movement-related points of concentration within the urban landscape. They may be conceived and envisioned with greater emphasis on their visual impact within the urban landscape, since they are the only elements that can take on the role of organizing point or local monument, if you will. And the institution must be understood both in terms of the types of institutions we already know and in terms of open areas of ground, in the form of the sports field, the city square, the urban garden, the park and the green.[33]

## The rebirth of the hierarchical structure?

One can then ask whether that which is being argued for, with this strategy, is merely, in the final analysis, a return to the concept of the neighbourhood unit, with the institutions as the organizing and community-bearing elements, and with a hierarchical cell structure as the ordering system? Is that which has been presented above a line of reasoning that coincides with the New Urbanism models[34] and their arguments for a re-introduction of the concept of the neighbourhood unit in the form of urban villages?

Is it thus a strategy that can and ought to be confronted with David Harvey's critique of 'the Communitarian Trap',[35] or with Hajer og Reijndorp's[36] critique of an all too simple and mechanical understanding of the public space,[37] or with Thrift and Amin's[38] critique of the dominant understanding of the social exchanges and meetings and the formative processes that are supposed to be linked up with the public space?

In his critique of New Urbanism, Harvey claims that the ideology on which the movement is building is based on: 'The presumption [...] that neighbourhoods are in some sense "intrinsic", that the proper form of cities is some "structure of neighbourhoods", that "neighbourhood" is equivalent to "community", and that "community" is what most Americans want and need [..]'. And Harvey continues: 'But can 'community' really rescue us from the deadening world of social dissolution, grab-it-yourself materialism and individualized, selfish, market-oriented greed? [...]. New Urbanism in fact connects to a facile contemporary attempt to transform large and teeming cities, so seemingly out of control, into an interlinked series of "urban villages", where, it is believed, everyone can relate in a civil and urbane fashion to everyone else.'[39]

When I propose to strengthen the welfare institutions' urbane role, am I going to end up ensnared in the 'trap' that Harvey is speaking about? Or, to put this question more generally in relation to urban planning's specialized traditions: Have architecture and the urban planning profession become so steeped in modernism's way of thinking in hierarchies and in the profession's over-simplified picture of neighbourhood communities and in a unity-cultural way of thinking that we are always going to wind up in the same place, even though we may believe we are moving in a new direction?

If we are going to address ourselves to these questions, what our response is going to have to be based on, for starters, is *where* in the urban landscape we happen to be standing. If we may coax an old warhorse out of its stable and make use of Ferdinand Tönnies' *Gemeinschaft-Gesellschaft* distinction,[40] and look closely at the small town, then we can say that we are standing in *Gemeinschaft* land. We are there, where the dense and controlling social relations prevail. And we can then move ahead and assume that the fundamental figure in the concept of the neighbourhood-unit, in the form of 'the urban village', may be categorized in the same way in relation to Tönnies' conceptual pairs. And in any event, that's what Harvey is doing when he maintains that the concept of the neighbourhood unit and 'the urban village' constitute the reintroduction of the village's controlling and oppressive social community.

The *Gesellschaft* category stands as the antithesis, as the city that offers access to and choices among the many non-binding social relationships that are attached to different spaces and institutions. In the work of urban theorists like Richard Sennett,[41] the public space is seen as the setting for many different kinds of social meetings, which generate acceptance and a sense of understanding for other individuals and other groups, and thereby builds up the metropolitan culture, which is a prerequisite for the civil society's being able to function. In several of their books, however, Amin and Thrift have been contesting the validity of the notion[42] that what takes place through the meeting with 'the stranger' in the public space is a form of democratic formation, where one learns to associate with other people with social and cultural backgrounds that are other than one's own. They believe these descriptions are too simple and generalizing. Amin and Thrift place a great deal of weight on the importance of the public space in the creation and the maintenance of the civil society, but they also believe that there are more specific processes than those that Sennett is describing, processes that have to be called into play in the understanding of the place's[43] and the public space's importance in socialization- and democratization processes. In his article 'Re-thinking the Urban Social'[44] which discusses what urban studies really ought to focus on, Amin writes about *the place*: 'New spatialities have become decisive for the constitution of place. The varied processes of spatial stretching, interdependence and flow, combine with in situ trajectories of socio-spatial evolution and change, to propose place as a site of intersection between network topologies and territorial legacies. The result is no simple displacement of the local by the global, of place by space, of history by simultaneity and flow [..]. Instead it is a subtle folding together of the distant and the proximate, the virtual and the material, presence and absence, flow and stasis into a single ontological plane upon which location – a place on the map – has come to be relationally and topologically defined.'[45]

Amin thus rejects the simple distinction between *Gemeinschaft* and *Gesellschaft*, and advances an argument for what he, in another article, calls 'Consideration of spatial juxtaposition in urban life'.[46] In doing so, he is drawing near to the way in which Doreen Massey[47] identifies that which she calls an open and 'progressive sense of place'. Massey sees the place as being construed through certain constellations of societal relationships that become woven together into a specific locus. With this, it supposedly becomes a meeting place that is not only for individuals but also for global relationships. According to Massey, this understanding encompasses an understanding of place and 'a sense of place, which is extroverted, which includes a consciousness of its links with the wider world, which integrates in a positive way the global and the local.'[48]

Can one, then, make use of such an understanding of place and public space in the discussion about the welfare institution's role and importance in the city of tomorrow and as a strategy for strengthening and activating the social life in the welfare city? Amin and Thrift suggest that we start with an overriding recognition that: 'Our emphasis falls on institutionalized actions which can, on the one hand, enhance individual and social capabilities, and, on the other, build solidarities across the society of difference.'[49]

And they maintain, moreover, that: 'We see the city, more specifically its institutions, providing the opportunity for citizens to become something else and for mutuality to be strengthened.'[50] [...] 'For example, schools have a vital role to play by re-energizing, debating societies, but covering issues of everyday concern [...] the key is to spark engagement as a means of building critical ability, voice and argument. Defined thus, there is no reason why the principle cannot spill over into afterschool centres, evening courses, workplaces and other sites of gathering, etc.'[51]

Although it can be asserted that these statements are moving around on a level of abstraction that is situated above the concrete institution, I would like to take the liberty of using them as a form of rendering plausible that the strategy I have been arguing for, in what has heretofore been presented in this article, is on the right track. I am interested in urban planning and in how we can develop and improve our cities, and here, even more specifically, I am interested in the role that the welfare institution can play in this connection. A strategy cannot be scientifically proven. It is a choice and a wagering. However, what have to be the pre-conditional requirements for good planning are that the understanding of the city's dynamics and way of functioning are well-described and that a relevant understanding- and discussion space has been constructed, as it were: such a space that can qualify the choice of strategy. And it is here, I believe, that the way in which Thrift and Amin, Massey and many others understand the regional city's processes and way of functioning will render it likely that the sketched-out strategy will point in the right direction.

I also believe that in the discussion about this strategy, one can lean against some of Hajer and Reijndorp's observations.[52] They are saying, that we, when we are talking about public space, exhibit a marked tendency to demand that they are open for everybody and that all groups will really and truly be present. But they correct this perception by saying that a public space ordinarily obtains its quality as place by being occupied by specific groups. And it is thanks to these dominant groups' social practices that the place becomes a place, with a special atmosphere and rhythm. What really matters, according to Hajer and Reijndorp, is whether this taking in of the place excludes others or opens up for others. And then they go on to argue that a way of achieving this balance, between the captured and the open, has a lot to do whether the city's stream of life passes through or passes around the spaces under consideration: Are the individual places connected through publically accessible passages? Or are they positioned in such a way, in terms of their spatial structure, that they can be allowed to close around themselves?[53]

When we move further and include Lieven De Cauter's discussion of 'The Capsular Civilisation',[54] we find that he uses the cell-structure as the picture of a society where different social and ethnic groups shut themselves in, within their own respective cells, and define themselves negatively in relation to other cells, and, in doing so, gradually undermine the civil society. There are many studies that point in a similar direction,[55] and speak about a rising compartmentalization or about the emergence of gated communities. I would argue that the strategy that is based on the welfare institutions is also a way of countering these tendencies, as far as it is still possible to accomplish this.

The contention being put forth[56] in this article is, thus, that reinterpreting and further developing that which could be called the welfare city's points of concentration, understood as meeting places and points of orientation, is of vital importance. It is important because the points of concentration with which the welfare city was spawned have now become weakened. If we are in a position to give the welfare institutions a new and expanded role in the urban landscape and to open them up, both physically and socially, as parts of a network of points of concentration, then it is going to be possible, in my opinion, to parry off and counter a number of the challenges facing the post-war suburbs and it is going to be possible to assign a new and more important role to the welfare institutions, a role that does not exclusively have to do with supplying services but also has to do with standing as a point of concentration for some of civil society's principal processes. However, this is going to require that the welfare institution and the welfare city will be discussed and understood within this large-scale societal and regional context. And it is going to require that each of the institutions will be examined for the specific possibilities that it offers in terms of setting up local spatial, aesthetic and social points of concentration and in terms of becoming coupled within a network of institutions. And this is going to require that we deal with the concepts of the local and the regional with a greater degree of dialectics.

Now we can summarize and generalize, in accordance with Ash Amin. According to him, what this has to do with is: 'the subtle folding together of the distant and the proximate, the virtual and the material, presence and absence, flow and stasis into a single ontological plane upon which location – a place on the map – has come to be relationally and topologically defined.'[57]

Notes

1 The concept *node/point of reference/meeting point* is primarily used to characterize the places where the city's social life condenses, i.e. the places where there is a relative intensification of social exchange processes. But the term is also used for visual accumulation points, i.e. places that achieve an importance because of their visual impact.

2 G. Viby Mogensen defines the welfare society in terms of prosperous, democratic societies with market economies and a comprehensive social security system. Starting from this definition, the welfare city can be defined as the spatial manifestation of the welfare society. The welfare city can geographically be limited to the urban formations that cropped up after the Second World War, i.e. predominantly those that would be referred to in everyday jargon to as 'suburban areas'. It is this delimitation that corresponds most fittingly with the present article's array of problems. However, the term can also be used to cover all of the welfare state's conurbations, on the basis of the consideration that older urban areas are also supplied with the institutions and accordingly come to resemble the way of functioning that characterizes the newer areas. G. Viby Mogensen: *Det danske velfærdssamfunds historie* (2010).

3 See, for example, G. Viby Mogensen, who, in this connection, builds upon the work of Esping Andersen.

4 During the inter-war period, the urban principles of modernism were represented especially by the three CIAM reports (see the literature list) and through the methodology that was constructed in conjunction with the CIAM conferences – the so-called 'CIAM Grid'. However, it was also the projects and reports that were handed down from the urban plan administrations in Frankfurt (Das Neue Frankfurt) and Berlin, which emerged and subsequently functioned as instructive tutorials for the planning of the modern city. See, also, note 7. See also J. Kvorning's article in *Modernismens Genkomst* (2001).

5 The American contribution to post-war planning systematics stemmed from the concept of the neighbourhood unit, for which Clarence Perry, in particular, had been advocating (cf. Lewis Mumford, and supplemented by the latter), but which was also being advanced by English planning's principal figure, Raymond Unwin, and which also appears, albeit in embryonic form, in both the City Beautiful Movement and in the Garden City movement's manifestos.

6 There is quite a voluminous body of literature on the English New Towns. For obtaining a survey on the topic, the reader is referred to F.J. Osborne: *New Towns* (1977) and to P. Hall: *Cities of Tomorrow* (2002).

7 'New beginning' was an oft-used term to characterize the understanding of the problem that was dominant in the urban and societal debate going on in Great Britain after the war. See, for example, L. Mumford: *The Social Foundations of Post-war Building* (1943).

8 The cell structure as ideal and as principle of organization has been put forward both in the 1920s (see, for example, Saarinen) and in the early post-war area. See, for example, The 1958 Plan for London.

9 Hilberseimer was working, at one point in time, as an assistant to Mies van der Rohe in the final phase of the Bauhaus School, and he followed Mies to the United States. Once there, Hilberseimer further developed his reflections on the organization of the modern city as a question of rationality and clear hierarchies.

10 As head of the architecture department at the Bauhaus School, Hannes Meyer promoted a radical functionalism, where the identification of the city's and the building's constituent elements constituted the central approach to the project.

11 Already in *The City of To-Morrow and Its Planning,* Le Corbusier is talking about road hierarchies.

12 CIAM (Congrès Internationaux d'Architecture Moderne) was founded in 1928 by the leading modernist architects, with Le Corbusier in the forefront. The organization held a series of international conferences. Before the Nazis took over power, conferences were held and reports were published: for example, Bauen für das Existensminimum. Rationelle bebauungsweise. Finally, in 1933, the so-called Charter of Athens was created; this is a document that put forth a cogent argument for the division of the city into specialized areas for living, for working and for recreation.

13 What were set up in almost all the Western European countries after the Second World War were building research institutes, which focussed attention on industrialized construction technology, on housing, and on cities – especially residential neighbourhoods. The Danish Building Research Institute was established in 1947.

14 London County Council: *Hook – The Planning of a New Town*. Greater London Council, 1965.

15 Architect Niels Thougaard, who was the leader of the Køge Bay planning secretariat, has confirmed this coupling in an interview. See the master plan for Køge Bay.

16 The 'Radburn system' refers to the plan that Clarence Stein hammered out, in 1929, for the new urban quarter, Radburn, in New Jersey. The system separates cars and pedestrians as two oppositely-directed cam systems. The

Radburn Plan carries further many of the principles that were developed in the early English garden cities.

**17** See the Hook Report and the plan documents for the Køge Bay Plan.

**18** Niels Salicath, who, for many years, manned key positions in connection with residential construction, as Director of KAB, has maintained that, 'The quantitative had its very strong position (in housing policy and in the housing debate).'

**19** Statistics Denmark.

**20** The number of child-care centres increased from around 1,100 in 1960 to around 3,500 in 1975 and, further, to 7,500 at the turn of the millennium. Statistics Denmark. BUPL. See also, G. Viby Mogensen: *Det danske velfærdssamfunds historie* (2010).

**21** In 1981, the sociologist, Leif Thomsen, wrote 'Den autoritære by', in which he advances the argument that the new suburbs are structured in such a way that they lay out and determine certain ways of living and certain rhythms of everyday life.

**22** See, for example, Chr. Mohr and M. Müller: *Funktionalität und Moderne. Das Neue Frankfurt* (1984). Reproduced in the book, there is a picture from the monthly magazine *Das Neue Frankfurt* which, accompanied by the caption, 'Die Moderne Frau', shows a tennis-playing woman (liberated from the kitchen and the housework by the modern architecture and the modern institutions). See also: *Betænkning om moderne hjælpemidler i husholdningen.*

**23** See *Das Neue Frankfurt* or the Danish Building Research Institute's publications on kitchen layouts.

**24** See, for example, sociologist Erik Høgh's concise teaching compendium for the urban planning programme at KADK. Erik Høgh was connected, for a period of time, with the school's urban planning department. In his compendium, he presented a few very simple statements about the relationship between form and social life. *Sociologi. Kompendium til Byplanuddannelsen ved KA.* KADK (1965).

**25** T. Ærø & H. Vestergaard: *Boligpræferencer og boligvalg*, Danish Building Research Institute, and *Ny by ved Store Rørbæk* (2006).

**26** The 'urban life concept' was advanced, in this country, especially avidly by Jan Gehl, who focuses on the interaction between the city's form and the city's life. Cf. the book *How to Study Public Life* (2013). In addition to its being bandied about in the study of this physical-social relation, this term is, ordinarily, also associated with the demand for lively and vibrant city life.

**27** Ærø & Vestergaard (2006), op.cit.

**28** See, for example, competition programmes for Realdania's suburban competitions and the book *Fremtidens forstæder.*

**29** See, for example: C. Bech-Danielsen and Gram Hansen: *Urban Lifescape* (2004).

**30** A.M. Kirkeby: *Skolen finder sted* (2006).

**31** See *The Capsular Civilization*. Here, De Cauter discusses the cell not as a hierarchical element within a social organization, but rather as a way of becoming isolated from the surrounding society.

**32** See P.H. Nielsen & T. Næss: *Bæredygtige forstæder. Bæredygtighed, tæthed og bystruktur* (2008).

**33** Ibid.

**34** See, for example, E. Talen: *Charter of the New Urbanism* (1999).

**35** D. Harvey: *The New Urbanism and the Communitarian Trap* (1997).

**36** M. Hajer and A. Reijndorp: *In Search of New Public Domain* (2000).

**37** Ibid.

**38** A. Amin: *Collective Culture and Urban Public Space* (2008).

**39** Harvey (1997), op.cit.

**40** F. Tönnies: *Gemeinschaft und Gesellschaf* (1897).

**41** See, for example, Richard Sennett: *The Conscience of the Eye (*1991) and A. Lane: *Flesh and Stone* (1994). See also: Sharon Zukin: *Cultures of Cities* (1995).

**42** Amin and Thrift have taken an especially critical stance in relation to Richard Sennett's description of the exchange processes in the public-space.

**43** 'Place' arises, by definition, when somebody takes it up and occupies it, and carries out a certain social practice in the space.

**44** A. Amin: 'Rethinking the urban social' (2007).

**45** Ibid., p. 103.

**46** Ibid.

**47** D. Massey: *Space, place and gender* (1994).

**48** D. Massey. 'A Global Sense of Place', in *Space, Place and Gender* (1994), p. 8. See: http://www.unc.edu/courses/2006spring/geog/021/001/massey.pdf Accessed on January 24, 2017.

**49** A. Amin and N. Thrift: *Reimagining the Urban* (2002).

**50** Ibid.

**51** Ibid.

**52** M. Hajer and A. Reijndorp: *In Search of new Public Domain* (2000).

**53** Ibid.

**54** L. De Cauter: *The Capsular Civilization in the Age of Fear* (2004).

**55** See, for example, D. Massey: *For Space* (2005).

**56** The proposal being put forth must necessarily take on the character of contention or claim. The proposal must be as well-underpinned with relevant experiences as possible. In any case, however, it remains a claim, and an experiment, *until* it is activated and can be tested for its effects.

**57** Amin (2007), op.cit., p. 103.

Literature

- Amin, A. & N. Thrift: *Reimagining the Urban*. Polity 2002.
- Amin, A.: *City. Analyses of urban trends, culture, theory, policy action*. Routledge 2007.
- Amin, A.: 'Collective Culture and Urban Public Space' in *City, vol 12. 2008*. Routledge 2008.
- Amin, A.: *Re-thinking the urban social*. www.scribd.com/document/182362765/Amin-2007-Rethinking-urban-social-pdf
- Bech-Danielsen, C.: *Urban Lifescapes*. Aalborg Universitet 2004.
- Bech-Danielsen, C., & J. Schjerup Hansen (eds.): *Modernismens Genkomst*. The Danish Building Research Institute and The Danish Architectural Press, 2001.
- Bæk Pedersen, P.: *Arkitektur og plan i den danske velfærdsby 1950-1990*. Aarhus School of Architecture, 2005.
- Cautier, L. De: *The Capsular Civilization in the Age of Fear*. NAi Publishers 2004.
- CIAM: *Atlas of the Functional City*. Thot Publishers 2014
- CIAM: *The functional City*. Kees Somer. Nai Publishers 2007
- Gehl, J., & Svarre, B.: *How to Study Public LIfe*. Island Press 2013.
- Hall, P.: *Cities of Tomorrow*. Blackwell 2002.
- Hajer, M. and A. Reijndorp: *In Search of New Public Domain*. NAi Publishers 2000.
- Harvey, D.: 'The New Urbanism and the Communitarian Trap'. *Harvard Design Magazine*, Spring 1997.
- Hays, M.K.: *The Architecture of Hannes Meyer and Ludwig Hilberseimer*. MIT Press 1995.
- Høegh, E.: *Sociologi. Kompendium til Byplanuddannelsen ved KA*. KADK 1965.
- Kirkeby, A.M.: *Skolen finder sted*. Danish Building Research Institute 2006.
- Kvorning, J.: *Bæredygtige forstæder*. Realdania and the Ministry of the Environment 2012.
- Kvorning, J., Tournay, B., & Poulsen, L.: *Tæthed / Bystruktur / Bæredygtighed*. KADK 2009.
- Køge Bugt Planen. Masterplan for the Køge Bay Area 1970.
- Køge Bay Plan. Development of the Køge Bay Area. 1975.
- Le Corbusier: *The City of Tomorrow and Its Planning*. Dover Publications 1929.
- London County Council: *Hook – The Planning of a New Town*. Greater London Council 1965.
- Massey, D.: *Space, Place and Gender*. Blackwell 1994.
- Massey, D.: *For Space*. Sage 2005.
- Mohr, Chr., & Müller, M.: *Funktionalität und Moderne. Das neue Frankfurt*. Rudolf Müller Verlag 1984.
- Mumford, L.: *The Urban Prospect*. Harcourt, Brace & World, N.Y. 1956.
- Mumford, L.: *Det sociale grundlag for byggeriet i efterkrigstiden*. Nyt Nordisk Forlag, Copenhagen 1946.
- Nielsen, P.H., & Næss, T.: *Bæredygtige forstæder. Bæredygtighed, tæthed og bystruktur*. Centre for Urban Planning at KADK 2008.
- Osborne, F.J. et al.: *New Towns*. Leonard Hill, London 1977.
- Realdania: *Fremtidens forstæder*. Bogværket 2013.
- Saarinen, E.: *Projects 1896-1923*. Ginko Press, Hamburg 1990.
- Salicath, N.: *Byplanhistorisk note 19*. Dansk Byplanlaboratorium 1989.
- Sennet, R.: *The Conscience of the Eye*. (Danish edition) Samleren 1996.
- Sennet, R.: *Flesh and Stone*. Allan Lane 1994.
- Spaeth, D.A., & Harrington, K.: *In the Shadow of Mies. Hilberseimer: Architect, Educator and Urban Planning*. Chicago Institute of Art / Rizzoli 1988.
- Stein, C.S.: *Towards New Towns for America*. M.I.T. Press 1957/1966.
- Talen, E.: *Charter of the New Urbanism*. McGraw-Hill 1999.
- Thomsen¸ L.: 'Den Autoritære by' i *Kultursociologiske skrifter 14*. Akademisk Forlag 1981.
- *Traffic in Towns*. Her Majesty's Stationery Office 1963.
- Tönnies, F.: *Gemeinschaft und Gesellschaft* 1897.
- Tönnies, F.: *Community and Civil Society. Ed. Jose Harris*. Oxford University Press 2001.
- Unwin, R.. *Nothing Gained by Owercrowding*. Routledge 1912/2014.
- Unwin, R.: *Town Planning in Practice*. London 1920.
- Viby Mogensen, G.: *Det danske velfærdssamfunds historie*. Gyldendal 2010.
- Zukin, S.: *Cultures of Cities*. Blackwell 1995.
- Ærø, T.: *Boligpræferencer, boligvalg og livsstil*. Danish Building Research Institute 2002.
- Ærø, T., & Vestergaard, H.: *Ny by ved Store Rørbæk*. Danish Building Research Institute 2006.

Jørgen Møller

# Planning and the Welfare Society

**Throughout the ages, planning, and especially the planning of the physical layout (a synthesizing term covering land-use planning, physical structures and connections in cities and in the countryside), and legislation surrounding this have undergone significant changes, which must be attuned to the needs of society and to prevailing political ideologies. A spot check on Danish planning calls attention to the fact that society's perceptions and the societal development of the welfare state, and concomitantly public planning, are undergoing major changes which have had significant implications for a portion of the Danish population.**

## A glance at history

Since 1938, we in Denmark have had a comprehensive urban planning legislation, which has been continuously revised: for the first time in the early 1970s; for the second time in the early 1990s; and most recently, in the spring of 2016, when a number of parties hammered out an agreement around considerable revisions in the Planning Act.[1]
The Danish welfare society was constituted and expanded in the period that spans from the end of the 1950s until the beginning of the 21st century, the first 25 years of which can be characterized as the welfare society's 'Golden Age'. The starting point coincided with a moment in time when an upswing in prosperity began to be noticeable, and when the contours of modern Denmark started to emerge. Employment among the work force was high, and more and more women were coming out onto the job market. Analogously, the educational system was expanded, and residential expenditures steadily increased. Many people acquired summer houses and eventually, also, cars. The welfare state was being extended and built up, at full throttle,[2] and in the course of the 1960s, there was an upsurge in urban planning in Denmark on the whole. Up until that point in time, urban planning had predominantly been a Copenhagen phenomenon, where especially Fingerplanen [the Finger Plan], from 1947, and Copenhagen's overall plan sketch dating from 1954 were distinctive and renowned plans. Out in the countryside it had not proved necessary, especially in the wake of the war, to follow up on The Urban Planning Act of 1938.[3]
The key players in the development were mainly Keynesian-inspired government constellations that, through the vehicle of an active, expansionary fiscal policy, invested in society's enlargement of the requisite infrastructures, which the modern welfare state needed for education, health, public transport and many other infrastructure and social welfare areas. The actual implementation took place through, inter alia, National Perspective Planning (PPI and PPII), where efforts commenced in 1968.
With a point of departure in the foregoing historical outline, I will – in the present article – be taking a closer look at welfare design which, in my

definition, is deeply rooted in the development of the public sector in Denmark. My angle of approach is primarily the planning of the physical layout as an implement for societal development, transpiring on several levels over a period of time that spans a few generations. The article is built around a series of impacts occurring in important periods, where society's perception and the development of the welfare state and public planning undergo noticeable changes. Naturally, what we are going to present here could hardly be said to be fully exhaustive descriptions, analyses and explanations. In the final part of the article, the theme of the Peripheral Denmark will be discussed, along with the situation in rural regions in relation to the formative development and, conversely, the phasing out of small towns and villages. This can be regarded as both a new and a comprehensive planning-related challenge, but it is also being viewed as an arena for the citizens' active involvement in the creation of the villages' futures.

## The construction of the requisite plan systems

Up through the 1970s, large sector-planning systems were being built up in Denmark: in principle, these were supposed to bind the developments in the infrastructure together, down through the three newly established administration and planning levels: national, county and municipal. Last but not least, what were set in motion were a burden- and task-allocation reform and a municipal-level structure reform, which reduced the number of municipalities from 1,364 to 274, and reduced the number of counties from 25 to 13 counties, with democratically elected county councils.
As the crown of these efforts, what Denmark was endowed with during the period 1969-74 was an entirely new planning legislation, which served to empower the counties and the municipalities with potent, statutory planning tools, where three important factors are especially conspicuous in the objects clause found in the Act on National and Regional Planning from 1971: namely, the *equal development* of the society as a control target; *the synthesizing planning* as implement; and *public involvement* in the planning, as the democratic anchoring of the planning of the physical layout in the new large municipalities and the newly formed counties.
Behind these reforms, however, covertly lurks a long-standing debate on the development of – and on solutions to – the complex of problems that we now call 'the Peripheral Denmark' or 'the lop-sided Denmark'.[4] This discussion harks all the way back to the 1950s, when widespread and chronic unemployment was a genuine problem, a problem that was dealt with through, among other things, an advance of regional development support,[5] and under the banner of the Planning Act's motto about *'equal development'* in all of Denmark. In a more recent version of the Planning Act, however, this formulation was removed and was re-cast into the notion of 'a suitable development'.[6]

## Planning as implement comes under pressure – 2001-14

Today, when – ever since the early 2000s – a neoliberal competitive state[7] has given the place of pride to economy and growth in the private sector, and when faith in the all-encompassing societal welfare development and planning is being put under pressure, it becomes possible to delineate a period that is essentially different from the welfare state's Golden Age. This has come to take on noticeable consequences that bear on the development of the public sector's common property, on the development of infrastructures on four

Danish town.
Photo: Andreas Houmann.

geographical levels, and, to a certain extent, on the development of the planning of the physical layout.

In what follows, I will present a overview, in summary form, of the development in the social infrastructure on four geographical levels, characterized as the national, the regional, the municipal and the local levels, laying particular emphasis on the latter two.

For the governments that held power in this particular period, policy formulation around regional politics had different objectives and different contents, but the basic view has been that the cities are growth engines, and centralization on all levels has characterized Realpolitik as a restructuring principle in the public sector. In the period from 2001 until the change of government in 2011, when the Thorning-Schmidt government took over the reins of political power in the Parliament, we witnessed an extensive series of dramatic structural reforms within the governmental sector: in this vein, we can mention police reform, juridical reform, structural reforms in barracks and in teachers' colleges, and the centralization of middle-range training into larger 'University Colleges'. These reforms effectively reduce the amount of jobs for people with longer-term educational backgrounds and also affect educational opportunities, in the wrong direction, in the nation's outskirts.[8]

Two features that appear to be common to these reforms have been geographical centralizations and a service level for ordinary citizens that is perceived as being unsatisfactory, and which actually *is* much worse than before.

Within a historical context, the renowned and infamous national planning memorandum from 2006 constitutes an important milestone:[9] here, for the very first time, the then-reigning government drew a map of Denmark that contains both growth and decline areas. The memorandum can accordingly be regarded as an acknowledgement that Denmark is regionally developing in very different ways. Five years earlier, researchers and

social commentators had already started to use terms like 'the rotten banana', 'Peripheral Denmark' and other vivid designations signifying the situation that Denmark, geographically speaking, was marked by severe disparities when it came to all kinds of meaningful welfare-related parameters.[10]

What can be cited here as a concrete example is that the users on the regional scene have experienced significant restructuring and centralizing initiatives, especially within the hospital sector, where a number of smaller and medium-sized hospitals have been closed. In some places, they have been replaced by health clinics and the like. As far as the public transport system is concerned, there have been appreciable paradigmatic changes in mass transport policy, which are now being implemented under the motto that resources ought to be concentrated and staked wherever the largest number of potential users derive benefit from using the buses and the local trains. What this entails is that the route network and the number of departures is dwindling, with the result that people in the smaller communities are experiencing either a drastic reduction in services or the total elimination of public transport service altogether.

Gathering the threads, it could be said that the synthesizing planning of the physical layout, pursuant to the Planning Act, has not been playing any significant role in governmental structural reforms during the aforementioned period. And because the regional planning of the physical layout, for all intents and purposes, died out when the counties were disbanded for the sake of establishing 'the five regions', I will try to shed some light on the developments and the situation in the municipalities.[11]

When we turn our attention to the municipal scene, the municipal reforms that were adopted in 2006 led to fewer and larger municipalities.[12] The severe governmental control of the municipalities' economy, through budgetary cooperation between Kommunernes Landsforening [Local Government Denmark] and the Ministry of Finance led, together with the municipal reform's simultaneous reduction in the number of municipalities from 273 to 98, to drastic sector-structure- and urban-pattern changes. A good many small towns and large villages shifted their status from being 'large cities in small municipalities' to being 'small cities in large municipalities'.[13]

The task for the new large municipalities was, around the time of 2007, a highly complex and composite planning, phaseout, development and restructuring task. On the one hand, the task involved a requirement that involved, first, the rethinking of the new municipalities' geographic urban pattern structures and, second, developing a new system of central cities of different sizes. On the other hand, the pronounced tendency towards urbanization led to a declining population and to a falling off in the number of children in both the smaller and the very smallest communities – with all of this transpiring under stringent budgetary discipline and municipal-economic cutbacks and reprioritizations.

In the first city council period, 2005-09, a number of municipalities took these tasks on their shoulders and, thus, also the ensuing discussions and the people's protests, while other municipalities waited until the 2009-13 period. The vast majority of municipalities, by far, have now managed to plan out the future urban pattern and, concomitantly also, the most important prerequisites for the future's municipal localization of welfare benefits like schools, kindergartens, senior citizen's homes, sports facilities, etc.

The experiences that have been gained from this process bear out that a good many municipalities are still working with a rigid, column-divided sector structure and are still characterized by a cer-

Map of Denmark from the
National Plan Report 2006.
Danish Business Authority.

tain stance of hesitancy in relation to the physical aspects of the municipal planning's forces. What is missing is a simple, comprehensive and holistic strategy in a geographical and physical perspective.

## The municipalities' welfare infrastructure

The municipalities' welfare infrastructure includes schools, childcare institutions, care for elderly, public libraries and public transport. What also form an important part of the welfare society's infrastructure are sports halls, clubhouses, sports facilities and new large multi-functional association-, sports-, health- and community centres, which proliferate in the peripheral municipalities. It is statistically possible, to some extent, to document the number of changes and stoppages in the municipal sector: from 2010 to 2015, the number of primary schools has diminished from 1,503 to 1,290;[14] in the years following the reform in 2007, the number of public libraries has been reduced by approximately 200 across the country; and moreover, many of the remaining libraries in the smaller towns or in the suburbs have been turned into buildings where, most of the time, one lets oneself in by using the social security card as a 'key', because no staff are present. Since the year 2001, there have been significant changes in the municipalities' care of children, and there have been structural changes entailing that more children are now being cared for in age-integrated institutions. In addition, the institutions have become larger, and we are seeing other types of institutions where children of various ages are being looked after together. Combined with the striking shortage of children in the smaller rural

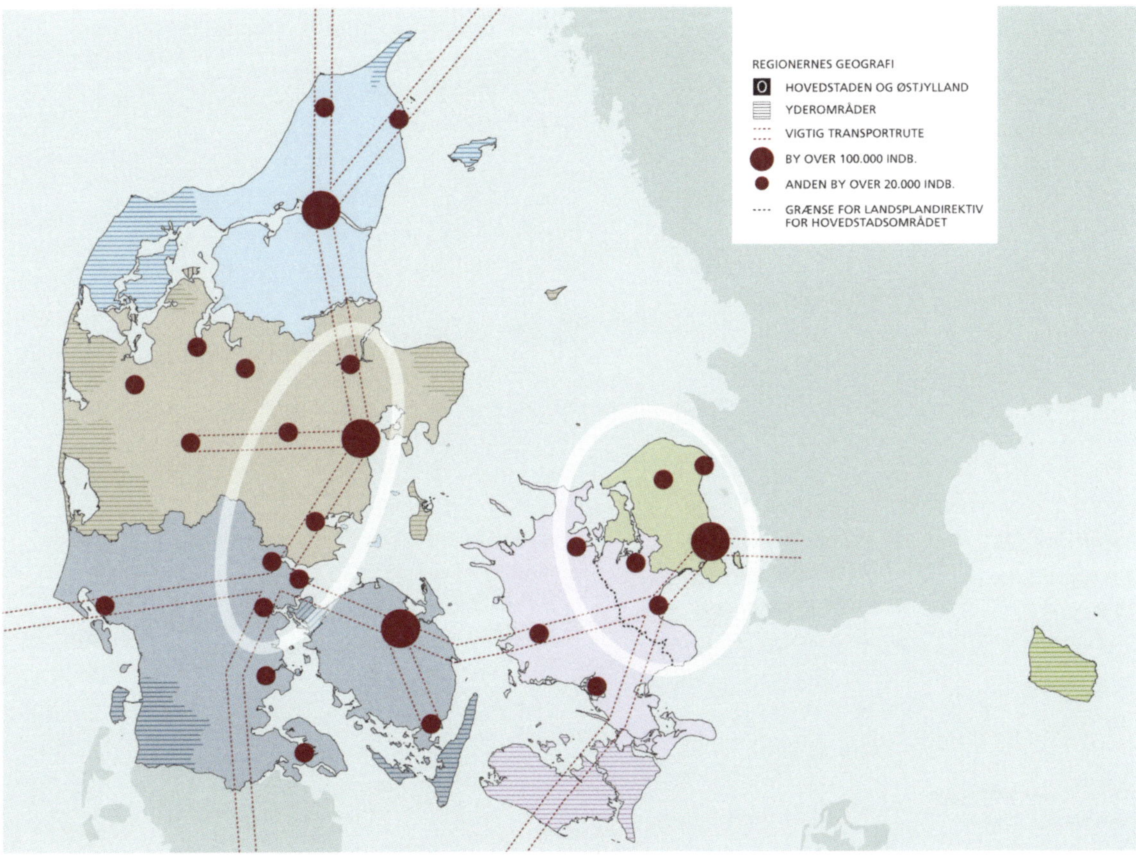

communities over the years, this had led to the closing of around 850 childcare centres in Denmark.

Within the elderly persons' sector, it is more difficult to tabulate just how many smaller nursing homes have been closed because people are working with other categorizations. However, it can generally be said that assisted-living facilities and homes for the elderly are replacing nursing homes and sheltered housing.[15] In addition, work is being carried out with alternative localizations, where the elderly persons will come to be living in the city or within the village's vibrant areas.

In a report from the Danish Association of Consulting Engineers, the need for investments has been taken stock of, and has been categorized into nine different infrastructural areas, and the summary shows that:

*Since 2012 there has been a positive improvement in Danish ports, railway lines and national and private roads, with the consequence that they now, together with airports and the waste sector, are assessed to be in good condition, corresponding to Grade 4.*[16] *Only the energy sector was, in 2016, assessed at Grade 4.5, following the further diversification of the energy sources after 2012. Within the sewage and wastewater sector, we can see both a centralization of the purifying plant structure and approximately 25% higher investments in the sewage system since 2012, which translates into a higher condition assessment (3.5) of the sector, when compared with the results in 2012. The water supply and the public buildings have also been evaluated as having the condition grade of 3.5, in conformity with the analyses in 2008 and 2012. Within these sectors, there is a need for substantial investments if the condition is going to be maintained in the future. In line with the expectations from 2012, the analysis ascertains an increase of 30-40% in the energy- and maintenance backlog of public buildings. All public buildings, however, are still assessed as having the condition grade of 3.5, with the consequence that there still should be an intense focus on implementing renovations – including energy renovations and indoor-climate improvement in the public building mass. At the very bottom, the municipal road network has been evaluated, where the condition grade of 2.5 reflects an acute need for efforts, so as to counter threats to the road network's functionality. What is estimated is that, across the nine sectors, there will be a need for investments in the order of 125 to 195 billion Danish crowns if all of the sectors are going be brought up to a satisfactory standard corresponding to grade 4. It must be emphasized that this* estimate *is subject to a high degree of uncertainty.*[17]

## Uproar from the outskirts and a politicized debate about the Planning Act

As a consequence of the growing dissatisfaction with the emergence of 'the lop-sided Denmark', a number of zealous souls initiated an 'uproar' from the outskirts. About the background of this, the authors Finn Slumstrup and Viggo Mortensen write:

*The prevailing warped twisting of Denmark is scandalous. It has either arisen as a result of erroneous political decisions or because nothing has been done. The advent of competitive business policies have brought about a number of decisions that elicited frightening consequences in the form of a centralization, which is devastating to a harmonious development. Now it's time to think in new ways and to create a comprehensive plan for a Denmark in balance.*[18]

The initiative received wide media coverage, and a number of reports and books on the subject were subsequently published. Other village organizations were founded in the wake of the com-

The landscape around the Danish town Klitmøller. Photo: Tobias Stidsen.

motion: Landsbyerne i Danmark [The Villages in Denmark] and the much larger organization, Landdistrikternes Fællesråd [Rural Municipalities' Joint Council] were actually amalgamated while the iron was hot. The latter organization, in turn, set up the action organization, Danmark på Vippen [Denmark on the Seesaw], which was supposed to ensure that the debate would transpire on the basis of facts and not unsubstantiated assertions.[19]

Peripheral players in this heated debate, who resolved, furthermore, to run for office in the parliamentary elections of September 2015, singled out, as a special theme, the Planning Act as the most important cause of almost of the ills in Peripheral Denmark.

However, not everybody agreed with the insurgents, and I threw my hat into the ring and took part in the debate by contributing the following views:

*We might start out by arriving at a consensus that what is sorely missing, and to the utmost extent, is an overriding political vision for Denmark's physical development in the many years to come: a vision that municipalities, people and investors can understand and that regions and municipalities, to some degree or another, ought to take as a jumping-off point when they crystallize their plans for the future. I expect to put forth these kinds of physical and developmental visions in the next national planning memorandum in 2017. The regional overview and a plan that can control a wide range of important municipal-boundary transgressing planning fields, such as the future's housing supply and localization, climate, energy, retail trade, tourism, infrastructure, higher education, etc., are sorely missing. We need a powerful planning instrument in order to ensure robust functional connections among the cities, and between the cities and the rural regions. They are not competitors, but rather each other's preliminary conditions.*[20]

The criticism of the Planning Act has now been orchestrated and has also been placed on the political agenda in the Ministry of Business and Growth Denmark's growth plan from 2015, which is entitled 'Vækst i hele Danmark' [Growth in all of Denmark]: in Chapter 3, 'Liberalization of the Planning Act'. Here, it becomes clear that more liberalism-oriented rules for, among other things, commercial development and housing in villages and rural areas now situates municipalities, villages and neighbours outside of making any appreciable influence on the development of the Danish cultural landscape and of rural-zone villages in Denmark. In the government's proposal, the so-called production imperative, trumps everything else; this could prove to be a fatal mistake in relation to a village development that builds on community fellowship, on social capital, and on taking into consideration all interests within a process of planning that balances all considerations.

## The planning of the physical layout in the municipalities and the citizens' initiatives in the villages

In the final part of this article, I will examine the role and position of the planning of the physical layout in the preservation and the expansion of a municipal-level and local welfare society that more adequately matches the future's developmental challenges and, for one thing, effectively works towards a concept I would like to call 'the good everyday life' and, for another, appreciates the initiatives that people in smaller towns and rural communities are coming up with, on their own steam, under a new welfare paradigm, where the civil society takes up the reins after the municipalities have pulled out as suppliers of welfare benefits and infrastructure, within a compass of quality and with a localization that the citizens find to be satisfying.

The municipal-oriented planning arsenal consists today of the economic planning, with fiscal years and projected fiscal years, where work is being carried out with a four-year rolling process. Analogously, the planning of the physical layout works with a four-year plan process, with strategies and main structures that extend 12 years, or more, into the future. The sector plans for welfare and infrastructure areas will become incorporated, also routinely, into the laying of the budget. If people would also look routinely at the geographical and physical relationships and contexts, *the municipalities would have a fantastic plan system* that could be used for a holistically oriented and comprehensive planning of all the municipality's physical and sectorial areas, for the benefit of the citizens and under the preservation of the necessary economic realism.

The developmental and phaseout-related challenges that the smaller local communities and the small towns are facing can, in all probability, only be turned to profitable use if the municipal planning seriously takes up the challenge. In my work with analyses of the development in rural municipalities and villages, it is a basic assumption[21] that we cannot stop urbanization, even though we may be able to stave off a number of deleterious and negative effects of this process by deploying the entire arsenal of planning implements and methods.

Here, planning concepts and concerted efforts turn up, and in this connection turnaround planning, decline management, theme villages,[22] the removal of buildings and villages and village cluster collaborations can be mentioned. Urban planning consultant Mogens Knudsen, lecturer Lea Louise Holst Laursen and myself were the first to define the village cluster concept: 'A village cluster can be defined as a number of villages, in relative proximity to each other,[23] that work together, in a network structure, making use of each other's strengths, along with the citizens' skills, knowledge and experience, for purposes of developing the individual village beyond its own potentials and beyond the whole cluster.'[24]

I regard the aforementioned initiatives as adequate parrying-off measures, which can serve to potentialize 'The Good Life' in the countryside, in the future, even under a cutback and saving paradigm. The aforementioned planning-related grip around the task focuses on adapting and downscaling the small-scale societies' physical structures within businesses, institutions, residences and other infrastructures, in order to meet the future's challenges through, among other things, a village cooperation. 'Cooperation in village clusters is in vogue and is far more widespread than is generally assumed. In the villages and in the municipalities, there is a great interest in cooperation between villages and a strong belief that this can make a positive difference.'[25] At the same time, it will also be necessary to prioritize in a hard-nosed way in order to create economic latitude for development. Such processes will, in all likelihood, bring about a certain degree of centralization in the municipal institutions and systems. The point in this is that *this* is the only realistic option for preserving an intact network of villages with such a high quality that it will also prove attractive in the future to do business and to settle down in the rural municipalities and the villages.

## The privatized village and embryonic forms for a new village-based 'cooperative movement'

The political solutions to the challenges posed by altered demographic, economic, production-related and need-related conditions are still packed into a development paradigm that locks regions and municipalities tightly into specific, cheap(er)



The coast at Klitmøller.
Photo: Tobias Stidsen.

solution options around welfare's infrastructures. Often, savings and cutbacks routinely trigger off local civil society protests,[26] but they also give rise to initiatives where people take the development into their own hands as a reaction and as a counter-move. This is thus an implicit criticism of the long queue of cutbacks and closings in the municipal sector that has led, in certain places, to greater distances and to a quality in the supply being offered that villagers do not find to be particularly gratifying.

Characteristic of these very different reactions from the villages is that they can be divided into two different albeit complementary groups of initiatives. Common to both approaches is an understanding that is commensurate with the theoretical concept of Localism,[27] which stresses the importance of the villagers' own achievements, both the economic and the organizational ones, and also stresses practical activity, on the part of zealously committed individuals, in the preservation and development of the local communities.

In *the privatized village*, we have witnessed that a number of private measures have been set up, such as private independent schools, independent kindergartens and independent nursing homes, within the frames of current legislation, and with economic profit in mind. Perhaps there is also a Free Church/Union Congregation Church in the village. Current legislation makes it feasible and relatively easy to set up such institutions.

I find, however, the development to be even more promising in *the modern cooperative villages*, where the citizens, on a village basis, amass capital for various purposes. This might involve capital for the continued operation of a convenience store; for the modernization of a community hall; for the establishment of a village investment fund that can be used for buying up empty, unsightly homes, which can either demolished, converted for being rented out, or sold; for the establishment of an entrepreneurs' nursery in a farm building that has fallen into becoming superfluous; for establishing up a car-sharing arrangement or an intelligent car-pool arrangement; or for setting up foodware co-ops, etc.

The most manifest examples of the realization of the cooperative movement's way of thinking, with its point of origin in amassed local cooperative capital, can be found in the category of multi-purpose communal dwellings, where projects are being developed in relation to a worn-down sports hall dating from the 1970s. Here, there will be ample room for sports activities, educational instruction, health and wellness, culture and business – all in the same building. Thereby, one can say that the ring has been closed and that the way of thinking underlying the classical cooperative movement, which developed and served to advance the rural communities at the closing of the 1800s, with an ideological foundation that was based on fellowship, democracy and efficiency, finds its contemporary form in today's future- and re-alignment-ready cooperative movement villages.

## Summary

If we look back over the period that this article treats of, what comes to light is that there has been a period (1958-85) of dramatic expansion in the society's infrastructure, which was supposed to stimulate the development of the whole country. This period was succeeded by periods where there has subsequently been an impetuous centralization of the social infrastructure (2001-16). At the same time, my assessment is that the welfare society's buildings and facilities, on the whole, are (intensely) worn-down, aside from a very few exceptions. There is accordingly an enormous need for investment in the re-establishment and development of these. At the same time, I can spot a clear line of evolution leading from a situation where, previously, the planning of the physical layout was considered a powerful implement for the development of society, to today, where the planning of the physical layout *in the societal discourse* is becoming articulated as a stopper of an otherwise desired development.

On the scene of the municipal level, there are enormous potentials in the existing planning systems and, as I see it, there is an existing possibility for the development of the smallest local communities to unfold themselves in a relatively unproblematic way, especially if a symbiotic interaction between the municipal and the village can be established, in an equal cooperation, where both the municipality's and the village's strengths and potentials can be brought into play. This planning system and the results thereof can easily be rendered fertile through new forms of organization and new funding methods, where the village's fiery souls will spring into action. Today it is not only embryonic forms that exist. No, there are *also* fully developed and reality-checked models and procedures in the smaller local communities that are there for facing up to the local development's needs and challenges, in a more sustainable – and conditions-of-life ameliorating – direction.

**Notes**

1 This particular change, however, is not discussed in the present article.

2 Dansk Byplanlaboratorium: *Hvad gjorde vi ved Danmark?* Byplanhistorisk Skriftserie no. 70 (2012).

3 J. Harvest: Centerplanlægning. Udvalgte byplanopgaver udført i konsulentfirmaet Institut for Center-planlægning i 1960'erne. Dansk Byplanlaboratorium (2004).

4 J. Møller: *Yderområdeudpegning – velsignelse eller forbandelse?* Økonomi og politik. April 1, 2012. 85. årgang. (2012), pp. 38-39.

5 H. Kiib, E.H. Knudsen, G. Marling and J. Møller: Levevilkår og Regional Politik i Nordjylland (1978).

6 For further examination of this matter, the reader is referred to Miljøministeriet, Skov- og Naturstyrelsen, Landsplanafdelingen 2004 or Galland et al. 2016.

7 O.K. Pedersen: Konkurrencestaten (2008).

8 Møller (2012), op.cit., p. 46.

9 In my opinion, the two most important national planning memorandums are Landsplanredegørelsen [The National Planning Memorandum] from 1979 and the ensuing debate in Parliament on January 29, 1980. This particular debate came close to costing the reigning government its power. The heart of the dispute was the question of centralization vs. decentralization of the future increase in population. Planstyrelsen: *Folketingets forespørgselsdebat om landsbyer* January 29, 1980 (1980).

10 J. Møller: Mellem udvikling og afvikling – en minianalyse af de danske landdistrikter og landsbyer. *Tidsskriftet PLAN* (2009).

11 The planning of the physical layout on the regional level was significantly altered and six generations of regional planning were consequently thrown onto history's dung heap when the guidelines and the open terrain were transferred to the municipal's planning. In the period from 1975 to 2007, six generations of high-quality plans were hammered out and were continuously fine-tuned and adapted to the societal and regional development. From 2009 and all the way up to 2014, the five regions worked up the called 'RUPs' (regional development plans), and ever since then, the resolutions have been removed completely from the Planning Act. What is presently being prepared are the so-called 'REVUSs' (Regional Growth and Development Strategies), which are aimed at business development and support for commercial projects. For further details, see Region Nordjylland 2015. The lack of any regional or inter-regional plan level is continuously being discussed in planning circles. See J. Møller: *Forsimplet debat om planloven.* Altinget (2015) and Dansk Byplanlaboratoriums Årsmøde, 2015.

12 Møller (2012), op.cit., p. 48.

13 Daniel Galland Garcia de Quevedo, Stig Enemark, Jørgen Møller, Line Træholt Hvingel, Anne Lise Schrøder & Esben Munk Sørensen: *International Manual of Planning Practice* i *International Manual of Planning Practice* (2016).

14 (*Jyllands-Posten*, 2016.)

15 *Nyt fra Danmarks Statistik*. No. 668, December 2012: *Pleje og ældreboliger* (2012).

16 The grading scale spans from 1 to 5, and half-grades (i.e. x.5) can also be used when assignment grades. 1.0 is such a poor grade that what is indicated herewith is that the layout in question is simply not fulfilling or sustaining its intended function: a major renovation or new establishment altogether are reasonably to be expected. 5.0 is a condition corresponding to 'like new', for which, over the course of many years, what might be anticipated is nothing more than minimal and ongoing maintenance efforts in order to uphold the condition.

17 Foreningen af Rådgivende Ingeniører. FRI: *State of the Nation* (2016).

18 F. Slumstrup. & V. Mortensen (eds.): *Oprør fra udkanten. Mulighedernes land* (2014).

19 Landdistrikternes Fællesråd: *Danmark på Vippen* (2014).

20 Møller (2015), op.cit.

21 Ibid.

22 A theme village is a village where the citizens, in cooperation with the municipal, are developing a special 'village profile', which could be a 'guild village', a 'horse village', a 'school village', or anything else that provides a sense of direction to what are strategically the most important initiatives that municipalities and zealous souls set in motion. At the same time, this will also be an opportune 'branding platform' for the village.

23 A salient feature of the Danish system of villages, which has descended down from the early medieval town- and village-formation process is that the distance between the villages is rarely more than 3-4 kilometers. Therefore, the physical distance between functions does not constitute a major problem for the cluster cooperation.

24 Knudsen, Laursen & Møller: *Landsbyklynger-netværk og samarbejde* (2014).

25 L.H. Laursen, M. Frølund, P.H. Johansen & E.M. Christiansen: *Landsbyklynger som mulig udviklingsstrategi – Muligheder og Barrierer. En forundersøgelse for DGI og Realdania* (2014).

26 Jørgen Møller: 'Big Changes in the Local Welfare System'. *Nordregio* (2012).

27 'Localism describes a range of political philosophies which prioritize the local. Generally, localism supports local production and consumption of goods, local control of government, and promotion of local history, local culture and local identity. Localism can be contrasted with regionalism and centralized government.' Wikipedia. Retrieved on May 3, 2016.

**Literature**


- Dansk Byplanlaboratorium: *Hvad gjorde vi ved Danmark*. Byplanhistorisk Skriftserie no. 70. Copenhagen, 2012.
- Foreningen af Rådgivende Ingeniører. FRI: *State of The Nation*. Copenhagen, 2016. Retrieved 12.03.2016: http://www.frinet.dk/sotn_2016
- Galland Garcia de Quevedo, Daniel; Enemark, Stig; Møller, Jørgen; Hvingel, Line Træholt; Schrøder, Anne Lise & Sørensen, Esben Munk: *International Manual of Planning Practice* Published in: *International Manual of Planning Practice*, 2016.
- Harvest, J.: *Centerplanlægning Udvalgte byplanopgaver udført i konsulentfirmaet Institut for Center-planlægning i 1960'erne*. Dansk Byplanlaboratorium, Copenhagen 2004
- Kiib, H., Knudsen, E.H., Marling, G., & Møller, J.: *Levevilkår og Regional Politik i Nordjylland*. Copenhagen. DSF. Forlag, 1978.
- Knudsen, Laursen & Møller: *Landsbyklynger-netværk og samarbejde*, 2014. Retrieved March 12, 2016 http://fjordklyngen.dk/om-fjordklyngen/om-projektet/
- Landdistrikternes Fællesråd: *Danmark på Vippen*, 2014. Retrieved March 12, 2016 http://landdistrikterne.dk/ikke-kategoriseret/danmark-pa-vippen-vil-skable-vaekst-i-hele-danmark/
- Laursen, L.H., Frølund, M. & Johansen, P.H., Christiansen, E.M.: *Landsbyklynger som mulig udviklingsstrategi – Muligheder og Barrierer*. En forundersøgelse for DGI og Realdania, 2014.
- Liliegreen, Curt: *Byudviklingsforums debatmøde 'Den store omstilling', 21. januar 2015*. Retrieved June 22, 2016. https://www.realdaniadebat.dk/byudviklingsforum/Pages/Affolkningen-er-godt-for-%C3%B8konomien.aspx
- Miljøministeriet, Skov- og Naturstyrelsen, Landsplanafdelingen: *Bidrag til regionplanlægningens historie*. Prepared by Vilhelm B. Michelsen, Karsten Bay Christensen and Ib Ferdinandsen, 2004.
- Møller, J.: *Mellem udvikling og afvikling – en minianalyse af de danske landdistrikter og landsbyer*. The journal *PLAN*, Universitetsforlaget Oslo, 2009.
- Møller, J.: *Big changes in the local welfaresystem*. Nordregio. Stockholm, 2012. Retrieved July 7, 2016: *http://www.nordregio.se/en/Metameny/Nordregio-News/2012/Quality-of-Life-in-an-Urban-Rural-Perspective/Big-Changes-in-the-Local-Welfare-System/*
- Møller, J.: *Yderområdeudpegning-velsignelse eller forbandelse?* Økonomi og politik. April 1, 2012. Vol. 85. Jurist og Økonomforbundets Forlag. Copenhagen 2012.
- Møller, J.: *Forsimplet debat om planloven*. Altinget. 2015. Retrieved March 12, 2016: http://www.altinget.dk/by/artikel/forsker-forsimplet-debat-om-planloven
- Nyt fra Danmarks Statistik. No. 668. December 2012: *Pleje og ældreboliger* 2012. Retrieved March 12, 2016: http://www.dst.dk/pukora/epub/Nyt/2012/NR668.pdf

- Planstyrelsen: *Folketingets forespørgselsdebat om landsbyer 29.01.1980,* 1980.
- PP II: *Perspektivplanredegørelse 1971-1987.* Økonomi- og Budgetministeriet. Copenhagen 1973.
- Pedersen, O.K.: *Konkurrencestaten.* Hans Reitzels Forlag. Copenhagen 2008.
- Region Nordjylland: 'Mulighedernes Nordjylland: Regional Vækst- og Udviklingsstrategi 2015-2018', 2015. Retrieved March 12, 2016: http://www.rn.dk/Regional-Udvikling/Strategier-og-planer/REVUS
- Slumstrup, F. & V. Mortensen (eds.): *Oprør fra udkanten. Mulighedernes land.* Lindhardt og Ringhof, Copenhagen 2014.
- Vestergaard, Morten: 'Bølge af protestfriskoler er forsvundet-kommuner siger de vil beholde de små skoler', in *Jyllands-Posten,* March 12, 2016.
- Vækst- og Erhvervsministeriet: *Vækst og udvikling i hele Danmark,* 2015.
- Wikipedia. Localism. https://en.wikipedia.org/wiki/Localism. Retrieved May 3, 2016.

Deane Simpson

# Between 'Circumscribed' Neoliberalism and Welfarism:

## Copenhagen under the Metric Regimes of the 'Competitive' and 'Attractive' City

**How can we interpret contemporary notions such as the liveable city and sustainable city in relation to those of the post-war welfare city – particularly in the context of Copenhagen's position as an international emblem of all three urban paradigms? This article addresses the metrics attached to liveable and sustainable city rankings, and explores their role within wider forms of attractive and competitive city production. In doing so, it points to the complicity of these systems within the general 'turn' the city has undergone since the 1990s.**

## Introduction

"[By 2015] Copenhagen will have become the Eco-Metropolis of the World, thus demonstrating that environmental concern adds an extra dynamic to urban development."

Municipality of Copenhagen, *Eco-Metropolis: Our Vision for Copenhagen 2015*, 2007[1]

"...the philosophy behind all the development in the city [of Copenhagen] comes down to the question of liveability."

Copenhagen's Lord Mayor Frank Jensen, 5 May, 2016[2]

During the past two decades, in Denmark and much of the global north, notions of the *liveable city* and the *sustainable city* – and to a lesser extent the *smart city* – have become dominant as drivers in the production of the contemporary *competitive* and *attractive city*.[3] And it is through related discourses and measuring instruments that Copenhagen has established and actively promoted itself internationally as a model city – to be marketed and exported globally. If, for example, *liveability* is at the centre of considerations of urban development, how is it defined, measured and represented, by whom, and toward what ends? Is it possible to conceive of such drivers as an extension of, or in continuity with what has been historically presented as the dominant paradigm in Nordic and Danish urbanism – the *welfare city*? In the sense that *sustainability* might represent a form of responsibility to the maintenance and protection of our future collective welfare;[4] or that *liveability* may define, in relation to the broader Nordic understanding of the term *welfare (velfærd* in Danish), the propensity of the city to deliver 'the good life'?[5] How can we understand such notions through the lens of ranking indexes, particularly in relation to those of the *welfare city*, and how do they map onto the city itself? And what actual impacts do such notions and agendas have on the city? It will be suggested that the emergence in recent decades of the concepts of the *liveable or sustainable city* as framed through the metrics of ranking indexes – and by association, the notions of the *attractive* and *competitive city* – are deeply embedded within a wider neoliberal restructuring of urban development within Copenhagen, a restructuring that is particularly evident in the housing sector. This is the case even in a Nordic context where the ethos of universal welfare still remains central to the national political and public discourse, particularly in sectors such as healthcare and education – just as welfare plays a defining role in the identity of the Nordic countries from an international perspective. The resulting condition, between a form of 'circumscribed neoliberalism' (to use David Harvey's term) and what could be called 'circumscribed welfarism', may be presented as both an urban model with important accomplishments, in relative terms, and as an urban model facing considerable challenges. In these terms the distinctions between the *competitive*, the *attractive,* and the *welfare city* as different notions of the city will be discussed, as well as their framing as distinctly bounded objects in space and time.

## Copenhagen Acclaim

The international status of Copenhagen with respect to sustainability and liveability has become increasingly evident post-2000 through labels circulating internationally such as: "the World's Most Liveable City",[6] "World's Most Green City",[7] "European Green Capital",[8] "Eco-Metropolis of the World",[9] "Sustainable Transport Mecca";[10] "City with the Happiest People in the World",[11] "Bike-Friendliest City on the Planet",[12] "Paragon of T.O.D." (Transit-Oriented Development).[13] This contemporary status represents an extraordinary contrast to the municipality of Copenhagen and its urban core in the 1980s and 1990s when the municipality approached bankruptcy after decades of decline characterized by "de-industrialization, suburbanization, high unemployment rates, high welfare costs, an outdated housing market, strong segregation and various other factors."[14]

Perhaps most critical to the international positioning of the Copenhagen brand is the city's top ranking across a range of international city indices, from *Siemens European Green-City Index* (2009) and *Tree Hugger's Best City for Cyclists* award (2009), to *Monocle's World's Most Liveable Cities Index* (2008, 2013, 2014). With a shorter history than their nation state-focused counterparts, indices such as these, comparing the relative performance of cities, have become ubiquitous in recent years. Such city-ranking indexes emerged from the first global city indices that focused largely on establishing the relative economic influence of cities, and to a lesser extent their political and cultural influence and infrastructural connectivity, such as the *A.T. Kearney Global Cities Index*, for example. In recent years, clusters of indices have emerged addressing themes such as the relative 'sustainability' or ecological performance of cities (e.g. *Siemens Green City Index* or the *Mercer Eco-City Ranking)*; and the relative urban 'liveability' or 'quality of life' (e.g. *Monocle's Liveable Cities Index* or *Mercer's Quality of Living Ranking*). The emergence of these more recent frameworks for both defining urban agendas and measuring urban performance, have been framed in positive terms by some critics for their shift in emphasis away from economic growth and techno-rational optimization metrics toward ones that are more environmentally, socially, and humanistically centred.[15] In further exploring these indices and the roles they play in a larger set of dynamics, it is possible to identify opposing assessments of their value and impact. On the positive side, it has been argued that indices are effective in gaining media and public attention and in generating debate over particular urban issues. An effectiveness – according to Nick Ennis and Birgit Stöber[16] – that lies in their ability to simplify and as a result make highly complex conditions comparable. Similarly, it has been suggested that indices can also support urban governance and decision-making by supplying specific data/measurement addressing relevant issues. It has also been stated that they can support competition for improvement; supplying recognition, support (and economic opportunity) to successful pro-active actors; and potentially placing pressure on inactive actors to take action. In these terms, it is important to point out the coupling that the indexes are capable of enacting between 'soft' qualitative values (which can define the social, cultural and spatial experience of the city), on the one hand, and 'hard' quantitative ones (that are often framed in economic or financial terms), on the other. In other words, they facilitate a form of economic quantification of social, cultural and spatial qualities – which can in turn supply relatively new and potentially powerful arguments for valuing 'soft' qualities in the public debate and in urban policy- and decision-making.

On the other hand however, the indices raise a number of concerns. In their tendency toward oversimplification, it has been argued that they tend to provide misleading or inaccurate portrayals of diverse and complex conditions, also in their potential exaggeration of differences between cities. Related issues include the potential arbitrariness – or imposition of bias – attached to measurement assumptions (and the agendas behind the indices), and questions over the relative (and often arbitrary) weightings of the various index components. For example, whereas international indices comparing nation states have been most commonly produced by supranational organizations such as the UN, EU, OECD, or WHO from data supplied largely by national statistics offices – the more recent city-ranking indices have been produced predominantly by private sector interests, with more varied data sources and data production techniques, and with more focused commercial agendas behind them – with greater potential for bias and conflicts of interest.[17]

Related issues exist with respect to the possibility for cities 'gaming' indices; and in the diversion of focus that potentially comes with attention to competitive urban performance in areas specific to indices.[18] Some of these issues may be unfolded in a closer look at specific city-ranking indices.

## Siemens Green City Index

The *Siemens Green City Index* raises particular issues. Envisioned by its sponsor, the German multi-national engineering and electronics conglomerate – and its commissioned researcher, the London-based magazine *The Economist*'s *Intelligence Unit* – it is intended to address "urban environmental sustainability by creating a unique tool that helps cities benchmark their performance and share best practices."[19]

The coincidence of the presentation of Copenhagen's top positioning in the European index in 2009 with the COP15 meeting in Copenhagen the same year provided important international marketing opportunities for the Municipality of Copenhagen's commitment to $CO_2$ neutrality – promoting the city on an international stage – while at the same time profiling Siemens sustainability commitment at COP15.[20] This form of benchmarking, however, and the promoted competition between index achievers and non-achievers alike, appears to be strongly motivated by the sponsor's own corporate interests and agenda – evident in the near-perfect mapping of subcategories of the index[21] onto Siemens' own business sectors.

## Monocle Liveability Index

Perhaps the most frequently quoted index addressing Copenhagen's liveability performance, *The Monocle Magazine Liveable Cities Index* is sponsored, researched and published by the London-based lifestyle magazine of the same name. Since the index was founded in 2007, Copenhagen has excelled in the ranking, being positioned in 2nd (2007), 1st (2008), 2nd (2009), 2nd (2010), 3rd (2011), 3rd (2012), 1st (2013), 1st (2014), 10th (2015), and 4th (2016) place in subsequent years.[22] The description of the research methodology behind their rankings raises clear questions over the scientific objectivity and comparability of the index – as well as the potentially arbitrary or biased weightings between the various elements of the index: "Both scientific (a few of our key metrics are listed in our ranking that follows) and subjective (it's difficult to measure whether a city is cosy or inclusive so you have to get out on the streets and experience it)."[23] Researcher Birgit Stöber has questioned how qualified a lifestyle magazine is to adjudicate on the performance and ranking of complex urban systems – asking how it managed to secure this position? One of the answers she provides is the notion of *mutual authority,* exemplified in the 'happy hour' celebration of Copenhagen's top ranking in the first *Monocle* Index in 2008 on the city hall square, presided over by the Lord Mayor at the time, Ritt Bjerregaard, with the *Monocle*'s editor in chief, Tyler Brûlé, as the guest of honour. Here, the magazine gains considerable authority and publicity in the municipality-sponsored promotion of its index, while the city itself gains authority from its top ranking position.
As with the Siemens index, top-ranking cities are consistently more affluent ones, and – with the exception of Tokyo which reached the top ranking in 2015 and 2016 – the leading cities are modest in size. Sam Jacob has provocatively claimed – in questioning the lesser positioning of large cities such as London or Paris – that the more successfully ranked cities "barely qualify as cities."[24] Further reservations have been raised over the objectivity of self-interested ranking producers from the private sector – which is possible to address at two levels. Firstly, the business model and revenue generating streams to maintain and develop magazines can create conflicts of interest. This is evident when supplementary national survey issues of *Monocle* are funded by those nations, and associated cities that are also ranked within the indexes. This occurred in 2012 with the release of "The Monocle Denmark Survey" funded by the Danish Ministry of Foreign Affairs and supported by tourism promotion agencies Visit Denmark and Wonderful Copenhagen to the tune of 700.000 Danish Kroner.[25]
Secondly, the indices raise questions concerning their relation to targeted readership segments which influence metrics defining notions of liveability and 'the good life' – with obvious leanings toward that specific readership. This is evident when metrics such as retail mix, the quality of cocktails, and the interior design of the airport are included, while issues such as social segregation or spatial inequalities are not. This is particularly relevant, when the Mayor claims that the 'liveability agenda' is so central to the decision-making of the city, and the metrics behind the index inform the city's branding strategy. And it is this decision-making logic – directed largely toward more affluent citizens – that produces *a series of by-products and unanticipated outcomes.*[26]

## The City-Size Problem

Just as the indices raise questions over the construction of the concept of liveability or sustainability, and how those notions are measured within the indices, they also raise similar questions regarding what we understand to be the city as an object of measurement. Each of the indices described above, for example, is based on the Copenhagen municipality alone, rather than Greater Copenhagen, the urbanized area, metropolitan area, or metropolitan city region – which in turn opens up questions as to what constitutes the conceptual and territorial limits of the 'city' as a distinct object. As an urban territory, the municipality contains less than half of the population of the urbanized area commonly known as Greater Copenhagen and less than a quarter of the population of its functional metropolitan region. This represents what could be referred to as a *'city size' measurement problem* common amongst indices.[27] As such, the Siemens' Green City Index's presentation of a 'sustainable Copenhagen' is based on a dense territory constructed largely prior to the Second World War, of quite different character and performance to that of the larger metropolitan area. KADK Professor Jens Kvorning refers to this split condition as a "Jekyll and Hyde town – a double city" characterized by a sustainable dense inner city, on the one hand, and a large unsustainable post-war periphery, on the other.[28] This is reflected in considerable variations in statistics across various indicators such as $CO_2$ emissions, district heating connectivity, social housing provision, and so forth between the Copenhagen municipality and the larger metropolitan area. *Monocle* magazine's Livable Cities ranking is similarly focused on the territory of the Copenhagen municipality – evident in the video documenting 'liveable' spaces and qualities of the inner city. It articulates quite distinct spatial conditions and atmospheres from those of the larger post-war welfare city.

Not only does this suggest a range of different scales and periodizations of Copenhagen – from the historical urban fabric of the inner city and municipality, to the post-war territories of Greater Copenhagen, to the post-millennium metropolitan trans-border region – the latter operating as the main economic scale framing Copenhagen. It raises the question as to the feasibility of defining a city's environmental responsibility and green performance according to its geographical area, particularly as post-industrial transformations have seen a high proportion of the production of the goods and services it consumes shift to the other side of the globe? And, similarly, a number of vital and large-scale urban structures such as logistics centres, industrial and office parks, highways, and a range of structures highly reliant on and dominated by private automobile mobility are excluded from the assessments of the city's liveability or sustainability.

## Local and Global Ambitions

Ranking-based representations of the Municipality of Copenhagen are often used as validation of the local municipal project to improve the everyday 'welfare', life quality, or 'liveability' of citizens (and voters), and towards realizing ambitions for the sustainable performance of the city.[29] But they are also intimately linked to the validation and support of broader, global ambitions – two aspects of which will be addressed here. Firstly, in terms of ambitions to export Danish know-how in the internationally competitive fields of 'green growth' and 'liveable city innovation'; and secondly, in terms of the broader global-scale project of producing a competitive city-region.

## Global Ambitions: Liveability, Sustainability, and Green Growth

Global ambitions are directed toward the communication of Copenhagen's leading position of expertise in the area of sustainable and liveable city innovation – as one of the key sectors of 'green growth' development articulated in the municipality's *Copenhagen Solutions for Sustainable Cities*[30] document, for example, a part of the *State of Green* initiative.[31] It is also present in others such as *Eco-Metropolis: Our Vision for Copenhagen 2015*,[32] and in *The City of Copenhagen's Business and Growth Policy 2015-2025*.[33] The latter document emphasizes this focus, stating that "*A liveable city is the driver of businesses' innovation and growth.*"[34]

Supported by entities such as the Danish Ministry of Foreign Affairs, which markets Denmark's expertise in areas related to green-growth based on Danish and Copenhagen experiences – this agenda is underwritten by the notion that economic growth and environmental sustainability are not mutually exclusive. The central role of Copenhagen in its ambition to hold the position of 'Eco-Metropolis' of the world is linked to a number of other commercial initiatives, such as Copenhagen Solutions, Sustainia, State of Green, and BLOXHUB. BLOXHUB, for example, is an association initiated "... by Realdania, Denmark's Ministry of Business and Growth and the City of Copenhagen underscor[ing] their ambition to establish Denmark as an exporter of sustainable urbanization solutions for the world's major cities."[35] Expertise in architecture, urban design, and urban planning associated with declared humanist goals such as liveability, quality of life, etc., represents an aligned export – as Tom Nielsen has described in "Exporting Humanist Architecture".[36] These broad positioning efforts have been highly advantageous for practices such as Gehl Architects and BIG – and the ongoing performance of the city in indices such as Siemens's and *Monocle*'s are essential components in establishing the authority of Copenhagen as a world centre and market leader in green and liveable city innovation.

## Global Ambitions: Competitive Metropolitan-Region Production

Further to these ambitions; the international positioning of Copenhagen played out in the indices is tied to the broader dynamics of competitive metropolitan-region making – and the increasing role attached to city performance within competitive national and global (knowledge-based) economies. In particular as engines of economic growth in competition with other regions to attract international tourists, businesses, capital investment, and qualified labour/knowledge workers.[37] This has been framed as a broader paradigm shift in urban planning and the production of the city, as well as coinciding with a transformation in the spatialization of the welfare system.

David Harvey describes this broad global shift as a condition emerging at the end of the 1980s – from a managerial planning paradigm of urban govern*ment*, focusing on the delivery of welfare and public social services, to an entrepreneurial planning paradigm of urban govern*ance* directed toward inter-urban competition.[38] In recent decades, this has evolved, in the words of Jamie Peck, into an urban toolbox of: "[...] neoliberalism's now-customary forms: privatized governance and public–private partnerships; the outsourcing and localization of risk; an orientation to speculative investment, along with the commodification of place and place assets; and heightened competition across the spheres of production and consumption, as well as in the distribution of public resources"[39] – in addition to other important tools such as "the promotion of international events, infrastructures for connectivity, urban renewal and sustainability policies, cultural and housing interventions."[40] The rhetorics and ethos attached to this shifting landscape tends to frame the role economic competitiveness plays in benefitting the population as a whole – linking according to Harvey to the role of the neo-liberal state in creating a "good business climate [...] because it will foster growth and innovation and that this is the only way to eradicate poverty and to deliver, in the long run, higher standards to the mass of the population."[41] While such approaches have, in Roberta Cucca's words, been "... quite successful in attracting the creative class, talents, foreign investments, new populations"[42] to Copenhagen, they have on the other hand been realized at a considerable cost.[43]

A number of sectors in Denmark, such as healthcare and education, have to a large extent maintained their status as components of a universal, de-commodified welfare system (despite undergoing considerable restructuring since the 1970s). However, the urban development sector, and that of housing in particular, has undergone a considerable shift toward what has been described by Harvey in his 2005 *A Brief History of Neoliberalism* as a form of *'circumscribed neoliberalism.'*[44] Here, with reference to similar conditions in Sweden under politicized rhetorics that positioned the welfare state in the 1970s and 1980s as: "[...] the fundamental cause of economic stagnation",[45] what took place was described as a 'partial implementation' of the neoliberal agenda, including: "'deficit reduction, inflation control and balanced budgets rather than full employment and an equitable distribution of income [as] cornerstones of macroeconomic policy'." However, in the Scandinavian countries, such as Sweden, "The public still remained broadly attached to its welfare structures. Inequality certainly increased, but by no means to the levels seen in the US or the UK. Poverty levels remained low and levels of social provision remained high."[46]

The geographer Eric Clark, a decade after the release of Harvey's *A Brief History*, would question the extent to which neoliberalism is actually circumscribed or moderated in the Nordic context, particularly with respect to the housing sector.[47] "Now it seems plausible that the Nordic welfare state has offered more latitude for radical neoliberalization than in places where privatization, commodification and marketization had already transformed societies. Housing was the first sphere of the neoliberal revolution [...]. With the helping hands of both social democratic and right-wing governments (more aidez-faire than laissez-faire), spheres of commons built up and institutionalized during the middle decades of the twentieth century have rapidly been privatized, commodified and marketized, while 'exchange value considerations' have become the primary drivers of urban policy and development."[48]

Ole B. Jensen and Ib Jørgensen, for example, similarly describe Denmark's: "[...] remarkable turnaround from the situation in the 1960s and the 1970s when spatial planning was institutionalized [...] as the spatial expression of the welfare state- [...] Planning strategies now addressed the new socio-spatial context of increased urban competition, and looked towards the European Union and its emerging spatial visions."[49] This approach to planning in the earlier period is described by Helen Carter, et al. "[...] as a distinct, spatial-political dimension of the wider welfare state project [...]. This involved among other things an up-scaling of planning politics to the scale of the entire state territory, in which the socio-spatial trajectory re-emerged in debates about spatial inequality. Planning at that time could be understood as a territory-wide spatialisation of the welfare state objective of material growth and social equalisation. Appropriating Harvey's notion, this territory-wide 'managerialism' became a hallmark of planning politics until the end of the 1980s."[50]

An important historical document representing the subsequent shift of policy in the Danish context is the report *Hovedstaden: Hvad vil vi med den?* (The Capital: What do we want to do?) produced in 1989 by the Stallknecht committee appointed by conservative prime minister Poul Schlüter. The committee's report would make several influential suggestions addressing the: "[...] desire for greater growth and a stronger international profile for Copenhagen, including a fixed connection across the Øresund to Sweden."[51] The report's recommendations were based upon the assumption that: "... 'the capital region again has the possibility to become a dynamo in the development of the country' and the bridge would give Copenhagen a 'unique chance for a new prosperity for the benefit of the whole of Denmark'."[52] The report's recommendation of considerable infrastructural investments including new highways, rail links and expansion of the airport – in addition to the Øresund Bridge – was informed by the perception that for some years Copenhagen had been short-changed on infrastructural investment.[53] It was strongly influenced by the larger context of changes taking place in Europe in the late 1980s, including the dissolution of the former Soviet bloc, and Finland and Sweden's application for EU membership, which would, in a Scandinavian context, reposition Copenhagen geo-politically and economically in a more central position.[54] According to John Andersen and Gestur Hovgaard, this would translate into a "shift away from the former dominant orientation in Danish regional policy, which had emphasized on interregional equalization, hence disfavoured the capital in the ongoing struggles over public infrastructure and other investments."[55] As a result, in the early 1990s, the Danish Parliament would approve not only the fixed bridge link between Copenhagen and Malmö, but also the establishment of a larger urban development area, Ørestad.[56]

The later Würtzen committee was tasked with detailing these plans in terms of their financing and realization. At this time, "... not only did Denmark as a state face huge debts [...] that could hinder its financial integration into the European Monetary Union, history had also shown that it was always very difficult to acquire approval of the national parliament for infrastructure investments in the Copenhagen area. Furthermore, [...] the weak financial situation of the city government itself prevented it from taking any substantial initiatives."[57] Within such a context, it was deemed necessary to find 'creative financing solutions' that did not rely on large-scale public expense.[58] Stan Majoor describes how this would "focus on a large-scale urban development project that could work, at the same time, as an economic development zone and as a means to create investments for a new public transport system for the whole city. The origin of this idea links back to the concepts furthered in the British New Town developments at the turn of the century. The huge increase in value of a plot of land that was jointly owned by the national government and the municipality would be capitalized to finance a new public transport system for the city."[59] This would become the blueprint for the development of Ørestad, and later Nordhavn, whereby the private-public entity and land owner, By & Havn, majority-owned by the Municipality of Copenhagen, would realize the urban infrastructure and sell the land for predominantly high-end housing, with the responsibility of maximizing profit to pay for the metro infrastructure. Together with other related transformations, this would concretize further movement towards the 'competition state'

including the increasing neoliberalization of the housing sector from a 'welfare state' – based on national planning and the goal of equal or balanced spatial development.[60]
According to Carter, Larsen, and Olesen, this represents a considerable shift in the role of the state in housing provision when post-war housing politics "[...] was a question of providing housing for the rising and increasingly urban population, but it was also a reflection of growing wealth and an increasing acceptance of adequate housing as a public responsibility."[61]

## Competitive Trans-Border Region: Economies of Scale and Sectorial Specialization

Economies of scale would function as one of the central logics in developing the competitive state and competitive advantage of the metropolitan city-region of Øresund – as the largest metropole in the Nordic region in competition with other larger North European cities such as Stockholm, Hamburg, and Berlin. This understanding of scale – within which a doubling of regional size, for example, implicates approximately a 15% rise in value added per unit[62] – has been, and continues to be, supported politically at the level of urban governance. Frank Jensen, Copenhagen Lord Mayor, for example, stresses in a 2015 interview that: "Size matters. [...] Together [Denmark's Zealand and Sweden's Skåne] will have 3.8 million people, 11 universities with 150,000 students and many PhDs, so we will come up as an interesting place to locate your European or Scandinavian HQ," says Jensen. "That is what it's all about."[63]
Per Tryding, the vice-president of the South Sweden Chamber of Commerce, buttresses this argument in the same article, suggesting that "A metropolis needs 4–5 million people to be 'Somebody' on the world stage."[64]

Arguments around economies of scale are similarly entwined with the logic of regional sectorial specialization. In the context of the Denmark-Sweden cross-border regional development project, this addresses a range of industries from transportation and logistics, to processed food and business services, to biopharmaceuticals and the medical devices sector. The latter two, collectively framed as the life sciences sector, are viewed as one of, if not the most important sectors for Copenhagen.[65] In the biopharmaceuticals sector, Denmark is ranked 12th in the world in export value, with Copenhagen and the Øresund Region in direct competition with city regions such as Basel, Paris, Rome, and Frankfurt. In the production of medical devices, Denmark is globally ranked 15th, with Copenhagen competing with Freiburg, Paris, and Lyon, etc.[66] According to the OECD Territorial Review Copenhagen, the challenge of attracting international qualified labour/knowledge workers to sectors such as this in particular represents the greatest challenge to the competitive performance of the region and emphasizes the hinge between intra-urban competition and the metric regimes of liveability.[67]

## Medicon Valley

One of the 'flag-bearing' initiatives central to the development of these competitive sectoral clusters has been Øresund's Medicon Valley Alliance, formed "... in 1997 as an EU Interreg II project under the name Medicon Valley Academy."[68] It was initiated by both Lund University and the University of Copenhagen, with the support of the region's major pharmaceutical companies, including Novo Nordisk, Astra-Zeneca, and Lundbeck, as "a platform where Danish and Swedish life science actors could meet."[69] The naming and branding of the Medicon Valley concept emerged with reference to Northern California's ICT clus-

medicon Valley
BIOTECH/PHARMA ORGANISATIONS
WWW.MEDICONVALLEY.COM
Höganäs
Ängelholm
Ängelholm Airport
Helsingborg
Helsingør
Hillerød
Landskrona
Hässleholm
Kristianstad
Kristianstad Airport
Eslöv
Hörby
Sjöbo
Ystad
Lund
Malmö
Malmö Airport
Trelleborg
SWEDEN
SKÅNE
COPENHAGEN
Copenhagen International Airport
Holbæk
Roskilde
Roskilde Airport
Kalundborg
Køge
DENMARK
Sorø
Næstved

ter known as Silicon Valley.[70] This reference is not only based on the clustering of advanced industries within the knowledge/service economy, but also on the geographical and infrastructural comparisons that can be traced back previous decades.[71]

While Medicon Valley continues its programme supporting networking and knowledge-sharing, since the late 2000s the organisation's focus has been largely directed toward "[...] boosting Medicon Valley's ability to attract talent."[72] As a non-profit membership organization of approximately 250 members, collectively employing around 140,000 people, Medicon Valley defines itself as "the region's triple helix and include[s] universities, hospitals, human life science business, regional governments and service providers. We exist to make Medicon Valley an attractive destination for the best talent within life science. We do this because talent is the single most important and valuable resource in a knowledge-intensive sector such as life science. We create value for our members by launching and driving initiatives that put Medicon Valley firmly ahead in the global race for talent."[73] Central to the initiatives to attract talent is the Medicon Valley Beacons project which focuses on the attractiveness of Copenhagen. It employs Copenhagen's position on liveability indexes as a key aspect of this: "In Medicon Valley, you are never far from nature or big city life and you actually get to enjoy it due to the excellent work-life balance that is part of our DNA. You will also access the benefits of the Scandinavian welfare system, which includes free healthcare. Medicon Valley is family friendly and offers a safe and clean environment. In 2014, Copenhagen was named the most livable city in the world for the third time by *Monocle* magazine."[74] A spread of the 2011 Medicon Valley brochure, for example, depicts a woman and child on a Christiania (cargo) bike on the recently opened Bryggebroen bicycle bridge with the former industrial silo building in the background repurposed by MVRDV – popular Dutch architects of the 1990s and 2000s . It is accompanied with the caption: "A Perfect Work/ Life Balance: In Medicon Valley."[75]

## 'Eco-Gentrification' and 'Liveability-Gentrification'

While Copenhagen's urban resurgence since the city's most challenging period in the 1990s is depicted in attractive images like that above; as well as in urban liveability and sustainability rankings; and in the metrics of employment levels, income and population[76] – less positive consequences of these accomplishments have been described by several commentators. Sociologist Roberta Cucca has been one of the more outspoken in her framing of a process of 'Eco-Gentrification' – a term that may be supplemented with that of 'Liveability-Gentrification' – in Copenhagen and other cities at the top of international ranking indexes in sustainability and liveability. According to Ranci and Cucca, the economic resurgence of those cities in recent years has intersected with rising inequality. "Social and economic disparities have increased as consequence of two main trends: the rise of prices for housing, and the increase in the share of highly skilled workers attracted in the most innovative economic sectors. Urban policies have actually contributed to this trend, to the extent they supported both these trends. In Copenhagen, this policy orientation was quite explicit as the local government wanted to attract new functions and new population to the city in order to contrast the previous trend towards impoverishment of the city."[77]

Cucca describes three main contributing factors to the 'Eco-Gentrification' process, related in particular to the conditions of the housing sector in Copenhagen.



Medicon Valley Map (excerpt from Medicon Valley brochure, 2011).

# A PERFECT WORK/ LIFE BALANCE

In Medicon Valley, combining work and family life is easy – and highly appealing to expatriates. Companies offer flexible working hours so you can balance a successful career with a rich, fulfilling family life.

**AN ATTRACTIVE PLACE TO LIVE**

Free schools, free healthcare, easy access to childcare, a safe, healthy environment with a low crime rate and good leisure facilities – these are just some of the benefits of living and working in Medicon Valley.

With a rich heritage and modern facilities, the region's principal cities, Copenhagen and Malmö, offer unique cultural experiences and plenty of opportunities for outdoor activities. What's more, forests and beaches are never more than half an hour's drive away.

International, trendsetting magazine Monocle recently declared Copenhagen the world's second most attractive city to live in. Monocle's 2010 survey, which assessed 40 major cities on criteria such as public transport, education, ease of doing business and hours of sunshine, commended Copenhagen for its compact town planning, good regional transport network and clean, safe environment.

Denmark: trends in Gini Coefficient (disposable income) (Source: OECD).

←
Medicon Valley: a perfect work/life balance (excerpt from Medicon Valley brochure, 2011).

1) *Sale of municipality-owned rental housing*
Under the threat of bankruptcy, the municipality of Copenhagen sold the majority of its rental housing stock in the mid-1990s. This stock was offered to tenants willing to purchase their apartments and establish cooperatives. This resulted in a shift between 1994 and 2004 in which: "[...] the housing stock managed by the public authorities declined from more than 20,000 units to approximately 4,000, while cooperatives increased from approximately 60,000 to more than 80,000 units."[78] According to Cucca, this diminishing of public housing stock corresponds to a general shift towards housing policies concerned with "urban competitiveness and attractiveness [...] supporting real estate developments and requalification projects mainly driven by private interests." A shift favouring "the access of the new affluent social classes to highly priced housing supply. In Copenhagen this policy has been considered a priority in order to re-balance the city's public budget."[79]

2) *Neighbourhood gentrification focus*
Copenhagen's urban redevelopment policies in recent decades have focused more on the "renewal of deprived neighbourhoods than on promoting housing affordability." Cucca links this to the promotion of "home ownership in an attempt to capture high income groups and solve the financial crisis of the local public budget." It is in these terms that "public intervention aimed at renewing deprived neighbourhoods (es. Vesterbro) and at fostering private investments in new development areas (Oresund) worked out as drivers of gentrification and increasing costs of housing."[80] This led to a population change in which "[...] entire neighbourhoods once populated by the working class (the most famous example is the redevelopment of Vesterbro), [were] during the time replaced by populations belonging to middle-class, much less demanding for services and grants offered by the generous Danish welfare system."[81] [82]
The inherent ambiguity and 'mystifications' attached to terms such as 'gentrification' and 'improvement' in the contemporary shift toward entrepreneurial planning is addressed by Eric Clark. "Assumed to be universally positive (who in their right mind would wish to argue against improvement and investment?), critical examination of their historical usage reveals how problematic implications of some kinds of improvements and investments become hidden behind reasonably positive characteristics of other very different improvements and investments."[83] Clark refers to Karl Polanyi's concerns between the terms 'habitation' and 'improvement': "it was improvement on the grandest scale which wrought unprecedented havoc with the habitation of the common people", which in turn suggested the necessity for "legislative acts designed to protect their habitation against the juggernaut, improvement."[84]

3) *Increasing concentration of vulnerable populations within deprived housing areas*
The mechanisms described above – a considerable contraction in the number of affordable rental accommodations in Copenhagen and the higher cost of the remaining private housing stock (generally 40-50% higher at the beginning of this decade) – are linked to a third tendency: "extremely favourable conditions for the growing of segregation processes in the remaining areas of social housing: [...] despite policies focused on fighting against residential concentration."[85] This has been the case as social housing (known as 'almene boliger' in Danish) has become "the only affordable chance to settle in Copenhagen for many immigrants." Contributing factors to these concentrations, according to Cucca, are "the discriminatory attitudes in the cooperative sector, as well as the

Socio-spatial segregation map (excerpt from *Analyse: Segregering i de fire største danske byområder*, Ministeriet for By, Bolig og Landdistrikter, 2014).

MINISTERIET FOR
BY, BOLIG OG
LANDDISTRIKTER

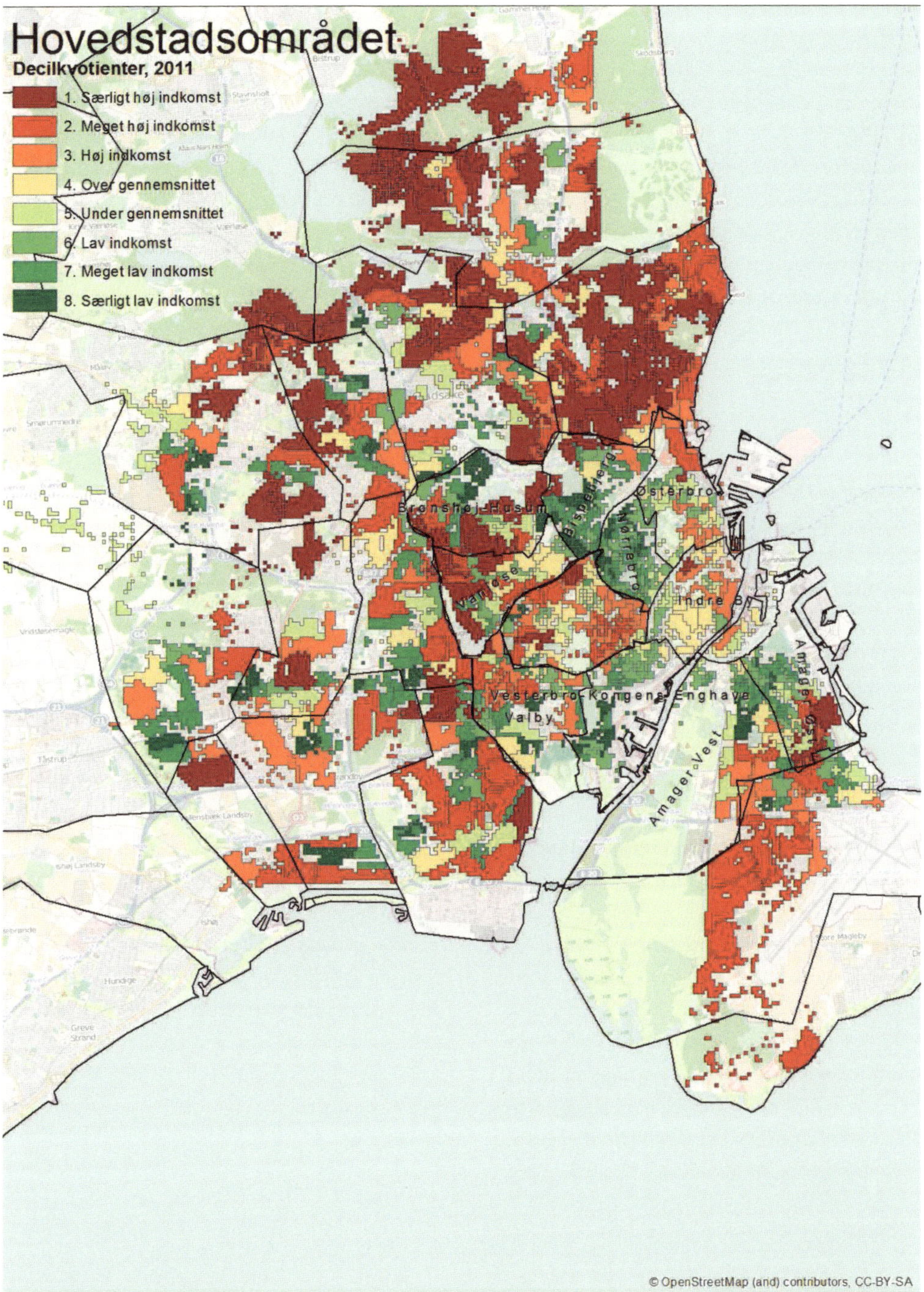


Kilde: Egne beregninger baseret på data fra Danmarks Statistik, Geodatastyrelsen og Rockwool Fondens Forskningsenheds boligområder.

attitude to self-segregation among members of the host society."[86] "This situation of social and economic disadvantage of immigrants is strongly linked to the housing condition, especially in the social housing sector."[87] This tendency has been characterized in terms of a "transition from a universalistic system of social housing to a residual one, where mainly refugees and unemployed are concentrated."[88]

The three factors described here have contributed towards in and out migration at the municipal level, leading to a population substitution within Copenhagen through an outflow of low-middle-income level residents and an inflow of high-income residents.[89] The general increase in spatial segregation of lower income groups extends to the wider development of socio-spatial segregation of both deprived and affluent groups – as documented in recent studies by the former Ministry of Housing, Urban and Rural Affairs.[90] "During the period 1985-2007 an increasing concentration of respectively low income and high income groups has occurred in all four cities [Copenhagen, Aarhus, Odense, and Aalborg]. The capital is most pronounced in relation to segregation among high-income earners."[91]

According to the Danish journalist Lars Olsen, this increased spatial segregation represents a considerable threat to the social coherency and solidarity of Danish urban society. Olsen suggests the consequences of this spatial fragmentation when he asks: "How can we have a social contract in a welfare society, without social contact in the everyday?"[92] Such a challenge is not only a specific Danish condition, but to a certain extent, a European-wide phenomenon resulting from economic liberalism and policy shifts. European cities, as the European Commission has suggested, "[...] have traditionally been characterized by less segregation and less social and spatial polarization compared to, for instance, US cities. This has been especially true for cities in countries with strong welfare systems. However, there are many signs that polarization and segregation are increasing. The economic crisis has further amplified the effects of globalization and the gradual retreat of the welfare state in most European countries."[93]

These processes are evident in recent statistics documenting levels of inequality at country and city level. While Denmark has in the past decades been amongst the countries with the lowest rates of inequality, it is in recent years amongst the countries with the highest increases in inequality. EUROSTAT for example, documents an increase in 5 GINI index points between 2001 and 2009 – placing Denmark in the top two countries for this metric.[94] Euromonitor International ranks Copenhagen a close second to Frankfurt at the top of the rankings for Cities with the Most Severely Widening Income Inequality between 2008 and 2013 with a more than 4.5 point change in that period, compared to the national change in the same period which is less than one point.[95] A 2016 report by Copenhagen Economics addresses the economic implications of inequality taking place in spatial contexts – addressing the condition of increasing socio-spatial segregation in Denmark: "Over the past two decades there has been an increasing breakdown of the Danish population across of income, both between city and countryside and within the cities."[96] Similar mechanisms are described, including "[...] the high housing prices in major cities, making it difficult for low-income groups to afford to live in cities which increases the division between high and low income groups within cities."[97] The report goes further to outline the costs such socio-spatial segregation inflicts on cities including the limits that this imposes on social mobility and economic growth.

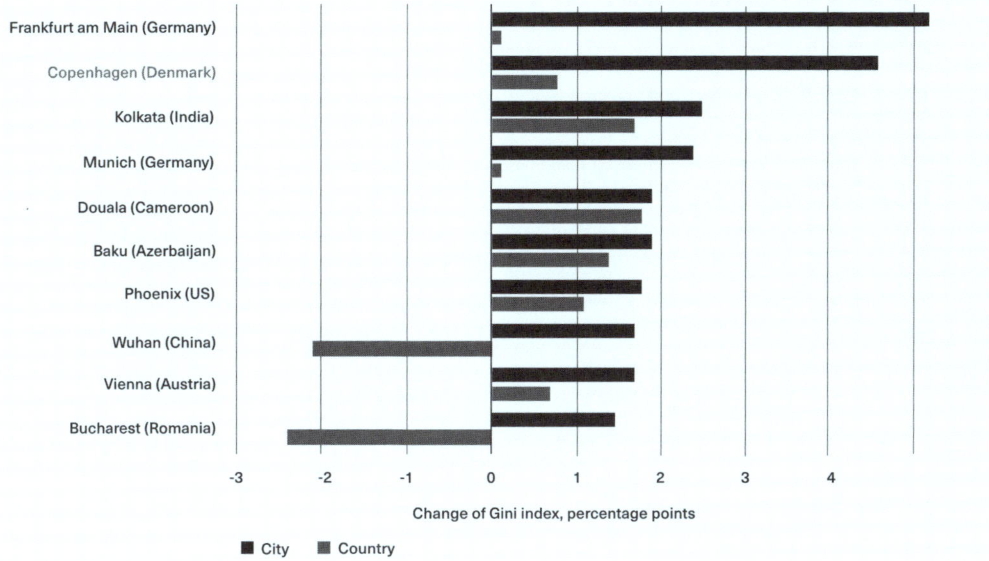


The emerging unevenness related to the contemporary liveable/sustainable city model, and its related mechanisms, presents clear contradictions to the ethos of universal and even distribution of welfare services and resources across the country and within the spaces of the post-war welfare city. Answers to the question of inclusiveness – "liveability, but for whom?"[98] – are perhaps offered then in the figure of the contemporary life sciences knowledge workers represented in the Medicon Valley brochure imagery; or in the imagery of the urban creative class represented in the *Monocle* liveability rankings videos; or most vividly expressed in the singular focus of the Mercer Quality of Living Rankings, directed exclusively towards mobile employees of multinational corporate firms.



Cities with the Most Severely Widening Income Inequality, 2008-2013) (Source: Euromonitor International).

## The Municipality of Copenhagen and the Coherent City

The Municipality of Copenhagen has been keenly aware of these challenges in recent years and has attempted to react to them – most visibly in the 2014 Municipal Planning Strategy entitled *The Coherent City* – which outlines strategies to realize the municipality's political intentions for a socially mixed and socially sustainable city. The document portrays several ambitions including: expanding the housing stock in general to expand supply and affordability; and within areas of expanded housing stock (particularly in areas of resourceful inhabitants) to ensure the presence of 25% social housing, as allowed by the law negotiated in 2014 and passed in 2015.[99] The municipality focuses its neighbourhood regeneration (kvarterløft) projects in districts with deprived housing areas and has supported a range of strategies and investments in deprived housing areas that have been directed against the concentration of vulnerable inhabitants. This has included: job creation in the areas; altered apartment provision rules intended to reduce the proportion of residents on social benefits; and incentives for vulnerable residents to move into other areas.[100]

Other strategies have been employed broadly across the city, including using school district borders as a framework to ensure a greater social mix and integration possibilities.

There are currently considerable structural barriers to the general success of these strategies and measures, however. While the municipality is able to demand 25% social housing provision in new local planning areas, the profit motive of the operating logic of the predominantly municipality-owned enterprise By & Havn, involved in those areas, leads to the remaining 75% of housing being largely directed toward the very high end of the housing market. The challenges of this model are addressed in architect Charles Bessard's recent research presented at the 2016 Venice Biennale.[101] Without a structural shift in the legal organization and economic framework of an organisation like By & Havn, there is limited possibility for alternate outcomes. Furthermore, the municipality is legally restricted in its activities such as offering the sale of municipality-owned land below market rate. According to the Copenhagen-based International Federation for Housing and Planning "[...] since the municipality does not have very cheap housing available, it can be difficult to place disadvantaged people in housing in Copenhagen. [...] it is not possible for the municipality to buy normal housing and become a landlord. The municipality has no legal possibility of giving extra support, and as a municipality, it is not allowed to compete with private investors. It will not be in accordance with the law if the city buys cheap apartments and sublets them to marginalised groups. The municipality can only refer tenants to the social housing organizations and the city doesn't have access to the other typologies (that are also very expensive). In general, the City of Copenhagen is dealing pro-actively with social segregation, but lacks tools to regulate the market and provide cheaper housing."[102]

So while the Ørestad development, as an outcome of 1990s planning and economic reality, has since been criticized for its lack of human scale and lack of spatial and programmatic diversity, Nordhavn has been judged as an effective answer to those specific concerns. However, while it has been heralded in terms of environmental performance, and its high-quality 'liveable' neighbourhood and public space structure – its largely singular social composition has led to criticisms of a 'rich person's ghetto.'[103] It is in this sense that Copenhagen, and the structure of By & Havn may learn from other structural formats of urban planning. For example, the French ZACs, and the alternate German developments such as HafenCity in Hamburg where transport infrastructure funding and urban development funding are intertwined within a single 'break-even' strategy.

## Conclusion

In touching upon conditions and characteristics of Copenhagen as a contemporary urban system under the developing metrics of liveability and sustainability, this article points to those metrics as a component of the general shift from the post-war welfare city logics of managerial planning and universal welfarism. A product of Fordist-Keynesianism predict-and-provide planning, the post-war *welfare city* famously structured according to the 1947 Finger Plan was conceived of as an egalitarian structure for distributing resources and inhabitants across the urban territory, based upon the logics of transport-oriented development. Aimed at urban decongestion and the 'good life in the suburbs' supported by infrastructure for the private car and commuter rail, and informed by the framework of the subdivided 8 + 8 + 8 hour day. In contrast to the welfarist image of the post-war Finger Plan, it is suggested that entrepreneurial planning logics focused upon inter-urban and inter-regional competition have contributed to the production of two distinct but coexisting urban objects and spatial visions. On the one hand the *competitive* city and on the other the *attractive city.*

Emblematized in *Monocle* magazine's presentations of the city, highlighting the attractive 'creative' and historical urban core, the contemporary *attractive city* corresponds to the bounded object of the Copenhagen municipality measured in the *liveable* and *sustainable* city ranking indexes. The image of the *attractive city* in particular is in contemporary terms attached to humanist and welfarist rhetorics, and in the ongoing presentation internationally of the humanist urban focus – one with considerable public investment in: high-quality public space (e.g. Amager Strandpark, Superkilen, etc.); upgraded neighbourhoods (e.g. Vesterbro, Nørrebro); public transport infrastructural upgrades and expansion (e.g. Metro lines with new circle line extension); extensive biking infrastructure (e.g. bicycle parking, superhighways, etc.); expanded cultural infrastructure; but also the ongoing non-spatial achievements of the Danish welfare system including the maintenance of universal free access to education and healthcare, paid maternity leave, relatively low inequality and relatively high social mobility, etc. And it is these spaces, of a contemporary affluent and increasingly socially sorted city, that contrast to the prior post-war welfare city described as the "city of the poor."[104]

In contrast to the *attractive city*, the contemporary *competitive city* may be understood as the territory of the regional urban system that emerged from the fundamental shift in the late 1980s in the approach from equitable managerial planning logics to competitive entrepreneurial ones. In the case of Copenhagen, emblematized by the image of Medicon Valley, this involves the recently infrastructurally connected Øresund Region. It describes a predominantly centrifugal distribution of polycentric industrial/commercial nodes/clusters argued through a focus on economies of scale and aggregation and in terms of regional sectorial business specialization and competition.

Whereas the *attractive city* model, and the urban liveability and sustainability metrics that underwrite it, are placed at the core of city branding and marketing efforts as an *image* to attract international tourists and knowledge workers – the *competitive regional city*, on the other hand, operates at the scale of the functional *content* of the urban system of scalar aggregation. It is in the space or gap between these two cities, and between a range of welfarist and humanist drives, on the one hand, and entrepreneurial and competitive ones, on the other, that the contradictory conditions of this territory become evident. Here it is possible to experience these gaps or spaces, similar to those Carsten Juel-Christiansen would already hint at in 1985 as the architecture of the new city in *Monument and Niche* or those suggested also in the spaces between the schizophrenic sustainable/unsustainable city(ies) referred to by Jens Kvorning; or between what Tom Nielsen has described as the first and third scales of Copenhagen.[105] These spaces are unlikely to figure in the pages of *Monocle* or other ranking index publicity images, but consist of the office/science parks and campuses of the large biotechnical and pharmaceutical concerns; in the big-box logistical spaces of the large commercial chains; in the expansive toll plaza spaces of the Øresund Bridge; in the global carbon footprint of the Maersk shipping company; or in the passport control line-up at the entrance to the trains to Sweden at Copenhagen Airport.

While the ranking view of Copenhagen as an internationally acclaimed Nordic welfare/design utopia – describes a far more attractive, affluent, and environmentally and economically competitive city than that of the 1980s and 1990s – it is, nonetheless, a considerably more unequal city and an increasingly spatially segregated one. One that reinforces the ongoing expansive circumscription of the notion of the welfare city – and the decreasing circumscription of the neoliberal one. Facilitating the 'good life' particularly for those with sufficient resources to live within it; and promoting a common responsible environmental future, particularly for those within the historical boundaries of the compact city. It is this set of conditions that necessitates a more deeply critical stance toward the ranking indexes, their assumptions, their terms of focus, and their influence on the future of our great, dynamic cities.

**Notes**

1 City of Copenhagen (2007).

2 https://www.theguardian.com/cities/2016/may/05/story-cities-copenhagen-denmark-modernist-utopia

3 The *Smart City* functions as the third, and most recently discussed model. It will be suggested here that it represents predominantly a means toward achieving greater liveable and sustainable urban outcomes.

4 The actual and less commonly known name of the 1986 *Brundtland Report* was *Our Common Future*.

5 The context for the introduction of liveability indexes and rankings has been argued as a shift from economic focused, or technical/functional-optimization approaches to the city, to ones incorporating subjective well-being and more 'humanistic' parameters and considerations. See for example: http://www.livablecities.org/blog/value-rankings-and-meaning-livability

6 https://monocle.com/film/affairs/most-liveable-city-copenhagen/

7 https://www.theguardian.com/cities/2015/apr/02/where-is-the-worlds-greenest-city-ecofriendly

8 http://ec.europa.eu/environment/europeangreencapital/winning-cities/2014-copenhagen/index.html

9 http://kk.sites.itera.dk/apps/kk_pub2/pdf/674_CFbnhMePZr.pdf.

10 J. Greenfield: "Danish History: How Copenhagen became bike-friendly again", http://gridchicago.com/2012/danish-history-how-copenhagen-became-bike-friendly-again.

11 http://www.spiegel.de/international/europe/europe-s-coolest-cities-copenhagen-cool-cultural-and-creative-a-502512.html.

12 http://www.treehugger.com/slideshows/cars/best-of-green-cars-transportation/page/2/#slide-top

13 R. Cervero: *Transit-oriented Development in the United States: Experiences, Challenges, and Prospects* (2004), p. 61.

14 H.T. Andersen and L. Winther: "Crisis in the Resurgent City? The Rise of Copenhagen" (2010), p. 693.

15 R. Rojas: The Measurement of Quality of Life: Conceptualization Comes First. A Four-Qualities-of Life Conceptual Framework and an Illustration to Latin America. ISQOLS Conference: Measures and goals for the progress of societies, Florence (2009), p. 16.

16 See for example: N. Ennis: "City Ranking Indices – Handle With Care", (July 2011); and F. Csaba and B. Stöber: *Copenhagen is hot, Denmark is not: On the Authority and the Role of Place Branding Image Rankings* (2011), p. 13.

17 See for example: Ennis (July 2011), op.cit.; and F. Csaba and B. Stöber: *Copenhagen is hot, Denmark is not: On the Authority and the Role of Place Branding Image Rankings* (2011), p. 13.

18 B. Stöber: "Place Branding – How the Private Creates the Public" (2008), p. 179.

19 Siemens and The Economist Intelligence Unit: *The Green City Index* (2012), p. 4.

20 The report describes several features: "The city finishes among the top five for all categories, except one – waste and land use. Copenhagen is also very ambitious on limiting carbon emissions. In 2009 it set a target to become CO2 neutral by 2025, which if met would make it the first large carbon-neutral city in the world. The city aims to achieve 10% of its CO2 reductions through construction and renovation projects, with plans to upgrade all municipal buildings to the highest standards for energy efficiency. Copenhagen also has an extensive public transport system, including a metro system, suburban railway and bus networks, and virtually all residents live within 350 metres of public transport." Economist Intelligence Unit "The Green City Index", Siemens (2012), pp. 12-14. The report continues: "In addition, the Danish capital aims to become the 'world's best cycle city' by raising the share of residents who regularly use a bicycle to commute from 36% in 2009 to 50% by 2015. The city has outstanding green land use policies as well. Between 2000 and 2009, 80% of new developments were built on brownfield sites."

21 Index categories: $CO_2$ emissions; energy; buildings; transportation; water; air quality; waste and land use; and environmental governance. Siemens own business sectors: Energy; Building Technology; Mobility; Energy from Waste; Water Technologies; Air Pollution Technology; Safety Management Systems. Siemens, Press Release "Copenhagen – The Greenest Major City in Europe" (2009), p. 1.

22 The 2008 report describes the city in the following terms: "Good looks, brains, perfect proportions, a sunny disposition and a sense of humour are always a winning combination – no matter what the competition. In the urban quality of life stakes a mix of all these, plus a firm grasp of environmental issues, regional transport and a variety of subjective elements (food culture, housing design, retail mix and quality of cocktails) all helped pull the city up from second place last year to global leader for 2008. Copenhagen treats residents to a lifestyle that's hard to match: manageable scale, a clean harbour for brisk dips and abundant green space. The development of the Metro system and a commitment to cycling makes urban navigation swift and seamless. Some recent residential developments have created neighbourhoods lacking the street life that makes the rest of the city tick but it appears that developers have learnt from these mistakes. We'd happily move house if the right offer came along." *Monocle*, "The World's Top 25 Most Liveable Cities – 2008" (2008), p. 19.

23 *Monocle*, "The World's Top 25 Most Liveable Cities – 2008" (2008), p. 18. These particular perspectives informing the construction of the index bring to the foreground the contested nature of sustainability, and sustainable urbanism as socially constructed terms and concepts. Terms and concepts defined in this context according to what Simon Guy and Graham Farmer would describe as a dominant techno-rational orthodoxy of the *eco-technical* logic of sustainability (see S. Guy and G. Farmer: "Reinterpreting Sustainable Architecture: The Place of Technology" (February 2001), pp. 140-48) – in contrast to other competing logics that define how sustainability is conceptualized or constructed such as the eco-social, or eco-political, or the eco-cultural and eco-aesthetic aspects that are almost entirely absent from the Siemens Green City Index. (See for example: Guy and Farmer (February 2001), op.cit., p. 141; or P. Pyla: "Counter-Histories of Sustainability" (December 2008), pp. 14-17).

24 S. Jacob: "Cities that score well barely qualify as cities" (2014).

25 "Magazine's Denmark tribute paid for by Ministry: DKK 700,000 for positive coverage to modernise the Danish 'brand'." http://www.b.dk/english/magazine-s-denmark-tribute-paid-for-by-ministry

26 On the other hand, the influence of particular index metrics can also affect positive pressure for transformation. This is evident for example with the dropping of Copenhagen's status from the top ranked city in 2014, to tenth place in 2015, due to the introduction of 22 new metrics, including affordable housing as a component of the index. According to Brulé "The most dramatic result of this year's survey is that Copenhagen, which won in both 2013 and 2014, dropped down to the bottom of the top 10. As our correspondent in Copenhagen says: the city is just too expensive," "We have added 22 new ranking criteria to the study, including housing and living expenses. They include the price of a three-room house, a cup of coffee, a glass of wine and a decent lunch." *Monocle* (2015).

27 According to Statistics Denmark (2012-update), the population of the Municipality of Copenhagen is 565,253; and the population of the urban area (also known as Greater Copenhagen) is: 1,307,469 inhabitants. The population of the Copenhagen Metropolitan Area according to the OECD's Territorial Review (2009) is 2,390,000 inhabitants.

28 Kvorning quoted in O. Lowenstein: "A green reckoning" (2009).

29 "We will become the world's most liveable city: a sustainable city with urban space inviting people to a unique and varied urban life. We will become a metropolis for people." Copenhagen Municipality, *A Metropolis for People* (2009), p. 1.
30 City of Copenhagen (2014).
31 "Denmark has decided to lead the transition to a Green Growth Economy and aims to be independent of fossil fuels by 2050. As the official green brand for Denmark, State of Green gathers all leading players in the fields of energy, climate, water and environment and fosters relations with international stakeholders interested in learning from the Danish experience", p. 55.
32 City of Copenhagen (2007).
33 City of Copenhagen (2015).
34 "The City of Copenhagen will give businesses an even better chance to utilise the commercial potential of Copenhagen's continuous investments in green, healthy and creative solutions. The City of Copenhagen will enter into more partnerships with businesses and knowledge institutions about the development, testing and implementation of innovative solutions to support Copenhagen becoming an even more liveable and green city. This concerns collaborations about climate- and environmental solutions, next generation welfare technology and new solutions to develop city spaces and city culture to the residents' benefit. The City of Copenhagen will do its best to ensure that these future city solutions become known to the world, thus increasing the export potential for the region's businesses." p. 2.
35 http://www.realdania.org/grants-and-projects/bloxhub/nyheder/pm-nu-aabner-bloxhub_03062016
36 T. Nielsen: "Exporting Humanist Architecture" (2016).
37 See for example: L. Winther and H.K. Hansen: "The Economic Geographies of City-Regions: Remarks from Copenhagen" (2007:02).
38 D. Harvey: "From Managerialism to Entrepreneurialism: The Transformation in Urban Governance in Late Capitalism" (1989), pp. 3-17.
39 Peck, J.: "Entrepreneurial urbanism: between uncommon sense and dull compulsion" (2014), pp. 396-401.
40 R. Cucca: Paper presented at the RC21 International Conference on "The Ideal City: between myth and reality. Representations, policies, contradictions and challenges for tomorrow's urban life", Urbino (Italy), 27-29 August 2015, pp. 4-5.
41 D. Harvey: "The Global and the Local: D. Harvey, Spaces of Global Capitalism: Towards a Theory of Uneven Geographical Development" (2006), p. 25.
42 Cucca (2015), op.cit., pp. 4-5.
43 Anthropologist Julian Brash offers a similar description of neoliberal urban planning approaches and techniques including: "...the privatisation of public services and public space, the public subsidization of downtown commercial development and luxury housing, and heavy-handed approaches to social control and policing, as well as shifts in urban culture and urban imaginaries that highlight the importance of consumption, 'creativity,' and entrepreneurialism."
44 D. Harvey, *A Brief History of Neoliberalism* (2005). See also Clark, p. 392.
45 Ibid., p. 113.
46 Ibid., p. 115.
47 Peck (2014), op.cit., pp. 396-401.
48 E. Clark: "Good urban governance: making rent gap theory, not true" (2014), p. 392.
49 O.B. Jensen and I. Jørgensen: "Danish Planning: The Long Shadow of Europe", *Built Environment (1978-)*, (2000), p. 37.
50 H. Carter, Larsen, H.G., & Olesen, K.A.: "Planning Palimpsest: Neoliberal Planning in a Welfare State Tradition" (2015), p. 9.
51 Ibid., p. 13.
52 Ibid., p. 13.
53 S. Majoor: *Disconnected innovations: new urbanity in large-scale development projects: Zuidas Amsterdam, Orestad Copenhagen and Forum Barcelona* (2008), p. 123.
54 Ibid., p. 123.
55 J. Andersen and G. Hovgård: "Welfare and Urban Planning in transition – A Copenhagen Case Study", Research Paper (2003), p. 39. Cited in Majoor (2008), op.cit., p. 123.
56 Majoor (2008), op.cit., p. 123.
57 Ibid., p. 128.
58 Ibid., p. 128.
59 Ibid., p. 128.
60 J.H. Petersen, Petersen, K. & Christensen, N.F. (eds.): *Dansk velfærdshistorie* [Danish Welfare History]. (2011).
61 Carter, Larsen & Olesen (2015), op.cit., p. 9.
62 Copenhagen University Prof. Emeritus Christian Wichmann Matthiessen, interview with author, 16 October, 2016.
63 D. Crouch: "Denmark wants to rebrand part of Sweden as 'Greater Copenhagen'" (2015).
64 Ibid.
65 According to the Danish Ministry of Foreign Affairs, Life sciences is one of seven key industries that Denmark is focusing on developing in the coming years (others include cleantech, creative industries, financial, food, ICT, and transport and logistics.)
66 OECD Territorial Review Copenhagen (2009).
67 Ibid.
68 http://mva.org/about-mva/mvas-history/
69 Ibid.
70 Reinhold Martin has referred to Silicon Valley as a kind of urban 'phantasm', "something like a valley stretching west of the San Francisco Bay between two ridges in Northern California and running southward from San Francisco's hilly streets, through the campuses – academic, military

and industrial [...]." R. Martin and K. Baxi: *Multi-National City: Architectural Itineraries* (2007) p. 19.

**71** A 1959 map drawing in the Swedish Källa labeled as "Detta är Nordens San Francisco" or "The San Francisco of the North" showing a future Øresund bridge and an Elsinore-Hälsingborg bridge connecting the bi-nation area. Källa (1959.11.30).

**72** http://mva.org/about-mva/mvas-history/

**73** Ibid.

**74** Medicon Valley Alliance, 'Access Medicon Valley' (2015), p. 16. http://mva.org/wp-content/uploads/2015/01/Access-Medicon-Valley.pdf

**75** The text continues: "...combining work and family life is easy – and highly appealing to expatriates. Companies offer flexible working hours so you can balance a successful career with a rich, fulfilling family life. An Attractive Place To Live: Free schools, free healthcare, easy access to childcare, a safe, healthy environment with a low crime rate and good leisure facilities – these are just some of the benefits of living and working in Medicon Valley. With a rich heritage and modern facilities, the region's principal cities, Copenhagen and Malmö, offer unique cultural experiences and plenty of opportunities for outdoor activities. What's more, forests and beaches are never more than half an hour's drive away. International, trendsetting magazine *Monocle* recently declared Copenhagen the world's second most attractive city to live in. *Monocle*'s 2010 survey, which assessed 40 major cities on criteria such as public transport, education, ease of doing business and hours of sunshine, commended Copenhagen for its compact town planning, good regional transport network and clean, safe environment." Copenhagen Capacity/Invest in Skåne, *Medicon Valley* (2011), p. 10.

**76** See for example: Andersen and Winthur: Crisis in the Resurgent City? The Rise of Copenhagen (2010).

**77** C. Ranci og Cucca R:: "(Un)equal cities in Europe: the challenge of post-industrial transition in times of austerity". Paper presented at the RC21 International Conference on "The Ideal City: between myth and reality. Representations, policies, contradictions and challenges for tomorrow's urban life", Urbino (Italy), 27-29 August 2015, p. 31.

**78** R. Cucca: *Stigmatized, peripheral and residual: patterns of spatial segregation among recent immigrants in Copenhagen, Toronto and Milan* (2011), pp. 6-7.

**79** C. Ranci and R. Cucca: "(Un)equal cities in Europe: the challenge of post-industrial transition in times of austerity" Paper presented at the RC21 International Conference on "The Ideal City: between myth and reality. Representations, policies, contradictions and challenges for tomorrow's urban life", Urbino (Italy), 27-29 August 2015, p. 25.

**80** R. Cucca: Paper presented at the RC21 International Conference on "The Ideal City: between myth and reality. Representations, policies, contradictions and challenges for tomorrow's urban life", Urbino (Italy), 27-29 August 2015, p. 23.

**81** Cucca (2011), op.cit., pp. 6-7.

**82** "Additionally, in many renewal projects non-profit co-operatives were prevented to build low cost apartments in order to avoid providing housing for the less affluent. This policy has successfully attracted new high income and highly skilled workers to Copenhagen, but has also increased dualization in the housing market. In the last years local authorities have elaborated a new Social housing Masterplan [...] The houses should have been located on publicly owned land in order to reduce the total costs. However, sale under market price of publicly owned properties has been decided illegal by the government and consequently the plan could not start so far." Ranci C., Cucca R.: "(Un)equal cities in Europe: the challenge of post-industrial transition in times of austerity". Paper presented at the RC21 International Conference on "The Ideal City: between myth and reality. Representations, policies, contradictions and challenges for tomorrow's urban life", Urbino (Italy), 27-29 August 2015, p. 22-23.

**83** Clark (2014), op.cit., p. 393.

**84** Karl Polanyi quoted in ibid.

**85** Cucca (2011), op.cit., pp. 6-7. The term 'social housing' refers here to the Danish 'almene boliger.'

**86** Cucca (2011), op.cit., pp. 6-7.

**87** Ibid, pp. 6-7.

**88** Kristiansen (2007) og Skifter Andersen (2010) referred to by Cucca (2011), op.cit., pp. 6-7.

**89** Ibid, pp. 6-7.

**90** Ministeriet for By, Bolig og Landdistrikter 17. marts 2014 *Analyse: Segregering i de fire største danske byområder*, p. 5 [author's translation].

**91** Ibid.: "In terms of education, we see in the period 1985-2003 that residents of Copenhagen, Aarhus and Odense generally live more in areas according to their level of education than in the past [...]."

**92** Presentation at Dansk Byplanlaboratorium's Annual General Meeting, Malmø October 6, 2016.

**93** European Commission Report 2011, 22 quoted in Cucca (2015), op.cit., p. 23.

**94** See for example: J.S. Juul: "Rutsjetur: Danmark er ikke længere Europas mest lige land, Arbejderbevægelsens Erhvervsråd" (2011). For Eurostat data see: http://ec.europa.eu/eurostat

**95** U. Saltenyte: "Growing Income Disparities Challenge Business in Both Developed and Developing Cities", Euromonitor International, 2014, http://blog.euromonitor.com/2014/02/growing-income-disparities-challenge-business-in-both-developed-and-developing-cities.html

**96** Copenhagen Economics: *Billige boliger i storbyerne – bidrag til vækst og velstand* (Affordable housing in the large cities – contributes to growth and prosperity), 2016, p. 26.

**97** Ibid, p. 26.

**98** Discussed for example by architect Charles Bessard at In-Between Economies LiveabilityMAX debate 27 January 2016; or at IFHP Nordic Housing Lab's "Nordic Liveable Cities. For whom? Exploring spatial segregation and housing policies in the Nordic countries" http://www.ifhp.org/event/ifhp-nordic-housing-lab

**99** L 89. Forslag til lov om ændring af lov om planlægning og lov om almene boliger m.v. http://www.ft.dk/samling/20141/lovforslag/l89/index.htm

**100** R. Cucca: *Stigmatized, peripheral and residual: patterns of spatial segregation among recent immigrants in Copenhagen, Toronto and Milan* (2011), pp. 6-7.

**101** See Charles Bessard interview in B. B. Jensen and K. Weiss (eds.): *Art of Many* (2016).

**102** International Federation for Housing and Planning, *Nordic Livable Cities Lab*, 2015, pp. 18-19. (http://www.ifhp.org/sites/default/files/staff/IFHP_ones_NordicLab_040116.pdf) "Since marginalised groups often have a limited income as well as limits on housing allowances, it can be very difficult to find housing for groups such as homeless people because of the general price level and the limited tools used to regulate the market and housing situation. Building costs are very high and rent costs cannot meet the social demand. That means that there are many structural barriers."

**103** See for example: Karsten Ifversen, architecture editor for the newspaper *Politiken*: "Nordhavn is a new ghetto for the wealthy: It can be difficult to understand how a social democratic city government can afford such a socially skewed urban profile to grow." *Politiken*, March 10, 2017. http://politiken.dk/kultur/arkitektur/art5867741/Nordhavn-er-en-ny-ghetto-for-velhavere.

**104** Jens Martin Skibsted interviewed in *Monocle*, 0.34 *Monocle* Issue 65 2013. Skibsted continues: "This was changed by systematically improving conditions for families with kids. They used to move to suburbia, but with the new kid-friendly environment they stayed and shared their riches as they grew older. With more money comes more culture, and a more attractive environment."

**105** T. Nielsen: "The Sustainable City Region" (2017) (forthcoming at time of publication).

**Literature**


- Andersen, H.T., & Winther, L.: "Crisis in the Resurgent City? The Rise of Copenhagen", in *International Journal of Urban and Regional Research*, Volume 34.3: 693–700 2010
- Andersen, J., & Hovgård, G.: Welfare and Urban Planning in transition – A Copenhagen Case Study, Research Paper no. 8/03, Roskilde University 2003.
- Andersen, J., & Pløger, J.: *The Dualism of Urban Governance in Denmark, European Planning Studies*, 15:10 2007, pp. 1349-1367.
- Carter, H., Larsen, H.G., & Olesen, K.A.: "Planning Palimpsest: Neoliberal Planning in a Welfare State Tradition", Refereed Article No. 58, June 2015, *European Journal of Spatial Development.*
- City of Copenhagen: *A Metropolis for People*, 2009.
- Clark, E.: "Good urban governance: making rent gap theory, not true", *Geografiska Annaler*: Series B, Human Geography 96 (4): 392–395. 2014, p. 392.
- Copenhagen Economics: *Billige boliger i storbyerne – bidrag til vækst og velstand* (Affordable housing in the large cities – contributes to growth and prosperity) 2016.
- Crouch, D.: "Denmark wants to rebrand part of Sweden as 'Greater Copenhagen'", *The Guardian*, 5 March, 2015.
- Csaba, F. and Stöber, B.: *Copenhagen is hot, Denmark is not: On the Authority and the Role of Place Branding Image Rankings* (Unpublished working paper: Copenhagen Business School, 2011), p. 13.
- Cucca, R.: *Stigmatized, peripheral and residual: patterns of spatial segregation among recent immigrants in Copenhagen, Toronto and Milan.* Cities Centre – University of Toronto, Lunch and Learn Series, Sept 7, 2011.
- Cucca, R.: Paper presented at the RC21 International Conference on "The Ideal City: between myth and reality. Representations, policies, contradictions and challenges for tomorrow's urban life", Urbino (Italy) 27-29 August, 2015.
- Cucca, R.: "The Unexpected Consequences of Sustainability: Green Cities Between Innovation and Ecogentrification", *Sociologica,* 2/2012.
- Ennis, N.: "City Ranking Indices – Handle with Care", *GLA Economics Current Issues Note* 31 (July 2011).
- Graaf, R. de: "Look past the liveability ranks", *The Financial Times*, April 6, 2010.
- Guy, S. and Farmer, G.: "Reinterpreting Sustainable Architecture: The Place of Technology", *Journal of Architectural Education* 54/2 (February 2001), pp. 140-48.
- Harvey, D.: "From Managerialism to Entrepreneurialism: The Transformation in Urban Governance in Late Capitalism", *Geografiska Annaler. Series B, Human Geography,* Vol. 71, No. 1, The Roots of Geographical Change: 1973 to the Present, 1989, pp. 3-17.
- Harvey, D.: *A Brief History of Neoliberalism,* Verso, 2005.

- Harvey D.: The Global and the Local: in David Harvey, Spaces of Global Capitalism: Towards a Theory of Uneven Geographical Development. London and New York: Verso, 2006.
- https://www.dezeen.com/2014/09/04/sam-jacob-opinion-city-rankings-flawed-way-to-judge-best-cities-in-the-world/
- Jensen, O.B. and Jørgensen, I.: "Danish Planning: The Long Shadow of Europe", *Built Environment (1978-)*, Vol. 26, No. 1, Nordic Planning meets Europe 2000.
- Juul, J. S.: *Rutsjetur: Danmark er ikke længere Europas mest lige land*, Arbejderbevægelsens Erhvervsråd, 2011. For Eurostat data see: http://ec.europa.eu/eurostat.
- Lowenstein, O.: "A green reckoning", *Financial Times*, December 12, 2009.
- Majoor, S.: *Disconnected innovations: new urbanity in large-scale development projects: Zuidas Amsterdam, Orestad Copenhagen and Forum Barcelona*, Eburon Uitgeverij; 01 edition 2008.
- Ministeriet for By, Bolig og Landdistrikter, 17. marts 2014: *Analyse: Segregering i de fire største danske byområder.*
- Nielsen, T.: "Exporting Humanist Architecture" in B.B. Jensen and Weiss, K. (eds.) *Art of Many.* The Danish Architectural Press, 2016.
- OECD Territorial Review Copenhagen 2009.
- Pyla, P.: "Counter-Histories of Sustainability", *Volume*, 18 (December 2008), pp. 14-17.
- Peck, J.: "Entrepreneurial urbanism: between uncommon sense and dull compulsion", *Geografiska Annaler*: Series B, Human Geography 96 (4), 2014, pp. 396-401.
- Petersen, J.H., Petersen, K., & Christensen, N.F. (eds.): *Dansk velfærdshistorie* [Danish Welfare History]. Volume 2. Odense: University Press of Southern Denmark, 2011.
- Ranci, C., & Cucca R.: "(Un)equal cities in Europe: the challenge of post-industrial transition in times of austerity", paper presented at the RC21 International Conference on "The Ideal City: between myth and reality. Representations, policies, contradictions and challenges for tomorrow's urban life", Urbino (Italy), 27-29 August 2015.
- Saltenyte, U.: *Growing Income Disparities Challenge Business in Both Developed and Developing Cities, Euromonitor International*, 2014, http://blog.euromonitor.com/2014/02/growing-income-disparities-challenge-business-in-both-developed-and-developing-cities.html.
- Stöber, B.: "Place Branding – How the Private creates the Public" in Hansen, H.K. and Salskov-Iversen, D. (eds.): *Critical Perspectives on Private Authority in Global Politics.* Palgrave: Macmillan 2008.
- Winther, L., and Hansen, H.K.: *The Economic Geographies of City-Regions: Remarks from Copenhagen*, TAPAS Working Paper 2007:02.

Kirsten Marie Raahauge

# Towards the Outskirts

## Welfare Spaces in Tønder

**The provinces have undergone great changes. These changes are connected with the spatial and material conditions that influence the everyday lives of many people, and also on how these areas are understood. It is as if the distinctive landscapes and towns that once constituted the provinces have now come to be parts of a more generic and repetitive form, where it is becoming increasingly difficult to tell the differences between the places. This movement is taking place while, at the same time, some of the provinces have changed their name to 'outskirts'.**

The provinces' changes is a global phenomenon; both architectural competitions and social media are focusing on *shrinking cities* and *abandoned cities*. These implosions happen at the same time as *megapolises* are growing, and the *blue bananas* of European growth areas are singled out,[1] and are being reflected in the *rotten banana* of the Danish debate.

During the development of the welfare state in the 1960s and 1970s,[2] the Danish provincial towns were provided with a number of institutions, as part of the efforts to extend welfare to the whole country.[3] These institutions constituted important spatial and physical aspects of welfare, especially in the form of a more expanded infrastructure and a distribution of hospitals and schools, along with a wave of new town halls,[4] and sports centres and swimming baths. In recent years, several of these functions have been combined in larger units like 'super hospitals' and district-administration halls, which have left large parts of the provinces in a new situation.

With Tønder as the paradigmatic example, the change from provincial town to outskirt town will, in what follows, be contemplated from a physical-spatial perspective, which will come to touch upon institutions[5] and infrastructure, and their role in Tønder's outskirting.[6] The overriding relationship between centre and outskirts will also be considered.

## Tønder, from centre to outskirts

Tønder is situated in the marshland, by the German border, and close to the North Sea. The city became a borough in 1243. For centuries thereafter, it was a strategically important city.[7] The Tønder marshland is criss-crossed by a network of dikes that define the area. They were constructed as protection from flooding and storm surges. The protruding dike, from 1981, now ensures the Tønder marshland against flooding.[8]

The city of Tønder is man-made, and so is the landscape: not only has it been cultivated, it has also been reclaimed by human beings. Previously, there was sea; now it has become marshland. The marshland has always been arable land; in 2014 another dimension was added. The Wadden Sea National Park has been added onto UNESCO's list of World Heritage Sites. The marshlands have accordingly become an enormous museum piece, and a landscape of experience, in addition to a landscape of farming.

Tønder is well defined. It is a 'place', or a 'locale', in the sense that Frederik Stjernfelt employs this term in his article 'Sted, gade, plads. En naiv teori om byen' [Locale, street, square – a naïve theory of the city] (1996/2008), where he presents a phenomenological-semiotic theory of the city. Stjernfelt proposes 'the locale' as the destination, which somebody is drawn towards – via the street's course and through the square's options. The typical 'locale' is the ultimate goal, and it is often associated with a certain cosiness (like the bodega) or homeliness (like home).[9] Tønder's quality of being a place is accentuated by the fact that the city possesses a specific architectural style and a demarcated border between the city and the countryside. One can even speak of a certain atmosphere that may be connected to the architecture, the demarcated border, the proximity to the landscape, or something else, such as tourism, the inhabitants, their way of speaking, or the many disparate affiliations that are flourishing among them, most of whom are Danish-minded, while some are German-minded,[10] many are South Jutlanders, while still others have 'come up from the old country.' For a long time, Tønder was a centre for its hinterland, as the only borough in the region, famed for making and selling lace, for silversmith's work, for producing sepulchral tablets and other kinds of wood cuts, and for its af-

Braunius' map of Tønder from the end of the 1500s. It comes from *All Kinds of Cities* (in Latin *Civitates Orbis Terrarum*), describing cities around the world, but mostly European cities. The book contained descriptions, panoramas or maps of approx. 130 cities. The pictures were made as engravings. *From All Kinds of Cities* (*Civitates Orbis Terrarum*) from 1572 to 1617. Museum Sønderjylland.

Panorama of Tønder.
All photos by the author 2016.
→
H-City.
Illustration by Claus Peder Pedersen and Claudia Carbone.

fluent merchants and markets, where oxen were bought and sold.[11]

Over the years, Tønder has served as an infrastructural hub for roads, later on, for railroads, and up until the 1500s, there was a port here. More curiously, this was a base for German Zeppelin traffic during the First World War.[12] Denmark's most extensive railway line, and later on, the nation's motorway network, has the shape of an 'H', which conjoins the largest cities in Denmark. A position inside or outside the 'H-city'[13] has become important when it comes to the cities' respective developments. This strip city runs from Aalborg in the north through Aarhus and the Triangle Region (Fredericia, Kolding and Middelfart), to Padborg in the south, on the western vertical axis; and from Helsingør in the north through Copenhagen to Køge in the south, on the eastern vertical axis. Running transversely to these axes the 'H''s horizontal central axis extends from Esbjerg in the west, and runs through the Triangle Region and Odense, to Copenhagen in the east.

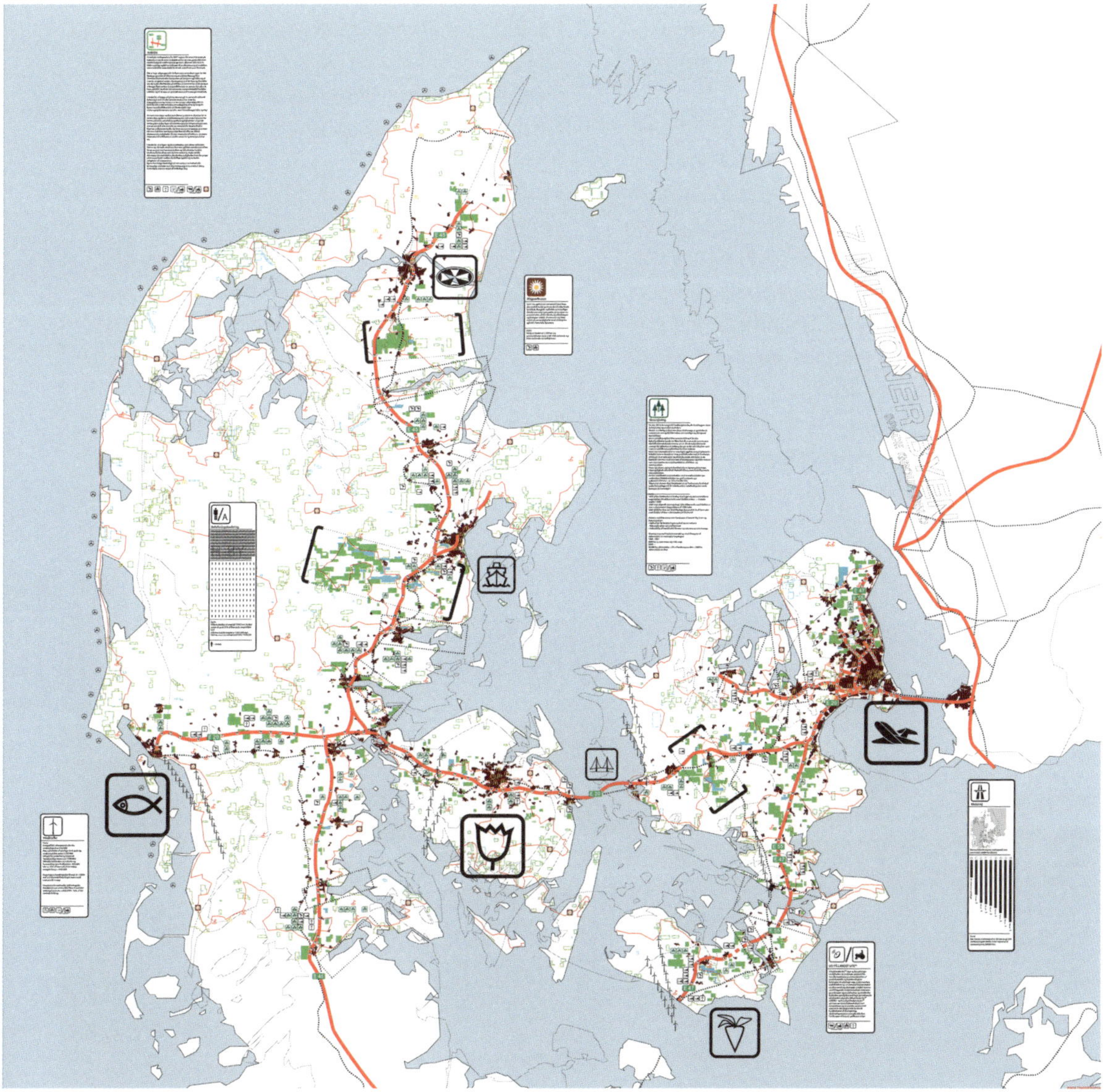

Placed outside 'the H-city', Tønder has been cut off: now it is situated in the outskirts.[14] It is odd that a small country like Denmark would be affected by such a syndrome: places become outskirts merely by virtue of being outside of the Capital Region or outside 'the H-city'. It may seem ridiculous to worry about such a brief interval of travelling time, when viewed from the perspective of the United States, Sweden or Germany; this point is also made frequently. This disproportionate relation between the small nation and the powerful impact of the outskirting leads to the question of how small a place can be and still have a centre and outskirts.[15] The short travelling time, which feels like a long time in Denmark, evinces the global impact on the Danish micro-level.

Tønder has undergone a profusion of calamities: wars, due to the city's strategically important placement in Schleswig, where counts, dukes and kings from the south and the north were fighting over power; conflagrations, exacerbated by the town's narrow streets; and worst of all, storm surges, when the dikes would burst and the sea would wash in over the marshlands and the city. The most engulfing storm surge of all was *Grote Mandränke* in 1362, where many thousands, maybe even hundreds of thousands, of people drowned along the North Frisian coast. Rungholt was the name of a large town situated on the Hallig Strand, it was swallowed up by the sea during a storm surge. Legend has it that, when there is clear weather, you can hear Rungholt's church bell ringing. Between catastrophes, Tønder has enjoyed extended periods of prosperity.[16] Only 20 years ago, the city was lively, but now it has become somewhat still, on the streets, in any event. There are just as many people living in the city as there were 20 years ago, about 8,000, but they are not so visible anymore. Among other things, this is related to the fact that the population has aged. Moreover, the institutions now closed used to inspire people to move around from place to place. Recently, new life has come to the city: in the old dormitories are now living youngsters and children who have come to Denmark unaccompanied, as refugees. They can be seen riding bicycles to and from school and hanging out in the town after school.

From the reunification in 1920 and until the 1990s, Tønder, like other provincial cities, prospered from many institutions and a vibrant urban life. Tønder, as a matter of fact, was especially privileged because it was a border town being Danicized[17] and displayed as specifically Danish. However, with the Schengen Agreement, which Denmark ratified in 1996, the city lost this aspect of its identity. Suddenly, the international boundaries were not going to be marked out – now they were supposed to be crossed, and the city to be

integrated into a larger project. In the years after the structural reform in 2007, the city, like so many others, was deprived of many of its institutions.

Professor Nils Gunder Hansen is a Tønder boy. In his memoirs, *Lille dreng med rejseskrivemaskine* [Little boy with portable typewriter] (2011), he calls attention to the city's transformation from being 'a world in itself' to being 'outskirts'[18] and to how many aspects of life this change has affected, especially when it comes to the change from multiplicity to sameness, from vivacity to stagnation. I am a Tønder girl. I have been watching the city for many years, both as a resident and as a visitor, and I can recognize much of what Hansen writes. The present article's empirical material stems from the *native knowledge* I possess, but it also makes use of written sources pertinent to Tønder, along with conversations I have had with Tønder-dwellers and a body of material that students from the Royal Danish Academy of Fine Arts, Schools of Architecture, Design and Conservation (KADK), have collected and transformed into proposals as part of a project, carried out in 2014, on Tønder, as a paradigmatic example of outskirts.

## Speed and outskirts

Contrary to the concept of province, the concept of *the outskirts* is essentially spatial.[19] Moreover, novel and mutually incompatible ways of understanding the spatial, of which outskirting forms a part, are emerging.

On the one hand, the understanding of space and time is undergoing change because of the speed, with which we can move from place to place. The concept of *timespace compression* was put forth by the geographer David Harvey (1990) and was later employed by the sociologist Mark Gottdiener (2001), in an attempt to explain the uncomfortable effects it has on people when they travel at high speeds in aeroplanes over large distances without being able to keep up with the speed and without having any chance to readjust themselves to the new places as quickly as is required before having to leave again. The urbanist Paul Virilio's notion of *dromology* (see for example 1993) has for several decades been a key to understanding such movements, since it calls attention to speed's influence on developments in all registers: one of the overriding effects of the accelerating speeds is that the world seems to be shrinking. The concrete movement from place to place transpires with greater speed; virtual approaches to the concrete world also make it faster and easier to reach even remote places. Furthermore, virtual and concrete spaces can be combined and can even mediate one another in novel ways. In contemporary architecture and planning, the effect of these mediations is clear to see when buildings are presented from their best angle when viewed from an aeroplane or through the virtual representation of Google Earth, that is to say, not via the perspective of the human gaze: consider for example the National Aquarium Denmark or Palm Jumeirah in Dubai. The world thus simulated highlights the concrete presence of places, and the space is sensed as being smaller with the dromological acceleration of speed.[20]

On the other hand, the concrete, physical place has come to take on greater significance, inasmuch as it has become far more essential than it was only 50 years ago whether or not the place is hooked up to this rapid movement and situated spatially so that it lies within and not outside the infrastructural tissue: in these years, without Wi-Fi coverage and Internet possibilities, and with only a limited road network which does not include motorways or airports, places become disconnected. In the same movement that gathers the world together and makes it smaller, with



Border patrol, Sæd.

ever increasing speed, there is, then, also a separating movement, since the parts that do not enter into the speed network with the same easiness as the coupled parts turn into segregated *compartments*.[21] They turn into *outskirts*, and accordingly into peripheries, in relation to something else, which is central.

## Welfare's outskirting

This mega-trend of simultaneous acceleration and outskirting operates in synchronicity with the physical placement of welfare distributions. The wide effect is that the province has turned into outskirts. This is a discoursive movement insofar as the provinces are being referred to more and more as 'outskirts', and stagnating and negative qualities are being attributed to them,[22] along with what is simultaneously an economic-political movement, insofar as funds and attention are being drawn away from the outskirts and into the bigger cities. Finally, this also articulates a socio-cultural movement, inasmuch as the inhabitants of the outskirts are living someplace else than they were living only 20-30 years ago, so to speak, in terms of economic resources, media coverage and also welfare distribution, which can be seen on the quiet streets and in the empty buildings.
Tønder, the border town, which was so privileged after the reunification, could, over the course of several decades, make a display of the welfare society, hosting frequent visits by The Royal Theatre, presenting major concerts and having several music venues. There were also many shops, especially butchers' shops, and even, for some years, an Irma supermarket.[23] Besides, there were institutions: an art museum and a historical museum, the barracks, the teachers' training college and other educational institutions, a hospital, a new town hall, sports centres and swimming baths, a police station with a chief constable, a courthouse and a jail, a prefect, a land law committee; many of these were already placed in the city at the time of the reunification. The many institutions played a role in creating a vibrant commercial life, with a thriving pedestrian shopping street and luxury restaurants, already in the 1980s. Here lived the small shopkeeper who was listening to Coltrane and Parker and filming starling murmurations for documentaries; as a matter of fact, he was not really fond of the more popular jazz that was being presented during the yearly folk music festival. Here lived the farmer who was requesting that works by French philosophers be brought back to him from the French bookstore on Badstuetræde in Copenhagen, when the students were coming home for Christmas, preferably Lyotard and Baudrillard and Serres, all pronounced with South Jutlandish diction by the bachelor from the large Frisian farm, who started each day by standing on his head for a few seconds. And here lived prestigious chefs who were being garnered with all of the 'chef's caps' that *Politiken* could award in its restaurant reviews in the days back before the Michelin era.[24] Many students came from here, students who became theologians etc. Unlike other of the provinces' cities, Tønder was always amicably disposed towards Copenhagen. Nobody was talking about the 'Devil's Island' or cormorant nests: Copenhagen was Danish, and it was attractive when seen from the borderland. The artist Claus Jensen once told me that he knew somebody who had pieces by Donald Judd and other great masters hidden away in his barn at a Frisian farm in Sæd, just outside of Tønder. And on a *varf* in the marshlands,[25] a few kilometres south of Tønder, lies Emil Nolde's home and museum. There was, in other words, a rather multifarious life that was being unfolded here. Nils Gunder Hansen even suggests that the city was situated 'centrally':

'Perhaps the historical consciousness was indirectly present: there was a certain laid-back self-awareness about Tønder – there was no ambience of the provinces or the periphery, and there were no inferiority complexes or self-loathing, even though we, all things considered, constituted one of the most remote one-horse towns in the kingdom. I have subsequently been many places in Denmark that seemed far more provincial and peripheral. Was it history's weight that was the buoyant factor here? Was it because Tønder was situated "centrally", with only an hour's drive to Flensburg, and two to Hamburg?'[26] Mega-trends and smaller-scale circumstances are commingled, and different times are woven into one another. So when Tønder Statsseminarium [Government Teachers' Training College] was founded in 1788, as the first of its kind in the Nordic countries, it was particularly significant for Tønder, on a micro-level, but it was also the start of a mega-trend in the Nordic countries, which served as a pre-condition for the welfare society's Danish amplification. The many institutions that were planned, made their effect, and were eventually demolished, are thus specific to Tønder, which, by all means, hereby became hyped, coddled and Danicized; but they are also typical of most Danish provincial towns.

## The institutions' demise

In a way, Tønder is a microcosm. Hansen writes:

*Tønder is a world in itself. Far away and deep down. The trip across the flat land can feel like it's almost infinite. But then you catch sight of the church's tall spire, long before you get a presentiment of the city itself. This is the city's landmark. My father has often said that when we approached the city by car, the church looked like a rocket that was ready to launch.*[27]

A few years after its 200th anniversary, in 1992, the Teachers' Training College was closed. Until then, it might have been the most important institution as far as life in the city was concerned, with the many training college students and student teachers that were studying and practising their craft on pupils at the 'Practice School'. I was one of those whom they were practising on, and when

The central square in Tønder.

I changed schools, from Rødding to Tønder, what came as a surprise to me was how progressive and modern the teaching had suddenly become, with 'integrated Danish' and teamwork. My mother wrote in the school magazine about her being surprised that Helga, Hans and Lars were able to manage the school camp outing by themselves until she figured out that this was a school where the teachers were not addressed by their last names. Traditions were being challenged, and society as such was being put up for discussion, and there were major concerts, parties and vivacity in the town, as if this were a big city. The buildings of the teachers' training college were rather large, and after the training college was closed, they were put into use for, among other things, holding language classes for immigrants. Now there is a cultural centre with lectures and courses being offered.

Tønder Hospital was built in 1889 by Tønder County. In her article 'Sønderjysk sygehusvæsen: fra fattiggård til moderne sygehus' [South Jutland hospital system: from poorhouse to modern hospital], nurse Dagmar Bork writes:

*The decentralized model operating in Tønder County was underscored by the fact that, at the same time, hospitals were built in Leck, in Niebøll, in Wyk and in Westerland immediately south of the present-day national border. It was the objective to provide the citizens in these sparsely populated areas with proximity to treatment sites. The largest hospitals contained, after its expansions, almost a hundred beds. As the smallest of the hospitals, however, Højer Hospital had room for only twelve patients.*[28]

In the late 1800s, the decentralized principle was replaced by Tønder Hospital. This was a large workplace, and when my mother was working there, doctors and nurses swarmed into and out from our home, for parties and dinner festivities, or because they just happened to be passing by: there was a hustle and bustle of substantial character in the city. The hospital was expanded on several occasions, but now its activities have been curtailed and the place has been reduced to being a day hospital; patients that have to be hospitalized are now referred to the large Sygehus Sønderjylland [Hospital of Southern Jutland] in Aabenraa. The buildings are still being used in connection with the healthcare services: practising specialists can rent space within the buildings. In order to visit a patient, you will have to go to Aabenraa, which is 40 kilometres away; it is best to do this if you have access to a car, because it takes a lot of time to get there by the bus, and there are no other options.

The courthouse was built in 1914-16, when the city was German. It is one of the predominant buildings in the heart of Tønder, with its imposing entrance area. The courthouse was previously also a police station; the police station, however, was moved to the Alexandrine School's building, a few house numbers away. In *En fælles kulturarv. Tyske og danske bygninger i Sønderjylland 1864-1920* [A common cultural heritage. German and Danish buildings in South Jutland 1864-1920], Peter Dragsbo writes:

*In the years 1907-15, with the county house, the state school, the courthouse, the Alexandrine School and the agricultural college, Tønder was embellished with a string of pearls consisting of large and beautiful buildings in the native country style. Notwithstanding its slightly conventional baroque style, the well-preserved courthouse holds its ground exquisitely in the five-leaf clover.*[29]

The judge's residence was situated behind the courthouse, and the county jail, dating from 1916, was situated next to the courthouse, facing the judge's garden. I was in the same school class as the judge's daughter, and when we were playing together at her home, we could look up from her garden towards the barred prison windows on several floors, and we knew they could see us and were thinking about how their own children were doing. That is what I imagined, anyway. Now, the judge's residence and the courthouse have been sold off by the State, into private ownership. The entire judiciary institution was closed in Tønder in the 2000s and was transferred to Sønderborg. The county jail is still in use, but many of the prisoners are being moved to more secure prisons. The police station is still there. Not so long ago, there was a chief constable and there was a crew on duty, on a 24/7 basis. Now the place has turned into the 'Tønder Local Police', which is open for business from 9:00 AM to 4:00 PM from Monday to Wednesday, until 5:00 PM on Thursdays, and until 1:00 PM on Fridays. Should crimes be committed outside these intervals of time, one needs to call the Southern Jutland Police in Esbjerg, which is 80 kilometres away, and hope that a police car is driving somewhere in the vicinity of Tønder. That was certainly not the case on the autumn evening that I tried to get hold of the police, when a man, who was simply plastered, fell over right in front of me after he had been inside Centralhalle, bowling with his friends; he had no chance of finding his way home in the pouring rain.

The open-air swimming pool was inaugurated in 1951, and Tønder Hall in 1965;[30] since then, they have been expanded many times. Now it has all turned into one very large complex, expanded, rebuilt, as part of a collaboration with the high school.

The slaughterhouse was shut down in the 2000s. It became Tønder Andelsslagteri [Tønder Co-operative Abattoir] in 1950, merged with other co-operative slaughterhouses in 1970, and was subsequently taken over by the Danish Crown food company. As the marshlands are abounding in cattle and lambs, it was especially these animals that were being slaughtered, and with the proximity to German culinary traditions, it was obvious to built a sausage factory here. Now, the buildings are unsalable, because a proviso stipulates that they must not be used for slaughtering livestock.

Tønder State School, now Tønder Gymnasium, which was mentioned by Peter Dragsbo as part of the beautiful 'five-leaf clover' from the German time, has undergone many conversions and rounds of renovation. This institution, with its 670 students and its staff of 70 teachers, is still going strong with activities being carried out in cooperation with Niebüll in Germany, around an international line. The presence of both German-minded and Danish-minded citizens has brought about a doubling of kindergartens and of schools into both German and Danish institutions. Even the ministers and the sextons are found in duplicate and are, by turns, serving the Christ Church in German and Danish.

Tønder Post Office was erected during the German era, in 1899, by the architect, Schantze. In *Post- og Telekommunikationens huse 1880-1930* [Postal and telecommunication houses 1880-1930], Elisabeth Buchwald has been writing for the Heritage Agency about Danish post offices, also about Tønder Post Office:

*The post office is a tall, detached, five bays' long, two-storey building, with a high basement and a robustly constructed square stair tower in the building's eastern gable end. The building, which has been designed in a historicizing Nordic 'castle style', replete with references to both the Gothic and the Renaissance, has exposed red brickwork with decorative fasciae of glazed bricks. The hipped roof has been tiled with newer red tiles.*[31]

Like every place else, the post office is now closed, and its functions have been moved to a supermarket. Its buildings are standing empty, in the middle of the city.
The barracks were erected in 1936 and were closed in 2002. They established a bastion of defence in relation to the border, and gave rise to a stream of young people coming to the city, in ensemble with the agricultural college, the chimney sweepers' school, the teachers' training college, and the other educational institutions. These barracks' soldiers were not only used for marital activities. In the late 1940s, during a severe winter, parts of Tønder were suffering from an overflow from the Vidå stream. The marshlands have a high groundwater level, and now it was so high that the sewage system did not work. Colonel Jensen, also called Morocco-Jensen, then organized explosions of the ice in the Vidå stream, and managed thereby to obtain outward flow for the water. For a long time, the barracks remained important, largely because of Germany's proximity after 1920, and after the Second World War, but also as a cursor of Danishness. Now the barracks are standing empty, although parts of the buildings are still in use in connection with various kinds of commercial leases, including one being held by the Danish Tax Department.
The city hall in Tønder used to be situated on Tønder Square, but in 1981 a new town hall was designed and built by Halldor Gunnløgsson and Jørn Nielsen. In 2014, this new building was expanded by Sleth Architects, supplementing the low-density red structure with a steel and glass building. The edifice was erected on top of a large Viking find, which, according to historical experts, ought to have been excavated. There were neither time nor means for doing this.
The art and culture museum in Tønder is the whole of South Jutland's museum. The art museum is rather large, with extensive historical and contemporary art collections and changing exhibitions, while the culture museum, situated inside the remains of the old Tønder Castle, documents Tønder's history through the prestige objects and other items that were locally produced, and also acquired over the years, such as pieces of lace, tiles, dower chests and silver objects. Moreover, the old water tower has become a Wegner Tower, where Hans Wegner's chairs have been put on display. This institution has been expanded. Here, between old Tønder relics and an exhibition of large photostats of Per Bak Jensen's 'Udkantsdanmark' [Outskirts Denmark], design and architecture students from KADK exhibited their projects about Tønder in 2015-16.
Hovedbanegården [The Central Railway Station], or Marskbanegården [The Marshlands Railway Station], was erected in the German era, in 1890, in Prussian style. It once had a restaurant and offered train connections to Højer and the tourist

The pedestrian street in Tønder.
←
The new town hall, Museum Sønderjylland and the railway station.

destination Sild, and also to Tinglev and consequently the 'H-city', in addition to offering train connections to Niebüll in the south and Bramming in the north. Now there are no services operating on the site, the building is for sale, and the private company Arriva has taken over the operations of railway traffic between Niebüll and Bramming.

## The effects of transformation

Tønder was 'the institutions' city',[32] and each of the buildings reflected an architecture, a time and a society. Aside from the rich hinterland of marshland farmers, there was a wide diversity of human beings, and also a flourishing trade, which could be credited to the many institutions that were situated here.[33] Some of these people have moved away, to larger and more central hubs, which is why the previously so self-aware, peculiar and funny borough has become quieter. It has also come to resemble the other towns that have become quiet. Little by little, as Tønder's picturesque streets come to be dotted with more and more empty shop windows and fewer and fewer people in the streets, the city is, to some extent, losing its distinctive quality and is drawing nearer and nearer to a generic form. The city still possesses its distinctive well-preserved architectural culture, and the socio-cultural distinctive features that have been described are still present, but there is something, as far as the buildings are concerned, that is becoming less indispensable as time goes by; the city is taking on more the character of a tourist attraction or a museum, perhaps, and less of a changing city, and as far as the socio-cultural aspects are concerned, they are still to be found, albeit less vibrant. This line of advance has features of what anthropologist Marc Augé calls 'non-place' (1995). Augé relates 'non-place' to the spaces of 'super modernity', such as malls, airports and motorways, defined by a lack of social relations and history. As he writes, they are the antitheses of an 'anthropological place'. This cannot be said about Tønder, but in spite of Tønder's intense place character, the city has recently obtained a touch of something else, with its abandoned institutions, its less lively traffic and its empty windows with but a few antiques to put a damper on the cheerlessness. This 'something else' carries within itself something of the non-place's emptiness.

Østergade 8 in Tønder.

→

Uldgade.

## When KADK came to town

In the fall of 2014, 26 international design and architecture students from the KADK were given an assignment that involved focusing on Tønder. How could outskirting be changed for the better? Whether discoursively, socio-culturally, politically or economically, the change towards the periphery served as the springboard for their design and architectural proposals. Which physical-material possibilities could they envision in their solutions, proposals and projects, related to this specific context in Tønder and also contributing to a larger discussion of the development on the global level? After the study tour to Tønder, nine of the students chose, on their own initiative, to live in Tønder for the five months in which the project was unfolded, while the rest of the students went back to Copenhagen. The nine who remained living there thought that Tønder had a need for young people; this is why they were staying. It also gave them the opportunity to familiarize themselves with the place and to understand its specificity. All the projects took their points of departure in the specific and sought to see the potentials in the distinctive, while at the same time reflecting on the general through this particular paradigmatic example. The projects concerned: the conversion of an old German hangar to a pre-university, inspired by the folk high school idea; an artist's residence in the marshlands; a tourist's walk through the city, with a dramatic use of the Vidå stream; ornaments for one of the small alleys; a labyrinthine urban garden; a cooking school; the conversion of a furniture shop; a lace facade for the Town Hall; shelters in the UNESCO-protected marshlands; a mega-sized lace ornament encircling the city; a repository for forgotten crafts and artefacts; temporary housing for elderly and otherwise hospitalized people; rendezvous points in the city; a Tønder immigrants' centre, where they could obtain a pair of Ecco shoes and drop off a souvenir; a communication channel between Copenhagen and Tønder; a Tønder movie; holiday cottages and installations on Rømø and in Tønder; a thermal bath in the marshlands; a nature centre; a marketplace; Tønder left to the devices of nature; and Tønder's pavements transformed.[34] The projects were not focused on welfare institutions, and yet, several of them were nevertheless mimicking these institutions, albeit upon postmodern conditions of a more aestheticizing and wild character.

These projects were related to the distinctive character of the place and thereby threw the city into relief from a site-specific perspective. At the same time, these ways of highlighting the city have the effect that the area comes to enter into competition with other regions and cities. Back in the 1990s, many cultural researchers were speaking about the return to the Middle Ages' economically, politically and socially strong cities. That is what is happening these years, and this can be rediscovered in the student projects' highlighting of specific effects. This movement also holds, within itself, a process of rendering things uniform; this is what is happening simultaneously for many cities. In these years, architects and designers are becoming interested in the specific, but necessarily from a generalizing perspective, for this is part of the global trend that is related to finding, polishing and post-modernizing the specific. By this means, the specific gets run through a machine that renders it more uniform and more like other specific sites. In this way, the students' projects pointed toward the site's specific distinctiveness but were also accentuating something generic.

Moreover, the students' circling around the site-specific implied a renewed focus on institutions. This encompassed not only welfare's institutions (mimicking those that disappeared in the 1990s: like the pre-university, the cooking school, the hospital/senior housing and the thermal baths) but also the projects which were promoting tourist economy (like the nature centre, the UNESCO shelters, the market place and the renovation of a huge furniture store). Moreover, an interest in improving everyday life was evident in the form-focused projects (such as the new town hall facade, the lace trimming surrounding the city, the alley's decoration, the urban park labyrinth, the repository and the transformations of the pavement). These were specific-and-generic-proposals and they touched upon fellowship and the establishment of community in what has suddenly become a hushed town. In this way, the projects were concerned with re-reading a welfare notion which could come to supersede what the former institutions, only 20 years ago, were unfolding, with their solutions to welfare tasks in the city, and also through the variety that was educed by having a host of nurses, civil servants, teachers, etc. in the city.

## Welfare spaces in the provinces

Many of the buildings described here are today being used for something else than what they were originally built for; they have been carefully thought through with respect to their intended function and with respect to the aesthetic references that such institutions are supposed to bear. So it is strange to see these buildings which, in their exterior appearance, used to show what was happening inside, but which now are housing something else or nothing at all. Both the previous institutions and many of the shops in Tønder are now standing with vacant windows. Most of the women's clothing stores and cafés are are still there. This adds to the sensation that specific distinctiveness is undergoing transformation towards repetition, albeit on a small scale. In his book *Disjuncture and Difference in the Global Cultural Economy* (1990),[35] the anthropologist Arjun Appadurai wrote about how the increased connections between places, through the intensified rapid global flow of 'scapes' (ethnoscapes, technoscapes, finanscapes, mediascapes & ideoscapes) change the world and give rise to greater uniformity, but on a structural level produce greater differences and inequalities. These early diagnoses are visible in Tønder and in others of the outskirts that used to be provinces: being dependent on large-scale flows, these areas are becoming subject to global forces instead of to regional or national forces, as far as their classification as centre or periphery is concerned, and furthermore, with respect to their form-related interchange between being rendered special (global trend that focuses on local distinctivenesses) and being pushed towards something generic (global trend that converts local distinctivenesses into generically recognizable forms).[36]

Perhaps the repetitive is the new modus for the provinces, and perhaps this is one of the spatial reasons why the provinces turn into outskirts. The one city has a tendency to resemble the other, and when the specific peculiarity fades away, spatially as well as socially and culturally, the magnificence also dwindles. The repetitive, the ligated, the empty and the silent are moving slowly and are pushing the sites towards a sensation of non-place, and the provinces out towards the outskirts – *or what?* Is this just a passing wave, like so much else in Tønder's tumultuous history?[37] It may well be that welfare has to be given new forms. It may well be that it is a form that can glide into the present. And it may also be that this is a form whose qualities we must first get to know, a form that is on the way out there, in the provinces.

Notes

1 See also P. Allingham & K.M. Raahauge: 'Introduction: Post City Represented' (2008).

2 O.K. Pedersen calls attention to the fact that 'welfare state' and 'welfare society' are often used interchangeably, as synonyms, which they are not. The state is the means for attaining utopia, i.e. society O.K. Pedersen: 'Efterord' (2015), pp. 243-44. This is discussed in Pedersen's afterword in *Tidsskriftet Antropologi's* second special issue on the welfare state (2015). What is being examined, analysed and discussed in this double issue are various examples of the welfare state's (and of welfare society's) projects (such as the school, psychiatry, the home, the university, the kindergarten, the healthcare system, care of the elderly and animal welfare). Moreover, a dialogue is carried on with political science and its concept of the state and traditions of analysis that are markedly different from those of anthropology, while at the same time, there are certainly areas of research that the two disciplines have in common. The both empirically broad and analytically challenging presentations of the welfare state and the welfare society fashion background knowledge for the present article.

3 See also Jørgen Møller elsewhere in this anthology.

4 All of Denmark's 275 town halls from that time have been described and photographed by Pablo Llambías: *Rådhus* (1997).

5 This glance at the institutions has been inspired by Mette Jerl Jensen and Kjeld Vindum's concept of *the small monuments*, by means of which they allude to institutions as underexposed albeit significant architectural contributions to the welfare society.

6 'Outskirting' (the transformation from provincial town to peripheral fringe region) is a neologism that I am taking the liberty of introducing here, since the concept accentuates the movement towards the outskirts, and the state of turning into or becoming outskirts.

7 For a description of Tønder's history, see, for example, C. Eskildsen: *Tønder 1243-1943* (1943).

8 The protruding dikes were granted by the Danish government and were built after a storm in 1976, when things came very close to having the former dikes burst, as a result of a storm surge and with the ensuing flooding of Tønder and the marshlands.

9 F. Stjernfelt: 'Sted, gade, plads – en naiv teori om byen' (1996).

10 'Hjemmetysker' [German-minded] is a term that is used to describe Danish citizens living in Denmark, who understand themselves as being Germans in Denmark. German associations and institutions gather the 'German-minded' together in Denmark; a corresponding thing can be said about Danish-minded citizens living in Germany: for example, in Flensburg. The many national and regional affiliations have to do with the fact that the area has been both German and Danish, and also that the area has enjoyed special status as a duchy under the Danish crown.

11 C. Eskildsen: *Tønder 1243-1943* (1943); H. Becker-Christensen: *Byen ved grænsen. Tønder 1920-1970* (1993).

12 I. Lauridsen: *Zeppelinbasen ved Tønder* (2002).

13 About 'the H-city', see C.Carbone & C.P. Pedersen: 'HBY. Byer' (2005); on the infrastructure, see H. Dahl: *Den usynlige verden* (2008).

14 Line Schmidt Hendriksen, who has written a thesis on *Udkantsdanmark* [Outskirts Denmark] from a discoursive perspective (2012), has been conducting fieldwork at three places in the country: namely, Rødding, Samsø and Hannæs. She notes that there are two ways in which the

outskirts are defined in relation to something else: namely, Copenhagen *versus* the rest (also known as outskirts); or the major cities (which correspond roughly to the cities in the H-city) *versus* the rest; L.S. Hendriksen: *At leve med 'Udkantsdanmark' – Diskursens magt i problematikken omkring udkantsdanmark* (2012), p. 25 and 31. Thanks to Katja Kvaale, who has referred me to this thesis.

**15** Places can only be understood in the context of other places, as Greimas (1974) suggests: for example, centre as opposed to periphery, where *periphery's* etymological root is the outer surface of a wheel H. Fink: 'Om grænsers måde at være grænser på' (1992). In contrast to 'periphery', the relative location of the outskirts, in relation to the centre, is typically ascribed with negative connotations.

**16** Much of this has been discussed in K.M. Raahauge: 'Into Tønder: Field Specific in the Marshlands' (2015) and K.M. Raahauge: 'Out of Tønder: Lost Fields in the Marshlands' (2015).

**17** Upon the reunification in 1920, 76.5% of Tønder's population voted German. See H. Becker-Christensen: *Byen ved grænsen. Tønder 1920-1970* (1993), p. 38.

**18** 'Tønder was a world in itself. It had everything that your heart could desire. Shops, sports halls, county officers, wise men and pretty girls, good teams in soccer and handball, the barracks, the teachers' training college, the hospital, the rock concerts, Tønder hippies: there was nothing that wasn't there. And there was a dynamics. Many children were newcomers like myself, and at the top class in the *realskole,* and immediately afterward, at the high school, we met those who were coming "from out there in the parishes". "Everybody was a stranger in Tønder", I came close to saying. It was a melting pot. (//) Today, perhaps it doesn't have everything anymore. That's what it looks like when I go to visit there. It's all a bit worn down and diminished when I compare it with how things were way back when. Tønder SF doesn't even exist anymore. For that matter, it wound up getting moved back to Series 2, from where the club ascended during its heyday. The teachers' training college was closed; the barracks had fallen into disuse; the county officer disappeared; and the hospital, too – well, almost; lots and lots of small shops – bakeries and butcher shops – have disappeared and given way to a few supermarkets. The political and economic community development and centralization has not been in Tønder's favour. But the outskirts are something the city has become and is being turned into, and not something that it has been in a somewhat longer temporal perspective.' N.G. Hansen: *Lille dreng med rejseskrivemaskine. Erindringer* (2011), pp. 76-77.

**19** 'Province' signifies that a place has been conquered by somebody (from ancient Rome). 'Outskirts' signifies that something is not the centre, but is farthest away from the centre.

**20** Moreover, Michel de Certeau calls attention to this simulation- and absence point already in *Walking in the City* (1984) where he stresses that cities always carry references to other places in themselves, in the form of street names and memory embedments as well as through other displacements and phantasmagorical machines.

**21** 'Compartment' was used by the anthropologist Niels Fock in his article 'Med Einstein i rummet' [With Einstein in Space] in order to illuminate how the indigenous people in Australia think synthetically, while we in the West think in terms of differences, in *compartments*, and thereby posit a separation between, for example, religion and kinship. I have transported this figure to Denmark, and specifically to Lyngby as being spatially compartmentalized. See also Fock (1994) and Raahauge (2001).

**22** See Pagh & de Neergaard, in the present anthology on the significance of the discoursive aspect. See also Hendriksen (ibid.), who describes how 'outskirts' has evolved from being a demographic and geographic definition up until, in 2010, when, with the media's use of the term, it became a fluid and derogative term for 'outer areas'. L.S. Hendriksen: *At leve med 'Udkantsdanmark' – Diskursens magt i problematikken omkring udkantsdanmark* (2012), pp. 10-19.

**23** Hansen writes: 'My parents were very enthusiastic about the fact that there was an Irma shop in Tønder. Irma was 'the real deal' for conscious consumers in the late 1960s. For reasons that I am not fully cognizant of, the major South Jutland cities were the only places outside Sjælland where the Irma chain was materializing. After a few years, however, Irma withdrew from the region, and the goods to which we had become accustomed, we now had to re-stock when, on rare occasions, we were in Copenhagen.' N.G. Hansen: *Lille dreng med rejseskrivemaskine. Erindringer* (2011), p. 71.

**24** The herbs were plucked by the chef, Stig Henriksen – from the Savoy in London, right in our garden: ergo, an early appearance of the *Noma*-movement.

**25** Varf: Frisian term for a man-made hill. The farms were constructed on top of the *varf* in order to have a 'small island' for your farm in the event of storm surges.

**26** Hansen (2011), op.cit., p. 72.

**27** Ibid., p. 98.

**28** D. Bork: 'Sønderjysk Sygehusvæsen: fra fattiggård til moderne sygehus' (2007).

**29** P. Dragsbo: *En fælles kulturarv. Tyske og danske bygninger i Sønderjylland 1864-1920* (2011), p. 42.

**30** H. Becker-Christensen: *Byen ved grænsen. Tønder 1920-1970* (1993), pp. 312-13.

**31** E. Buchwald: *Post- og Telekommunikationens huse 1880-1930* (2002).

**32** H. Becker-Christensen: *Byen ved grænsen. Tønder 1920-1970* (1993), p. 216.

33 'The many hundreds of civil servants and other public officials came, together with their families, to strongly place their mark on the life in Tønder (...) whether you were German or Danish, you could take delight in the economic boost that the city obtained as a result of this.' H. Becker-Christensen: *Byen ved grænsen. Tønder 1920-1970* (1993), p. 216.

34 See The Tønder Project: Observations (2015) & The Tønder Project: Design Projects (2015).

35 See A. Appadurai: 'Disjuncture and Difference in the Gobal Cultural Economy (1990).

36 Thesereflectionsareinspiredby R. Koolhaas: *The Generic City* (1995).

37 Thanks to the research councils, a research project about Danish welfare's spaces, among these the outskirts, has been initiated at KADK.

**Literature**


- Allingham, P. & Raahauge, K.M.: 'Introduction: Post City Represented, in Post City' in *Semiotic Explorations of the City, Knowledge, Technology, and Policy*, Springer Journal 21(3), 2008, pp. 99-103.
- Appadurai, A.: 'Disjuncture and Difference in the Gobal Cultural Economy' in *Theory, Culture & Society,*1990 7, pp. 295-310.
- Augé, M.: *Non-Places – Introduction to an Anthropology of Supermodernity*. Verso, London & New York 1995 (1992).
- Bruun, M.H., Kristensen, D.B., Krøyer, S., Møller, J.R., & Rytter, M. (eds.): *Velfærdsstaten 1, Tidsskriftet Antropologi*, 2015, no. 72.
- Bruun, M.H., Kristensen, D.B., Krøyer, S., Møller, J.R., & Rytter, M. (eds.): *Velfærdsstaten 2, Tidsskriftet Antropologi* 2015, no. 73.
- Becker-Christensen, H.: *Byen ved grænsen. Tønder 1920-1970*. Institut for Grænseregionsforskning. Aabenraa 1993.
- Bork, D.: 'Sønderjysk Sygehusvæsen: fra fattiggård til moderne sygehus' i *Sygeplejersken* 2007, nr. 19, pp. 56-59.
- Buchwald, E.: *Post- og Telekommunikationens huse 1880-1930*. Danish Heritage Agency, Ministry of Culture, 2002.
- Carbone, C. & Pedersen, C.P.: 'HBY. Byer' in *Abomey – Mumbai. Tidsskriftet Antropologi* vol. 2005, 47, p. 43-57.
- Dahl, H.: *Den usynlige verden*. Gyldendal, Copenhagen 2008.
- de Certeau, M.: 'Walking in the City, Part III: Spatial Practices, Chapter VII' i *The Practice of Everyday Life.* University of California Press, Berkeley 2002 (1984), pp. 91-130.
- Dragsbo, P.: *En fælles kulturarv. Tyske og danske bygninger i Sønderjylland 1864-1920.* Museum Sønderjylland. Sønderborg Castle, 2011.
- Eskildsen, C.: *Tønder 1243-1943*, Guldhorn, Tønder 1943.
- Fink, H.: 'Om grænsers måde at være grænser på' i *Grænser. Kulturstudier 15*. Centre for Cultural Research. Aarhus Universitetsforlag, Aarhus 1992, pp. 9-31.
- Fock, N.: 'Med Einstein i Australien. Rummet i etnografisk belysning'. Rum. *Tidsskriftet Antropologi* vol. 30:5-15.
- Gottdiener, M.: *Life in the Air. Surviving the new Culture of Air Travel*. Rowman & Littlefield Publishers, Lanham & Oxford 2001.
- Greimas, A.J.: 'Toward a Topological Semiotic. Chapter 7' in *The Social Sciences. A Semiotic View.* Minneapolis: University of Minnesota Press, 1990 [1974], pp. 139-60.
- Hansen, N.G.: *Lille dreng med rejseskrivemaskine. Erindringer.* København. Kristeligt Dagblads Forlag, 2011.
- Harvey, D.: *The Condition of Postmodernity: An Enquiry into the Origins of Cultural Change*. Blackwell, Cambridge, MA, 1990.
- Hendriksen, L.S.: *At leve med 'Udkantsdanmark' – Diskursens magt i problematikken omkring udkantsdanmark.* Thesis from Dept. of Anthropology, Aarhus University, 2012.
- Koolhaas, R.: 'The Generic City, Guide 1994' in *Small, Medium, Large, Extra-Large*. Office for Metropolitan Architecture. 010 Publishers, Rotterdam 1995, pp. 1238-1770.
- Lauridsen, I.: *Zeppelinbasen ved Tønder.* Sønderjyllands Kulturmiljøer nr. 5. Det regionale faglige kulturmiljøråd for Sønderjyllands Amt, 2002.
- Llambías, P.: *Rådhus*. Gyldendal, Copenhagen 1997.
- Møller, H.J.: *Tønder Kaserne 1920-2002. Samspillet mellem en by og en kaserne*. Tønder Museum, 2004.
- Pedersen, O.K.: 'Efterord' i *Tidsskriftet Antropologi 72, Velfærdsstaten,* 2015, pp. 137-51.
- Raahauge, K.M. (a): 'Into Tønder: Field Specific in the Marshlands' in *The Tønder Project: Observations*, KADK, 2015, pp. 7-17.
- Raahauge, K.M. (b): 'Out of Tønder: Lost Fields in the Marshlands' in *The Tønder Project: Design Projects*, KADK, 2015, pp. 7-11.
- Raahauge, K.M.: *Lyngby her og der.* Part of: *Lyngby og omegn i antropologisk belysning* (with Katja Øder Hansen), KADK, 2001.
- Stjernfelt, F.: 'Sted, gade, plads – en naiv teori om byen' in *Byens Pladser* (Martin Zerlang ed.).
- Urbanitet og Æstetik. Borgen, Copenhagen 1996, pp. 11-31.
- Virilio, P.: 'Véhiculaire' in *L'insécurité du territoire*. Éditions Galilée, Paris 1993 [1976], pp. 243-73.
- The Tønder Project: *Observations*, KADK 2015.
- The Tønder Project: *Design Projects*, KADK 2015.

# Institutions

Peter Thule Kristensen

# A Coherent Whole

## Gottlieb Bindesbøll's Mental Hospitals, Regarded from a Welfare-Historical Perspective

**In the middle of the 19th century, the Danish historicist architect Gottlieb Bindesbøll designed three mental hospitals. Not only do the hospital projects testify that the state was taking more and more responsibility for the treatment of persons with mental disorders; they also testify to a faith in the healing effect of architecture. If we want to understand what eventually crystallized into the welfare state, where the citizens' health and well-being is a central dimension, it makes sense to study Bindesbøll's hospital architecture. In addition, his work stands as a manifestation of a romantic world view, which can have left its mark on the welfare state to a greater degree than has previously been discussed.**

Many of the public institutions that characterize the 20th century's Western societies came into being during the 19th century, when their establishment coincided with major social and political upheavals. One of the foremost pioneers in this process of genesis is, in the Danish context, the architect Gottlieb Bindesbøll (1800-56). Not only is Bindesbøll experimental in his idiom, he is also the architect who, in the wake of the democratic movements in the middle of the 19th century, designs some of the period's most important new institutional buildings: the Thorvaldsen Museum, Denmark's first genuine museum building; three mental hospitals; 19 railway stations in Schleswig; the nation's first academic agricultural college; a number of town halls, courthouses and prisons; philanthropically financed workers' housing, and much more. For this reason, if one wants to understand the historical circumstances that were antecedent to the later era's welfare state's institutional buildings, it makes a good deal of sense to take a look at Gottlieb Bindesbøll's architecture.

I have chosen to focus here on Gottlieb Bindesbøll's three projects for the design of mental hospitals: Jydske Asyl [Jutland Asylum] in Riis Skov, a wooded area of Aarhus (1850-52); Oringe, in Vordingborg (1854-58); and Kurhuset at Sankt Hans, in Roskilde (1852-60). The specific medical intentions underlying these hospitals are well documented, and most certainly, the hospital architecture serves to illustrate one of the later welfare state's central domains, namely the health sector.

At the same time, the hospitals – and, for that matter, architecture on the whole – are a somewhat overlooked chapter in Danish social history, which often focuses myopically on legislation. Even the otherwise thorough *Dansk Velfærdshistorie,* in six volumes, which appeared in 2010-15, makes no mention whatsoever in its first volume (covering the period 1536-1898) of Bindesbøll's pioneer hospitals.[1] In Danish architectural history, on the other hand, the hospitals have certainly been the object of discussion, especially in my own monograph-dissertation, *Gottlieb Bindesbøll – Denmark's First Modern Architect*, published in 2013, from which I draw throughout the course of this article.[2] However, to a greater extent than was attempted in my dissertation, the present article puts Bindesbøll's work into a context that conceptually subsumes the development of the later Danish welfare state. It is the article's thesis that Bindesbøll was working purposefully with the hospital building's semantic level. Through this means, he was demonstrating a romantic notion that the individual, the architecture and the society are 'organically' linked together, and also that this connection can be read – and can be felt – in the architecture. Accordingly, I will attempt to show that a romantic world view may very well have exerted an influence on the development of the later welfare state. What I understand about the term 'romantic' has to do with a broad cultural stream that bourgeoned in Europe sometime around 1800. It was characterized by, among other things, an ambition to recreate, through art, a spiritual experience of coherence in the world without taking refuge in earlier times' religious and aesthetic dogmas, which appeared to be devoid of meaning in this turbulent and modern era.[3]

## Harald Selmer's system

A decisive prerequisite for the idiom in Bindesbøll's three mental hospitals is the specifically medical context. At this point, there was one figure that served as the leading arbiter: the doctor, Harald Selmer (1814-79). In 1846, Selmer published a treatise on the fundamentals of ordering the care of the insane, *Almindelige Grundsætninger for Daarevæsnets Indretning*,[4] which had an impact to bear on the fact that the consultative provincial assembly in Viborg resolved, in 1846, to erect the Helbredelsesanstalten for Sindssyge i Nörrejylland [The Curative Institution for the Mentally Disordered in Northern Jutland] – which was also known as the Jydske Asyl [Jutland Asylum] in Riis Skov. Selmer became the institution's chief physician and was simultaneously a member of the building commission, which was supposed to keep an eye on the course of construction. For this reason, he made a study tour in the winter of 1847-48 to a number of modern mental hospitals

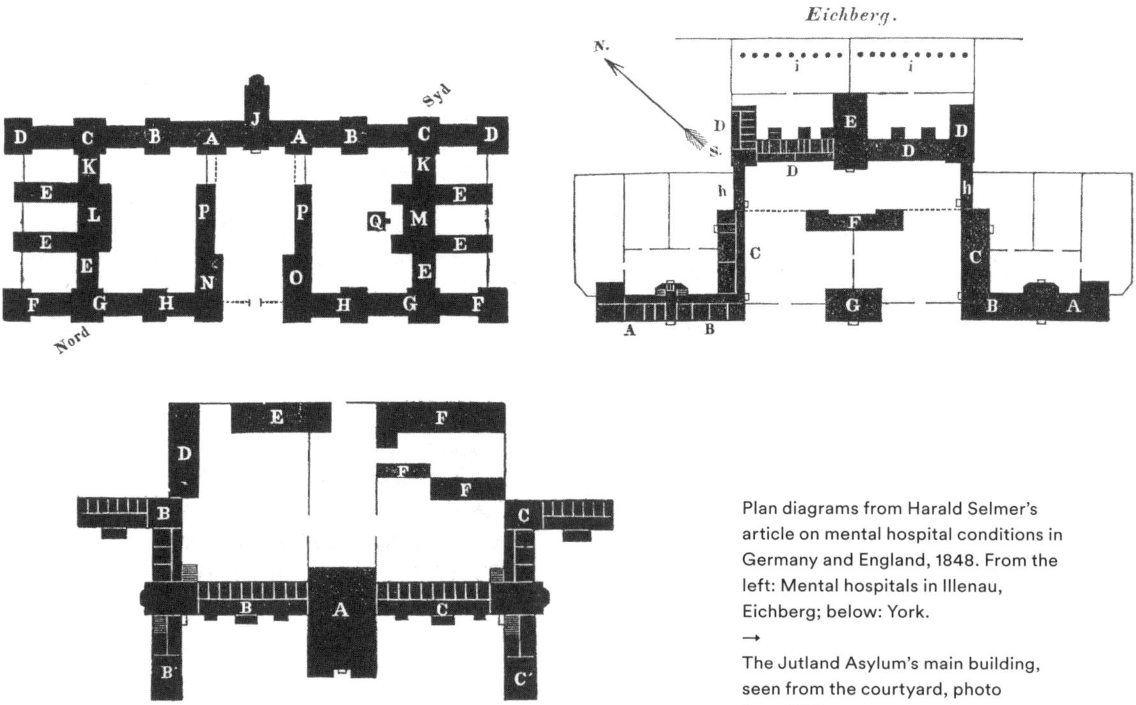


Plan diagrams from Harald Selmer's article on mental hospital conditions in Germany and England, 1848. From the left: Mental hospitals in Illenau, Eichberg; below: York.

→

The Jutland Asylum's main building, seen from the courtyard, photo from 1902.

in England and Germany. The trip resulted in a small paper about their architecture, *Daareanstalternes Bygningsforhold i Tydskland og England*,[5] which included a critical review of foreign models. Furthermore, after the erection of the Jutland Asylum, Selmer penned another article about the building project itself and about the spatial organization of the hospital.[6] Later on, Selmer came to serve as a member of the reorganization committee behind the new sanatorium at Sankt Hans, the architectural competition for which was won by Bindesbøll. Selmer also took part in submitting a recommendation to the Ministry of Justice which eventually resulted in the erection of the mental hospital in Oringe.[7] Seeing as there are virtually no descriptions about the buildings that issued from Bindesbøll's hand, it makes sense to study Selmer's writings.

To put it succinctly, Harald Selmer propounded a new treatment concept which, as a matter of fact, assigned an important role to the architecture: 'The insane asylum ... must do away with the unnatural isolation of the lunatic's life and once again place him in sensible interaction with the world. According to its fundamental concept, the treatment of the insane is not a question of separating, but of once again bringing the separate together. This concept has not, however, found a corresponding expression in a site plan that is essentially based on isolation. The concept must seek its medium specifically in building conditions that unite diverse elements, isolated in relation to one another, into a cohesive whole.'[8] In Selmer's writings, this was followed by a series of concrete proposals: the asylums ought to be established someplace with 'a completely rural and peaceful character';[9] they ought to accommodate all classes of society, so that patients from the 'working classes' can 'carry the higher classes along with them, via the force of example';[10] cleanliness and ventilation were crucial, and the security measures should not have a prison-like character, although the asylum should not appear to be 'masking life's gravity'.[11] The asylums, on the whole, should be characterized by a minimum of fixation and compulsion.

The architecture should function, in the words of the 19th century French psychiatrist Jean-Étienne Esquirol, as 'a therapeutic instrument'.[12] With Selmer, this was to be supplemented by a kind of occupational therapy, where the mentally disordered persons were occupied with everyday routines that were tailored to their original backgrounds. Male patients from the 'third class', who had backgrounds as smallholders, were activated doing fieldwork on the adjoining lands, while women from the 'first class' could embroider on canvas or play the spinet. All of the hospitals were publicly funded, but they operated also with private payments. Impecunious patients were granted the possibility of obtaining free room and board for the first three months of their stay and subsequent to this, room and board for a reduced fee. Similarly, patients could be paid for their labours.[13]

With this, we meet, and at an early stage, an example of partially publicly financed welfare, which was meant for all classes of society – i.e. with universalistic character, in other words, a system of welfare where solidarity was disseminated to the whole population.[14] This universalistic model is precisely what characterizes the Scandinavian welfare state and stands in contrast to a model where welfare benefits are, to a greater degree, distributed via the labor market.

The therapy's form was a manifestation of the so-called 'somatic' school in psychiatry, which proceeded in a more scientific way than what had prevailed in the past and which imputed to mental disorder various physiological factors, running along the lines of other diseases.[15] In keeping with this, Harald Selmer was not particularly inclined to lean up against religious models of explanation, either.[16]

## Differentiation and joining

Harald Selmer's overall aims and instructions were manifest in Bindesbøll's architecture in the form of a series of miniature worlds that offered an interesting interaction between, on the one hand, delimited building sections within a well-defined hierarchy and, on the other, a tendency for all the building components to be interconnected and contain the same symbols. By this means, the facilities were transformed, quite precisely, into 'a coherent whole'.

All three hospitals were organized as vast symmetrical installations, with room for more than 120-130 patients. In the centre were the chief

Bindesbøll's plans and designs, c. 1850.

F.F. Friis's facade elevation on the park, presented in 1849.

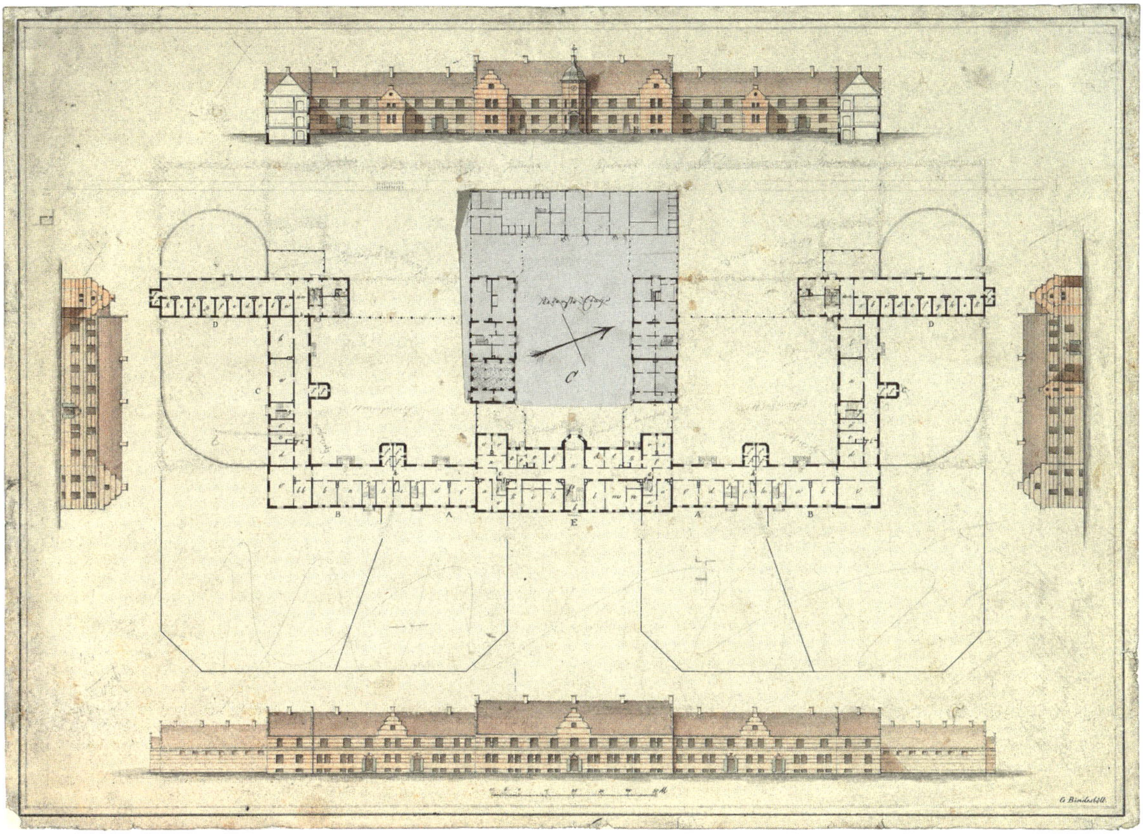

physician's residence and common spaces like the assembly hall and the chapel, and from there, the patients' wings spread out, with the women on the one side and the men on the other: a principle that was also being deployed in many of the foreign examples that Selmer had studied on his journey. At the same time, patients were also divided up according to class and to their respective degrees of disturbance. This manifested itself in a series of delimited albeit interrelated building sections, where the first class lived closest to the chief doctor, followed by the second and the third class. Farthest from rationality's centre were found the veritable 'cell wings' for the most troubled patients. These wings were also the only ones that had, for reasons of safety, bars in front of the windows. Otherwise the motto was that visible coercion should be avoided: for example, by placing walls that had been set up in front of sections with the more troubled patients out of sight, and recessed in a kind of ditch, a so-called 'ha-ha', or by using sturdy mullions instead of metal bars.

If the three plan arrangements are considered, it is possible to spot an evolution in Bindesbøll's overall way of organizing these kinds of institutions. At Riis Skov, in Aarhus, Bindesbøll took over an already ongoing project from the architect Frederik Ferdinand Friis, who was also making his design in a way that complied with Harald Selmer's instructions. The final facility was constructed around a 140 meter long backbone with a main building that faces the institution's large park area. The main building has official residences, an assembly hall and a chapel in its middle, and two side wings with rooms for, respectively, calmer female and calmer male patients. From here, new wings jut out further, towards the facility's vehicular approach. Obviously, Bindesbøll found the 140 meter long facade to be monotonous. When we consider Friis's original barracks-like facade proposal, this is most certainly the

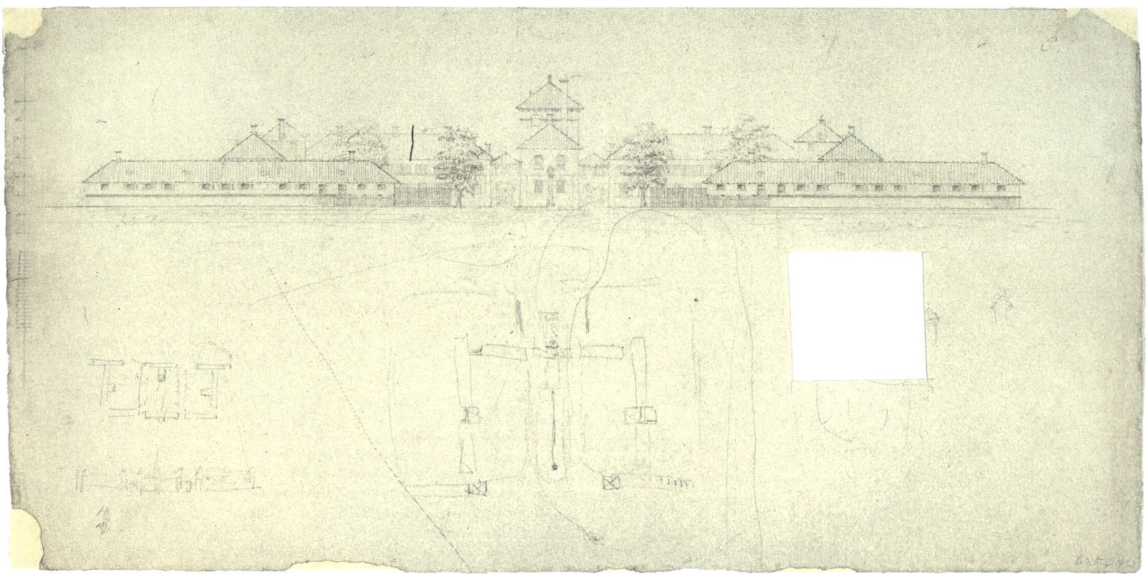

Bindesbøll's proposal for the sanatorium, *Kurhuset*, 1853. Facade elevation of the entire complex seen from the driveway and sketches of site plans.

→
Bindesbøll's Therapeutic Institution for the Insane at Oringe, near Vordingborg, inaugurated in 1858. Photo: Jens Lindhe.

case. At the time in question, though, Bindesbøll was not able to manage changing the plan arrangement,[17] while, on the other hand, he did get a chance to redesign the facades, which he partitioned into more differentiated sections, with different roof elevations and a more varied and complex fenestration.

In the next of the projects, which involved the design of a new sanatorium for the existing Sankt Hans hospital in Roskilde, the so-called *Kurhus*, Bindesbøll, on the other hand, was given the opportunity to make his own sketches for a floor plan, starting from scratch. In the *Kurhus*, the long garden facade from Riis Skov was jettisoned for the sake of creating a number of wings that appear more independently, more equal, and simultaneously offer greater contrast to each other.

The autonomy is accentuated by the fact that the wings are not immediately adjacent to each other, but are joined instead through the help of partially recessed intermediate buildings, which lie in extension of the corridors. The facade's flush line facing the park was interrupted – most especially in the form of a central building that is positioned

perpendicularly to the main facade. Correspondingly, the wings jut out on the main facade's garden side and introduce a displacement motif which emerges in the plan by virtue of the fact that the facility's many wings are seemingly ready to disentangle themselves from one another. The *Kurhus*, with its displacement motif, is less conventional than Riis Skov and was possibly inspired by the floor plans of the foreign mental hospitals that were discussed in Selmer's article. Due to a disagreement that arose between Bindesbøll and the building owner, the *Kurhus* project was taken over by the aforementioned Frederik Ferdinand Friis, who, among other things, changed the facade's expression.

In the last of the three hospital projects, Oringe, in Vordingborg, we meet again the same overriding organization that we met in the two previous examples. Just as he did in the *Kurhus*, Bindesbøll was attempting to divide the vast installation into well-arranged building wings, which are linked together by intermediate buildings. The main building itself, in this case, is very short compared to the facility's vast expanse, but Bindesbøll manages nonetheless to provide it with clout by virtue of differentiated building elevations and a fenestration with more wall surfaces in the central parts. In its final execution, it is *this* facility that comes closest to Bindesbøll's own intentions (even though he died before its completion).

Generally, the organizational form in all three hospitals reflects a hierarchical class society, where the respective person categories are placed in separate building parts, which then, in turn, form part of a larger hierarchy, culminating in the chief doctor's residence. If you take a closer look, however, it becomes clear that Bindesbøll, at certain spots, also breaks down the hierarchy and then gathers the separate parts together again – into one homogeneous composition. In principle, the chief physician lives under the same roof as the most demented person. The interaction between hierarchy and uniformity is, on the whole, a central theme running through Bindesbøll's architecture. In Bindesbøll's Thorvaldsen Museum, from 1848, one meets, for example, both a hierarchical spatial sequence, culminating in the hall where the sculpture of Christ is displayed, and repetitive spatial sequences that are ultimately bound together with the rest by virtue of certain few recurring motifs, like barrel vaults and slanting frames around all of the wall openings.

## Under the same symbol

Up until Harald Selmer's reform of Danish psychiatry, people with mental disorders typically lived at the same facilities as, for example, disabled people and mentally handicapped people. Or they were kept inside the home. Selmer's reforms signalled a more targeted medical effort against mental illness and simultaneously instigated the need to come up with a suitable architectural framework that could, for one thing, elevate the mentally ill persons' status in the society, and could, for another, offer these people a well-ordered and idealized microcosm where they, through everyday routines, could gradually regain their sanity. Selmer himself, in this connection, described the style behind the first of the mental hospitals in Riis Skov as the 'older manor style'.[18] We could, however, also push the point further than this and assert that hospitals are miniature societies where all the elements from the classic city are present: monuments, anonymous buildings, streets and squares. It is noteworthy that Bindesbøll, in his architecture, has simultaneously attempted to boil down the number of architectural motifs to very few, which are reused in different scales and situations. Herewith, the hierarchy that

Bindesbøll's facade elevations of the complex in Oringe, undated.

Plan of the first and the second floor in Oringe, undated.

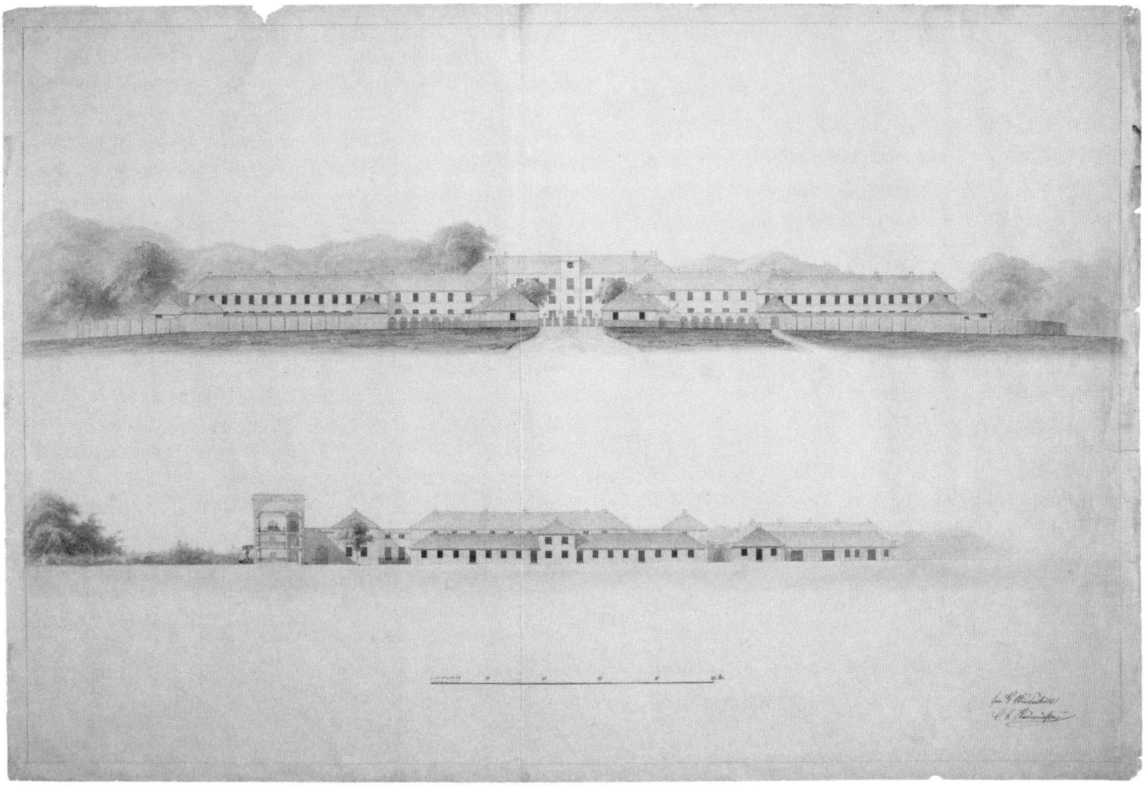

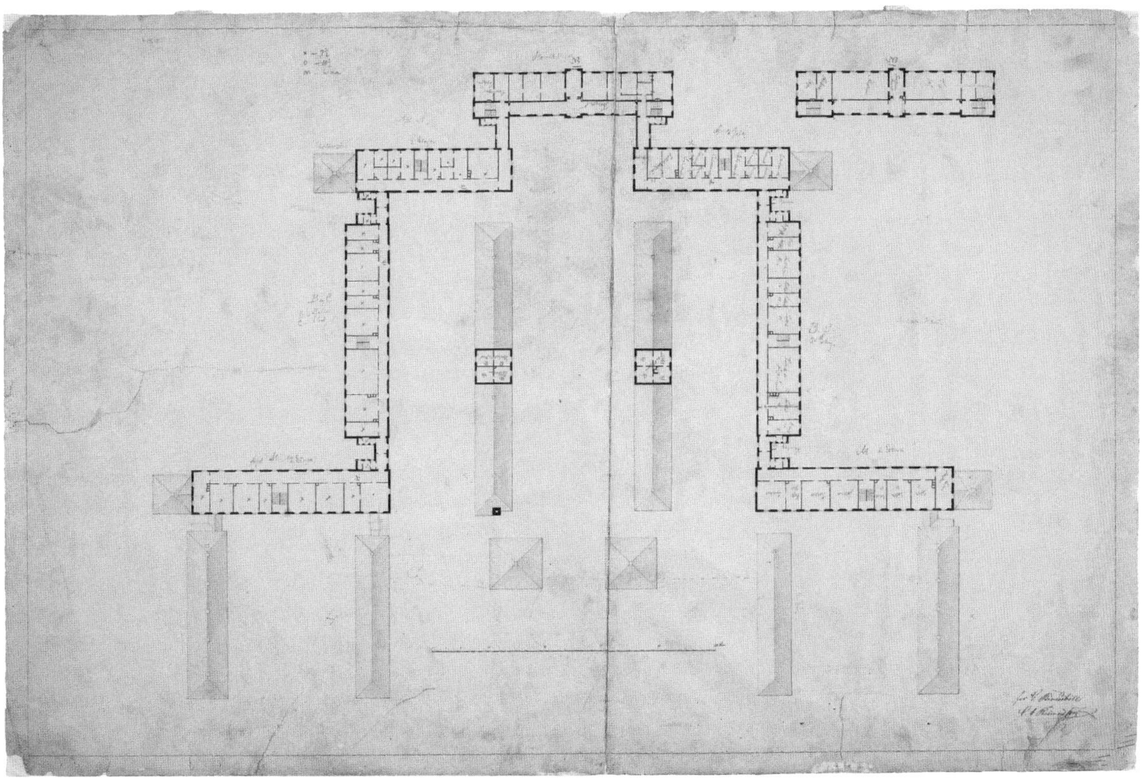

we know, for example, from the traditional manor is broken down.

At the Jydske Asyl in Riis Skov, Bindesbøll most clearly reaches back to a style that was inspired by Danish manor houses dating from the Renaissance: we meet the brickwork with horizontal stripes, the gables and the tower. But at the same time, Bindesbøll, instead of the traditional red brick, has chosen a yellow brick which, at that point in time, was ordinarily being used in more secular buildings. Similarly, he refrains from using the otherwise typical classicist pediments over the windows, except for the one at the entrance door. In many ways it is, quite precisely, the gable that comes to be the installation's recurring symbol: it appears no less than 25 times throughout the facility.

In *Kurhuset* at Sankt Hans and in the institution in Oringe, the facilities' recurring symbols become more commonplace. In these places, Bindesbøll has chosen a hipped roof as the recurring figure, which surmounts all of the building sections, from the main building to the cell wings. This everyday-like symbol is given the chance, both in Oringe and in Bindesbøll's original project proposal for *Kurhuset,* to stand forth in a pure and almost abstract way, inasmuch as any ornamentation that might refer to a particular style or construction detail, such as exposed rafters or socles, is avoided, by and large. Although these layouts, in their symmetry and in their emphasis on a main building, especially call to mind the Baroque era's castle layout, Bindesbøll is not operating here with the differentiation in decoration and details that one would otherwise know from this epoch. The main buildings, for example, do not have copper roofs: they rather have the same tiles as do the most humble parts of the installation. And at both Sankt Hans and Oringe, centrality is rejected: in Sankt Hans, inasmuch as the entrance is not to be found in the main building's central axis but rather in the sides; and in Oringe, by virtue of the fact

Bindesbøll's designs for pavilions and gateway in Oringe, undated.
→
The roofscape at Oringe, seen from the courtyard. Photo: Jens Lindhe.

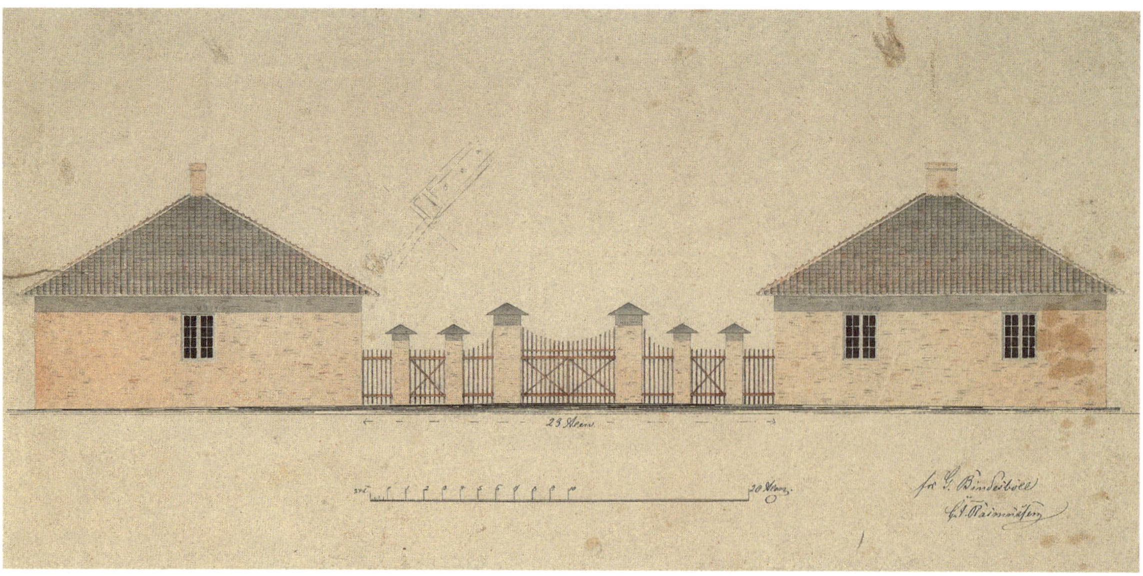

that the main building's windows' rhythm continues, unchallenged, right on past a tower-like middle section.

Seen from the outside, both Sankt Hans, in Bindesbøll's original proposal and Oringe appear as crystalline compositions, where one and the same geometry is repeated in different situations. The hierarchy is just barely retained. But most of all, what we have here is a hierarchy like that of a medieval town, where the surrounding houses follow the same growth principle as that of the cathedral. This can most clearly be seen in Oringe's entrance gate, where a series of piers with different pyramid terminations introduces the narrative and the building's recurring symbol: a commonplace house symbol, the hipped roof.

The last two of Bindesbøll's mental hospitals are idealized urban communities, where all classes, healthy and ill, are living together within the same house type.

## The hospitals in a context of social policy

The architecture in the three hospitals is not merely an expression of a particular societal order but also of a notion that the building's construction was related analogously, and in an organic way, to the patient's inner 'architecture'. A coherent architecture brought forth coherence in the mentally disordered person's life and mental apparatus. This manner of thinking is close to the romantic organicism concept, where society is regarded as a totality of component parts that cannot function alone. In this case, however, because of the particular jumping off point, with its specifically medical foundation, the spiritual dimension that otherwise characterizes the organicism concept has been toned down.

At the same time, the example with the hospitals shows that public-sector initiatives were being

taken to solve a societal problem in a way where both users' fees and public financing were woven together. A sense of public responsibility for the healthcare system has, in a Danish context, been a fact of life since the Reformation, when the state power took over the church's obligations in this area. As political scientist Tim Knudsen has discussed, the construction of the Scandinavian, publicly funded welfare state must in fact be regarded in this long-term perspective.[19] Normally, mention is made, in Danish social history, of the introduction of publicly financed old-age provisions in 1891 as the first step in the construction of the welfare state. But if we want to understand the preliminary conditions antecedent to the Danish welfare model, it makes sense to turn our gaze even further back.

The extensive hospital construction in the 1850s stands as an exception in relation to the economic liberalism which, headed up in part by Denmark's National Liberal Party, sets its mark on Denmark following the introduction of democracy in 1848. However, this does not mean to say that the ideology behind the hospitals was socialistic, social-conservative or ecclesiastical philanthropy, as was often the case with the somewhat later critique of liberalism during the latter half of the 1800s.[20] The hospitals, what with all their retention of a class system, are far from being 'socialistic'. But at the same time, on account of their scientific and progressive approach to the treatment of mental illness, they cannot be said to be conservative, either. And with their scientific approach, nor can they be said to have sprung forth from a Christian way of thinking, in the manner of the English Quakers' asylums that date from the end of the 1700s, and in the manner of certain segments of the prison system in the 1800s.

What we have here instead is a distinctive mindset that combines a scientific jumping-off point with a romantic conception of art. A similar mixture can be found in the work of Gottlieb Bindesbøll's mentor, the physicist Hans Christian Ørsted (1777-1851), who took the young Bindesbøll along with him in 1823 on his European tour. Separate natural forces like magnetism and electricity were, in both Ørsted's and Bindesbøll's projects, wonderfully linked together, in much the same way that the romantics' graceful Gothic cathedrals were linked up with nature.[21] In both worlds, thousands of tiny parts, functioning together, form a totality of 'vegetable-like' character. This romantic way of thinking about society and wholeness characterizes Bindesbøll's and Selmer's early welfare machines.

When we contemplate the architecture, what we meet in Bindesbøll's work is a vision of society where hierarchy and solidarity, community and individual, therapy and building have all been conceived into one and the same formula. Bindesbøll's use of a few recurring symbols in all situations, the remarkable interplay between hierarchical and uniform order and the unostentatious expression in, for example, Oringe are extraordinarily radical – also in relation to contemporary time's architecture. As my dissertation demonstrates, by virtue of a project like Oringe, Bindesbøll comes to influence an entire generation of Danish architects in the 20th century who played a role in shaping the welfare state. As the architect Ivar Bentsen (1876-1943) put it in 1924: 'For such a superior master of decoration like Bindesbøll, this 'stylelessness', this stringent, economic, structural, democratic realism compared with the past, must be due to a restraint conditioned by taste, a deliberate break with the past.'[22] The collective attitude underlying the later Danish welfare model cannot be found solely in the economic and political spheres: it is also seated there within the domain of architecture.

## Notes

1 J.K. Petersen, K. Petersen & N.F. Christiansen (eds.): *Frem mod socialhjælpsstaten. Dansk Velfærdshistorie, bind 1, 1536-1898* (2010). Within a Danish context, the development in 19th century psychiatry has, on the other hand, been more specifically described in, among other works: A. Mortensen: 'Den første psykiatriske debat', in: J. Nielsen & E. Danielsen (eds.): *Fra Jydske Asyl 1852 til Psykiatrisk Hospital i Århus 2002* (2002); J.L. Jakobsen: 'Fra Galehus i Middelalderen til Jydske Asyl i 1852', in Nielsen & Danielsen; M. Mellergaard: *Psykiatriens historie*. Published by Sankt Hans Hospital's Museum (2008); T.F. Nielsen: 'Fra dårekiste til terapeutisk anstalt. Dansk psykiatri 1800-1850', in J.V. Kragh (ed.): *Psykiatriens historie i Danmark* (2008), pp. 59-87; J. Møllerhøj: 'Sindssygdom, dårevæsen og videnskab. Asyltiden 1850-1920', in Kragh (2008), op.cit., pp. 88-119.

2 Peter Thule Kristensen: *Gottlieb Bindesbøll – Danmarks første moderne arkitekt/Gottlieb Bindesbøll – Denmark's First Modern Architect* (2013), pp. 346-77.

3 This definition has been inspired by G. Schulz: *Romantik. Geschichte und Begriff* (1996), which describes 'the romantic' as a broad and complex cultural stream.

4 H. Selmer: *Almindelige Grundsætninger for Daarevæsnets Indretning* (1846).

5 H. Selmer: 'Daareanstalternes Bygningsforhold i Tydskland og England', in *Bibliothek for Læger*, rk. 3, vol. 4, 1848, pp. 35-113.

6 H. Selmer, 'Den jydske Daareanstalt', in *Bibliothek for Læger*, rk. 3, vol. 11, 1852, pp. 381-463. The article, in an abridged form, was subsequently published with the title, *Den jydske Helbredelsesanstalt for Sindssyge*.

7 H.I. Gøtz & H. Gøtz: *Oringe – der var engang* (2003), p. 46.

8 Selmer (1848), op.cit., pp. 49-50.

9 Ibid., p. 45.

10 Ibid., p. 46.

11 Ibid., p. 109.

12 B. Edginton, 'A space for moral management: The York Retreat's influence on asylum design', in Topp, Moran & Andrews: *Madness, Architecture and the Built Environment. Psychiatric Spaces in Historical Context* (2007), p. 88.

13 H. Selmer (1852): 'Bilag A. Regulativ for Helbredelses-anstalten for Sindssyge i Nörrejylland', § 17 and § 26, in ibid., p. 443 and p. 446.

14 This definition is found in T. Knudsen (ed.): *Den nordiske protestantisme og velfærdsstaten*, Aarhus 2000, p. 23.

15 T.F. Nielsen, 'Fra dårekiste til terapeutisk anstalt. Dansk psykiatri 1800-1850', in Kragh (2008), op.cit., p. 64.

16 V. Lyhne, 'Kropsarkitekten', in: *Slagmark*, no. 27, 1997/98, p. 130f.

17 H. Selmer (1852), op.cit., pp. 386-87.

18 Ibid., p. 394.

19 T. Knudsen: *Den nordiske protestantisme og velfærdsstaten* (2000), p. 48.

20 See, especially T. Knudsen: *Den nordiske protestantisme og velfærdsstaten* (2000); Petersen, Petersen & Christiansen (2010), op.cit., p. 83f.

21 Cf. Kristensen (2013), op.cit., p. 16f.

22 I. Bentsen: 'G.M. Bindesbøll', in *Architekten*, vol. 26, no. 13, 1924, p. 157.

## Literature


- Bentsen, I.: 'G.M. Bindesbøll', in Architekten, vol. 26, nr. 13, 1924, p. 157.
- Edginton, B.: 'A space for moral management: The York Retreat's influence on asylum design', in Leslie Topp, James E. Moran & Jonathan Andrews (eds.), *Madness, Architecture and the Built Environment. Psychiatric Spaces in Historical Context*, New York 2007.
- Gøtz, Heidi Inger & Gøtz, Henning: *Oringe – der var engang*, Næstved 2003.
- Jakobsen, J.L.: 'Fra Galehus i Middelalderen til Jydske Asyl i 1852', in Nielsen & Danielsen; Mogens Mellergaard, *Psykiatriens historie*. Published by Sankt Hans Hospital's Museum, Roskilde 2008.
- Knudsen, T.: *Den nordiske protestantisme og velfærdsstaten*, Aarhus 2000.
- Kristensen, P.T.: *Gottlieb Bindesbøll – Danmarks første moderne arkitekt/Gottlieb Bindesbøll – Denmark's First Modern Architect*, Copenhagen 2013.
- Lyhne, V.: 'Kropsarkitekten', in *Slagmark*, no. 27, 1997/98.
- Mortensen, A., 'Den første psykiatriske debat', in Johannes Nielsen & Eddie Danielsen (eds.), *Fra Jydske Asyl 1852 til Psykiatrisk Hospital i Århus 2002*, Aarhus 2002.
- Møllerhøj, J.: 'Sindssygdom, dårevæsen og videnskab. Asyltiden 1850-1920', in Jesper Vaczy Kragh (ed.): *Psykiatriens historie i Danmark*, Copenhagen 2008, pp. 88-119.
- Nielsen, T.F.: 'Fra dårekiste til terapeutisk anstalt. Dansk psykiatri 1800-1850', in Jesper Vaczy Kragh (ed.): *Psykiatriens historie i Danmark*, Copenhagen 2008, pp. 59-87.
- Petersen, J.H., Petersen, K., & Christiansen, N.F. (eds.): *Frem mod socialhjælpsstaten. Dansk Velfærdshistorie*, Vol 1, 1536-1898, Odense 2010.
- Schulz, G.: *Romantik. Geschichte und Begriff*, Munich 1996.
- Selmer, H.: *Almindelige Grundsætninger for Daarevæsnets Indretning*, Copenhagen 1846.
- Selmer, H.: 'Daareanstalternes Bygningsforhold i Tydskland og England', in *Bibliothek for Læger*, rk. 3, vol. 4, 1848, pp. 35-113.
- Selmer, H.: 'Den jydske Daareanstalt', in *Bibliothek for Læger*, rk. 3, vol. 11, 1852.

Loa Kristine Teglgaard Christensen

# When the Institution Steps in over the Threshold

**Today, the home occupies an undisputed position as the preferred spatial frame around the care of frail and vulnerable elderly people in the welfare state. This status has been borne forth especially by normative conceptions of the home as an autonomous zone, where the individual, despite impairments and dependency, can live a more dignified life. In practice, however, what often happens is that the experience of autonomy and control is challenged when care is carried out within the setting of the home. The home, in other words, is not left unaffected.**

The important position that the home occupies in the contemporary Danish welfare state becomes clear when we take a closer look at the services and interventions by means of which the welfare state attempts to take care of its citizens and create the frames and the possibilities for 'the good life'. If we stop and consider, for example, the field that I am investigating, namely the care of the elderly in Denmark, we find that a common prefix is 'home-': 'preventative home visits'; 'home care'; and 'home-based rehabilitation', to mention only a few.

In a Danish context, from the early 1980s, the phrase 'For as long as possible in one's own home' ('Længst muligt i eget hjem') was introduced as the guiding principle for the provision of elder-care. It signalled an intention to deinstitutionalize the care of elderly people in favour of stepping up efforts to support their option to remain living within their own homes for as long as possible and receive the requisite care there.[1] More than three decades later, this principle still applies.[2] In an international perspective, the Danish policy motto, 'for as long as possible in one's own home', can be coupled to a much broader tendency that often goes under the umbrella term 'ageing-in-place'. Many of the policies that are currently being developed globally to accommodate the needs of the growing populations of elderly citizens have 'ageing-in-place' as their strategic backbone. The underlying premise is that the home and the local community are the optimal spaces for providing care and support to elderly people in order for them to remain as independent and self-reliant as possible for as long as possible.[3]

But where does this notion of *the home* as the optimal site of care originate from? How does it manifest itself? And what actually happens with the home when care is undertaken within its physical space? Through a series of empirical observations from an ongoing ethnographic field-work examining municipal eldercare in Denmark, I will try in what follows to answer these questions.

## Home rather than institution

The discourse of deinstitutionalization and the efforts to promote ageing-in-place build on certain key notions of 'welfare', 'home' and 'institution', and on the interconnections between them. When I asked a care worker what it meant to the encounter between the citizen and the municipality that such a meeting would take place within the older person's own home, he replied:

*Within the world of ball games, you have what's called 'home grounds' and 'away grounds'. And I know, of course, that the same rules apply* [when you play at home as when you play away]. *But in this particular context, we probably ought to think that when we are inside the home, it's the citizen who, to a greater degree, defines the rules.*

This understanding of *the home* as the place where the resident has determinative rights and control over what happens within the four walls can be linked to a well-known cultural notion of the home as a special autonomous zone. The home is typically associated with self-determination, with privacy and with control.[4] Generally speaking, the professionals whom I have met during my fieldwork ascribe a great deal of value to the fact that the encounter between them and the citizen takes place in the citizen's own home.[5] They express a fundamental desire to respect the autonomy, control and privacy that are associated with the home, and most of them strive to comply with this principle. Several have told me that they, upon stepping into the citizen's home, take on a role comparable with that of a guest. The professionals also express the view that the citizen is endowed with more 'dignity' when the meeting takes place on his or her 'home ground'. The underlying rationale seems to be that dignity is promoted because the encounter is more *equal* when it takes place in the older person's own home. The professionals have the power, by virtue of being representatives of a vested authority, to influence the granting or the withdrawal of benefits. But when the citizen, on the other hand, has the control that is associated with being at home, there seems to be an assumption that the relationship of power becomes more balanced – it becomes more equal. In this vein, the Norwegian anthropologist Marianne Gullestad points out that the home in a Scandinavian context is associated with equality, in marked contrast to the State and the market, which are associated with hierarchy and formality. The home is the place where many feel that they have control: 'In popular belief,' she writes, 'the home is a last, closely defended bastion still unconquered by bureaucracy and the market economy.'[6] The institution, on the other hand, is traditionally conceived of as being characterized by an uneven power relation and by social differentiation between the staff and the residents.

In addition to being associated with control, privacy, autonomy and equality, the home is typically associated with *authenticity*.[7] For instance, during my fieldwork I have often come across the idea that as a professional you meet more authentic versions of the citizens when the encounter takes place on their 'home ground'. The home is generally perceived as being the place where one really 'can be oneself'.[8] There is a widespread assumption that this situation is quite the opposite of what we see with the institution: "Institutional care' has for a long time been associated with a set of de-individualizing characteristics', as formulated by Dorrer and colleagues .[9] Institutions are generally perceived as uniformizing and consequently as being oppressive to the resident's individuality and opportunity to be his/her authentic self: the resident has to adapt to the institution, and not vice versa. The professionals whom I have met seem to subscribe to this ideal, but moreover they express the view that the home as a frame around the encounter gives them an advantage in relation to the specific task they are supposed to solve. When, for instance, they are assigned to assess a particular citizen's situation, they experi-

The bedroom of a home-care recipient.

ence that they obtain a more integrated and genuine picture of the person inside the home. This, they explain, is partly because the person being visited feels more secure at home and thus to a greater degree can 'be him/herself', and partly because the materiality of the home itself can be decoded as signs and thereby contribute towards forming the most undisturbed and authentic picture of the citizen and his/her condition.[10] As a professional who specialized in performing preventive home visits once explained to me, it was already out on the road, as she approached the driveway and could see if the area around the house was well cared for and that the lawn had been mowed, that she started forming a picture of the person whom she was going to visit.

The close links between the respective ideas about welfare, home and institution also emerge in Susanne Højlund's anthropological study of a particular type of children's home that is known in Denmark as the 'mini-institution'.[11] At these children's homes, the concept of 'homeliness' constitutes the explicit ideological principle on which the everyday pedagogical practice is founded. In situations where the physical institution cannot be avoided, homeliness continues to stand forth insistently as the ideal for how the institution is organized, socially as well as materially. In the event that a 'real' home cannot be the physical frame around the welfare state's attempt to take care of its citizens, homeliness is to be pursued.[12] The staff of social workers wish to dissociate themselves from everything perceived as institutional and are trying, fundamentally, to organize the institution as a non-institution.[13] In relation to this dichotomized discourse, Højlund concludes:

*In a recurring motif, homeliness is described as a response to the idea of the large, anonymous institution, which is seen to represent rationality, instrumental reasoning, bureaucracy, distance, and non-authenticity.*[14]

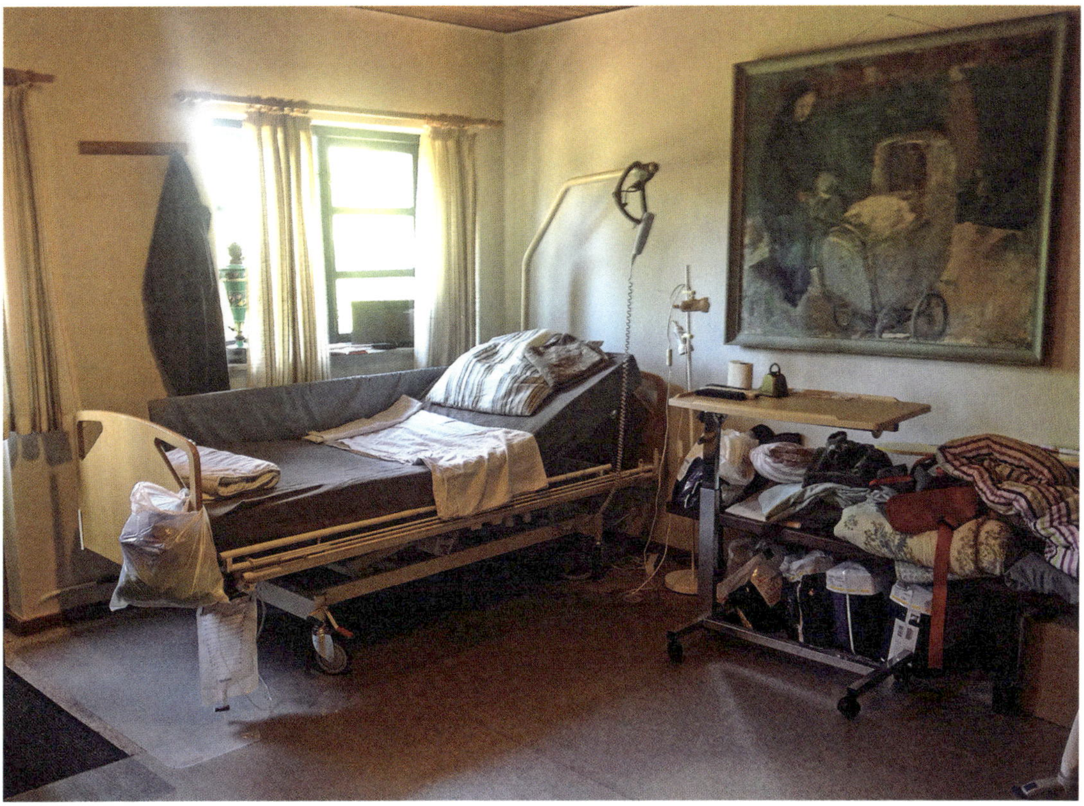

It's as if the home, in the context of the Danish welfare state, cannot fully be conceived without an often-implicit reference to its imagined antithesis: the institution. And conversely, the institution cannot be fully understood without having the home in mind.[15] They relate reciprocally to each other: as ideas, they have become each other's 'standard "Other".'[16]

## The porous home

But what actually happens when the home is turned into the space where care is given and received? What happens when the ideal of home (rather than institution) runs up against practice? Let me illustrate, by way of example, with Gyda's story.

For 40 years, Gyda lived in a small first floor flat in a housing association in a Danish provincial town. Up until six months ago, Gyda was managing her everyday life without receiving any kind of assistance from the municipality. But then she fell and broke her hip. From that moment on, her life changed dramatically. Our first meeting took place at the municipal respite-care ward, where she had been staying for about a month following her hip operation. I visited her together with a physiotherapist from the municipality, who routinely asked her about the physical framework in her flat, to where Gyda, according to the plan, would soon be moving back. 'What about the doorsteps? And do you have many carpets? It has to be possible for you to move around with the walker, you know.' At one point in the conversation, the therapist broaches the question of whether it might be possible for Gyda to put in a request for a flat on the building's ground floor, so that she would not have to stress and strain about climbing all the stairs whenever she wants to go out. The question triggers off a reaction that I think surprises both the therapist and me. Gyda replies promptly and with a great degree of fury that nobody is going to take her home away from her. She knows well that this is what everybody

wants to do, she says, and starts to cry. She wants to go *home*.

My encounter with Gyda served to corroborate Mark Vacher and Maja Højer's statement that the home, 'for many people [is,] the most solid reference point in life'.[17] They write that the home, in different ways, can 'constitute an ontological foundation which, if it should collapse, runs the risk of shaking life beyond recognition.'[18] If we take Gyda's situation as an example, the converse appears to be the case: When one's life becomes insecure, when illness and misfortune threaten one's feeling of control, the home can become the ontological mainstay that one can cling to. Seen in this light, the feeling of impotence that Gyda expressed, and which initially surprised me due to its vehemence, may not be all that surprising. She had experienced the fractured hip and the ensuing months of treatment and rehabilitation, first at the hospital and, later on, at the respite-care ward, as a sweeping loss of control. For her the longing to *come home* again was connected to a longing to regain control.

Gyda did eventually come home. When I interviewed her again, she had been home for a few months. Although she expressed satisfaction with being at home, my meeting with her left me with the impression that the home she had come back to was not the same as the one she left when she was transported to the hospital. In contrast to what had been the situation in the past, she was now receiving home care on a daily basis, help with the cleaning every other week and additionally, for the first few months, she was visited intermittently by a physiotherapist whose task was to evaluate and follow up on the home training programme which Gyda was supposed to carry out on a daily basis. As a consequence, there was a daily flux of people coming in and out of her apartment. Even though the planners in municipal eldercare strive towards continuity of care workers, meaning that the individual eldercare recipient only should be met by the same few primary home carers, it is not always possible to achieve this in practice. As is frequently the case at any workplace, at any workplace, sick days and other factors mean that every now and then, temporary staff workers come to take the place of the steady personnel. Gyda expressed a perception that there was 'a crush' of many different people. She confided in me, in a moment of obvious frustration, that one day, 'somebody from the municipality' had dropped by for the purpose of replacing something or other – some article of equipment that they use for cleaning. Now, this might seem to be a fairly innocuous incident: an isolated unannounced, albeit short, visit. For Gyda, however, it took on a great degree of importance. The experience of order and predictability, which had (to a greater degree) characterized her life before she was injured, had not been re-established. The autonomy and control that the home stood for were not intact, after all. 'The institution' was present in her home as a not always predictable flow of people, objects and practices, and this had rendered her home porous.

## When the boundaries between public and private are transcended

As previously described, the 'guest role' becomes an ideal for the professionals, because it represents certain broader notions about the home as an autonomous zone that must not be violated. What is regarded as paramount is that the privacy and control, which, as we have seen, are generally associated with the home, are respected and maintained. Accordingly, seeing oneself as a guest in the citizen's home is a manifestation of an ethical standpoint.[19] In practice, however, it is not always possible for the professionals to act in accordance with this ideal: being a professional



The blue plastic slippers signal 'institution', efficiency and hygiene.

at work, you will inevitably come to do things that an 'ordinary' guest would never do. This could be keeping one's shoes on when walking into the house, or wearing latex gloves or the characteristic blue 'plastic slippers' which, at least in a Danish context, unequivocally signal 'institution' and institution-related rationales concerning, for example, hygiene and efficiency.

When stepping in from the outside, it can be difficult to navigate one's way into where the boundaries are drawn in this landscape of different rationales. I experienced this myself one of the first times that I was accompanying a home care worker on a home visit; while standing in the entrance hallway, I customarily bent over to untie my shoelaces. 'Don't take off your shoes!' said the employee to me, brusquely, in a hushed albeit determined tone. 'Well, ummm, okay,' I managed to mutter, and straightened myself up. The elderly woman who lived in the house was now on her way towards us, and I felt somewhat embarrassed because I had inadvertently come to draw the attention to this non-action that indicated 'institution' rather than 'home'. On the one hand, we were entering her home as guests; on the other hand, the care worker I followed was on the job, and had to comply with hygiene-related guidelines and a tight schedule.

Another practice that plays a part in blurring the boundaries between public and private and between the roles as guest and as professional are the key boxes that many home-care recipients have mounted next to their front doors. The home care workers have a master key that can unlock the various key boxes, and inside each of the key boxes is a key to the house. This solution is meant to be an aid for the care recipient, who may struggle to get out of bed in the morning hours, and it is convenient for the professionals who do not have to wait around while a resident who may be both hard of hearing and slow to walk responds to the doorbell and manages to open up the front door.

The key box is a widely used technology in Danish home care.

→

The 'paraphernalia of care' taking up space in a home-care recipient's bathroom.

Both of the practices that I have chosen to put forth here as examples unfold themselves around the door's threshold, which precisely marks out the home's boundary. 'The threshold,' states Gullestad, 'is the most important boundary between the private and the public. The entrance door, the locks, the nameplate, the doormat and the bell can all be regarded as practical and symbolic markings of this boundary. It is, at one and the same time, both a barrier and a defence.'[20] 'The barrier and the defence' are transcended when institutional logics and practices enter into the home, in practice resulting in a series of dilemmas. When the home becomes increasingly significant in the everyday lives of older people whose mobility is constrained, paradoxically it is simultaneously becoming more 'public'.[21] The vulnerable body often implies that the home, as a zone for autonomy, control and privacy, becomes vulnerable.

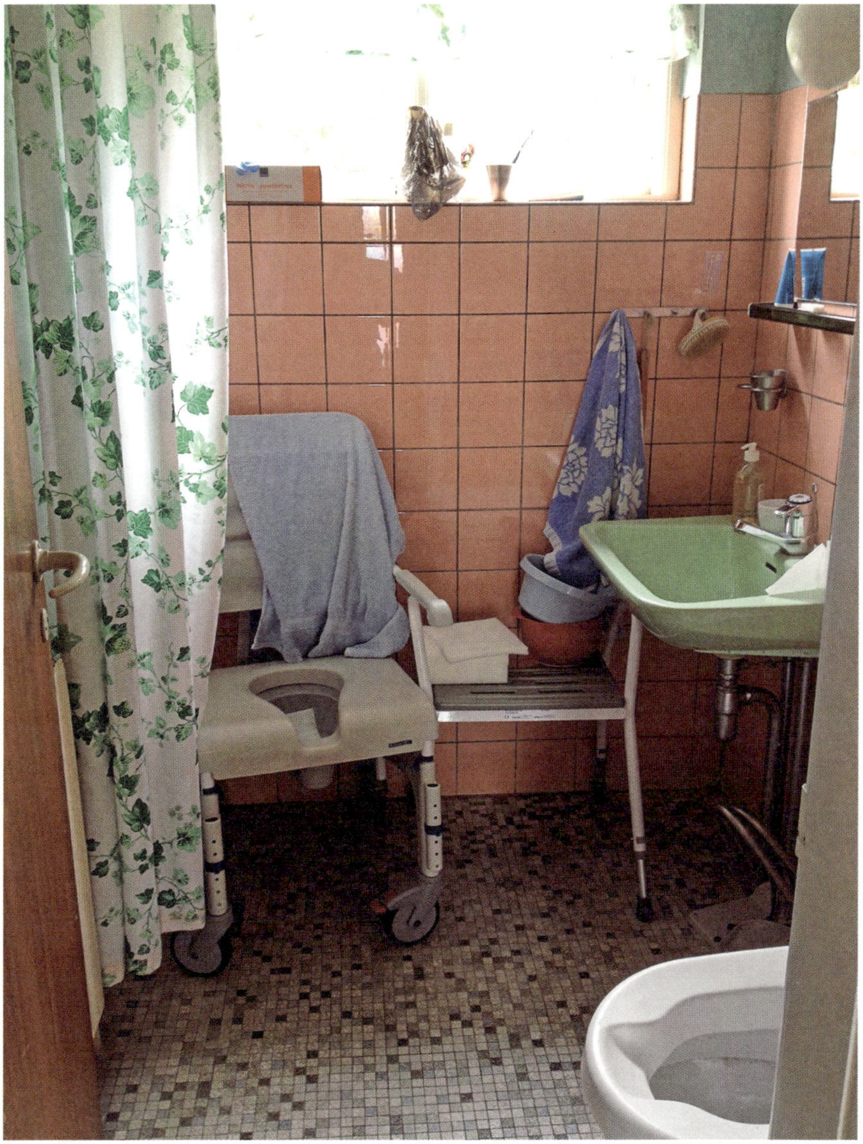

## The material manifestation of the institution within the home

The walker. The compression stocking applicator. The hospital bed. The bedside commode. The threshold ramp. The hoists. Frequently, the objective that older people should be able to remain living in their homes for as long as possible requires the importation of the 'paraphernalia of care' into the domestic home. Even though many people feel that they benefit from these aids and experience them as being 'enablers'[22] in their everyday lives, it is not always without ambivalence and some degree of resistance that they offer them a place in their homes. During my visits to elderly persons' homes, I was occasionally amazed to witness some of the strategies used to conceal or even negate the aid's presence; compression stocking aids were put away in invisible nooks and crannies and bedside commodes were camouflaged. The latter I experienced during a home visit, when I was about to make myself comfortable in what to me looked like an (admittedly somewhat tall) easy chair, but proved to be a commode that was covered with a brilliantly coloured fabric. The woman we were visiting was living in a densely furnished cottage, with a small bathroom, which left no room for a bedside commode. For this reason, it had been allocated space within the living room. It was only because the home-helper whom I was accompanying on

this visit discreetly made signs to me at the very last moment that I dodged sinking down into the commode. Henriette Langstrup (2013) uses the term 'chronic care infrastructures' to denote the different socio-material elements (activities and objects) that form part of – and produce – the treatment of chronic illness at home. One of her points is that these elements, in addition to the effect of treatment, also in practice elicit 'place-making effects'. When for instance the bedside commode is covered, or when other kinds of assitive aids are hidden away, this can be understood as an attempt to deal with and negotiate the 'placemaking effects' that a given object elicits within the home.

## Extitution – from the territorial institution to complex care arrangements

In Denmark we have seen an ideologically motivated deinstitutionalization of society's care for the elderly. For more than three decades, the ideal that ageing citizens are supposed to remain 'for as long as possible in their own homes' has been a guiding principle for the welfare state's organization of eldercare, and the home has gradually come to take on a naturalized status as the the optimal place for caring for and treating frail elderly people. The home, and homeliness, are associated with notions of 'the good life' and concomitantly, there have been attempts to integrate them into different spheres of welfare provision – spanning from pedagogy to eldercare. In many ways, the ideal of home-based care arose as a response to the notion of the large and anonymous institution characterized by de-individualizing and disempowering institutional practices. In this article, I have engaged with the question of how the home is affected, socially and materially, when the welfare institution, as it were, 'steps in over the threshold'. As a consequence of making up the physical frame around formal care, professional intervention and labour, the home becomes a paradoxical space. The underlying ideal is spatial continuity for the elderly as well as the autonomy associated with it. However, care and health-related interventions performed at home in the context of eldercare in Denmark do not leave the home unaffected. Implying the emplacement of objects and activities, home-based care and treatment often have placemaking effects, which are then negotiated in the encounter between different actors such as the elderly themselves, the professionals, other residents in the house and the home's materialities. Deinstitutionalization and the circumstance that care and treatment is undertaken within the citizens' own homes do not necessarily entail that 'the institution' disappears entirely from the lives of the people who are in need of care. It merely manifests itself in other kinds of spaces. In order to capture this particular paradox, Christine Milligan, inspired by Vitores (2002), makes use of the notion of *extitution*. Extitution represents the idea that processes of deinstitutionalization do not necessarily imply a complete cessation of the institution, but rather a *virtualization* of it. The institution, at one and the same time, is de-territorialized and re-manifests itself in other care arrangements which are constituted by both physical and virtual elements, be they the physical space of the house, electronic journals, alarms, telecare-technologies, telephones etc.[23] – in other words, care arrangements that are generally characterized by a far greater complexity in time and space than what can be seen in the traditional territorial institution. In the context of the discourse expressing that elderly people ought to remain living for as long as possible in their own homes, architects and designers might see fit to work with a kind of re-establishment of the threshold. With the purpose of

Many older people rely on walkers to move across the threshold between the home and the outside world.

supporting the possibility of ageing-in-place, a rather impressive multiplicity of aids has been developed, spanning from very low tech to highly advanced technologies. The vast majority of these, however, have been targeted towards facilitating bodily functions and the performance of activities. One could pose the question, however, whether these efforts should be aimed not only at enabling elderly people, physically and practically, to remain living for as long as possible at home. Perhaps the focus should also be on how to assist elderly people in upholding a sense of control in their own homes. This might be attainable through an increased attention on maintaining the threshold, for example, through different forms of gatekeeping technologies. By doing so, the task becomes one of not only supporting the frail and impaired body, but also of shoring up and sustaining a social role.

**Notes**

1 M. Lewinter: 'Developments in home help for elderly people in Denmark: the changing concept of home and institution', *International Journal of Social Welfare*, no. 13, 2004, pp. 89-96, H van der Boom: *Home nursing in Europe: patterns of professionalization and institutionalization of home care and family care to elderly people in Denmark, France, the Netherlands and Germany* (2009) and H.H. Petersen: *Velfærd for ældre. Holdning og handling* (2008).

2 H.M. Dahl, L. Eskelinen & E.B. Hansen: 'Coexisting principles and logics of elder care: help to self-help and consumer-oriented service?', *International Journal of Social Welfare*, vol. 24, 2015, pp. 287-295.

3 C. Milligan: *There's no place like home: place and care in an ageing society* (2009). This applies not only to the care of the elderly. 'Home-based care' is an ideal in the treatment and the care of many target groups with disabilities or chronic diseases, and the development of various forms of telecare- and monitoring technologies is supposed to support this ideal and render it feasible. I. Dyck, P. Kontos, J. Angus & P. McKeever: 'The home as a site for long-term care: meanings and management of bodies and spaces', *Health & Place*, vol. 11, 2005, pp. 173-185, A. van Hout, J. Pols & D. Willems: 'Shining trinkets and unkempt gardens: on the materiality of care', *Sociology of Health and Illness*, vol. 37, no. 8, 2015, pp. 1206-1217 and H. Langstrup: 'Chronic care infrastructures and the home', *Sociology of Health and Illness*, vol. 35, no. 7, 2013, pp. 1008-1022.

4 I. Dyck, P. Kontos, J. Angus & P. McKeever: 'The home as a site for long-term care: meanings and management of bodies and spaces', *Health & Place*, vol. 11, 2005, pp. 173-185; K.M. Raahauge: *En Århusantropologi*, PhD thesis (2007); D. Stones & J. Gullifer: "At home it's just so much easier to be yourself': older adults' perceptions of ageing in place', *Ageing and Society*, vol. 36, no. 3, 2016, pp. 449-81; A. Leibing, N. Guberman & J. Wiles: 'Liminal homes: older people, loss of capacities, and the present future of living spaces', *Journal of Aging Studies*, no. 37, 2016, pp. 10-19.

5 Cf. A. van Hout, J. Pols & D. Willems: 'Shining trinkets and unkempt gardens: on the materiality of care', *Sociology of Health and Illness*, vol. 37, no. 8, 2015, pp. 1206-1217.

6 M. Gullestad: 'The transformation of the Norwegian notion of everyday life', *American Ethnologist*, vol. 18, 1991, p. 488.

7 S. Højlund: 'Home as a model for sociality in Danish children's homes: a question of authenticity', *Social Analysis*, vol. 55, no. 2, 2011.

8 D. Stones & J. Gullifer: "At home it's just so much easier to be yourself': older adults' perceptions of ageing in place', *Ageing and Society*, vol. 36, no. 3, 2016, pp. 449-81.

9 N. Dorrer, I. McIntosh, S. Punch & R. Emond: 'Children and food practices in residential care: ambivalence in the 'institutional' home', *Children's Geographies*, vol. 8, no. 3, 2010, pp. 247-59, p. 254.

10 Cf. A. van Hout, J. Pols & D. Willems: 'Shining trinkets and unkempt gardens: on the materiality of care', *Sociology of Health and Illness*, vol. 37, no. 8, 2015, pp. 1206-17.

11 S. Højlund: 'Home as a model for sociality in Danish children's homes: a question of authenticity', *Social Analysis*, vol. 55, no. 2, 2011.

12 In Danish the word denoting homeliness is 'hjemlighed', a compound consisting of 'hjem' ('home') and the word 'lighed' ('likeness' or 'resemblance'), thus literally meaning home-likeness.

13 N. Dorrer, I. McIntosh, S. Punch & R. Emond: 'Children and food practices in residential care: ambivalence in the 'institutional' home', *Children's Geographies*, vol. 8, no. 3, 2010, pp. 247-59.

14 S. Højlund: 'Home as a model for sociality in Danish children's homes: a question of authenticity', *Social Analysis*, vol. 55, no. 2, 2011, p. 118.

15 Cf. K. Lützen: *Byen tæmmes: kernefamilie, sociale reformer og velgørenhed i 1800-tallets København*. Hans Reitzels Forlag, 1998, Copenhagen, and S. Højlund: 'Home as a model for sociality in Danish children's homes: a question of authenticity', *Social Analysis*, vol. 55, no. 2, 2011, pp. 106-20.

16 Cf. M. Douglas: 'The idea of a home: a kind of space', *Social Research*, vol. 58, no. 1, 1991, pp. 287-307.

17 M. Højer & M. Vacher: 'Om hjemblindhed og husets antropologi', *Tidsskriftet Antropologi*, *Hus og hjem*, no. 59/60, 2009, p. 10.
18 Ibid.
19 Cf. A. Santos Salas & B.L. Cameron: 'Ethical openings in palliative home care practice', *Nursing Ethics*, vol. 17, no. 5, 2010, pp. 655-65.
20 M. Gullestad: *Kultur og hverdagsliv* (1989), p. 53; quote translated by the author.
21 I. Dyck, P. Kontos, J. Angus & P. McKeever: 'The home as a site for long-term care: meanings and management of bodies and spaces', *Health & Place*, vol. 11, 2005, pp. 173-85
22 A. van Hout, J. Pols & D. Willems: 'Shining trinkets and unkempt gardens: on the materiality of care', *Sociology of Health and Illness*, vol. 37, no. 8, 2015, pp. 1206-17.
23 C. Milligan: *There's no place like home: place and care in an ageing society* (2009).

**Literature**


- Dahl, H.M., Eskelinen, L., & Hansen, E.B.: 'Coexisting principles and logics of elder care: help to self-help and consumer-oriented service?', *International Journal of Social Welfare*, vol. 24, 2015, pp. 287-95.
- Dorrer, N., McIntosh, I., Punch, S., & Emond, R.: 'Children and food practices in residential care: ambivalence in the 'institutional' home', *Children's Geographies*, vol. 8, no. 3, 2010, pp. 247-59.
- Douglas, M.: 'The idea of a home: a kind of space', *Social Research*, vol. 58, no. 1, 1991, pp. 287-307.
- Dyck, I., Kontos, P., Angus, J., & McKeever, P.: 'The home as a site for long-term care: meanings and management of bodies and spaces', *Health & Place*, vol. 11, 2005, pp. 173-85.
- Gullestad, M.: *Kultur og hverdagsliv*, Universitetsforlaget, Oslo 1989.
- Gullestad, M.: 'The transformation of the Norwegian notion of everyday life', *American Ethnologist*, vol. 18, 1991, pp. 480-99.
- Højer, M. & M. Vacher: 'Om hjemblindhed og husets antropologi', *Tidsskriftet Antropologi*, *Hus og hjem*, nos. 59/60, 2009, pp. 3-16.
- Højlund, S.: 'Hjemlighed som velfærdsparadoks: om iscenesat autenticitet i døgninstitutioner for anbragte børn', *Tidsskriftet Antropologi*, nos. 59/60, *Hus og hjem*, 2009, pp. 49-66.
- Højlund, S.: 'Home as a model for sociality in Danish children's homes: a question of authenticity', *Social Analysis*, vol. 55, no. 2, 2011, pp. 106-20.
- Langstrup, H.: 'Chronic care infrastructures and the home', *Sociology of Health and Illness*, vol., 35, no. 7, 2013, pp. 1008-22.
- Leibing, A., Guberman, N., & Wiles, J.: 'Liminal homes: older people, loss of capacities, and the present future of living spaces', *Journal of Aging Studies*, no. 37, 2016, pp. 10-19.
- Lewinter, M.: 'Developments in home help for elderly people in Denmark: the changing concept of home and institution', *International Journal of Social Welfare*, no. 13, 2004, pp. 89-96.
- Lützen, K.: *Byen tæmmes: kernefamilie, sociale reformer og velgørenhed i 1800-tallets København*. Hans Reitzels Forlag, Copenhagen 1998.
- Milligan, C.: *There's no place like home: place and care in an ageing society*, Ashgate, Farnham 2009.
- Petersen, H.H.: *Velfærd for ældre. Holdning og handling*, Syddansk Universitetsforlag, Odense 2008.
- Raahauge, K.M.: *En Århusantropologi*, PhD thesis, SBi's forlag, Hørsholm 2007.
- Stones, D., & Gullifer, J.: "At home it's just so much easier to be yourself': older adults' perceptions of ageing in place', *Ageing and Society*, vol. 36, no. 3, 2016, pp. 449-81.
- van Der Boom, H.: *Home nursing in Europe: patterns of professionalization and institutionalization of home care and family care to elderly people in Denmark, France, the Netherlands and Germany*, Aksan, Amsterdam 2009.
- van Hout, A., Pols, J., & Willems, D.: 'Shining trinkets and unkempt gardens: on the materiality of care', *Sociology of Health and Illness*, vol. 37, no. 8, 2015, pp. 1206-17.
- Vitores, A.: 'From hospital to community: case management and the virtualization of institutions', *Athenea Digital*, no. 1, pp. 1-6, www.raco.cat/index.php/Athenea/article/view/34097/33936, 2002, retrieved on March 15, 2016.
- Santos Salas, A. & Cameron, B.L.: 'Ethical openings in palliative home care practice', *Nursing Ethics*, vol. 17, no. 5, 2010, pp. 655-65.

Camilla Hedegaard Møller

# Colours for Welfare?

## The Controversy around Gernes's Decoration of Herlev Hospital

**Can art contribute to the welfare of patients? A discussion about this issue broke out in Denmark in 2012, when one of the floors at Herlev Hospital was refurbished; this public hospital had been the site of a 'total decoration', conceived and executed in the 1970s by Poul Gernes. In the course of time, Gernes's decoration has come to acquire the status of an artwork which is, moreover, beneficial to the patients. However, on the cardiac ward, the opposite impression emerged. The article describes, from an 'ANT-perspective', what it was that led up to the conversion project, how power was mobilized, and how the decoration, as such, became an active player.**

## Prologue

**When the artist Poul Gernes decorated Herlev Hospital,[1] in a project that started in 1968 and was completed in 1976, he contributed to one of the Danish welfare society's icons: the modern hospital. Here, new technology and whatever were the latest advances within medical science were supposed to heal the folk. However, Gernes found the day's concrete building constructions to be inhuman. For this reason, he executed a brilliantly coloured building-integrated decoration, which was supposed to bring joy and encouragement to the patients.[2] Ergo,** *colours for welfare.*

According to a conservation manual prepared by the Ministry of Culture's Agency for Culture in 2014, the hospital's lobby is adorned with decorated wall panels while the rest of the decoration consists of a total colour scheme, which is based on a colour system.[3] The system is linked up with the artist's practical ruminations on finding one's way around and being able to distinguish between functions. As described in my article, 'Gernes: Herlev Hospital. Integreret kunst med tiden' [Gernes: Herlev Hospital. Integrated art over time], the colour system is presented in a colour manual which, for years, to a relatively great degree, contributed to maintaining the decoration.[4] The colour principles were undoubtedly a stroke of genius because they allow the decoration to change in synch with the house, but Gernes was not able to foresee everything. For this reason, a number of the instructions have come to be impossible to follow.

According to Hans Edvard Nørregård-Nielsen, Poul Gernes (1925-96) was active in Den eksperimenterende Kunstskole [the Experimental Art School] from 1961; this posed an alternative to The Royal Danish Academy of Fine Arts, an alternative that was absorbed with the notion of collective expression, with whatever was non-commercial in art, and with a more direct contact with the viewers. Gernes was a pioneer within monumental and integrated art, and this was manifested in a most dramatic way with his decoration of Herlev Hospital. In this same period, several public decorations could be seen, against the backdrop of legislation that set up the Danish Arts Foundation: the art was now to be found, to a greater degree, right there where the citizens were.[5]

Both Peter M. Hornung and Ulrikka Gernes,[6] as well as Erik Steffensen,[7] define the decoration of Herlev Hospital as being a veritable masterpiece in Danish decorative art. The unique relationship between architecture and art has most recently been discussed by Anne Mette Rahbæk as '(...) one of the 20th century's Danish building- and decoration-related icons and an important part of our common cultural heritage, which is supposed to be preserved for posterity.'[8]

A vehement debate broke out in the Danish daily newspaper *Politiken* in 2012, when it was revealed to the public that the third floor of the hospital's 'bed tower' had recently been re-equipped as a cardiology unit. With sleek glass surfaces, with wood as material, with contemporary design and with fewer coloured elements, this section of the hospital looked very different than the other wards.

In the opinion of the chief physician of the cardiac unit, Gernes's decoration was no longer conducive to promoting good health. On the contrary, the physician felt, the colours contributed to bringing about a poor working environment. Now the question was whether Gernes's colours promote well-being. How should the welfare society's hospital be defined, in the first place?

When Gernes decorated Herlev Hospital, what was at stake was a building-integrated work. Subsequently, there are at least two very divergent expositions that can be traced about how Herlev Hospital, with Gernes's decoration, ought to be

Preparatory work by Poul Gernes. Courtesy of KØS – Museum of Art in Public Spaces.

→

Sketch by Poul Gernes. Courtsey of Museum of Artistic Process and Public Art, Lund.

understood, and two very divergent expositions about the effects that the decoration makes. If these expositions are viewed in terms of team- and network-formation, what emerge are at least two tendencies, which implicate widely different 'actors' in relation to the colours of the wards. What, within the one grouping, has become, in the course of time, tedious and increasingly pricey colours, has, within the other grouping, come to take on an attribution of value and has come to be regarded as a masterpiece in Danish decorative art: as a cultural legacy worthy of preservation. As encouraging art, for all the patients. Accordingly, as welfare, also for the future. The two tendencies have been asymmetric and have evidently been proceeding in parallel but segregated contexts until 2012.

## The decoration

With his decoration of Herlev Hospital there was an essential change of tack in Poul Gernes's practice. From then on, he worked intensively with large decoration assignments and distanced himself from the commercial circuit in the art world and from elitist art. Poul Gernes was of the opin-

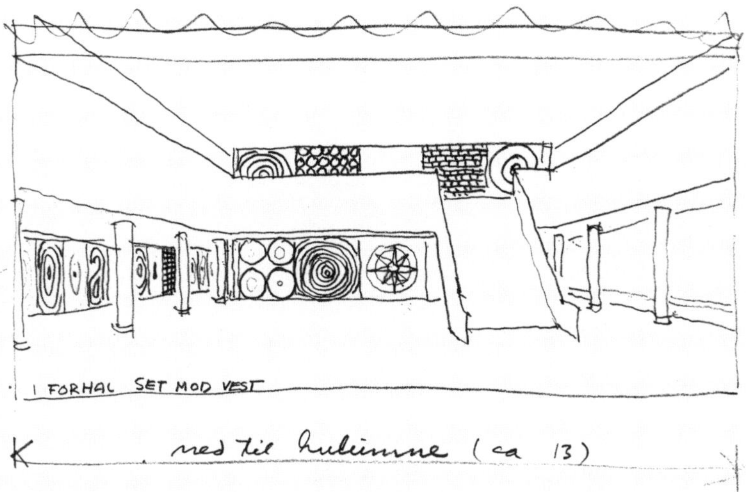


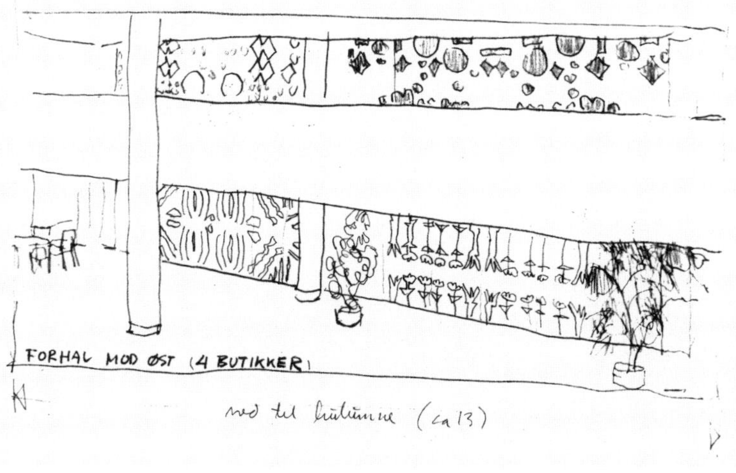

ion that art was supposed to enrich society, be useful and be present, right there where people were. He was an advocate of brilliantly coloured decorations, and he wrote that the scope and quality of decorations was quite possibly '(...) proportional to society's dynamics, welfare and vitality'.[9] The common and collective were also typically present in the actual execution of the building-integrated decoration assignments. For example, the textile painter and craftswoman Aase Seidler Gernes (born in 1927), who was married to Poul Gernes, held a significantly more prominent role than has generally been acknowledged.[10] Poul Gernes had a theory that colours affect people's moods in a positive way, largely because the sense of sight is associated with feelings. It was upon this theory that he based the decoration of Herlev Hospital. Sample modules were tested out, initially, at Gentofte Hospital, with mainly good results; this paved the way for giving the green light to the decoration of Herlev Hospital.[11] Along with its decoration, Herlev Hospital consists, in terms of composition, of three basic elements that are relevant here: the vertical bed tower, the horizontal treatment department, with its lobby, and the auditoriums.[12][13] The decoration is extraordinarily complex, but here I will present some of the main ideas: the bed tower is simply organized, with wards out towards the facade and a core of servicing spaces and functions in the centre. The walls behind the beds' headboards are white, but the wards are otherwise coloured in relation to the character of the incident light that their orientation provides: yellow is suited to the morning sun, emanating from the east; orange and red emphasize the warm light from the south; blue and green are becoming to the colder northern light; and the sunset is underscored by tones

in apricot. The horizontal treatment building is coloured according to its various functions: for example, the maternity ward is bright green while the blood bank is red. The lobby or arrival hall is characterized by storey-high wall friezes of pictorial fields filled with circles, patterns, a target, a poem and the like, in many bold colours. In addition to this, there are certain principles for the colours on the door frames and window frames, on the doors, on the floor-ribbons and on the linoleum, not to mention the use of 'confetti colours' for fittings like covers, shelves, handrails and much more.[14]

## Point of departure

In this article, I am examining[15] the process behind the conversion and the controversy around the hospital, by means of actor-network theory (ANT), which is a relational and object-oriented sociology.[16] Specifically, I am inspired by ANT in the field of architecture,[17] and I am using qualitative methods in order to produce[18] empirical data.[19] In ANT, work is done with human and non-human actors and with a description of actor-network as method. An 'actor' is defined as anything that makes a difference, and the decoration, which has been impossible to ignore for the past 40 years, is accordingly a non-human actor.[20]

What does the decoration actually do? In order to grab hold of this question, I make use of the concept of *non-human actors' agency*. To put this in a simple way, a non-human actor can get others to act, like when the hospital removes the decoration on the third floor. What this also implies is that action can be delegated out to a non-human actor, [21] as when the total decoration's colour principles are delegated out to the colour manual, or when a coloured stripe leads us along the correct path. By this means, both collective action and delegated responsibility between actors arise.[22] Objects and architecture are not passive entities,[23] and welfare can therefore be delegated out to architecture and colours.

One distinguishing feature of the Nordic welfare states is the principle of its citizens' equal access to social welfare benefits.[24] Logically speaking, a public hospital in Denmark must have a similar purpose: *welfare for all the citizens.* Seeing as not all of the citizens can concretely take part in discussions about what this means, somebody has got to *represent* the citizens. But who is going to do this? The *spokespersons*, who, in ANT, are speaking on behalf of others. In doing so, they contribute to establishing and stabilizing groups,[25] as can be seen when different actors are speaking on behalf of the patients in general. It will become obvious that the actors are struggling over the definition of the hospital. Is it, for example, a work of art or a workplace? In an ANT-perspective, architecture[26] can be considered an 'interactive network' of various actors.[27] Buildings are not regarded as passive, static objects, but rather as conglomerates. They cannot be reduced to an essence. For this reason, more composite concepts like 'a-building-on-the-move' or 'a complex ecology'[28] are employed. What this entails, quite simply, is that Herlev Hospital is *not* the same throughout the course of time, and that what Herlev Hospital 'is', once and for all, and forever, cannot be defined.

## Herlev Hospital, from the inside

From the lobby's colourful fields and patterns, moving via the corridor's coloured ribbons and ascending a narrow lift, I make my way to Knud Skagen (hereafter: 'Knud'), retired chief head doctor and principal figure in the remodelling of the third floor. He has been employed at Herlev Hospital, almost continuously, from 1983 until the

From the horizontal medical ward. 2016. Photo by the author.

end of 2014, in all types of posts for doctors, including as acting deputy director of the hospital. Now we're sitting in a small, compact office, with paper cups and rolls. Knud is far from being a Rindalist[29] and wishes to make it clear that, as a matter of fact, he has always been impressed with the decoration and has been proud to show it off to patients who themselves were well-known artists. However, it is to the colours on the wards that he has objections.

Knud sets the remodelling project into the situational context of the past 30 years. When people finally moved past the scandal that the construction of Herlev Hospital was underfunded, a sense of pride arose in the county of Copenhagen. If there was any hospital that was going to be shown off, it was going to be Herlev Hospital. There was enough money in the county and even an overdraft every year. The perception was, by and large, that the decoration might cost whatever it had to cost, in terms of maintenance, and that people would comply quite rigorously with the directives charted out in the colour manual. Knud further explains that because of the colour manual, he has, through the course of time, used an inordinate amount of time on tedious disputes about things like tables and chairs.

He cites one example illustrating just this:

*When we were up on the fifth floor, we noticed that there were lacking a few tables. Two of the staff workers went over to the county's local outlet and bought three tables, rather inexpensively. However, the tables had blue legs and should, according to the Operations Department, have green legs. We insisted that we were pleased with the tables, which had the same table top surfaces as the other tables we had, albeit with blue legs instead of green legs. Then the person who, at that time, was serving as head nurse got a phone call from the hospital administration and was told that if she did not see to it that the tables were at once thrown away, she might as well find another place to work.*[30]

The so-called 'table-leg affair' took on the status of a legend in the department and Knud feels that as things panned out, people working there started to feel differently about the whole building. Knud recounts, also, that when the administrative structure of the 'county' was superseded by the Capital Region of Denmark in 2007, projected budgets were supposed to be complied with, and what suddenly became a matter of dispute was whether things like colours and items of furniture were simply too expensive to maintain. Moreover, certain door knobs, electric switches, mixer taps and the like went out of production and were being replaced by current Danish on-the-shelf products. It was not only the economy that was getting tighter: people were streamlining, and very drastically, all the time. For example, the period of time that the patients were confined to their beds was being reduced each year. What this entailed was that the patients were actually not doing as well as before, and that working with them had become more labour intensive. At the same time, the number of employees was increasing tremendously.

The situation of labour on the wards, in other words, was intensifying drastically over the years, and as Knud sees it, this spells a poor fit with the many colours.

He explains:

*I've never been enthusiastic about the coloration of the wards, which, in my eyes, has made the hospital's personnel and the patients tired because of the chaos of colours. There mustn't be too many things standing about in the corridors before it gets even worse, and what with a staff that really needs to move around quickly, hustling about every which way – with stretchers and carriages. Beds on the way out, and beds on the way in. And the overcrowding, with people lying around on the corridors. In such a situation, it all appears to be something like a chaos. As the years rolled by, I became more and more convinced: it must be due to* the colours.[31]

At several points in our conversation, Knud stresses that there was an urgent need for tranquillity and order, and that people wanted to get away from noise, clutter and chaos. He is very precise in his criticism: the many colours were not well-suited to those areas where there was a lot of movement going on. What he also believes is that there was simply *all too much*, visually speaking, also when patients were being wheeled around inside the building. For this reason, he feels that the colour impressions should be dampened down.

The concrete aspect of the affair with the hospital building began, in Knud's assessment of the situation, when, at the end of 2009, funds were suddenly made available from the Capital Region of Denmark. The hospital management had previously tried in vain to obtain permission to rethink one of the storeys in the building, and now the chance was there. The cardiac unit had become very worn down, also in terms of its technical fittings and its equipment. As a result, Knud, working together with the staff, went to work rethinking the unit. He confirms that it was a deliberate move, on his part, that Poul Gernes's decoration was not mentioned in the call for tenders. The department wanted to avoid turning the hospital into a museum, and the people working there wanted to have a modern unit and workplace. Knud explains that the unit had purposely refrained from asking the Capital Region of Denmark, or anybody else, about this, but simply seized the opportunity to think along new paths. They were counting on the regional administration being positively disposed toward spotting an example of innovative thinking, with an eye trained on the new 'super hospital'. The person who was then the leading head nurse was the anchor person and represented the many internal working groups, consisting of personnel and representatives from the hospital's building department. Knud emphasizes that the internal working groups enjoyed an extremely good collaboration with the consultants (Arcrum, Ramboll and others) from the outside.

It is clear that the colours on the ward, and even on the table legs, were effective actors, which incited a long chain of other actors to act. What can also be observed here is a delegating of action from Gernes to the decoration, and further on to the colour manual and the Operations Department. All were active mediators[32] along the way.

It is difficult to determine just where the process that led up to the remodelling really commenced, but Knud – as spokesperson for the patients and the staff, as well as for the modern hospital, especially, and therewith, for all the citizens' health-related welfare – became momentously important.

## The new cardiac care unit

Architect Jan Knudsen (hereafter: 'Jan') greets me at JJW's studio on Finsensvej, in Frederiksberg, and we find an available conference room. How did the process move forward up until the time that the new cardiac care unit was finished and ready? When Jan was involved in the matter, it was as head of the design studio, Arcrum, a consulting firm that later merged with JJW Architects. In a team consisting of two engineering firms, Ramboll and Arcrum, and the German hospital specialists Heinle, Wischer und Partner, the collaborators won, in 2009, the European Union-tendered competition for the remodelling of the third floor. Jan stresses that they won the competition because of the price. In the tender letter sent out by Herlev Hospital,[33] what was stated categorically was this: 'The central criterion for awarding the contract will revolve around considerations about which tender is economically the most attractive.'

The task was, to put it succinctly, to convert the floor into a ward for 28 patients, with diverse servicing functions and technical upgrading. The hospital wanted to install as many wards as possible and new private rooms. They were supposed to be tested out as prototypes for further conversions in the rest of the bed tower and as forerunners for the coming 'super hospital'. The facades were supposed to be insulated further, and the heating of the building through warmed air was going to be replaced by heating conducted through radiators. In addition, the bed tower was very deep and featured unpleasantly closed spaces in its central area.

Jan explains that 'user involvement' was wide-ranging and that 'user involvement' was also a specific political requirement posed by the Capital Region of Denmark. In the organization, it was the hospital's administration that was the formal building owner, while for all practical purposes it was chief physician Knud Skagen who was 'the client'. Early on in the process, the collaborating consulting firms thoroughly photographed the premises. Upon an examination of these photographs today, there was an impression of worn down and – in some places – almost overgrown areas.

Jan goes on to explain that early on, the collaborating consulting firms had a clear sense that they, with Gernes's decoration 'were dealing with something iconic'. But what quickly crystallized was a genuine challenge, and this was something that emerged at the first of the workshops with the users and other stakeholders. Jan tells:

*With respect to the colour composition, we were, of course, well aware that it was Poul Gernes's manual that was supposed to serve as the basis. However, we were getting a crystal clear message from the hospital's side that the people there did not in any way want to have the same thing: this cacophony, you might say, of colours. All the people on the staff simply could not work within all the colours: they were getting completely dazed, and they were refusing to do it. This was one of the most important premises that we were given to work with in connection with implementing our project.*[34]

The members of the personnel to whom is Jan referring here were primarily those who were employed at the department. He recounts that they did not have anything against the colours as such, but that it was the sheer number – and the many clashes – of colours that they perceived as being the problem. In addition, they had come to experience that the patients were getting confused about the colour scheme. Jan calls the restricted economy 'our next problem'. In the colour manual, for example, specially manufactured drapes and custom linoleum were prescribed. The hospital had nothing at all in its storehouse. What this

An entry into the former cardiac unit. 2009.
←
Interior from the former cardiac unit. 2009.
Photos by Thomas Kröll, Arcrum.

entailed was that a new production for circa 2000 m$^2$ of floorage would have to be addressed – and this was financially intractable. For this reason, what was resolved was that the idea of setting any 'custom-made' production into motion would be shelved. And then the scenario grew even more dire: large portions of the existing piping (oxygen, water, waste pipes) were in a deplorable condition, due to lack of proper maintenance, and this placed an unexpected strain on the project's economy.

The task of both having to make use of the colour manual and simultaneously meet the personnel's demands for fewer colours, in order to bring about a more tranquil environment, most certainly posed a paradox. Jan explains that, for this reason, they chose a lesser number of colours from the colour manual, refrained from ordering the expensive custom-made elements and introduced

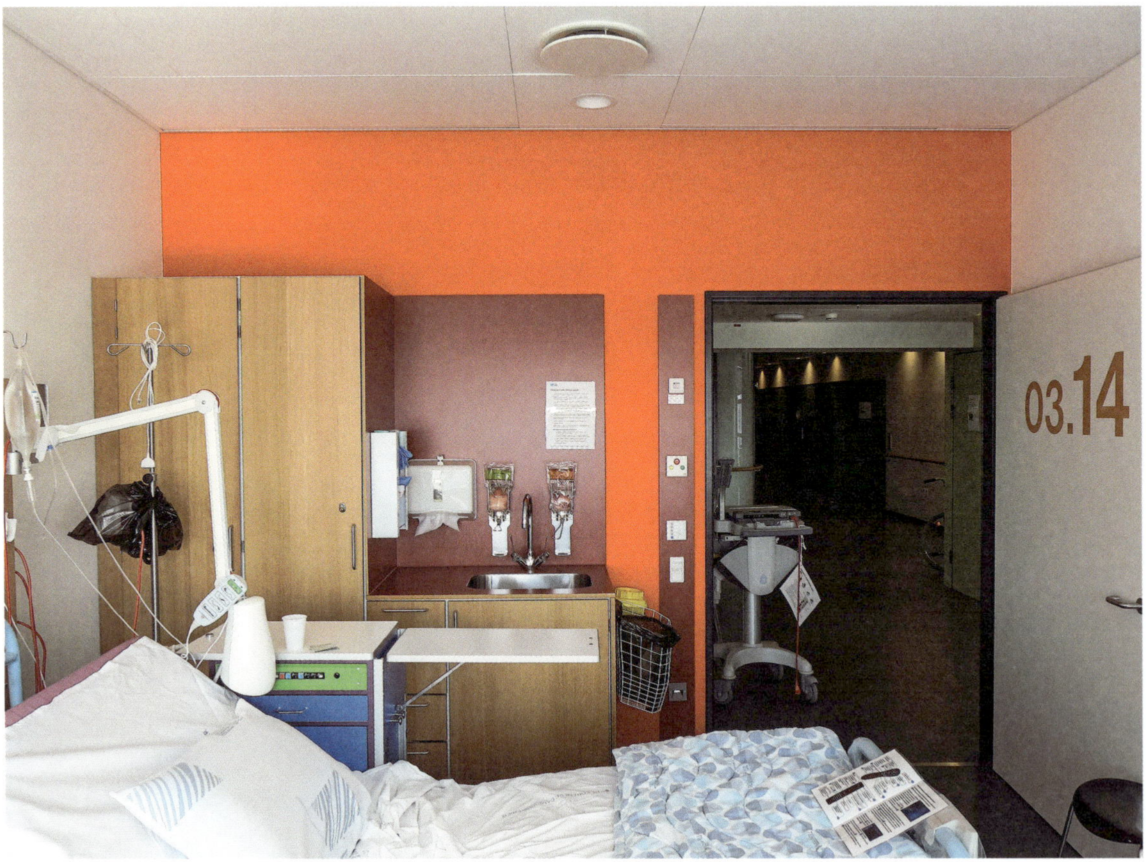


Bedroom in the new cardiac unit. 2016.
→
Interior in the new cardiac unit. 2016.
Photos by the author.

wood as material. It is wood that panels the walls behind the patients and that encases various technical connections. Jan lays special emphasis on the fact that you can still find strong Gernes-colours on the wards and in the bathrooms, but that the aggregate impression is calmer. One crucial detail here is that the new light sources which the architects were obliged to use do not reproduce the colours' values in the same way as did the former light sources. The project's head architect, Thomas Kröll, from JJW Architects,[35] remarks that it was impossible to reconcile all the divergent positions, but that the collaborating consulting firms placed the greatest weight the users' needs, because one of Poul Gernes's fundamental assumptions, namely that patients were going to be hospitalized for quite some time, was simply not the typical situation any longer. In the design of the building's core, the project's architects dissociated themselves from the 'colour explosion' and chose, instead, a 'less aggressive colour scheme' for the sake of the staff. Subsequently, the third floor, which housed a small church space, offices, guards' rooms and the like, was totally reconstructed and was then resurrected in the way that it can be seen today. Jan tells me that there was only praise and satisfaction among the personnel, the steering committee and the hospital management at the time the remodelling was completed.

Even though architect Jan Knudsen speaks about 'user involvement', what comes closer to the heart of the matter was that there was 'architect involvement', instigated on the part of the building owner. And as a commercial studio, the architects were compelled to solve the task on the existing basis. The 'user group' was comprised both of experienced specialists within their respective

fields and a contingent amalgamation of people, where discourses and attitudes were quite easily propagated within a hierarchical organization. Not only do the existing actors get the advisory group to act: also future actors make the group act.

The building was also surprising and was not fully controllable.[36] The architects were mediators who not only followed the colour manual, but also reduced it, and they acted along the way as spokespeople for, among others, 'Gernes's spirit' and, via the consulting team's composition, for German specialized knowledge. The wide-ranging actor-network of heterogeneous actors, with relations that hark back to the original colour principles, becomes stabilized on the new third floor with the sought-after lesser agency issuing from the colours. The responsibility was, along the way, distributed collectively and was widely bifurcated. However, they had not anticipated all eventualities.

## The controversy

In January of 2012, Ulrikka Gernes, the daughter of Poul Gernes, initiated a meeting[37] with, among others, the hospital's management, which eventually extended a promise that no similar conversion would take place. The Academy Council[38] then asked the hospital to 'put a halt to the over-painting' of the decoration, which they called a masterpiece that had garnered international attention.[39] Subsequently, *Politiken* published an article entitled 'Gernes' værk malet over' [Gernes's artwork painted over], wherein museum director Christine Buhl lodged a complaint about the remodelling project and broached the question of conservation. Also in *Politiken,* hospital director Søren Rohde explained, '(...) that they now understood and acknowledged that many people perceived the artwork as a cultural legacy which had to be preserved.'[40] In another column, fine arts editor Peter Michael Hornung wrote that the positive effect on patients had been documented.[41] Shortly afterward, this statement was refuted, on experiential grounds, by chief physician Knud Skagen, who voiced the objection that the new floor of the hospital had solved many years of problems bound up with the hospital's overall well-being.

He wrote: 'HEH is not a work of art, but rather a workplace which was coloured more than 35 years ago by one of that day's experimental artists.'[42]

Jes Fomsgaard, the former rector of Funen Art Academy, expressed astonishment about the intervention on the part of the medical profession into the realm of professional art practice. He took it as a given that the chief physician would hardly appreciate interference on the part of professional art practitioners when he was going about *his* work. Fomsgaard reminded the doctor that he only had the artwork *on loan,* and that '(...) the identityless and dismal characterizes the majority of our hospitals.'[43] Bjørn Nørgaard, chairperson of the Monument Council, informed – in another column – that a preservation was, theoretically speaking, possible.[44] In an opinion piece that appeared later on, Ulrikka Gernes expressed her astonishment at the fact that the hospital had not taken it upon itself to secure any professional advice from the art community. Similarly, she pointed out that the decoration, by virtue of the principles laid out in the colour manual, could certainly change in synch with changes in the rest of the hospital.[45]

According to Knud Skagen,[46] the criticism in *Politiken* emerged out of thin air and emanated from people whom he did not know, personally. Nor did he believe that many of these people could ever have visited the hospital. By way of response, he wrote a sound retort, which lay around at *Politiken* without being printed until the doctor phoned the newspaper and raised the question of censorship. Only then was his retort published. The debate in the media, according to Knud, resounded among politicians in the Capital Region of Denmark. Hospital management and the regional chairperson convened for a guided tour, and they were very satisfied about what they saw, on behalf of the patients. They were absolutely displeased about the public furore and they feared a suit involving listing something that would undoubtedly drive up the cost of future renovations.

The decoration at Herlev Hospital was subsequently designated as being worthy of preservation. After this, the hospital director announced to all the departments that no similar transformation would ever take place again. In Knud's opinion, this was really a shame, because the remodelling was very well received, by both the patients and the staff. He predicts that when, in a few years time, the cardiac care unit moves over to the new emergency hospital, there will, on the part of the hospital's departments, be a run on gaining occupancy of this third floor. Knud reports, moreover, that in the wake of the controversy, there was a lot of talk in administrative circles about limiting, as far as it is possible to do so, artists' influence on hospitals in the future.

The criticism also came as a surprise to architect Jan Knudsen,[47] and he emphasizes that if the floor in question were really supposed to have been like the existing floors, with regard to the decoration, then they should *not* have enlisted the aid of the hospital personnel in the process. In such a scenario, the whole affair would have amounted to a completely different assignment. But that would have been wrong, since it is expressly *for* the patients and the personnel that the consultants for the taxpayers' money are setting up the wards. He exclaims: 'We really did make an effort. We felt we had supplied a super product and something that was in Poul Gernes's spirit.'

As can be understood from the debate, what arose in various milieus, apparently outside the hospital, was a completely different perception of the situation. While Knud did not know the critics, they did know the hospital and its decoration, which they considered to be a masterpiece. In the criticism of remodelling, what was insisted upon was that the decoration had a positive effect on the patients and the negation was 'identityless and dismal' hospitals. Once again, the masterpiece, as actor, incited others to take action, this time around, for its own preservation. In this group's act to protect the decoration, other actors like specialized knowledge about art, the daily newspaper *Politiken*, a museum director, the colour manual's future-ready character, and least but not least, the potential conservation, became wrapped up within the network. The critics were speaking on behalf of art- and architecture history and on behalf of cultural heritage. They were spokesmen for the future generations of people who deserved to have this masterpiece preserved. Here, the argument about health-related welfare was less effective than was the argument related to cultural legacy. In Knud's view, it was finally the two actors *Politiken* and the spectre of listing which brought about the situation that the hospital director eventually declared the work of art to be a cultural legacy worthy of preservation. In this manner, the controversy became stabilized.

The Minister of Culture at the time, Uffe Elbæk, appointed a working committee,[48] and in 2014, *Herlev Hospital som kulturarv. Bevaringsvejledning*[49] appeared. Project Director at Herlev Hospital, Connie Barfod,[50] tells me that future conversions will be carried out with the conservation of the decoration in mind, but that there are currently no specific plans. The hospital's agreement with the Danish Culture Ministry's Agency for Culture and Palaces is that preservation instructions will have to be followed. Any doubts about the interpretation of conservation instructions have been delegated out to the hospital's Department of Building and Grounds.

## Discussion

When Poul Gernes harboured a theory about colours' positive effect, his thinking was based on *artistic experience and insight, as well as on ideology*. At the same time, Dr. Knud Skagen's *experience* with patients and his staff prompts him to declare that the colours do not have any practical effect. Whether or not the study of the test modules in Gentofte[51] can be said to be scientifically valid is difficult to determine. The statements about the colours are different. However, there is one thing about which they are all in agreement: they do *something!* When doctor Lars Heslet and architect Kim Dirckinck-Holmfeld[52] call for a new hospital paradigm, which they call 'Sansernes Hospital' [Hospital of the Senses], this is against the backdrop of more positivistic knowledge that architecture has more to bear on healing than has previously been assumed. Here, the ANT-analysis will be set in parentheses, and the question can be posed in this way: *are there other forms of scientific knowledge about colours in this area of inquiry?*

Architect and nurse Mette Blicher Folmer, who has earned her PhD in healing architecture, explains[53] that healing architecture came onto the agenda as a field of research in Denmark from around 2009. The colours' effect has never been systematically examined at Herlev Hospital, but people have studied, in other contexts, the rela-

tion between colours and patients' healing processes. However, it has not been possible to prove specific colours' effect on people's health. This is due to the fact that the experience of colour is influenced by many factors, such as the character of the space within which the colour is seen, the illumination and person's mental state. In other words: colours' effects are profoundly contextually contingent.

On this premise, we can no longer speak about health-scientific healing alone: we also have to take architecture and art into consideration, and the question of colours cannot be isolated.

## What can we learn?

How can the insights from this analysis be utilized in practice? My assessment is that it is impossible to define what Herlev Hospital 'is' once and for all. Is it a hospital? A coloured working place? A changeable work of art or a cultural legacy? It is impossible to say that it is not some of these things, for this is what the hospital has been turned into by the actors over the past 40 years. It has to be remembered that the hospital is public and not private. It belongs, in the most profound sense, to the community, and must be regarded as 'complex ecology' in continuous transformation.

If we accept this premise, then the following is implied: when it comes to the question of the hospital's development, *both* the medical aspects and specialized considerations related to art are relevant. However, the composite character imposes an obligation – and it changes. It is therefore essential to understand that the function for which the decoration was created has been changed. The question, then, becomes: *how can the total decoration be continuously updated in relation to changes in the hospital's function?* The colour manual is a good tool but there is going to have to be more. Similarly, another – seemingly converse – question needs to be asked: *how can the hospital's practices be developed in relation to the art's function?*

Herlev Hospital is a special place, with specific circumstances.

User involvement is, of course, central to a hospital, but it must be defined precisely in relation to what it is that is relevant. It seems obvious that the building owner and the authorities ought to be required to enlist the aid of art-specialized capacities in the formulation of tasks, in proposals for remodelling projects and the like – at any public hospital with such a highly valued decoration. Such advisers should *not* be employed by the building owner, but ought to be appointed, instead, by the Academy Council, and/or be working at the Historic Buildings Council or KØS Museum of art in public spaces. But the criticism cannot just be parked here, since, for as the report points out, there are many active 'mediators', including the decoration, the colour manual, and so on and forth, that play a role and help to bring about the situation as it crystallized in 2012.

Conservation runs contrary to the decoration's original idea. It is, to a great extent, based on the aforementioned colour system and thereby dynamic, and most deliberately created *for* the hospital's function. Poul Gernes has given us a challenging assignment and a weighty problem. The decoration and the building must be 'on-the-move', together. Gernes reminds us that doctors, artists and architects *can* do something together. But maybe it works best when we are not quibbling about the definition's law but acknowledge its complexity. We have got to continue carrying on an empirically grounded discussion about how colours and architecture also create welfare.



Entry into the new cardiac ward. 2016.
Photo by the author.

**Notes**

1 At the time it was constructed, the hospital presently known as 'Herlev Hospital' was named Amtssygehuset i Herlev [County Hospital in Herlev].

2 U. Gernes and P.M. Hornung: 'The Medicine of Colours' (2003) and Poul Gernes: 'Kunst, der ikke er brugskunst, er ikke kunst' (1986).

3 S. Felding*: Herlev Hospital som Kulturarv Bevaringsvejledning*, Kulturstyrelsen (2014).

4 C.H. Møller: 'Gernes: Herlev Hospital. Integreret kunst med tiden' (2012).

5 H.E. Nørregaard-Nielsen: 'De nye' in *Dansk Kunst, Tusind års kunsthistorie* (1983), pp. 555-76.

6 U. Gernes and P.M. Hornung: 'The Medicine of Colours' (2003).

7 E. Steffensen: 'Herlev', *Poul Gernes, Monografi* (2000).

8 A.M. Rahbæk in Felding (2014), op.cit., p. 5.

9 Gernes: *Forskningsforpligtigelsen 1*, (1988), p. 30.

10 N. Hobolth: 'From a corner of the world' (2015) and Ulrikka Gernes: 'A mother is a history without a beginning' (2015).

11 U. Gernes and P.M. Hornung: 'The Medicine of Colours' (2003).

12 The brightly coloured red auditoriums were opened in 1982; they were *not* coloured by Poul Gernes (Krogh 1989).

13 S. Felding (2014), op.cit.

14 *Farvemanual*: *Københavns Amt Sygehus Herlev* (1998).

15 My investigation is based on interviews with the doctor, Knud Skagen, and with the architect, Jan Knudsen, as well as on comments made by Thomas Kröll from JJW Architects. In addition, I have been making use of archival material from the building project and a survey of Herlev Hospital. Due to considerations of the present article's format, it has not been possible to reproduce the full complexity of the matter.

16 B. Latour: *Reassembling the Social: An Introduction to Actor-Network-Theory* (2005).

17 A. Yaneva: '*How Buildings 'Surprise': The Renovation of the Alte Aula in Vienna*' (2008A); A. Yaneva: 'Understanding Architecture, Accounting Society' (2008B); K. Fallan: '*Architecture in action: Traveling with actor-network theory in the land of architectural research*' (2008).

18 All of the quoted material has been slightly re-phrased, on the basis of considerations regarding readability, and the revised quotes have subsequently been approved by the people who were interviewed. The 'hospital management' has been mentioned several times, and this body consists of a changing procession of persons, seeing as the investigation covers a long span of time. The leading persons have not been contacted in connection with this investigation. For this reason, they have been rendered anonymous. Statements made by those who were interviewed, then, tell *only* about how these persons have experienced and perceived the events.

19 L.N. Groat & D. Wang: *Architectural Research Methods* (2013).

20 Latour (2005), op.cit.

21 Ibid.

22 R. Beauregard: *We Blame the Building! The Architecture of Distributed Responsibility* (2015).

23 A. Yaneva (2008B), op.cit.

24 E.J. Hansen: 'Velfærdsstat' (2011).

25 Latour (2005), op.cit.

26 Here, I will take it as given that it does make sense, inasmuch as we speaking about building-integrated art, to include the decoration in this umbrella designation of 'architecture',

27 N. Albertsen: '*Arkitekturværkets netværk: tre samfundsteoretiske perspektiver*' (2002).

28 B. Latour & Y. Albena: '*Give me a gun and I will make all buildings move: An ANT's view of architecture*' (2008), p. 87.

29 Translator's note: 'So-called Rindalism (named after Peter Rindal, a warehouse manager from Herning) attacked experimental art and the newly-created Danish Arts Council for its support of the period's abstract and conceptual art. Rindal saw the Danish Arts Council's activities as scandalous for using state resources to support incomprehensible and strange art. The opposition against modern art was articulated in explicit nationalist terms where modern art was considered to be foreign and a threat to the healthy values of ordinary Danes.' Retrieved on August 7, 2016 from < http://www.e-flux.com/journal/on-the-turn-towards-liberal-state-racism-in-denmark/>

30 Interview with doctor Knud Skagen, conducted at Herlev Hospital on February 29, 2016.

31 Ibid.

32 Latour (2005), op.cit.

33 JJW Architects' archives.

34 Interview with Jan Knudsen, conducted at JJW Architects' drawing offices on February 22, 2016.

35 E-mail received on March 6, 2016.

36 A. Yaneva: '*How Buildings 'Surprise': The Renovation of the Alte Aula in Vienna*' (2008A).

37 '*Referat af møde på Herlev Hospital tirsdag den 24. januar 2012. Referat ved Ulrikka Gernes og Christine Buhl Andersen*'. Received in the form of an e-mail from Ulrikka Gernes, and discussed in a telephone conversation with the author in March 2016.

38 Akademiraadet [The Academy Council] is the Danish state's (actually, the Danish monarchy's) specially appointed body of qualified advisors in matter of artistic import. See: www.akademiraadet.dk

39 Akademiraadet: *Poul Gernes' udsmykning af Herlev Hospital*, 2012.

40 C. Stockmann: '*Gernes' værk malet over*' (2012).

41 Hornung (2012), op.cit.

42 K. Skagen: '*Herlev Hospital er jo ikke et kunstværk men en arbejdsplads*' (2012).
43 J. Fomsgaard: '*Herlev Amtssygehus er altså ikke et hjem, men et hus*' (2012).
44 B. Nørgaard: '*Husk, at når vi freder, er det for fremtiden – ikke for fortiden*' (2012).
45 U. Gernes: '*Gernesmanual fra fortiden til fremtiden*' (2012).
46 Interview with Doctor Knud Skagen conducted at Herlev Hospital on February 29, 2016 and subsequent follow-up e-mail exchanges with the author in March 2016.
47 Interview with Jan Knudsen, conducted at JJW Architects' drawing offices on February 22, 2016.
48 Danish Ministry of Culture (2012).
49 Felding (2014), op.cit.
50 E-mail correspondence between the author and Connie Barfod in the months of February and March 2016.
51 Gernes and P.M. Hornung: '*The Medicine of Colours*' (2003).
52 L. Heslet & K. Dirckinck-Holmfeld: 'Sansernes Hospital: Et nyt hospitalsparadigme' (2008).
53 Based on telephone conversations and e-mail correspondence between the author and Mette Blicher Folmer in March 2016.

**Literature**


- Akademiraadet: *Poul Gernes' udsmykning af Herlev Hospital*, press release. Det Kongelige Akademi for de Skønne Kunstner, Akademiraadet, Copenhagen, 2012.
- Albertsen, Niels: 'Arkitekturværkets netværk: tre samfundsteoretiske perspektiver'. *Nordisk Arkitekturforskning*, vol. 15. no. 3, 2002, pp. 7-22.
- Beauregard, R.: 'We Blame the Building! The Architecture of Distributed Responsibility'. *International Journal of Urban and Regional Research*, Vol. 39, Issue 3, 2015, pp. 533-49.
- *Farvemanual: Københavns Amt Sygehus Herlev.* Stæremose & Isager, Arkitektfirma K/S, 1998, scanned version from the archives of JJW Architects.
- Fallan, K.: 'Architecture in action: Traveling with actor-network theory in the land of architectural research'. *Architectural Theory Review,* vol. 13, no.1, 2008, pp. 80-98
- Felding, Sven: *Herlev Hospital som kulturarv. Bevaringsvejledning*. Kulturstyrelsen, 2014.
- Fomsgaard, Jes: 'Herlev Amtssygehus er altså ikke et hjem, men et hus'. *Politiken*, April 13, 2012.
- Gernes, Poul: *Forskningsforpligtigelsen 1.* Kunstakademiet, Copenhagen, 1988.
- Gernes, Poul: 'Kunst, der ikke er brugskunst, er ikke kunst', interview with A. Fuchs & K. Ortwed. *Skulpturelle synspunkter*, Esbjergs Kunstforenings Samling, 1986.
- Gernes, Ulrikka: 'A mother is a history without a beginning'. *Aase Seidler Gernes*, Alter Ego, 2015, pp. 136-42.
- Gernes, Ulrikka: 'Gernesmanual fra fortiden til fremtiden'. *Politiken*, April 15, 2012.
- Gernes, Ulrikka and Peter Michael Hornung: 'The Medicine of Colours: Poul Gernes and Copenhagen University Hospital', Borgen, 2003.
- Groat, L.N. & Wang, D.: *Architectural Research Methods*, 2nd Edition. Wiley, Hoboken, N.J., 2013.
- Hansen, E. J.: 'Velfærdsstat'. *Sociologisk Leksikon*, eds. S. N. Larsen & I.K. Pedersen, Hans Reitzels Forlag, Copenhagen, 2011, p. 750.
- Heslet, L., & Dirckinck-Holmfeld, K.: 'Sansernes Hospital: Et nyt hospitalsparadigme'. *Bibliotek for læger*, 2008, pp. 280-309.
- Hobolth, N.: 'From a corner of the world'. *Aase Seidler Gernes*, Alter Ego, 2015, pp. 56-69.
- Hornung, Peter Michael: 'Ikke for kunstens skyld alene', *Politiken,* April 3, 2012.
- Krogh, L.: 'Københavns Amts Sygehus'. *Kunst i rummet: Monumentaludsmykning i Danmark 1964-1988*, Borgen, Copenhagen, 1989, pp. 151-53.
- Latour, B.: *Reassembling the Social: An Introduction to Actor-Network-Theory.* Oxford University Press, New York, 2005.
- Latour, B., & Albena, Y.: 'Give me a gun and I will make all buildings move': An ANT's view of architecture'. *Explorations in Architecture: Teaching, Design, Research*. Geiser, Reto, Birkhäuser, Basel, 2008, pp. 80-89.
- Møller, Camilla Hedegaard: 'Gernes: Herlev Hospital. Integreret kunst med tiden'. *Arkitektur DK*, vol. 03, 56. årgang, 2012, pp. 24-30.
- Nørgaard, Bjørn: 'Husk, at når vi freder, er det for fremtiden – ikke for fortiden'. *Politiken*, April 12, 2012.
- Nørregard-Nielsen, Hans Edvard: 'De Nye'. *Dansk Kunst, Tusind års kunsthistorie*, 7th edition, 2nd printing, Gyldendal, Copenhagen, 2013, pp. 555-76.
- Rahbæk, Anne Mette: 'Forord'. *Herlev Hospital som kulturarv. Bevaringsvejledning, S. Felding,* Kulturstyrelsen, 2014, p. 5.
- Skagen, Knud: 'Herlev Hospital er jo ikke et kunstværk men en arbejdsplads'. *Politiken*, April 8, 2012.
- Steffensen, Erik: 'Herlev'. *Poul Gernes, Monografi.* Borgen, Copenhagen, 2000, pp. 135-52.
- Stockmann, Camilla: 'Gernes' værk malet over'. *Politiken*, April 3 2012.
- Yaneva, A.: 'How Buildings 'Surprise': The Renovation of the Alte Aula in Vienna'. *Science Studies*, vol. 21, no. 1, 2008A, pp. 8-28.
- Yaneva, A.: 'Understanding Architecture, Accounting Society'. *Science Studies*, vol. 21, no. 1, 2008B, pp. 3-7.

Mette Jerl Jensen & Kjeld Vindum

# The Waiting Room as Welfare Design

**What is 'welfare design'? Fundamentally, we construe it to be architecture and design with *the community* as programmatic intention. But what welfare design can signify in a more concrete sense is reflected on in this article. The focus is on social, institutional spaces, with the waiting room shown below as our point of departure and example.**

A waiting room in a Danish hospital, selected relatively randomly. The spatial delimitation seems to be fairly clear: a box-shaped volume, rectangular in its floor plan. And then again, not really. Stanchions divide the room's long sides into three bays. The two open bays at one end serve to connect the room with the surroundings, while the other bays' glass walls serve to expand the connection, visually. It's clear to us that the waiting room forms part of what supposedly is a central zone between the two main hospital corridors. In the end wall, there are two elevators, which tell

us that this building consists of several storeys, while a door in the middle of the end wall on the opposite side of the room opens up to the toilet. The space has been horizontally stretched out between infrastructural flows in the form of hospital corridors, while it vertically has been distended between infrastructural flows in the form of elevators and waste pipes. All of the walls are system partitions, the exposed divisions of which reinforce the impression of the room's being inscribed within a systemic grid while, at the same time, their lightweight, replaceable character underscores the transitoriness, the room's temporality, and accordingly, the grid's dynamics. These relations endow the room with a characteristic indeterminacy. On the one hand, this is a communicating påassage, situated between the primary hospital corridors, and also situated between the elevators and the toilets, which also happens to be a waiting area for the elevators, and thereby infrastructure and flow area. On the other hand, it is a room in itself, and apprehensible as such, by virtue of its size and its relative spatial definition. The room is an example of the more or less indeterminate spatialities, which the programming of large dynamic and systemic spatial structures always seems to leave behind. Too large, though, to merely tackle the aforementioned flows. Ergo, its role as corridor area, as infrastructure. And precisely in this way, receptive to apparently vaguely defined programmes like 'waiting area' and/or 'waiting room'. The room we are speaking about is thus dually programmed: it is both corridor area and waiting area. 'Waiting area' because the term 'waiting room' presumably calls for a primary programming as such; this something that we will be getting back to. Nonetheless, in what follows, we will simply call it a 'waiting room'.

← / → Waiting room.
Photo: Mette Jerl Jensen

The room has been furnished with 12 identical armchairs and nine identical round tables; a clothing rack mounted on wheels; a footstool; a rolling case with an automatic soda dispenser mounted on top; a socle-podium that supports an aquarium; another rolling table; a litter bag stand on rolling wheels; and two paper bins. On the stanchions, two magazine racks have been hung in place, along with a wall clock. And on the wall with the door to the toilet, there is a flat screen monitor. There is a tall plant in a floor pot, and on eight of the nine tables, there are flowers in blue plastic table pots. The materials are metal, plastic and melamine. Apart from table pots' blue, the predominant colours are white, shades of grey and black. On the walls, the institutional environment's ever so typical bulletins have been fastened in place with adhesive tape.

Everything is standard: colours, surfaces, fixtures, articles of furniture, objects and plants. Nothing inhabits the room in the sense that it appears to have been designed specifically for this particular room. With the possible exception of the aquarium, which potentially can be seen as a gesture, but supposedly a gesture that was originally intended for a different situation, and which has now, more or less provisionally, wound up being here. Like everything else, it also seems to be *in transit*.

## Institutional architecture

Much is being said about narratives, and all kinds of tales are being told for the time being. Often, even listening to architects talk about all the 'narratives' they have had built into their buildings can really become rather enervating. Nonetheless, all architecture talks and narrates. Or as the architect Mark Rakatansky expresses it: 'There is no mute architecture. All architects, all buildings 'tell stories' with varying degrees of consciousness. Architecture is permeated with narratives because it is constituted with and in a field of discourses and economies (formal, psychological,

and ideological), to any other aspect of which it cannot be reduced, from any one of which it cannot be removed.
The hierarchy and degree of definition of spaces, their relative size and location, and the sub-architectural apparatuses of each space (furniture, appliances, media services) – all these are defined by and give definition to the social and psychological narratives that influence the behaviours (encouraged, allowed, discouraged or forbidden) associated with each space.'[1]

Rakatansky also concerns himself with the narrative's temporal aspect, with the narrative's temporality. About this, he writes: 'Thus one could argue that the most significant temporal definition of architecture is not given by the physical experience of moving through a building, but rather by the temporality of institutional practices inscribed in architectural space.'[2] In other words, the temporal definition of architecture is articulated through the changes in and the replacement of the institutions' programmes. And Rakatansky continues: 'Institutions are the principal sites through which ideologies work, and thus, as in the case of ideologies (and conventional narratives ...) it is in the interest of institutions to effect (or at least give the illusion of) stable conditions.'[3]
It is in the institutions' interest to ensure the perception that the state, and in this context, the welfare state, will continue to uphold and sustain the institutions that take care of the community, notwithstanding the ideologies' shifts and changes.

It seems to be clear that an impression of stability has not been successfully established in the waiting room. There has not even been any attempt to sustain an illusion of stability: the load-bearing stanchions' presence is almost camouflaged, inasmuch as they are accordingly painted with the same bright colour as the mobile wall elements.
As architects, we surmise that the elevators are moving up and down within concrete shafts that are concealed behind the lightweight system partitions, and similarly we suppose that the recessed system ceiling hides a floor separation. However, whether or not people without building-technical knowledge share these intuitions is something we can only speculate about. In other words, there is an attempt to camouflage even the stable constructive elements that hold our waiting room together as being replacable. However, the floor's surface appears to be stable. On the other hand, we do not know its position relative to the earth's surface, inasmuch as the room has no windows. By the same token, access to daylight, as the possibility of reading the weather, and access to the doings of the world going on outside the institution are both absent. We are deprived of any opportunity to figure out where we are and all of the building elements appear to be replacable. The temporality is particularly significant here, and formlessness holds sway. The building materializes, in principle, as the infinite, systematic structure that the practices unfold. What we see taking effect within the waiting rum seems more to be the ideology of the welfare *system* than anything having to do with the welfare *society*.

## Welfare architecture and welfare design

The reason that we are speaking about the welfare society is to underscore welfare's relation to the community, 'welfare' being understood as a common concern and a shared project. And 'welfare' being understood as something different from – and something more than – a distribution logistic project. In this connection, there appear to be good grounds for calling attention to the standard of welfare design that was developed during the welfare society's coming into being in

the 1950s and 60s. During this upswing, the Nordic welfare states' institutions were especially characterized by a quality that, in terms of execution, in terms of materials, and in terms of design, very distinctly articulated a striking and thoroughly implemented solicitude for the users. Architecture and design had a character of gesture and celebration of the community, which promoted the citizens' confidence in and identification with the welfare state and welfare as a joint project. Qualities that were often manifestations of the designer's personal commitment to and identification with the welfare state, as a project.
In the meantime, welfare and the welfare state have come to be threatened by a scarcity of resources and by what appears to be declining backing. Apparently, welfare is being perceived, more and more, to be benefits and services that people feel entitled to receive, rather than a community that people want to contribute to. In our opinion, we feel that, in this connection, it is essential to the maintenance of welfare that the welfare society is once again seen as *a project*. A project for a community which looks ahead into the future.
That is precisely why the institutions of the welfare society will have to lay stress on the larger horizon and orientation towards the future, by expressing stability and by being built for the future. The institutions will have to stand forth as society's investments in the community's future and accordingly manifest their faith and confidence in the future. It is our fundamental perception and our thesis that the design of the welfare society's institutions is important to the citizens' understanding of the relationship between community and welfare, and that this design can contribute to strengthening the bond. But can architecture and design take effect as solicitude and care for the community? How can architecture and design contribute to having 'community' felt, discerned and construed as a quality? 'Community' not to be taken here as a matter of all of us being together all the time, but rather in the sense of an understanding of society and welfare as being a common concern.
An architect who has been working with these issues, in his authorship and through his architectonic output, is the Dutch architect and professor, Herman Hertzberger, whose special focus has been aimed particularly at the elaboration of welfare institutions, especially schools and childcare centres. And he has no doubts about architecture's potential when it comes to the community: 'We should not underestimate the importance of spatial conditions for social structures. Social cohesion arises primarily where people are gathered for social purposes, without exception in a spatial setting. It is not too daring to presume that an important origin of architecture lies in accommodating the coming together and keeping together of people in enclosed and covered structures and making communication possible through physical presence, in order to reinforce the sense of community.'[4]

## Temporality – the particular and the general

But how are these structures related to temporality? Hertzberger posits a distinction between provisional space and permanent space: 'Creating space is primarily about people living together and about the diversity in which this tends to be expressed. ... the dichotomy of what has always been true for all people everywhere on the one hand and what is more temporary, more local and more individual on the other. ... the conscious distinction between that which has a short lifespan, on the one hand, and the basis that represents the communal, on the other, which does not subsequently lose its validity and is thus long-lasting.'

Revealing 'what is ephemeral and what is enduring [...].'[5]
Hertzberger writes that, when all comes to all, it has to do with a balance between the two areas: space, which is formed, and space that is left over, i.e. that remains available. 'Ultimately it comes down to a balance between the two components: space that is made and space that is left over. [...] Whether we are dealing with good architecture is primarily determined by the degree to which social space has been created with architectural means.'[6] As far as the waiting room, which appears on this article's first page, is concerned, what we clearly have before us is a room that appears to us in a way that is more temporary than it is stable. A space that is not designed or made; a space that is left over, i.e. that is available.
Rakatansky also touches upon the distinction between the temporal and the stable when he starts to speak about how it is in the interest of the institutions to set up stable conditions. And about the experience of this, he writes: 'Our understanding of the (seemingly stable) types of institutional space (the domicile, the office, the school, the museum, and so forth), is such that, once we experience these types, we need not physically traverse a given building to have a sense of the temporal dimension of inhabitation likely to be found here.'[7]

What is adumbrated here is stability's consistency with typologies in a sense that corresponds to what Louis Kahn has enunciated with respect to the 'school' as a paradigmatic type: 'Reflect then on the meaning of school, *a* school, institution. The institution is the authority from whom we get their requirements of areas. A school or a specific design is what the institution expects of us. But school, the spirit school, the essence of the existence will, is what the architect should convey in his design.
The realization of what particularizes the domain of spaces good for school would lead an institution of learning to challenge the architect to awareness of what School wants to be which is the same as saying what is the form, School.'[8]
It can be said, then, that as far as institutional spaces are concerned, we have to distinguish between spaces of different paces, between different temporalities. We have to distinguish between spaces that are open to different practices and programmes undergoing changes and the more stable and durable social spaces, which have been formed in accordance with their programme, with their purpose.[9] As social spaces with special needs within the institutional context, the waiting room would have to be connected with stability, and it has to be formed (as opposed to being 'formless'). The design of a waiting room calls for a particular architectural form and articulation based on *what it wants to be*. A waiting room *has* to be a waiting room.

Lyngby City Library (architects Holm & Grut, 1994-68). Originally a connecting passsage and exhibition space, this waiting/reading area includes a small café and serves as an extension to the present lobby. As such, it tallies with Christopher Alexander's notions of a good waiting room, where staggered recesses provide opportunity for different activities and conditions: you can either be alone or mix with other people, you can read and/or drink coffee. However, it does not possess the other quality that he describes as important for waiting areas at doctors' surgeries, dental clinics or hospitals: the specific quality that, induced by the environment, makes the patient withdraw into his/herself, calm down and become meditative. "The right atmosphere will come naturally if the waiting area provides some places that are quiet, protected, and do not draw out the anxiety of the wait." Photo: Kjeld Vindum.

## The programme: waiting room

The programme of the waiting room is, however, shackled with a special problem, which the architect and architectural theorist Christopher Alexander has described in this way: 'How can the people who are waiting, spend their time wholeheartedly – live the hours or minutes while they wait, as fully as the other hours of their day – and yet still be on hand, whenever the event or the person they are waiting for is ready?
It can be done best when the waiting is fused with some other activity: an activity that draws in other people who are not there essentially to wait. ... Waiting can also be a situation where the person waiting, ... with the support of the surroundings, is able to draw into himself, become still, meditative ... The right atmosphere will come naturally if the waiting area provides some places that are quiet, protected, and do not draw out the anxiety of the wait.'[10]
Such a place could be the corner. About the corner, the philosopher Gaston Bachelard says: '[E]very corner in a house, every angle in a room, every inch of secluded space in which we like to hide, or withdraw into ourselves, is a symbol of solitude for the imagination; that is to say, it is the germ of a room, or of a house.' And further: '[...] the corner is a haven that ensures us one of the things we prize most highly – immobility. ... The corner is a sort of half-box, part walls, half door.'[11]
In the corner, you're protected, but you can still get away. The 'protection' is associated with immobility, permanence and stability.
A waiting room is thus a social space that simultaneously ought to afford the possibility for the individual to withdraw from the social, but nonetheless with the awareness of being a part of and being protected by the community. A balance between a certain surroundedness and a corresponding openness: a balance that could manifest itself architecturally in a kind of corner. Along

with an experience of stability, this could come to be an essential ingredient in what Alexander calls 'the right atmosphere', which the waiting room can offer. All in all, the concept of 'atmosphere' appears to embody important potentials in the situational context. Atmosphere can signify mood, in relation to a place or a situation, and consequently includes our experience of, for example, given spaces, certain people, or constellations thereof. The question now is: how to create an atmosphere that provides good opportunities for both conversation and silence, and which is instrumental in bringing forth an experience of protection and care?

## Atmosphere

But before we answer this question, let us look at a more detailed definition of what we mean by 'atmosphere'. In his definition, the philosopher Gernot Böhme, evokes the spatial aspect: 'atmospheres (...) are spaces with a mood, or emotionally felt spaces.'[12] And the architect and the architecture critic Mark Wigley speaks about atmosphere as emanating from the building, as something that can be constructed with architecture as medium: 'How is atmosphere constructed? Atmosphere seems to start precisely where the construction stops. It surrounds a building, clinging to the material object. ... the atmosphere of a building seems to be produced by the physical form. It is some kind of sensuous emission of sound, light, heat, smell and moisture; a swirling climate of intangible effect generated by a stationary object.
To construct a building is to construct such an atmosphere.'[13]
Meanwhile, the artist Olafur Eliasson follows up with a description that we find to be particularly fruitful for architects: 'Like the weather, atmospheres change all the time and that's what makes the concept so important. ... If you talk about an atmosphere in an public space, you can describe it as the coming together of numerous trajectories, the coming together of materials, of intentions, the buildings; it's a hovering, a resonance. It never stands still. It moves and changes. The idea of atmosphere that is dominant today sometimes suggests that aesthetics are separate from ethics. But when we talk about atmospheres, especially in public space, we cannot take away intentionality. And intentions – by city planners, governments, everyday users – inevitably embody an ethical stance, a suggestion about how to act and interact with others.'[14]
The intentional work with 'atmosphere' accordingly affects people who experience it in multiple ways, and especially as far as mood is concerned, but this work also has an influence to bear on our propensity to engage in activities like speaking with others or drawing into ourselves and falling into a reverie, as Christopher Alexander suggests. To a great degree, atmosphere is determinative of how we are doing, both in terms of how we feel about ourselves and in relation to others. And when architects and designers are working with the atmosphere of spaces, it is especially the phenomenological qualities – the qualities as they are sensed – with which architects are working, above and beyond all matters related to scale and differences, and above and beyond formal-aesthetic considerations like proportions, etc.
A decidedly atmosphere-conscious architect like the Swiss architect Peter Zumthor talks about how he is working with adjusting sensory expressions in relation to each other. That is to say, how he works with the relationships between sensory input from within itself, its surfaces, its colours, its lighting, and also how he works with relations between the room and the environment. Relations of the kind that might be commensurate with what Eliasson is calling 'trajectories'.

Florian Beigel and Philip Christou Architects: Youl Hwa Dong Book Hall Building, Paju Book City, Korea, 1999. Photo: Jonathan Lovekin

The architect and the interior designer's work with, for example, a waiting room's special and 'right atmosphere' is based on a scrupulous harmonizing of relationships. For one thing, the external circumstances of the building, and moreover, its organization, infrastructure and flow; for another, the internal relations among an extensive array of spatial-architectural means and agents like materials, surfaces, colours, incident light and artificial lighting, etc. Each of these being especially selected and treated with reference to their reciprocal and aggregate effect in relation to the intention concerning, for example, the waiting room's particular and special atmosphere and context.
In another context, the interplay between books' and people's lives is illustrated in a strikingly distinctive interior design, which was conceived by the architects Florian Beigel and Philip Christou, with their Youl Hwa Dong Book Hall Building, in Paju Book City, in Korea, which came forth in 1999.

Zumthor says: 'I try to make sure that the materials are attuned to each other, that they radiate; I take a certain amount of oak and a different amount of *pietra serena* and add something to them: three grams of silver or a handle that turns or maybe surfaces of gleaming glass, so that every combination of materials yields a unique composition, becomes an original.
I listen to the sound of the space, to the way materials and surfaces respond to touching and tapping, and to the silence that is a prerequisite of hearing.
The temperature of rooms is very important to me, how cool they are, how refreshing, the chiaroscuro of warmth that caresses our bodies ...
I love placing materials, surfaces, and edges, shiny and mat, in the light of the sun, and generating deep solids and graduations of shading and darkness for the magic of light falling on things. Until everything is right.'[15]
Zumthor, then, is speaking here from the specific space; he attunes it in relation to the social and emotional situation that he wants to elicit from the people who are going to be occupying the space for shorter or longer intervals of time. We are talking here about space that, as Hertzberger has voiced it, 'is made', as opposed to 'space that is left over'. In the 'made spaces', everything means something in relation to the intention. And things that are only situated within the space for a while also support or work counter to the intention.
The concept of 'atmosphere' thus refers to something specific, something that characterizes a special setting. Or, to be more specific, characterizes a location and contributes to making it a place.

Studioilse: Interior from the hotel and wellness sanctuary Das Kranzbach. Photo: Kai Knoerzer.

What is characteristic of the designer and the interior designer Ilse Crawford's interiors is that they are composite, and that they 'are not being subjugated to any formal or aesthetic frame or matrix, that they do not appear to be seeking to establish a conventional aesthetic harmony. [...] At first glace, the uninhabited interiors call to mind scenes with props which, suspended, are waiting for the actors to step in and put the plot in motion. Presumably, it is – quite precisely – the props'/furniture's diversity, their strength as individual characters, and their potential reciprocal relations that invest the interiors with this charge, this latency. It's as though the interiors were waiting for an action that they themselves had been staging. And maybe it is the props and the articles of furniture themselves that should rather be considered actors – that should be considered characters on the stage. [...] It is clear that such a reading of – and such notions about – these interiors are dependent on a very precise harmonization of the relationships between the objects [...], right up against the breach's limit. [...] In this sense, maybe it wouldn't be overdoing it at all to regard Ilse Crawford's interiors as explorations of new forms of balance, which include and embrace conflicts. [...] Notwithstanding their individualities and their differences, the rooms' objects, articles of furniture, textiles and so on seem nonetheless to be ready to engage in dialogue, and even ready to arrive at an agreement.'[17]
Nor does Ilse Crawford apprehend her own interior arrangements as finished designs. On the contrary: 'In Studioilse, we are not aspiring to make our houses completely finished. You've got to be a little hesitant in your design', and for Crawford, it has a lot to do with leaving behind spaces that are open for the user's co-creation, while at the same time, she is advocating that there has to be 'a strong structure in the things that you're actually making, which allows chance occurrences and coincidences to turn up within the rest. [...] it's about allowing a situation [...] that certain things can be under your control and other parts can be more dynamic. [...] It's about understanding how "life's rhythms' fit into a building." And it's wonderful if a house 'completely embraces [...] is built around the lives of the residents. [...] that it: is a life which has taken on a solid form. [...] I like the idea that what is airy takes shape. This is what constitutes the really special places.'[18]
Maybe these are precisely the places where life and space and form converge and create atmosphere, which in turn reacts to life and to the form. Where life, the airy and the physical are acting together.

## Atmosphere and temporality

Seeing that Zumthor is working with space and thereby with atmosphere '[u]ntil everything is right', his statement stands as a credo that he is operating with a definitiveness, with a finality. In comparison with this, Olafur Eliasson is underscoring the atmosphere's dynamics when he declares that atmospheres are changing all the time, just like the weather. In so saying, he is taking into account, to a certain extent, that atmosphere emerges in a meeting between a person and a room, at a certain moment in time, and under the specific conditions that apply to that particular moment in time, but also to the phenomenon that public spaces, in their exteriors as well as in their interiors, are in motion.

In continuation of this, it was our preliminary assumption that a building's materials and concomitantly its constituent parts and elements all have different velocities. That is to say, a kind of temporality that is associated directly with a building's materials and with their properties as well as with the situational contexts of which they form part and within which they are active. These are precisely the phenomena that the Austrian architect Adolf Krischanitz is aware of when he says: 'For me, the aspect of the different speeds inherent in individual construction parts is essential in so far as shapes contain time in several ways and thus evoke effects that may, for example, take up directionalities. Moreover, there are materials that are subject to ageing or not, that have fast or slow surfaces, colours that have a distance-changing or even dynamic effect – they all become part of this time-space fabric. ...

The idea is not to create frozen images, but conditions, spatial, colour, and lighting conditions which may effect something like an unfolding of the house with the changing sunlight in the

course of the day. This is what makes the house come alive.'[16]

When we compare his statement with Zumthor's description of his own work with the interior spaces, we come to see that Krischanitz is placing special weight on the aspect of time, on the materials' different velocities, on temporality as a crucial element in the work with space, inasmuch as he speaks about creating conditions. He opens up for the apprehension of interior design as a way of working with the elaboration of and with the crystallization of constellations of construction parts that are not only in motion and have different speeds, but that are active within the space, as co-creators of its atmosphere. However, what remains valid is that everything in the constellation – all the materials and surfaces, all of the elements – has significance to bear. Especially the articles of furniture and other movable elements.

If it is so that a waiting room can be designated an instance of 'welfare design', then its design may co-reflect relations between slow and fast; between permanence, solidity and flow; between the specific and the general/generic; between the made and the systemic. All of this with a view towards creating 'the right atmosphere'. Moreover, its design may be continuous and coherent – not necessarily in the sense of a harmonious coherence but more in the sense of a coherence that emerges, given that all things are interrelated, in the sense that all elements that contribute to the waiting room's configuration also contribute to its atmosphere and may therefore be designed and selected in relation to their reciprocal synergy, whether or not this is experienced as something harmonious, as something heterogeneous, or as something else again. The assignment's solution requires, of course, an artistic and, not least, an architectural intention and also the chance to make and to form and/or to select all items with care and solicitude in relation to this intention. When the intention and the opportunities are present, and when there is place for the afore-

Claus Pryds Arkitekter, Kræftrådgivning Livsrum ['Life-space' counselling centre for cancer-related questions] in Herning, 2015. Photo: Claus Pryds.

On a par with other social, institutional spaces, we see the waiting room as a particular social space. A room that not only offers the possibility of community, but also provides the opportunity to withdraw while still feeling included in and protected by the community. With its cancer centre in Herning, the studio of Claus Pryds Architects has designed waiting areas with spaces that open up towards the surroundings while they are enveloping and in full possession of form. These are spatialities which are, at one and the same time, divided and continuous. For example, there are the distinctive niches, where one can actually withdraw, without completely extricating oneself from the room.

mentioned reflections to unfold, then a waiting room can turn into welfare design.

## Epilogue: the specific vs. the generic

There are, however, good grounds for drawing attention to the manifestations of governmental management that act in a directly counterproductive way in relation to strategies for welfare design like those that have been discussed here. One policy that is making a particularly detrimental impact on the area of interior design, is the state's, the regions' and the districts' procurement policy. To put it succinctly, this has to do with governmental framework agreements for bulk purchases of a wide range of commodities and services, for the purpose of obtaining price reductions. Design elements are considered by the state, the districts and the regions to be, first and foremost, services. A chair is something you acquire with or without armrests, and the limited assortment of variations – blue, green or black upholstery – becomes transferred to the supplier who can come up with the best deal. Accordingly, the choice of central elements in the design of interiors is simply left to external actors and left open to circumstances issuing from outside the creative process. In this way, important and often decisive choices are extracted from the architect's and the designer's vocabulary in relation to the elaboration of specific environments, such as

a waiting room. And this is so, while at the same time, the same chairs, which might happen to be there only as a consequence of the bulk-purchase benefits, can therefore turn up in the canteen as well as in the offices. To put this succinctly, the procurement policies and the performance criteria that they promote ultimately operate in a counterproductive way in relation to the design of special places and atmospheres. The creation of the special social places within the institution is being thwarted by the national, regional and district procurement policies and the awarding of contracts. In other words: welfare design as interior design is being weighed down by the welfare state's centralistic management systems.

If we are correct in saying that interior design as welfare design in relation to social spaces is tantamount to all of its elements having to be designed, selected and processed with respect to their reciprocal and aggregate effects, in relation to the room's particular atmosphere and situational context, then we can consequently conclude that the waiting room we have been employing as an example is *not* welfare design. As a matter of fact, it is an antithesis of welfare design. The aforementioned example of a waiting room is a non-place. It is non-special. It is not formed, and it appears to be unstable. It incarnates centralized procurement policies and tenders that are based on all too narrow quantitative parameters, the sought-after economic viability of which is based on all too simple calculations. This is Excel architecture, this is non-architecture. Welfare Design, on the other hand, is based on differences and differentiation between areas. It is similarly based on social areas, like waiting rooms, being stamped by stability, specificity, situational coherence (atmosphere), care and solicitude and integrity. As far as the latter is concerned, we would now like to take the liberty of referring to the formulation voiced by Frank Lloyd Wright, a quote with which the Finnish architect and architectural theorist, Juhani Pallasmaa, chose to bring his book *The Eyes of the Skin. Architecture and the Senses*, to a close: 'What is needed most in architecture today is the very thing that is most needed in life – Integrity. Just as it is in a human being, so integrity is the deepest quality in a building [. . .] If we succeed, we will have done a great service to our moral nature – the psyche – of our democratic society [. . .] Stand up for integrity in your building and you stand for integrity not only in the life of those who did the building, but socially a reciprocal relationship is inevitable.'[19]

Integrity is consistency in 'actions, beliefs, methods, measures and principles,' and expectations and results.[20]

**Notes**

1 M. Rakatansky: 'Spatial Narratives' (1992), pp. 198-22. Quoted here from the reprint in: Architekturzentrum Wien (ed.): *Sturm der Ruhe – What is Architecture* (2001), p. 82.
2 Ibid., pp. 90-92
3 Ibid., pp. 90-92.
4 H. Hertzberger: 'Social Space and Structuralism' in *OASE #90*, 2013, pp. 17-18.
5 Ibid., pp. 18-20.
6 Ibid., pp. 18-20.
7 Rakatansky (1992), op.cit, p. 92.
8 L. Kahn: 'Form and Design' (1960) in R. Twombly (ed.): *Louis Kahn – essential texts* (2003), pp. 64-66.
9 Previously, in a project that was entitled *Det dynamiske monument*, we turned our attention to the monumental potentials in the slowness of social spaces. The project's intention was namely to come up with suggestions and proposals for possible architectural strategies that were focused on these relations: permanence (solidity) vs. flow, and generality vs. specificity, in relation to temporality – and with sustainability as a kind of driving force, inasmuch as the building, with respect to its resource efficiency, is being viewed as a constellation of elements and components with different life spans. For example, we are envisioning an institution whose overall constructive framework, its 'super-frame', has been conceived in ensemble with social programmes and has accordingly been carried into effect with an eye trained on a long life span, and consequently with relative permanence, and from materials of a high quality/high degree of

processing/finishing and with high robustness. M.J. Jensen and K. Vindum: *Form til velfærd: Det dynamiske monument, projektformulering*, KADK 2013.

**10** Chr. Alexander: 'A Place to wait' in Chr. Alexander: *A Pattern Language* (1977), pp. 708-09.

**11** G. Bachelard: *The Poetics of Space* (1964), pp. 136-37.

**12** From 'Atmospheres, Art, Architecture – A Conversation between Gernot Böhme, Christian Borch, Olafur Eliasson and Juhani Pallasmaa' (2014), p. 96.

**13** M. Wigley: 'The Architecture of Atmosphere' (2001), p. 41.

**14** 'Atmospheres, Art, Architecture', op.cit., p. 93

**15** P. Zumthor: *Thinking Architecture* (2006), pp. 87-88.

**16** A. Krischanitz in conversation with Markus Grob. Quoted here from: Architekturzentrum Wien (2001), op.cit., pp. 97-99.

**17** K. Vindum: 'Kammerspil – Studioilse' in *ArkitekturM* 1/2009, pp. 24-25.

**18** S. Bjerring: 'Interview med Ilse Crawford' in *ArkitekturM* 2/2009, pp. 24-25.

**19** F.L. Wright: 'Integrity' in 'The Natural House 1954'. Quoted here from: J. Pallasmaa: *The Eyes of the Skin, Architecture and the Senses* (2005), p. 77.

**20** *Wikipedia, the free encyclopedia*. <https://en.wikipedia.org/wiki/Integrity>. (Retrieved on December 15, 2016.) Also in the examination of this term, as posted on this website, we can read: 'One can describe a person as having [...] integrity to the extent that the individual's actions, beliefs, methods, measures and principles all derive from a single core group of values. [...] Integrity relates to [...] compliance to the rules as well as to social expectations, with morality as well as ethics, and with actions as well as attitude.' And also: '[...] integrity is the inner sense of "wholeness" deriving from qualities such as honesty and consistency of character. As such, one may judge that others "have integrity" to the extent that they act according to the values, beliefs and principles they claim to hold. [...] A value system's abstraction depth and range of applicable interaction may also function as significant factors in identifying integrity due to their congruence or lack of congruence with observation. A value system may evolve in a while, while retaining integrity if those who espouse the values account for and resolve inconsistencies.'

**Literature**


- Bachelard, G.: *The Poetics of Space*. Boston 1964, pp. 136-37.
- Bjerring, S.: 'Interview med Ilse Crawford' in *ArkitekturM* 2/2009, pp. 24-25.
- Borch, C. (ed.): 'Atmospheres, Art, Architecture – A Conversation between Gernot Böhme, Christian Borch, Olafur Eliasson og Juhani Pallasmaa' in *Architectural Atmospheres*. Basel 2014.
- Christopher, A.: 'A Place to wait' in *A Pattern Language*. Oxford 1977.
- Hertzberger, H.: 'Social Space and Structuralism' in *OASE #90*, 2013.
- Jensen, M.J., & Vindum, K.: *Form til velfærd: Det dynamiske monument, projektformulering*, KADK 2013.
- Kahn, L.: 'Form and Design' (1960) in Robert Twombly (ed.): *Louis Kahn – essential texts*. W.W. Norton & Company, New York & London 2003.
- Rakatansky, M.: 'Spatial Narratives' in Whiteman, J., Kipnis, J., & Burdett, R. (eds.): *Strategies in Architectural Thinking*, MIT, Cambridge/Mass. 1992, p. 198-222. Quoted from: Architekturzentrum Wien (ed.): *Sturm der Ruhe – What is Architecture*, Salzburg 2001.
- Zumthor, P.: *Thinking Architecture*, Birkhäuser, Publishers for Architecture. Basel, Boston, Berlin 2006.
- Vindum, K.: 'Kammerspil – Studioilse' in *ArkitekturM* 1/2009, pp. 24-25.
- Wigley, M.: 'The Architecture of Atmosphere' in Architekturzentrum Wien (ed.): *Sturm der Ruhe – What is Architecture*. Salzburg 2001.
- Wright, F.L.: 'Integrity' in 'The Natural House 1954'. Quoted from: J. Pallasmaa: *The Eyes of the Skin, Architecture and the Senses*, Wiley & Sons, Chichester 2005.
- 'Adolf Krischanitz i samtale med Markus Grob'. Quoted from Architekturzentrum Wien (ed.): *Sturm der Ruhe – What is Architecture*, Salzburg 2001.

Jesper Pagh & Maja de Neergaard

# Welfare's Spaces as Architecture-Historical Construction

**In the period 1957-2012, the journal, *Arkitektur DK,* continuously documented what of new Danish architecture was being built. Through these years, the journal functioned as a vital source of contemporary architectural history. Taking as point of departure a re-reading of all of the journal's issues, the article discusses how the history of architecture *documents* the accomplishments of the past as well as *constitutes* the present day's possibilities. Furthermore it is discussed what impact this makes on our understanding of what is possible.**

The journal *Arkitektur* (later called *Arkitektur DK*) was published for the first time in 1957 – the same year that approximately one half of Denmark's population was living in cities, and also the year that industry surpassed agriculture as Denmark's largest export business. Over the course of 56 years – up until and including 2012 – the journal documented – under the leadership of changing editors, in varying configurations, and through changing times – welfare's spaces, as they came into being. Without this being the direct intention, what was created through the journal was a kaleidoscopic portrait of the post-war era's development of the Danish welfare society as seen through the contemporaneous development in architecture – and vice versa. What appears in this picture is how the relationship between individual and community, between public and private, between room for diversity and attempts to bring about consensus, was continuously up for negotiation. Seldom does this come to light, directly, but through a closer reading of what was being told and what was not being told, of what it was that was given priority, and of what seeming accidents and coincidences of circumstances were ensuing along the way, what can be seen in *Arkitektur DK* is a surprising multiplicity of changing perceptions and often contradictory tales about the welfare society's spaces.

In this article, we will be taking a closer look at how these narratives were developed and came to take on significance, not merely as reflections of what had occurred, but also in the narratives' capacity as being co-determinative for our conceptions about what it is that *can* take place. The discussion here will be accompanied with a description of the work with editing the last two issues of *Arkitektur DK* as it is this process that have shaped the observations above. In the first section, some of the preconditions, preliminary assumptions and new insights that are linked up with the work will be discussed, along with reflections on the editor's role and influence, as he/she makes his/her choices. Next, we will focus on the history from building public elementary schools, as it unfolded in the period 1957-2012. We examine the way in which school construction was seen through *Arkitektur DK* as an example of how the presentation in the journal has impacted our perception of the school's architecture today.

The public school stands as example of how the architects – working in close cooperation with other occupational groups – give form to and create spaces for welfare. It is here that the future welfare society's citizens will be formed and educated, and the school is a topic that, especially in the first 25 years of *Arkitektur DK*'s life time, was given a great deal of editorial attention. In the article's latter section, we will be taking up a more theoretical discussion about how one can critically address oneself to the many and often contradictory narratives that turn up when one revisits the history of architecture, and we will examine some of the sources from which these contradictions originate. The purpose is to investigate whether this can contribute to the understanding of the correlation between architecture's and the welfare state's development, and to a continuous development of research, teaching and the practice through which the architects create spaces for welfare.

## *Arkitektur DK* 1957-2012

In the spring of 2013 Jesper Pagh, one of the authors of this article, edited the last two issues of *Arkitektur DK*. The two issues were collectively titled 'Velfærdssamfundets arkitektur' [The welfare society's architecture] and took on the character of an accumulation of the previous 56 years of publications, divided into two periods, 1957-1982[1] and 1983-2012.[2] The two issues contained a selection of all the buildings which had been shown in the journal over the years and wes sorted into six categories: *public administration and infrastructure*; *industry and commerce*; *culture and leisure*; *health and care*; *housing*; and *education and research*. Along with a timeline showing significant events and developmental trends in society, interviews and commentaries, the attempt was to outline, if not a total, then, in any event, a coherent picture of the society's, the architecture's and the journal's development over the years.

The starting point for the editing of the two issues of *Arkitektur DK* was the aspiration to illustrate and discuss the contribution of Danish architects to the development of the welfare society during the period that the journal had existed. The original assumption was that a review of all 56 annual volumes would make it possible to document the edifying coupling of architecture and welfare in the post-war period – a coupling that is prominent in contemporary architecture theory and -history.[3] Carrying this out, however, would prove to be not as straightforward a task as assumed to begin with. Certainly, one can rediscover the trails leading through the buildings and the contemporaneous presentation, debate and criticism, which were being written up in the dominant part of Danish architectural history, but there is also much else to be found. From a distance, the editorial choices and, conversely, what the editors chose to leave out are not immediately transparent: the original empirical material does not exist anymore; or else it is not possible to gain an overview of this material, and, even if such a scenario were to crystallize, this would require the involvement of many other sources grounded in a social scientific context – and this lies beyond the scope of the present article.

As a consequence of this, the presentation and the analysis that appears in the last two issues of *Arkitektur DK* came to constitute one more layer in the narrative instead of an elucidation of architectural history's established perspectives.

*Arkitektur DK* 2-2013. Odder Rådhus, Friis & Moltke 1970-71. Photo: Jesper Pagh.

*Architecture DK* 3-2013. Library on Rentemestervej, Copenhagen, Cobe and Transform 2010-11. Photo: Jesper Pagh.

## The Danish school – before, now and never

The presentation of school construction in *Arkitektur DK* largely traces the trajectory of the three Education Acts, respectively, of 1958, 1975 and 1993, each of which builds further on changes in the educational and organizational principles that fashion the bases for the schools and carries along a concomitant need for new construction, renovation and conversion. Most of the architect profession's debate in this area takes place in the expositions of competition projects, which were treated of and discussed in detail in *Arkitekten*, while *Arkitektur DK* concentrated on the presentation of the realized buildings. This led to extended special issues, with compilations of new examples of school construction, which were triggered by changes in the Education Acts (6-1963, 5-1975, 2-2003, 3-2007).

The three Education Acts of 1958, 1975 and 1993 were driven, when it comes to their key points, by a development that, in a somewhat generalizing way, can be described as setting the (individual) child more and more in focus and simultaneously giving priority to formative development instead of training and instruction. This is a course of development that is reflected especially distinctly in the movement from a decentralized and authoritative structure that existed prior to the Education Act of 1958 to the Education Act of 1993's description of the comprehensive school. Keywords in the objects clauses of all three Education Act are – albeit with different formulations and weightings – *formation*, *equal opportunities for everybody*, and *personal development.* What can be seen up until the passing of the Education Act in 1993 is the movement from a specialized to an interdisciplinary focus – a movement which, in subsequent revisions, recurs again, while at the same time, more and more weight is now, this time around, being placed on the instructional aspects than it is on the formative. These changes in the legislation reflect, as much as do the

Vangeboskolen [Vangebo School], Bornebusch, Brüel, Larsen & Selchau 1957-60. Photo: Birte Palle-Jørgensen.

Uglegårdsskolen [Uglegård School], Halldor Gunnløgsson & Jørn Nielsen 1972-74. Photo: Mogens S. Koch.

→

Stenvadskolen [Stenvad School], Fællestegnestuen A5 and Vandkunsten 1979-81. Photo: Foto C.

changing pedagogical ideals, changing societal tendencies and political ideals, on the whole. This can be spotted especially in the changing relationships between the individual and the community, between specialization and interdisciplinarity, and between edification and education. New construction, conversions and extensions of schools in this period can thus be seen as attempts to provide concrete, spatial responses to the changing tendencies and ideals of society, which manifest themselves in the legislation.
In the 1960s, where the major part of the writings on the issue is found in the special issue 6-1963, it is the Education Act of 1958 that is centrally positioned. Among other things, the adoption of this legislation effectively did away with the middle/intermediate school [≈ junior high school: classes 6-9 in the Danish system], as a separate institution, and led to the construction of a number of larger, centralized schools all over the country. Here, the development of the one-story *kamskole* ['kamskole' – crest school – is an emblematic expression for a variant of the pavilion school] is shown: one early example of this is Bornebusch, Brüel, Selchau and Henning Larsen's Vangeboskolen. This model, which was suitable for organizing the different parts of the school into clearly separated sections while simultaneously providing easy access to shared classrooms, is – in many different variations – dominant in the schools that were being shown in *Arkitektur DK* during the 1960s and the early 1970s.
The subsequent Education Act, which was adopted in 1975, did away with the *realskole* [lower secondary school], extended compulsory education to nine years and opened up the possibility for interdisciplinary teaching. This is reflected in the school construction from this period, and one aspect of this is that the one-story *kamskole*, in all its variations, evolves into the 'open plan' school, which offers more flexible spatial design programmes and, to an increasing extent, 'home areas' and 'workshop and specialty-subject areas' rather than fixed classrooms and specialty-subject rooms, which were dominant in the one-story *kamskole's* structure.
Halldor Gunnløgsson and Jørn Nielsen's Uglegårdsskolen, constitutes a stage along the way running between the one-story *kamskole's* class- and specialty-subject-divisions and the open-plan school's more flexible structure and, as editor Poul Erik Skriver highlights in his discussion of the building, it stands as a highly successful 'attempt to create a warm and robust learning environ-

ment, where the workshop-like interiors impose very few restrictions on the users.[4] The interplay here between inside and outside, as Skriver astutely points out, plays a part in generating a rich and varied environment, and contributes to creating life and sensuousness in what is otherwise a rigorously composed floor plan, which extends its way along a canal.[5]

Peder Lykke Skolen in Amager is another fine example of an admixture of an insistence upon the classroom structure and innovative experiments with the open, flexible plan. Here, by way of compensation for the fixed classroom structure, the door to the classrooms was removed in connection with the school's opening. These classrooms are openly connected with the outside-lying hallway and home-area sections. The open plan schools, which are, naturally, most typically built in one level, become very popular, and over the course of the years, a model has undergone development which is referred to, on several occasions, as 'the little school inside of the large', where the emphasis has been laid on a concentration of aspects of the school's life into smaller areas, of which Tegnestuen Vandkunsten and A5 Tegnestuen's Stenvadsskole in Farum are examples.[6]

After the appearance of Stenvadsskolen in 1982, there was – in the ensuing three decades – not more than one newly erected school that was featured in *Arkitektur DK* (namely, Dall & Lindhardtsen's Skovvangskolen, construction of which commenced in 1985 and proceeded, by phases, until 2000). It was not until 2003 that schools would appear again in the periodical's columns, and here it was the new Education Act of 1993,

which had replaced the Education Act of 1975, which was evidently making its impact. With the Education Act of 1993, the comprehensive school was introduced; this gave rise to degrees of differentiation in the education: new subjects were introduced; interdisciplinarity became a requirement; and project work came to be a new pedagogical form on the school level. These tendencies were reflected, particularly distinctly, in Trekroner Skole, which was designed by Vilhelm Lauritzen Architects based on one of three winning projects from the open competition, 'Rum Form Funktion i Folkeskolen' [Space, Form, Function in Elementary School], which was settled in 1999, and Thure Nielsen & Rubow's Kingoskolen in Slangerup.[7]

Special issues as editorial frames for presenting school construction constitute an approach that has made quite an enormous impact on how the development in these buildings is experienced, when you see them through the lens of *Arkitektur DK*. Special issues differentiate themselves from the continuous stream of communication about new architecture, and it thus appears, to a greater degree than is actually the case, as though the development were occurring in spurts, if one takes a look at *when* the schools were built – and also calls other sources into play. The differences from the one 'type' to the next become more pronounced: there is a greater homogenization taking place within the specific period, which thereby comes to stand in even greater contrast to the ensuing period. Among the results, there is a long and continuous development taking place, and this is also referred to, in dribs and drabs, in *Arkitektur DK*, but it is largely the editorial treatment (which often transpires against the backdrop of a more societally oriented critique in *Arkitekten*) that makes it relatively simple today to refer to the likes of the one-story *kamskole*, 'the open-plan school', and so on. As the journal, especially in its early years, had a certain authoritative weight, these types of schools simultaneously became points of departure for subsequent construction projects all over the country; they were specifically being sought after in connection with architectural competitions, and the projects that were consequently realized can subsequently be typologized, and can thereby serve to reinforce the point of departure. The building types were naturally not conjured up at random, and seeing as they take their point of departure in formal features like functional organization and spatial hierarchy, they nonetheless appear to be relatively robust.

Another feature that is characteristic of the presentation of school construction in *Arkitektur DK* (in any event, in the period leading up to 1982, when the aspect of materiality was most comprehensive) is that the development in the building types appears, to such an extraordinarily clear degree, to be coupled to changes in the existing legislation, which reflect, in turn, the changing views of the pedagogical and democratic principles for the school's organization. In-depth examinations of the school buildings are accompanied, in many instances, by altogether comprehensive explanations of the pedagogical principles underlying the different architectural solutions. A special editorial approach taken here is the great emphasis that is placed on documenting how new pedagogical principles are being translated into the school's spaces. This is especially striking because there is not anything similar to this that manifests itself, to the same extent, in the treatment of other types of buildings. Whenever hospital construction is shown, for example, a certain distance to medical science is maintained, and we understand that the architects have subordinated their impulses to the needs of this field. And whenever residential and commercial constructions are discussed, the editor himself comes for-

Trekroner Skole,
Vilhelm Lauritzen Architects 2001-05.
Photo: Thomas Schytt-Poulsen.

ward and, drawing on his own professional expertise (Poul Erik Skriver, who was the journal's editor from 1957 to 1982, had a background as a city planner) offers his own opinion on the apparently obvious qualities in the functionally-divided city and on large-scale urban renewal, and voices his own preferences for low-dense-construction rather than high-rise buildings.

In this way, the editor's altogether considerable power in his/her role as co-creator of the narrative about his/her contemporary time is also underscored, and this subsequently comes to be valid as an important source for historiography. There is selection and there is sorting away: some things are set into perspective while others are ignored. But in a subsequent rereading and redissemination, it is very difficult – and it is well-nigh impossible, in practice – to get a full overview about what it is that has been the original empirical material. What it is that has been sorted away and has thereby effectively been written out of history, already in is own time, is left to stand in is subject to considerable uncertainty.

## Architecture history in a discourse-analytical perspective

The thematization of and the present focus on how architects create space for new pedagogical principles are merely two examples of the many layers of priorities, interpretations, preferences and general interests that underlie the evocation of the general image of school construction in the period. A third, and equally interesting, perspective in this connection (one that has exerted a great deal of influence on the presentation in the preceding pages) is that in the last two issues of *Arkitektur DK,* schools were categorized – along with high schools, universities, etc. – into the category *education and research*, while kindergartens, for example, were displayed together with other types of institutions in the category *health and care.*

Perhaps the above picture would have taken on another nuance – or a completely different background – had the schools and the kindergartens been treated *together.* As mentioned in the introduction, these circumstances make it rather difficult to treat the edifying coupling between architecture and welfare in the post-war period unambiguously, even if this was the original intention.

In the final part of this article we will, taking our point of departure in discourse analysis, discuss how one way to critically address the many and often contradictory narratives that turn up when one revisits the history of architecture.

'Discourse' is understood here as 'a particular way of talking about and understanding the world (or an aspect of the world)'.[8] Discourses take the form of spoken language, written language and pictures, and they affect how we perceive social practices and institutions. At the same time, discourses – the ways in which we talk about and form our understanding of the world – are not merely a matter of *perceiving,* as a vehicle for reflecting our social practice. Much more than this: discourses play a part in constituting practice. In critical discourse analysis, special emphasis is placed on how, in the establishment of – and the adherence to – discourses, there is an essential element of power. Accordingly, discourses can play a role in securing and insisting on one particular view of the world in favour of another. In this effect – and by virtue of the influence – that discourses make on how the world hangs together, one speaks about discourses being *performative.* Seeing that in the theme issues of *Arkitektur DK*, the focus is aimed at different types of school buildings, this can be considered a case of how to establish a discourse upon which subsequent building constructions can be perceived (and

Kingoskolen,
Thure Nielsen & Rubow 2000-01.
Photo: Jan Juhl.

maybe even created) – both in their own day and in the future's historiography. Similarly, one can see the intense focus on the connection between the development of new pedagogical principles and new school buildings as a way of establishing a discourse around a special connection between the architects' efforts and the welfare society's development – a discourse that is subsequently co-determinative of how we perceive the acts of designing and building a school, then and now. Certainly, not all discourses are equally viable. The literature speaks of *discourse coalitions* that designate how a group of actors '*in the context of an identifiable set of practices*, shares the usage of a particular set of story lines over a particular period of time.' Discourse coalitions serve, for example, to consolidate the power that is seated in an already established discourse, by reproducing it or transforming it over time or across different domains.[9] In this connection, it is worth noting that precisely the way in which we have described school construction through *Arkitektur DK* lies in direct extension of some of the main points in Fisker and Millech's architectural history,[10] which was playing, in these very decades, such a dominant role in the establishment of Danish architects' understanding of being part of a historical and culturally conditioned tradition (see also, chapter 5.5).

By taking this one example, and by approaching it critically through discourse analysis, we can faintly glimpse the contours of how, through a particular presentation of architectural history and the contemporary practice, a considerably powerful discourse was established pertaining to a naturally advancing, pragmatic and functionally oriented architecture, which has, as one of its primary objectives, been compelled – together with other expert groups – to do its part in helping the welfare society further along in its development. Herein lies a possible explanation for why it is not immediately possible to separate the different layers of the architecture presentation and -history from one another; this is a very powerful discourse, which has been maintained, reproduced and transformed into a well-established discourse coalition over the course of a long period of time. However, had a different frame been constructed – had another discourse been established – the picture might have been something else altogether. As discourses and social processes are co-constitutive, they both influence what actions and perceptions are possible.

In the recent decade, we have seen the development of a critical historiography in the history of architecture. In a special issue of *Nordisk Arkitekturforskning* from 2006, with the title, 'Å se modernismen i bakspeilet' [Modernism in retrospect],[11] the editors describe this as a research practice that challenges the narrative form and 'takes the form of a rewriting – that embraces the nuances, the inconsistencies, the disparate traditions and the philosophical and formal tensions in what architectural history has made out to be a monolithic phenomenon.' Transpositions of the history as the focus of research is also reflected in the Swedish research programme, *Architecture in Effect – Rethinking the Social in Architecture*, where *Critical Historiography,* as one of four programme areas, is oriented around a study of the connections between architecture's history, education, research and practice, taking its point of departure in the notion that the architectural profession's identity is created through shared memories and discourses, and that the foundation for these must therefore always be exposed.[12]

With this one example and brief introduction to a possible theoretical understanding of how we can understand and change the world around us, it is our intention to instigate and spawn a critical assessment with respect to what role history plays in our understanding of the present. Can such a critical attitude fashion the point of origin for a new way of understanding the connection between architecture's and the welfare state's development? And can such a new understanding contribute to a sustained development of research, teaching and the practice through which the architects create spaces for welfare?

**Notes**

1 J. Pagh, S. Deis Christensen & H. Thomsen: *Velfærdssamfundet Arkitektur 1957-1982*, J. Pagh (ed.): *Arkitektur DK*, 57(2) (2013), pp. 1-87.

2 J. Pagh, S. Deis Christensen, H. Thomsen et al.: *Velfærdssamfundets Arkitektur 1983-2012*, J. Pagh (ed.): *Arkitektur DK*, 57(3), 2013, pp. 1-87.

3 See, for example: M. Keiding, M. Amundsen & K. Dirckinck-Holmfeld: *Dansk arkitektur siden 1754*, (2007); H.E. Langkilde, K. Dirckinck-Holmfeld & J. Hegner Christiansen: 'Arkitekten 100 år', *Arkitekten*, 1998 and N.-O. Lund: *Nordisk Arkitektur* (2008). See also, chapter 5.5.

4 P.E. Skriver: 'Uglegårdsskolen' in *Arkitektur DK*, 18(2) (1974), pp. 52-57.

5 J. Pagh: 'Uddannelse og forskning' in J. Pagh (ed.), *Arkitektur DK*, 57(2), 2013a, pp. 40-47.

6 J. Pagh: ibid., pp. 40-47.

7 J. Pagh: 'Uddannelse og forskning' in J. Pagh (ed.), *Arkitektur DK*, 57(3), 2013b, pp. 76-83

8 M.W. Jørgensen & L. Philips: *Discourse Analysis as Theory and Method* (2002), p. 1.

9 M.A. Hajer: 'Doing discourse analysis: coalitions, practices, meaning' in M. van den Brink & T. Metze, (eds.): *Words Matter in Policy and Planning – Discourse Theory and Method in the Social Sciences* (2006), pp. 65-74.

10 K. Millech: *Danske Arkitekturstrømninger,* K. Fisker (ed.) (1951).

11 M. Lending et al.: Å se modernismen i bakspejlet. *Nordisk Arkitekturforskning*, (1), 2006, pp. 5-6.

12 KTH: Architecture in Effect (2011).

**Literature**


- Fairclough, N., Jessop, B., & Sayer, A.: 'Critical realism and Semiosis' in Joseph, J. & Roberts, J.M. (eds.): *Realism Discourse and Deconstruction*. Routledge, London & New York, 2004.
- Hajer, M.A.: 'Doing discourse analysis: coalitions, practices, meaning' in van den Brink, M., & Metze, T. (eds.).: *Words Matter in Policy and Planning – Discourse Theory and Method in the Social Sciences*. Koninklijk Nederlands Aardrijkskundig Genootschap, Utrecht 2006, pp. 65-74.
- Jørgensen, M.W., & Philips, L.: *Diskursanalyse som teori og metode*. Roskilde Universitetsforlag, Frederiksberg 1999. [*Discourse Analysis as Theory and Method*. Sage Publications, London, Thousand Oaks, New Delhi 2002.]
- Keiding, M., Amundsen, M., & Dirckinck-Holmfeld, K.: *Dansk arkitektur siden 1754*, The Danish Architectural Press, Copenhagen 2007.
- KTH: Architecture in Effect, 2011. http://architectureineffect.se.
- Langkilde, H.E., Dirckinck-Holmfeld, K., & Hegner Christiansen, J.: *Arkitekten 100 år. Arkitekten*, 1998.
- Lending, M. et al.: Å se modernismen i bakspejlet. *Nordisk Arkitekturforskning*, (1), 2006, pp. 5-6.
- Lund, N.-O.: *Nordisk Arkitektur* 3rd edition, The Danish Architectural Press, Copenhagen 2008.
- Millech, K. & Fisker, K.: *Danske Arkitekturstrømninger.* Østifternes Kreditforening, Copenhagen 1951.
- Pagh, J.: Uddannelse og forskning in Pagh, J. (ed.): *Arkitektur DK*, 57(2), 2013a, pp. 40-47.
- Pagh, J.: Uddannelse og forskning in Pagh, J. (ed.): *Arkitektur DK*, 57(3), 2013b, pp. 76-83.
- Pagh, J., Deis Christensen, S., Thomsen, H., et al.: *Velfærdssamfundets Arkitektur 1983-2012*, Pagh, J. (ed.): *Arkitektur DK*, 57(3), 2013, pp. 1-87.
- Pagh, J., Deis Christensen, S., & Thomsen, H.: *Velfærdssamfundets Arkitektur 1957-1982*, Pagh, J. (ed.): *Arkitektur DK*, 57(2), pp. 1-87.
- Skriver, P.E.: 'Uglegårdsskolen' in *Arkitektur DK*, 18(2), 1974, pp. 52-57.

# Housing

Marie Stender

# Islands of Shared Identity

## An Anthropological Portrait of Lange Eng & 8 House

The architect called the 8 House 'a modern mountain village'. Many of the residents have embraced that story and address each other as '8'ers'. All photos by the author.

**Architecture, communication and social media coalesce in the new housing complexes' iconic enclaves. By this means, the architecture freezes a segmentation that is typical of the times – in glass and concrete. This brings about strong identity fellowship, internally, among the residents, who are simultaneously screened from the surrounding world. This article discusses the societal implications of this situation, and draws parallels to the welfare society where extensive redistribution and solidarity in the current discourse also seem to be conditional on homogeneity, internally, and on a clear delimitation, externally.**

## The return of the social – but not as we knew it...

Welcome to the modern mountain village! In Copenhagen's new urban district, Ørestad, 8 House's facades in glass and aluminium tower high, in dramatic contrast to the surrounding flat 'Amager fælled' terrain. The 500 modern flats have been stacked densely on top of each other in a gigantic complex, where a path winds its way up the building and renders it possible to walk right up to the top and greet your neighbours along the way. In the middle of all of this there are common rooms, allocated on five floors, and both

the architect and the residents speak about the place as 'a mountain village'.

For its socially oriented architecture, Denmark has come to be world-renowned: the collective dwelling form is said to have been invented here, and community-oriented ideals have left their distinct stamp on housing in general.[1] But society has changed since the 1970s, and so have its communities and the architecture that houses them. We are, according to Dutch architect and sociologist Arnold Reijndorp, playing witness to 'The return of the social – but not as we knew it'.[2] But what is it about the social dimension that has changed, and how does this coin itself in the new residential architecture?[3] In these years, the welfare state is being hailed, on the one hand, by politicians from all the political parties, while, on the other hand, what we in Denmark have traditionally understood as 'welfare' is simultaneously to a wide extent being phased out.[4] One consequence of this is a renewed emphasis on local social communities, on voluntary deeds, and on civil society as heirs to the tasks that the state is no longer able to cope with. It therefore seems relevant to take a closer look at whether and how architecture supports these kinds of local communities. What characterizes the social life that is being formed within the new residential architecture? And how is this related to the surrounding society?

In this article, light will be shed on these questions, on the basis of an anthropological fieldwork study conducted in 2012 in two rather striking new housing complexes:[5] first, 8 House, in Ørestad, designed by BIG (Bjarke Ingels Group); and second, *Lange Eng* [Long Meadow], a residential complex that was designed by Dorte Mandrup Architects and is located in Albertslund, a suburb west of Copenhagen. These two complexes were erected within the last ten years, they were designed by prominent Danish architectural offices, and they have both garnered recognition for their visionary and socially oriented architecture. Accordingly, they are obvious sites for con-

ducting an examination of the kinds of communities that are being fostered in the new architecture. In the article, initially, there will be a description of the two places' social life and identity.[6] Thereafter, the focus will be directed towards the relationship to the surrounding community that is mediated by the building. The argument is that they can be considered *designed communities,* which express a novel form of spatial segmentation. The societal consequences of this will be discussed in conclusion.

## Built-in identity communities

In 8 House's southern yard area, there is a fenced-in playground, where small children are romping about in colourful snowsuits. The adults are also wearing snowsuits, but their garments are black, sporting an angular, white '8 House' logo that has the same form as the building's floor plan. All in all, this logo reappears again in many places inside the complex: on information tablets beside each stairwell, which are supposed to make it easier to find your way around in the large complex; on posters in the café; and even on the spines of the ring binders that are kept in the bookcase in the kindergarten's office. As I interview the leader of the kindergarten, it comes to light, to my surprise, that the kindergarten's organization is completely independent of 8 House's. They have simply chosen the name and the logo, '8 House', in order to 'become part of the local environment', as he puts it. In Ørestad, people don't actually say what street they live on: instead, they say the name of the complex: V-Huset, Sejlhuset, Porthuset, 8-tallet (8 House), and so on. The iconic architecture provides identity, but also a sense of ownership, for better or for worse. The parents living in 8 House have, for example, a hard time understanding that their children do not have 'prior claim' to a place in the kindergarten, but have to remain on a waiting list for months, just like the children from the rest of the city. Similarly, Lange Eng's residents have, to the utmost degree, a sense of ownership when it comes to their building complex, which they call 'a modern co-housing complex'. Each family has its own residence, with a kitchen, a bathroom, a washing

←
Many different people live in the 8 House, but the architecture and branding of the place creates a common icon of identity. View over the southern courtyard and Amager Fælled.

The homes in Lange Eng sit in a ring with their backs to the surroundings: The outer facade is dark and closed, while the inner facade facing the yard is open, with lightweight polycarbonate and large windows.

machine etc. But above and beyond all this, they share a common house, which contains various leisure facilities, as well a dining room where community dining takes place six days a week. Lange Eng is much smaller than 8 House and it does not house any day-care institution, although some of the residents have certainly been thinking about starting up their own school, because they've run into certain difficulties with the quarter's elementary school. A good number of the residents have taken part, themselves, in establishing and designing the place. They were building owners and developers themselves, and it was, so to speak, *their* dream of living together that the architect Dorte Mandrup gave form. The 54 row house residences fashion one solidly cast block, with two narrow gates, with a small crease in the middle and with a distinctive black wooden facade. The complex's simple iconic form is a central element in the place's and resident group's identity. The residents heard, for instance, that some of the neighbours were calling the place 'the black hippie square'[7] and thereafter, they took on the nickname themselves. Although what we have here is not, as we have with 8 House, a professional *brandscape*,[8] where architecture and graphic communication have strategically been fused together, the architectural form in Lange Eng, as well, serves as some kind of icon for the community.

The greater part of Lange Eng's residents are younger families with children and two careers. They typically tell me that they have moved into the co-housing because of the practical benefits it offers in everyday life: you don't have to buy groceries and cook every day, but can walk up into the common house and eat, or you can even take the meal back home with you, as takeaway, and many of the families prefer to do this. There are plenty of playmates for the children, and the adults partake in mowing the lawn and doing other practical tasks, as well as getting together to play soccer and do yoga, after the children have been put to bed. Even though there is frequent community dining and even though there are shared facilities, co-housing set-ups like Lange Eng are essentially different from the communes of the 1970s. Whereas the driving force at that time, forty years ago, was an ideological urge to break with the very notion of 'the nuclear family' and re-organize socially in new and different ways, the motivation today is rather a wish to safeguard and ease the everyday life of the nuclear family.[9]

When we zoom in on Lange Eng's intranet, Forum, where the residents communicate about any and everything, it becomes altogether clear, that what

we are dealing with is not only a practical community. In 8 House, the residents' social media platform is called 8book, and even if the residents do not have daily community dining, as they have in Lange Eng, there is actually an animated communication here about food clubs and other social activities, as well as practical information and discussions. Even a cursory glance at the mailbox's stream of subject lines – 'Looking for rice pancakes – NOW', 'Is there an electrician in 8 House?' or 'I'm stuck in traffic – is there anybody who can pick up my child at the kindergarten?' – offers a continuous impression of the other residents' doings. Furthermore, on both Forum and 8book a common lingo arises, where the place's name and the complex's form become part of the residents' way of speaking to each other and become part of their way of speaking about the place's activities. In 8 House, for example, there are clubs like 'Blænde 8' [Dazzle 8] and 'Salon 8'. Similarly, in their e-mails, the residents address each other as '8'ers' or '8bookers', or they refer to 'our mountain village', or they say 'here in the village'. A corresponding trend can be seen on Lange Eng's Forum, where the residents sometimes address each other as 'Lange Eng'ers' or write 'here on the meadow' and might communicate about the running club that goes by the name 'Long Legs', the men's club, 'LEM – Lange Eng's Men' or the women's club, 'LED – Lange Eng's Damer' [Women]. This creative and specifically linguistic way of playing around with the complex's name and the lively communication on the social forums testify that what we have in the two complexes is not merely a matter of a practical community. Both Lange Eng and 8 House constitute contemporary identity fellowships, which the residents can also carry along with them, even when they are not home, via virtual platforms, where neighbours are constantly in contact.

## Sitting in a ring, with their backs to the world

That the social media play a central role in today's communities cannot come as any surprise. The interesting question, in this connection, is how the architecture interacts with the social media and how architecture – in addition to serving as a unifying identity icon – forms the place's sense of fellowship and the relationship to its surrounding environment.

Lange Eng's structural form, with a block that surrounds a common green courtyard area, is characteristic of Copenhagen's 'borough' quarters (e.g. Vesterbro, Østerbro, Nørrebro), where many

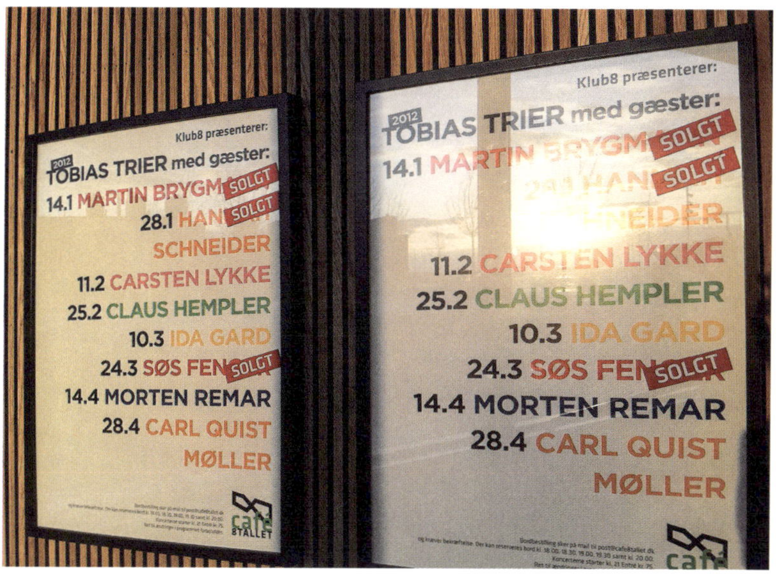


The 8 House logo can be found in many places around the house – here in the café. The building owner invested in establishing a café with concerts and a temporary gallery in order to create an atmosphere of urban life.

←

Many families choose to live in the new co-housing schemes due to the practical benefits. In Lange Eng there is common dining six days a week, but the residents can also bring the meal back home as takeaway.

of the residents were previously living. Conversely, the building complex's typology differentiates itself markedly from the otherwise typical Albertslund-ish suburban landscape within which it is placed. The residents actually had to apply for exemptions, since the complex's perimeter block-form deviated from the constructional principles that the municipality had stipulated for the area. However, this building complex also differentiates itself from Copenhagen's typical perimeter blocks, not only because it is less high, but also by virtue of the fact that it could be said to be turned inside out. While the classic Copenhagen perimeter block turns its 'face' to the street and its 'back' towards the yard, the private spaces in Lange Eng, like the bathrooms and the bedrooms, are placed out towards the outer facade, while the dwellings' representative zones – with their large windows, their double-high kitchen-family rooms, and their living rooms – are all facing the common yard space.[10] It is from here, and not from the outside, that the residence's large paintings, spectacular lamps and very best furniture can be seen. Similarly, it is from here that the home's life and rhythm is visible, when the lights are turned on and then off, and when the residents are moving around behind the large plate-glass windows.

In this way, the building complex's form establishes an introverted scene, but also fashions a distinctive framing of the common outdoor space and a safe, supervised playground for the toddlers. What is created is a clearly demarcated *inside* and *outside* in the building complex, partly through the perimeter block-form, and partly through the remarkable contrast between the dark and closed outer facade and the open interior facade, with its large windows and lightweight polycarbonate. The homes are virtually sitting in a ring, with their backs to the surrounding environment, and the residents are, for that matter, also themselves very attentive to the fact that their building complex can stand forth as a self-sufficient island, when seen from the surroundings. By way of example, one of the interviewed residents told, while laughing, that she had been attending a mothers' group with a woman who had the idea that Lange Eng was an extension of the nearby prison, while another one of the residents told me that she had friends who thought that the building from the outside looked like a castle.

Even though the character of enclave is most striking in Lange Eng, 8 House also steps out from its surroundings as an architectonic island. In this way, the building complex separates itself, albeit to a lesser extent, from the surrounding Ørestad, which is characterized on the whole by isolated building enclaves. 8 House's building complex is much larger and has been put together in a more complex way than Lange Eng: with business, flats, so-called 'townhouses', and penthouses, in what the architect has called 'an urban layer cake'.[11] Also, 8 house is basically a block that has, however, undergone a *twist* in its middle, with the result that two inner courtyards have been formed. The building complex's large windows, balconies and terraces are oriented more towards the sunshine and the views out over the Amager Fælled terrain than towards the common courtyard space, where the residents do not really spend a lot of time either. The path that makes it possible to promenade up to the top of the building, is, on the other hand, important to the place's social life, especially to those families that have terraces facing out to the path and who are able to chat with the neighbour on the other side of the fence. But, as a matter of fact, it is also important to the residents in the other apartments. They always take their guests along with them on 'the mandatory 8 House walk', where one obtains a most impressive view out over both the building complex and the surrounding area,[12] and accord-

8 House site plan: BIG Architects.

Lange Eng site plan:
Dorte Mandrup Architects.

ingly, the sloping path constitutes, also on a symbolic level, the very backbone of the 'mountain village' concept. The path was conceived, on the part of the architect, as a publicly accessible street, which could draw urban life right up to the top of the building complex. Massive media coverage, with photographs of, among others, the crown prince, the crown princess and Bjarke Ingels, who were all riding bicycles to the top of 8 House, gave rise to such a huge influx of architecture tourists that the public life has simply become 'too much' for the residents, and today, parts of the path are closed off, with locked gates.

Lange Eng's building complex is also pierced by a path. In order to grant permission to build all the way out to the edge of registered plot's limit, the municipality posed a demand that the two gates and the path leading through Lange Eng's yard space would have to be publicly accessible. Some of the residents would like to close off the gates, while others feel that the building is sufficiently closed up around themselves already. In practice, however, there are very few outsiders who dare step in through Lange Eng's narrow gates, and if they were to do so, their entrance would immediately be noticed by the residents, who can sometimes go as far as to ask unfamiliar faces what they're looking for. The courtyard is strewn with toys, and the hammocks, the potted plants and the rabbit hutches signal unequivocally that what we have here is a private garden rather than a public outdoor space.

## Segmentation in glass and concrete

Although both Lange Eng and 8 House are, in principle, publicly accessible, they appear as pseudo-public spaces, where outsiders are not really welcome. In practice, the complexes close up around the residents, even though few of the residents would ever dream of living in a gated

community. For, in fact, there is a specifically Danish aversion to high walls, fences and well-defined boundaries,[13] an aversion that is part and parcel of the Scandinavian egalitarianism ideal.[14] However, there is currently a tendency that can be seen towards what the Danish anthropologist Kirsten Marie Raahauge has described as 'invisible gated communities': 'The close sense of fellowship, which is conditional on the physical space within which one resides, is of consequence: the neighbour is your friend. A *revitalization* of the local is occuring (...),'[15] she writes, adding: 'Inside this sociocultural gating, no walls are needed. It is the social putty that gives rise to a sense of fellowship and to invisible filters.'[16] 8book and Forum can clearly be understood as virtual versions of this social putty, but the complexes' distinctive architectural-material screening-off nonetheless suggests that the Danish communities are also in the process of becoming more visibly gated.

However, it is important to emphasize that what we are dealing with, in both Lange Eng and 8 House, is not primarily a fear of crime, like we know it from American gated communities, where high walls and privately employed security guards are supposed to keep uninvited guests out of the complex. When the two settlements form a ring around their residents, this has more to do with shielding and safeguarding their sense of mutual fellowship. What the large windows and the subtle boundaries between private and public insist on, namely, is that it is not every Tom, Dick and Harry that can peer in, but for the most part, only your neighbours, whom you already know and whom you trust. Herein, a thought-provoking parallel to the welfare society, as such, delineates itself, In these years what is also being discussed is whether the extensive redistribution and solidarity is contingent on a certain homogeneity, internally, and a clear delimitation, externally.

As the Norwegian anthropologist Marianne Gullestad has pointed out, *sameness* in Scandinavian societies has long been a prerequisite for making friends and becoming good neighbours. In order to bring about sameness and a sense of community, internally, symbolic borders are drawn out, externally. As she writes:

*Norwegian men and women want sameness, but in the process of creating sameness they indirectly organize symbolic fences between themselves and the people who are not considered the same. The symbolic fences are not primarily established for shutting someone out, but first and foremost to protect and preserve a social identity which is defined within a reference group.*[17]

In Lange Eng, as a matter of fact, the residents was actually surprised about how similar they turned out to be. The word 'diversity' formed part of the written value foundation that was used for recruiting interested families. But paradoxically enough, this has resulted in a decidedly homogeneous community of people who are in favour of diversity. Conversely, it could be argued that in Lange Eng, the minor segregation counteracts the major segregation. This is to be understood in the sense that most of the residents, had it not been for Lange Eng, would hardly have settled in Albertslund, which is demographically characterized by a significantly lower educational and income level.[18]

The situation is somewhat different when it comes to 'sameness' in the 8 House's residents' group: for one thing, the many dwellings in various sizes and with many price levels result in a more diverse group of residents; for another, as a consequence of the financial crisis, the prices of the homes tumbled to the bottom, thus making the place accessible to a wider group than exclusively the creative class, which had initially been

Architecture-tourists have flocked to the 8 House to try bicycling on the path. The residents were fed up with it, so today cycling is banned and parts of the path have been fenced off.

targeted during the design and sales process. Through creative marketing campaigns and by investing in the café, the gallery and the delicatessen boutique located on 8 House's ground floor, the consortium of building owners was accordingly trying to attract what the manager responsible for 'branding' the complex referred to as 'the caffè latte segment'. However, he was subsequently surprised that the building's composition of residents was broader than that. After all, it is not all the residents that make use of the building's café or delicatessen boutique, that participate equally as much in the social activities, that express themselves on 8book, or that refer to the place as 'a mountain village'. Nonetheless, hand in hand with its thoroughly implemented branding, its virtual communication and its in-house clubs and activities, the place's architecture delineates a clear picture of a figure-8-shaped identity club: *for residents only.*

Rather than gated communities, these new Danish residential complexes can be described as 'designed communities'. It's not only the physical space but also its identity and social life that are being designed, with specific interest communities in mind. In reality, maybe this can be understood most of all as housing construction's answer to the segmentation that can also be seen many other places in society: in products that are targeted towards the one or the other consumer segment; or in policy-making 'designed' to please specific voter segments. In public spaces that are addressed not to the needs of the city's residents in general but rather to the needs of specific user groups: such as child-rearing families, skaters or shoppers.[19] Or on the Internet and on the social media, where not all users are presented with the same interface, but rather with ads and items of information that are tailored precisely to their particular user's profile, interests and 'likes'. It goes without saying that segmentation is not something that architects have come up with. But in the new building complexes, they are freezing the segmentation in glass and concrete. This generates strong identity communities, internally, in the complexes, where the residents are not only

sharing lawn mowers and taking part in collective cooking chores, picking up each other's children, but are also mirroring themselves in each other and bringing about a shared identity. In this respect, the new complexes are shoring up a society that is placing greater emphasis on civil society and on the local community. The question is whether this is actually transpiring at the expense of the larger community and at the expense of the welfare society's cohesion, when the architecture forms a ring around a group of like-minded people, turns its backs on the surrounding world and integrates a considerable portion of their social life as it is being lived *in-house.*

## Conclusion: islands of shared identity

A sense of community is in high demand in new Danish building complexes like Lange Eng and 8 House, but these are communities that have been formed and that function as designed communities or *islands of shared identity.* The point is that it is not merely the physical space, but also the place's identity and social life that are being designed for a specific group of people. Here, the architecture, hand in hand with virtual social forums, is playing a new role as identity icon. At the same time the building complexes open themselves up, internally, while externally, they screen the community off from its surroundings. Just as the welfare state's solidarity appears to be conditional on setting up delimitation externally, the residents' sense of mutual fellowship also appears to be contingent on being shielded off from the

In both residential architecture and the welfare society, the inward community appears to be contingent on an outward shielding off. The path of the 8 House is a pseodo-public space, where strangers are not really welcome.

←

The municipality demanded that there was public access through Lange Eng. Only very few outsiders, however, dare to step through the narrow gates.

surrounding environment. Such a shielding off was also seen in the early welfare society's housing projects. But where these were characterized by a functional division, the new housing projects rather bespeak a spatial version of the time-typical segmentation in cultural and social interest communities. The new enclave-like residential architecture can, in this way, capture and reinforce current segregational tendencies, where we tend to settle down close to those of our own ilk. Conversely, the somewhat self-sufficient complexes, with their built-in identity and social life, might also hold even sharper social contrasts to their surroundings: consider, for example, that Lange Eng is neighbour to a prison. Certainly, more striking enclave complexes like 8 House and Lange Eng will turn up in the Danish housing landscape in the time to come. The challenge for the future's welfare architects will therefore be to continue to forge connections and create junctures that will bind the islands together.

### Notes

1 There is no commonly accepted international definition of 'co-housing', and different countries have different forms of communal/collective residential situations. What is characteristic of Scandinavia, however, is that this movement has, to a great extent, been embraced by architects and professionals, as Egerö points out: 'The design of communal living has a strong utopian architectural and social engineering tradition in Scandinavia, especially Denmark and Sweden.' For example, inspired by the new collectivist ideas in the 1970s, the Danish Building Research Institute organized a nation-wide competition related to low-dense housing construction, where all the winning proposals were characterized by placing emphasis on common facilities and the involvement of the residents. B. Egerö: *Puzzling Patterns of Co-housing in Scandinavia* (2014).

2 A. Reijndorp & M. Hajer: *In Search of New Public Domain* (2001). Reijndorp has used this as the title for a series of recent lectures, among others, a lecture that was presented at the 'Housing & Welfare: Boundaries/Encounters/Connections' conference that was held at the Royal Danish Academy of Fine Arts, School of Architecture in Copenhagen in May 2015. Here, he draws on analyses from his book *In Search of New Public Domain (2001)*, wherein – in concord with the present article's point about spatial segmentation – an argument is advanced that rather than one common public space we increasingly have to deal with 'an archipelago of enclaves.' (Ibid.)

3 I have also discussed these issues in my article 'Social Living, Version 2.0', which analyses the new communities in relation to virtual forums and shared economy. What was pointed out here is that, in comparison to the 1970s' communes, the new forms of co-housing can be characterized by their *convenient sharing* and *brandscapes*. M. Stender: 'Social Living, Version 2.0 – An Ethnography of Three New Residential Complexes' (2015). The article has its empirical focus on Lange Eng and the 8 House, but additionally in the 'A house', designed by Holgaard Architects and located on Islands Brygge.

4 As the Norwegian anthropologist Thomas Hylland Eriksen has pointed out, the welfare state's current popularity can be associated with its being phased out: 'We see things more clearly when they are fading away (...). No one is going to call for the abolition of the welfare state, although only a generation ago, that would have garnered a substantial number of votes from people keen to reduce their tax bill. Today, there is an acknowledgement of vulnerability, threats, and uncertainty that makes us cling to what feels safe and provides stability and material security. And the welfare state is a symbol of that.' T.H. Eriksen (in conversation with Jesper Pagh): 'On Wolves and Owls and a Possible Sustainable Future' (2015).

5 The fieldwork was carried out in January-August 2012 and consisted, partly, of interviews with the architects, the planners and the building owners who had created the two buildings, and partly of interviews with residents and users. Moreover, I rented a dwelling for one month's stay in each of the two buildings, where I moved in, so as to be able to observe and take part in the life that was going on in the complexes, getting involved in joint events, in leisure activities and in discussions on the virtual platforms.

6 The concept of 'identity' is often used in architecture and urban planning in the sense of 'a distinctive feature', i.e. as a positive quality that a place can have more or less of, and which distinguishes it from other places. This article, however, leans more to an anthropological perspective, where identity is regarded as something relational and as something that has been socio-culturally constructed, which both has to do with the characteristics that differentiate one from the others and also with the common characteristics with which one group associates itself or becomes associated with by others.

7 The nickname refers to the complex's shape and colour, but also to Den Sorte Firkant ('The Black Square' ) - a term that was used in the 1970s to refer to one particularly disadvantaged residential quarter in the inner Nørrebro

section of Copenhagen. Many of Lange Eng's residents were also previously living in Nørrebro.

8 The American architect Anna Klingmann has introduced the concept of 'brandscape' as a strategic fusion of architecture and communication. She advocates that architecture ought to adapt to the experience economy: 'The focus of architecture has evolved from an emphasis on "what it has" and "what it does" to "what you feel" and "who you are" (...)'. For further discussion and criticism of Klingmann's concept, see M. Stender: *Nye steder med liv og sjæl? Stedskabelse i tre danske boligbyggerier* (2014).

9 This point is supported by sociologist Bella Marckmann's study of Danish eco-villages, see Marckmann, B.: *Hverdagslivets kritik:* Økosamfund *i Danmark* (2009).

10 The same trend can be seen in the way that many of the housing blocks in Copenhagen's borough quarters are currently being rebuilt. Here, many perimeter blocks have been refurbished with attractive green courtyards, with areas for playing, areas for barbecuing, etc. And today, many of the flats on the ground floor are being fitted with patio doors leading out to the courtyard, to which the residents also orient themselves socially.

11 The basic idea is that the various functions are placed in horizontal layers with businesses and shops at the bottom. Then, moving upward, are the so-called 'town houses', which are flats with their own terraces situated beside the path. Next, are more flats, and then, finally, the penthouses, which also have their own terraces right next to the path. See: www.big.dk/#projects-8

12 Not only does 8 House offer a built-in identity and a wealth of in-house social activities: the house in itself also contains 'a salver' in the form of presenting the chance to go for a walk in the neighbourhood and look at the surroundings. Thus, what has also been 'built-in' here is the typically Danish *go-for-a-walk* function, where one, as a guest, in Danish residential quarters with single-family detached houses and summer cottages, often takes a walk with the host, as comments on both the landscape and the height of the neighbour's hedge are bandied about all the while, as well as remarks about the new roof.

13 The Danish stance on physical fencing can perhaps best be described as *ambivalent*: on the one hand, Danish single-family detached housing quarters (and cemeteries!) are characterized by hedges, which clearly mark off the one family's plot from the other's. On the other hand, a vigilant watch is zealously kept over the height of these hedges, and very tall hedges or fences, not to mention walls, barbed wire and private security guards, are most certainly deemed to be socially unacceptable in a Danish residential area, and often, there will even be a ban on these measures, in the local plan.

14 M. Gullestad: 'The Scandinavian Version of Egalitarian Individualism (1991).

15 K.M. Raahauge.: 'Ved vejen – i komplekset. Om det globale, det lokale og det materielle' (2007), p. 40.

16 Ibid., p. 43.

17 M. Gullestad: 'The Scandinavian Version of Egalitarian Individualism (1991), p. 13.

18 When the municipality granted the exemption to the building development, despite its enclave character, this was also helped along the way by the prospect of attracting a group of more affluent families, which would ostensibly make a contribution to the municipality's economy and social life. The fact that co-housing residents are generally less 'picky' about the location, *as long as they have each other*, constitutes a certain potential in an urban planning context, which could possibly also be deployed when working with the regeneration of disadvantaged areas.

19 Architect Tom Nielsen analyses this kind of segmentation in relation to the welfare state's public spaces: 'While industrialism and the welfare city were characterized by the separation of functions, people and urban life, today's globalized society is characterized by the segmentation of everything and everyone into cultural and social subgroups.' T. Nielsen: 'Democratic urban spaces in the Nordic countries?' (2013).

**Literature**


- Egerö, B.: *Puzzling Patterns of Co-housing in Scandinavia* 2014 http://www.kollektivhus.nu/pdf/Bertil%20 Lidewij%20article%20corr%20aug%2014.pdf.
- Eriksen, T.H. (in conv. with Jesper Pagh): 'On Wolves and Owls and a Possible Sustainable Future' in *NORDIC Journal of Architecture,* No 4. Vol. 5. Summer 2015.
- Gullestad, M.: 'The Scandinavian Version of Egalitarian Individualism' in *Ethnologia Scandinavia* (21), 1991.
- Klingmann, A.: *Brandscapes. Architecture in the Experience Economy.* MIT Press 2007.
- Marckmann, B.: *Hverdagslivets kritik: Økosamfund i Danmark,* PhD diss., Museum Tusculanum 2009.
- Nielsen, T.: 'Democratic urban spaces in the Nordic countries?' i *Working Papers from AU IDEAS Pilot Centre: The Democratic Public Sphere – Challenges and Developmental Perspectives.* No 4, Aarhus University 2013.
- Raahauge, K.M.: 'Ved vejen – i komplekset. Om det globale, det lokale og det materielle' i *Dansk Sociologi* Nr. 4/18 årg. 2007.
- Reijndorp, A. & Hajer, M.: *In Search of New Public Domain,* NAi Publishers, Rotterdam 2002.
- Stender, M.: 'Social Living, Version 2.0 – An Ethnography of Three New Residential Complexes' i *NORDIC Journal of Architecture,* No 4. Vol. 5. Summer 2015.
- Stender, M.: *Nye steder med liv og sjæl? Stedskabelse i tre danske boligbyggerier.* PhD diss., Aalborg University Press 2014.

Masashi Kajita

# Re-Addressing the Social Dimension of Accessibility

## Towards an Inclusive Society

**Accessibility has to do not only with liberating disabled people from disabling built environments – as per the common interpretation. Accessibility also constitutes an essential foothold for realising and improving mankind's social existence by promoting the independence, participation and enjoyment of persons in the built environment. This article re-addresses the social dimension of accessibility and discusses how accessibility can more effectively be contextualized in spatial discourse. By doing so, it aims to provide a creative and alternative insight into the ways that difference, vulnerability and sensitivity can lead to environments with greater potential.**

## Introduction

**'...accessibility is the urbanistic equivalent of a less exclusive, more democratic attitude.'[1]**

Those who take part in the production of space must promote the active inclusion and full participation of all persons in society. In recent decades, there has been a growing recognition of the unequal and unjust position of disabled people in society. The European Commission's *European Disability Strategy 2010-2020,* adopted in 2010, and a more recent *European Accessibility Act,* which was proposed in 2015, both address this challenge; these followed the United Nations *Convention on the Rights of Persons with Disability* (2007). Article 9 of the Convention (UNCRPD) ensures a foothold which obligates State Parties to take appropriate measures to ensure that disabled people have access to facilities and services 'on an equal basis with others'. Accessibility plays a key role as one of the guiding principles that aims to ensure access to and use of the building and its facilities, and is underpinned in the Convention as a foundation for providing opportunities related to participation in society. Accessibility has indeed reduced inequalities of access caused by disabling built environments; and yet it is often experienced as dry, generic regulatory pressures that many architects consider to be restrictions rather than positive incentives. The realization of inclusive architecture, which begins with liberating persons from problems posed by disabling environments, relies largely on codified rules and standards that are intended to ensure the level of a building's function. This regulatory framework is based on an observation that, as in the case of the UNCRPD, ensures the minimum level of access is a prerequisite for reducing inequalities. The practices of building control, regarded as basic performance standards, seek to regulate the construction of buildings in the interests of public health and safety. With regard to access provisions, these rules provide the prescriptive specification of design elements as the minimum level of requirements in order to ensure the safety and independence of persons with impairments; these include the minimum 'clear width' of doors and corridors as well as the gradient of ramps. Through this process of codification, however, accessibility is reduced to a system of rules that associates itself with limited types of impairments, and this may lead towards the standardization of solutions, despite the fact that accessibility has much more to offer.

The intention of this article is to address the importance of accessibility and to further unfold its potential. In doing so, the article will be divided into three parts. First, I outline the concept of accessibility in architecture and go on to describe its evolution and the process of integration into legal frameworks, as well as to discuss problematic aspects raised by its codification. Second, I display an alternative and creative interpretation of accessibility by one particular architect, Herman Hertzberger, who interprets accessibility much more holistically – in a way that extends beyond the regulatory framework. Third, I conclude by underscoring the essential role of architects and spatial designers who could creatively transform codified rules and standards into positive incentives. A key is the (re)introduction of a social dimension into the framework of accessibility. By addressing the active role of architecture in social processes, this article unflods the significance of accessibility for realizing an inclusive society.

## Accessibility within the regulatory framework

Although the interpretation of disability took a turn from the 'social' to the 'biopsychosocial' model, which diminished the distinction between persons 'with' or 'without' impairments,[2] the environment remains an essential factor in the disablement process. Particularly in the built environment, the restriction of movement and access can easily result in people being excluded and segregated. Hence, there has been a conspicuous emphasis on dismantling obstacles or barriers as well as on fulfilling basic functional requirements in and around buildings. The term *accessibility* is the most widely recognized and is currently used in the field of architecture as the concept and tool that can ensure reasonable provisions to be made 'for people to gain access to; and use the building and its facilities'.[3] Accessibility embodies society's noble aim of offering equal opportunities for using architecture and the built environment. Continuous efforts to eliminate body-based discrimination in built environments have improved the everyday lives of many people and, yet, those who have benefited the most are persons with mobility impairment, particularly those who are using wheelchairs. When one considers the fact that accessibility – as a currently recognized legal norm – originates in the field of rehabilitation,[4] it is not so hard to acknowledge accessibility's inextricable associations with the reduced or lost ability of persons. After the Second World War, the practice of rehabilitation had immensely advanced its capacity to provide skills and technology for many people with reduced abilities so that they could regain independence in their everyday lives. Meanwhile, many practitioners as well as persons with impairments themselves came to discover the fact that barriers and obstacles need to be eliminated in built environments in order to sustain an independent everyday life, which was being improved at rehabilitation centres or similar facilities. This recognition sprouted and grew into the idea of making environments 'barrier-free', aimed at dismantling obstacles for persons who are mainly struggling to get around in built environments.

This transformation from the 'medical' model to the 'social' model articulated a crucial step in the evolution of the concept of accessibility. The medical model regards the disability which is the result of a reduced physical condition as being intrinsic to the individual; hence, society has to invest resources in its attempt to cure disabilities medically. In contrast, the social model views disability as being intrinsic to the interaction between a person and his/her environment, and therefore a social construction and a result of environmental barriers. Systemic barriers and poorly designed environments, which might reflect ignorance or even negative attitudes, serve to disable persons. It has long been considered, with this shift in focus towards the environment, that the success (and failure) of an accessible environment can be measured according to levels of the 'fit' between the individual abilities and environmental features.[5] It was, and still is, a central objective to intervene in the environment, in order to further enhance the independence of persons with reduced abilities. This social model forms a foundation for the current codified rules and standards which draw upon the first standards that presented criteria for designing facilities and programmes for the use of disabled individuals: *American National Standard A117.1*, codified in 1961.[6]

This linear causality between individual abilities and environmental features, however, exhibits a number of problematics. Its central drawback can be articulated by a general consensus among experts that an accessible environment is one in which individuals with impairments can 'function independently'; and that there is some level of function that can be defined as 'minimally acceptable'.[7] Not only does this observation suppress the differences of human bodies. Even more importantly, the attempt to define an accessible environment, through the measure of 'fit', simplifies the actual relationships between individuals and their environments. This generalization of diverse human bodies and their relations to the built environment further separates the lives of persons from their contexts. Accordingly, it can, and often does, lead to a situation where accessibility ends up being implemented as segregated and/or special access. Experts on disability and the built environment have highlighted that those design solutions are often 'add-ons', and they can be socially exclusive and offensively discriminatory.[8]

This critical view on generalizing human bodies and their relations to the built environment is reflective of the recent progression of official documents that seek to accommodate a broader definition of the population which could benefit from an improved environmental accessibility.[9] This challenge aligns with WHO's *International Classification of Functioning, Disability and Health* (ICF), which was approved in 2001. In this advanced 'biopsychosocial' model, disability is viewed as 'the outcome or result of a complex relationship between an individual's health condition and personal factors, and of the external factors that represent circumstances in which the individual lives'. Differences in individuals' functioning and abilities can be viewed as being equivalent to personal factors such as gender, ethnicity and age (Fig. 1). These differences between individuals are fundamental conditions of the human being; and therefore should not imply any inherent difference between a person 'with' or 'without' impairments. And even more importantly, this interconnected relation of complex attributes implies that abilities of individuals and possibilities of participation should be viewed contextually.[10]

A number of approaches have emerged that promote designed environments which are more responsive to different personal conditions and circumstances. The most significant is *universal design* (UD), coined by Ronald Mace in 1997 as 'the design of products and environments to be usable by all people, to the greatest extent possible, without the need for adaptation or specialized design.'[11] Since Mace's introduction, UD has secured an increasingly prominent position. The inclusion of the concept within the UNCRPD consolidated its status as an international governing term, and it has found its way into accessibility rules and standards. Similarly, the codification of UD itself has begun in an international context. UD, within the rapid process of institutionalization, is being shaped by the rationale of administrative functions and, in part, by the language of construction industries and values of consumerism.

Despite the advancement of the conceptual framework of disability, however, current codified rules and standards still draw attention to particular types of impairments; hence, this raises a question about the extent to which legislation can respond to the manifold interactions between diverse bodily varieties and material environments.[12] In addition, this regulatory framework, due to its nature of being perceived as rules that should simply be followed, may have been a drive bringing about the standardization of solutions with the potential to further stigmas and social exclusion. The notion of accessibility is tightly framed within legal systems, and it is certainly a matter of concern when accessibility causes exclusion, and moreover when it is perceived to be implemented at the expense of architectural and aesthetic quality, as has been claimed by many architects.[13] On the other hand, we ought to acknowledge that the minimum level of access specified in codified rules and standards has always provided the point of reference through which inequalities in the built environment are undoubtedly being reduced.

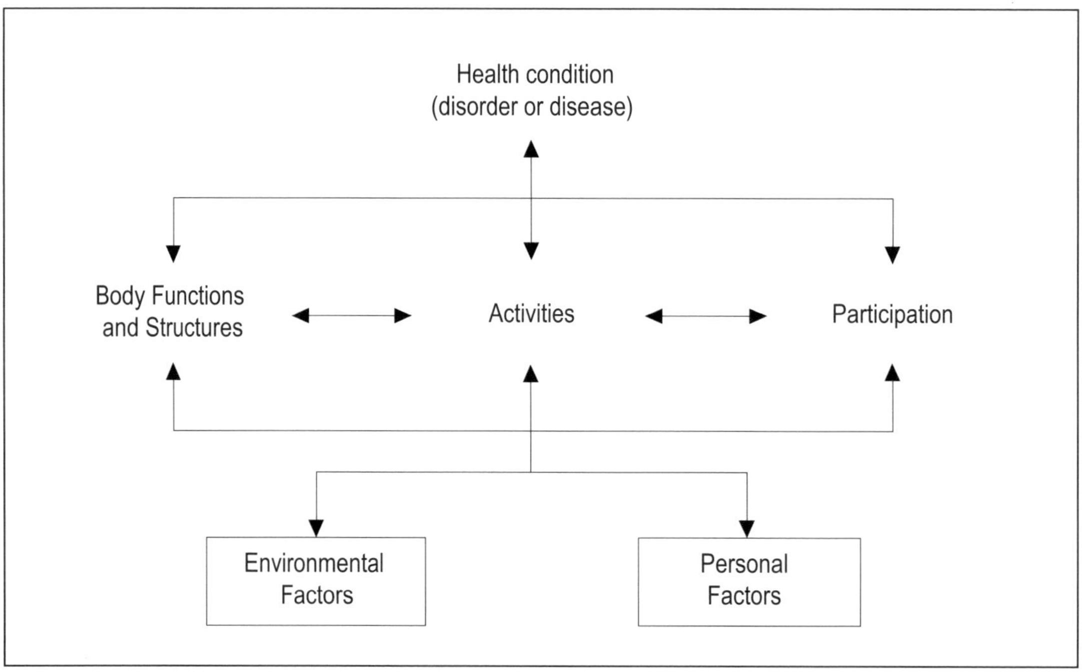

## A creative interpretation of accessibility

Standing in contrast to the current framework of the regulatory model, a more positive and creative interpretation of accessibility can be found in the writings of the Dutch architect Herman Hertzberger.

Accessibility has been a recurrent term in his writings since the 1970s, and has frequently been used to describe the social nature of architecture, wherein Hertzberger has employed the mode of two distinct and dichotomized territorial notions of 'public' and 'private' domains. Hertzberger once stated that 'accessibility is the urbanistic equivalent of a less exclusive, more democratic attitude', as part of his view that the built environment should 'open' itself up to a greater extent.[14]

Accordingly, in referring to urban life, Hertzberger sought 'a spatial organisation in which built form and exterior space (which we call street) are not only complementary in the spatial sense and therefore reciprocate in forming each other, but also and especially – for that is what we are primarily concerned with here – in which built form and exterior space offer maximal accessibility vis à vis each other.'[15]

In Hans van Dijk's words, Hertzberger was looking for 'optimal accessibility' by seeking the reconciliation of public and private realms, regarded not as 'two abstract opposites; rather they indicate domains that continually determine each other within a 'sequence of territorial tension''.[16]

Seeking productive relationships between users and built environments, Hertzberger addresses accessibility in relation to the disposition of rooms and the placement and proportion of architectural elements, such as widows, balconies, terraces, landings, and so forth; these represent physical properties which architects could affect through their professional practice. Notably, Hertzberger underlined that an architect 'always influences, intentionally or not, the most elementary forms of social relations. And even if social relations depend only to a limited extent on environmental factors, that is still sufficient reason to aim consciously at such organization of space that it is possible for everyone to confront the other on an equal footing.'[17]

Hertzberger's use of accessibility promotes the concept in two ways: In the first, he positions accessibility within a practice of architecture that aims to realize and improve mankind's social existence. Architecture provides – without determining the social outcome – opportunities for both individual and social use; and accessibility is a foothold upon which one gains opportunities for independence, autonomy and participation. Accessible architecture creates occasions for encounters with others and situations, but it also allows persons to withdraw when some form of privacy is required. Accordingly, Hertzberger

Fig. 1: Interactions between the components of ICF (WHO 2011, p. 18)

Environmental factors are constituted by the physical, social and attitudinal environment in which individuals dwell and conduct their lives. These factors are external to individuals and can have influence on the individual's participation in society, on the individual's ability to take action, or on the individual's body function or structure. Personal factors constitute the particular background of individuals. These factors may include gender, ethnicity, age, fitness, habits, education, profession, coping styles, and so forth – all or any of which may play a role in disability on any level. Such contextual factors interact with individuals who have different health conditions, influencing the functioning of persons on individual and societal levels. All the attributes are interconnected: interventions into one attribute have a potential to modify one or more of the other attributes; an emergence of disability might even modify the health condition of an individual.

Fig. 2 & 3: De Drie Hoven, Home for the elderly (Hertzberger 1991, p. 61 & 35).

This residential complex, completed in 1974 and eventually demolished in 2015, was designed for older persons who suffered from illness, injury and/or age-related impairments. Due to the restricted mobility of the residents, most of whom were not able to leave the prem without assistance, the primary intention of this building was to create an environment that approximated the nature of a city. Easy access and way-finding were essential factors; but social interaction was another essential focus. The dwelling units were organized along 'streets', which were integrated within a sequence of shared areas of varying size: ranging from porch-like areas of a more intimate character to a town square-like area with a strong sense of community. Fig. 2 shows the 'town square', where circulation routes were integrated within the area containing different recreational functions. A wide corridor provided enough space for accommodating the different speeds and paces of residents who enjoyed casual and spontaneous interactions with each other. In addition, the open structure of the area accommodated, when necessary, gatherings for communal events organized by the residents. Fig. 3 shows one of the porch-like areas where doors with two sections were installed. The residents were able to control the degree of accessibility. For example, the half-open door invited guests and facilitated casual conversations, while the closed bottom half of the door ensured the residents' privacy. The careful constitution of architectural elements encouraged the active participation of the residents, thus demonstrating the important role of accessibility when it comes to architecture taking an active role in producing an inclusive society.

seeks to 'create an environment in which each person, according to his (and her) limitations, would have the greatest choice of modes of exchange.'[18] He specifically addresses one essential value of architecture in its capacity to enable individuals to realize their collective existence as social beings.

Second, Hertzberger's interpretation promotes the active roles of users. It emphasizes that the material environment comes into existence in a social sense by means of human practice. Architecture and the built environment are subjected to the intrinsic human process of appropriating space. Accordingly, and inevitably, his approach supports users in determining the 'accessibility of areas', which will be adequate for their own demands and their respective responsibilities 'for upkeep'.[19] Accessibility forms a foundation for his interest in generous and inviting architecture as well as for his aspirations towards the social (and recurring conceptions of public and private). Here, accessibility is not only a matter of technique, solution and legislation, but also a question of convention: a matter of who uses, owns and takes care of the places, and how (Fig. 2 and 3). His approach looks at more subjective and embodied ways of occupying and producing space, which contributes to reducing the distance between the space experienced by users and space conceived by architects.

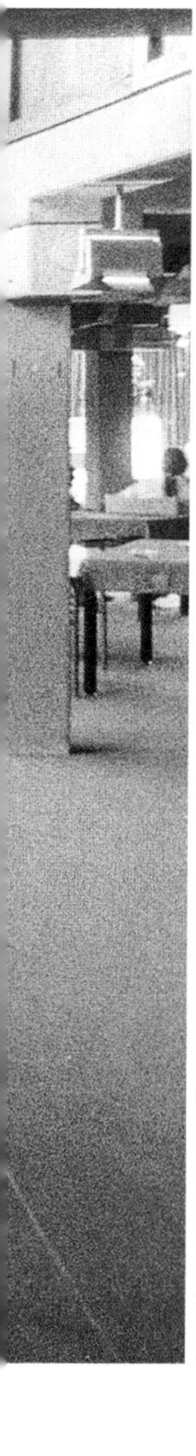

Bridging between the physical space of architecture, on the one hand, and the social practice, on the other, Hertzberger's quest for 'optimal accessibility' continues. However for most of us, it unfortunately appears that, by the late 1990s, accessibility had lost such positive and creative connotations. Corresponding to the growth of the welfare state and the emergence of welfare-related politics, and most of all, coinciding with enactments of disability discrimination legislation in many nations, accessibility became a legal norm within architectural practice and developed into comprehensive statutory requirements. And accessibility became a burden, rather than a creative incentive, for many architects, because it was charged with political meanings and its regulatory aspects were being emphasized. The partial interpretation of accessibility which emphasizes regulatory aspects now seems to have displaced the creative and holistic interpretation of accessibility, despite the fact that regulatory aspects should fundamentally be a *part* of the whole: and subsumed within creative interpretations of accessibility, as was so astutely demonstrated by Hertzberger.

## Conclusion: re-addressing the social dimension of accessibility

Hertzberger articulates that accessibility, beyond its regulatory profile, holds a great potential for influencing positively upon the life of us all as individuals as well as social beings. Not only does accessibility liberate persons from disabling built environments: it, moreover, has the potential to promote independence, participation and enjoyment in the built environment, through its fundamental relation to the mobility of the human body in space – noting that in certain circumstances, the *lack* of accessibility can also provoke persons to take positive action. Nonetheless, this latter role of accessibility, when viewed from the perspective of architects, becomes explicit by promoting users and their active roles, as well as by viewing their experience in relation to both the physical and the social properties of architecture. Architecture is not only produced but is also *re*-produced through the bodily experience of persons. Experiencing architecture and the material existence of architecture carry the presence of one another. Their reciprocal relation institutes the realm produced through bodily experiences. This architectural space, through the experience that people have of it, is one of the means through which social space is produced.[20] In other words, architectural space appears as a result of an interaction between its physicality and its social meanings as well as purposes. Architecture (and the physical environment in general) plays an active role in the construction of social life. Architecture can – and therefore must – aim to promote the active inclusion and full participation of all persons in society.

The UNCRPD underlines this essential position of accessibility by also emphasizing its social dimension. The Convention articulates the guiding intention behind the application of accessibility, which is to enable disabled people 'to live independently and participate fully in all aspects of life', and this ought to be 'on an equal basis with others'. Reflecting the evolution in the conceptual framework of the ICF, the UNCRPD removes the distinction between 'with impairments' and 'without impairments'; and importantly, it underlines the background for why it is essential to ensure access to – and use of – a building and its facilities. It clarifies the duty of accessibility and, by doing so, it goes beyond the existing regulatory framework in which accessibility is commonly interpreted and practiced. The UNCRPD places an emphasis on what is to be achieved by obtaining equitable access and use.

And still, the built environment continues to disable persons. Their lives continue to be delineated by buildings and products that are unusable or perhaps only accessible with third-party assistances and/or assistive devices. Such discriminations occur partly because of the insensitive attitude of architects whose design conception rarely conceives imperfect bodily functions and abilities as part of everyday habitation and being.[21] However, as this article has been discussing, the problem also lies in the underlying conceptual frameworks of the regulatory model, which needs to undergo further progress if it is eventually going to embody the complex relation between our diverse bodily performances and environments. Controversially, architectural practice is embedded in a complex system of codified rules and standards. Accessibility requirements and guidelines ensure the level of a building's function in order to reducing inequalities; however, their objective is to set basic performance standards as the essential point of references. The realization of inclusive architecture, including liberating disabled persons from a disabling built environment, relies on codified rules and standards; and yet their potential essentially derives from, and cannot be achieved without, the delimitation of their functions. The set of rules is not necessarily the ultimate tool in redressing the problems posed by disabling environments. Instead, those rules and standards need to be internalized into creative processes and practices, and not applied externally through the further enforcement of regulatory framework. A key is to make architects and spatial designers sensitized to diverse bodily variations, and their complex relations to the built environment must be viewed contextually. This contextualization addresses the importance of the social dimension of architecture.

Re-addressing the social into the framework of accessibility reiterates the knowledge of accessibility as a prerequisite for the achievement of an inclusive society. The realization of inclusive architecture cannot be left only to the development of the conceptual basis of accessibility and disability. Nor can it be left to the improvement of codified rules and standards and their practical applicability. Furthermore, this realization should be negotiated together with other contextual factors of place as well as personal factors, including diverse complexities of bodily ability and experience. This comprehensive approach, which amalgamates the physical and the social properties of architecture, can be expected to provoke the creativity of architects and bring the regulatory framework of accessibility within the positive and creative interpretation that Hertzberger demonstrated. Creative practitioners must rigorously recognize or even enjoy the complex reality of diverse bodies, experience and situations through which architecture that contributes to the enjoyment of bodily experiences and the social relations of everyday life could be produced. The current regulatory framework contributes to reducing inequality by dealing with vulnerable persons. But accessibility – when incorporated with the creative minds of architects – provides an alternative insight into the way that difference and sensitivity may lead to environments with even greater potential.

**Notes**

An extract from a text written in 1975 by Herman Hertzberger, which described his scheme for the University Library in Groningen. H. Hertzberger: 'Martinuskerk Groningen...Universiteitsbibliotheek?', 1975. In: *Space and the Architect: Lessons in architecture 2.* Rotterdam: Uitgeverij 010 Publishers (2000), p. 288.

**1** WHO: *International Classification of Functioning, Disability and Health* (2001).

**2** Great Britain, Office of the Deputy Prime Minister: The Building Regulation, access to and use of buildings: Approved document M (2010).

**3** S. Goldsmith og PRP Architects (Firm): *Universal Design: A manual of practical guidance for architects* (2000); E. Steinfeld og B. Tauke: 'Universal designing'. In: J. Christophersen (ed.): *Universal Design: 17 ways of thinking and teaching* (2002), pp. 165-90.

**4** E. Steinfeld og G.S. Danford (eds.): *Enabling Environments: Measuring the impact of environment on disability and rehabilitation* (1999).

**5** American National Standard Institute: *Accessible and Usable Buildings and Facilities* (2011).

**6** E. Steinfeld og G.S. Danford (eds.): *Enabling Environments: Measuring the impact of environment on disability and rehabilitation* (1999).

**7** S. Goldsmith og PRP Architects: *Universal Design: A manual of practical guidance for architects* (2000); R. Imrie: *Accessible Housing: Quality, disability and design* (2006); C. Ryhl: *Tilgængelighed – udfordringer, begreber og strategier* (2009).

**8** European Commission: *2010: A Europe Accessible for All* (2003); United Nations, General Assembly: *Convention on the Rights of Persons with Disabilities and Optional Protocol* (2007).

**9** WHO: *International Classification of Functioning, Disability and Health: ICF* (2001).

**10** North Carolina State University, The Center for Universal Design: *The Principle of Universal Design, version 2.0.* (1997).

**11** R. Imrie: 'Universalism, universal design and equitable access to the built environment'. *Disability and Rehabilitation* 34(10) (2012), pp. 873-82.

**12** A.K. Frandsen et al.: *Bygningsreglementets tilgængelighedsbestemmelser set i forhold til byggeprocessen – sbi.dk* (2012).

**13** H. Hertzberger: 'Martinuskerk Groningen... Universiteitsbibliotheek?'. In: *Space and the Architect: Lessons in architecture 2* (2000), p. 288.

**14** H. Hertzberger: 'The Public Realm'. In: T. Nakamura (ed.) *Architecture and Urbanism: Herman Hertzberger, 1959-1990* (1991), p. 16.

**15** H. Dijk: 'Hertzberger's Houses: The possibilities and limits of a leading theme.' In: T. Nakamura (ed.): *Architecture and Urbanism: Herman Hertzberger, 1959-1990* (1991), pp. 46-53.

**16** H. Hertzberger: 'The Public Realm'. In: T. Nakamura (ed.) *Architecture and Urbanism: Herman Hertzberger, 1959-1990* (1991), p. 30.

**17** H. Hertzberger: 'The Public Realm'. In: T. Nakamura (ed.) *Architecture and Urbanism: Herman Hertzberger, 1959-1990* (1991), p. 80.

**18** H. Hertzberger: *Lessons for Students in Architecture* (1991), p. 12.

**19** H. Lefebvre: *The Production of Space*. Malden, Mass: Blackwell Publishers (1991).

**20** R. Imrie: 'Designing inclusive environments and the significance of universal design'. In: J. Swain et al. (eds). *Disabling Barriers, Enabling Environments* (2014), pp. 287-96.

**Literature**


- American National Standard Institute: *Accessible and Usable Buildings and Facilities*. New York: American National Standard Institute, International Code Council 2011.
- Bloomer, K.C. and Moore, C.W.: *Body, Memory, and Architecture*. New Haven: Yale University Press. 1977.
- Boys, J.: *Doing Disability Differently: An alternative handbook on architecture, dis/ability and designing for everyday life.* London; New York: Routledge 2014.
- van Dijk, H.: 'Hertzberger's Houses: The possibilities and limits of a leading theme.' In: Nakamura, T. (ed.) *Architecture and Urbanism: Herman Hertzberger, 1959-1990.* April 1991 Extra Edition. Tokyo: A & U Publishing 1991, pp. 46-53.
- European Commission: *2010: A Europe Accessible for All.* Luxembourg: European Commission, 2003.
- Frandsen, A.K. et al.: *Bygningsreglementets tilgængelighedsbestemmelser set i forhold til byggeprocessen – sbi.dk.* Copenhagen: Danish Building Research Institute 2012.
- Great Britain, Office of the Deputy Prime Minister: *The Building Regulation, access to and use of buildings: Approved document M (2015 Edition).* London: NBS Publications 2010.
- Goldsmith, S. and PRP Architects (Firm): *Universal Design: A manual of practical guidance for architects*. Oxford; Boston: Architectural Press 2000.
- Goldsmith, S.: *Designing for the Disabled: The new paradigm*. Oxford; Boston: Architectural Press 1997.
- Hertzberger, H.: *Space and the Architect: Lessons in architecture 2*. Rotterdam: Uitgeverij 010 Publishers 2000.

- Hertzberger, H.: 'The Public Realm'. In: Nakamura, T. (ed.) *Architecture and Urbanism: Herman Hertzberger, 1959-1990.* April 1991 Extra Edition. Tokyo: A & U Publishing 1991.
- Hertzberger, H.: *Lessons for Students in Architecture.* Rotterdam: Uitgeverij 010 Publishers 1991.
- Hertzberger, H.: 'Martinuskerk Groningen... Universiteitsbibliotheek?', 1975. In: *Space and the Architect: Lessons in architecture 2.* Rotterdam: Uitgeverij 010 Publishers, 2000, p. 288.
- Hertzberger, H.: 'Flexibility and Polyvalency', *Forum* vol. 16 (no. 2, February-March), 1962, pp. 115-18.
- Imrie, R.: 'Designing inclusive environments and the significance of universal design'. In: Swain, J. et al. (eds.): *Disabling Barriers, Enabling Environments*. 3rd ed. London: Sage Publications, 2014, pp. 287-96.
- Imrie, R.: 'Universalism, universal design and equitable access to the built environment'. *Disability and Rehabilitation* 34(10), 2012, pp. 873-82.
- Imrie, R.: *Accessible Housing: Quality, disability and design.* Agingdon [England]; New York: Routledge 2006.
- Iwarsson, S. and Ståhl, A.: 'Accessibility, usability and universal design positioning and definition of concepts describing person environment relationships', *Disability and Rehabilitation* 25 (2), 2003, pp. 57-66.
- Lefebvre, H.: *The Production of Space*. Malden, Mass: Blackwell Publishers 1991.
- Lifchez, R.: *Rethinking Architecture: Design students and physically disabled people*. Berkeley: University of California Press 1987.
- North Carolina State University, The Center for Universal Design: *The Principle of Universal Design, version 2.0.* Available: http://www.ncsu.edu/ncsu/design/cud/about_ud/udprinciplestext.htm (Accessed 04-05-2016).
- Ryhl, C.: 'Accessibility and Sensory Experiences: Designing dwellings for the visual and hearing impaired.' *Nordic Journal of Architectural Research* Volume 22 (No ½), 2010, pp. 109-22.
- Ryhl, C.: *Tilgængelighed – udfordringer, begreber og strategier.* SBi report number 12. Copenhagen: Danish Building Research INstitute 2009.
- Steinfeld, E., & Danford, G.S. (eds.): *Enabling Environments: Measuring the impact of environment on disability and rehabilitation.* New York: Kluwer Academic/ Plenum Publishers 1999.
- Steinfeld, E. & Maisel, J.: *Universal Design: Creating Inclusive Environments*. Hoboken, N.J.: John Wiley & Sons, Inc 2012.
- Steinfeld, E., & Tauke, B.: 'Universal designing'. In: Christophersen, J. (ed.): *Universal Design: 17 ways of thinking and teaching.* Oslo: Husbanken, 2002, pp. 165-90.
- United Nations, General Assembly: *Convention on the Rights of Persons with Disabilities and Optional Protocol.* New York: United Nations 2007.
- WHO: *International Classification of Functioning, Disability and Health: ICF.* Geneva: World Health Organization 2001.
- WHO: *International Classification of Impairments, Disabilities, and Handicaps: A manual of classification relating to the consequences of disease.* Geneva; Albany, N.Y: World Health Organization 1980.

Heidi Jacobsgaard Schøbel

# Meetings between Generations

## A Re-Thinking of Welfare Institutions for Children and the Elderly

**By rethinking our welfare institutions' design and organization, architects can play a role in bringing about meetings between generations. Based on analyses of existing meetings between children and the elderly, I am putting forth a proposal related to how the institution, via four specific types of meetings, can operate as a social generator for meetings between generations; this will be further elucidated with diagrammatic sectional views. Finally, the architect's role in relation to contributing to the generations' meeting across the generation gap will be discussed.**

At the 'Forming Welfare' conference in September 2013, the sociologist Gøsta Esping-Andersen stated that Denmark's childcare centres have been a factor in bringing about the result that virtually all Danish women are part of the labour force. At the same time, this has elicited the concomitant effect that children and the elderly do not see so much of each other, since the need for having the children watched – and taken care of – by the family's elder members has dwindled down significantly. Consequently, Denmark is one of the countries in Europe where children see their grandparents the least.[1] The development in our society over the past 200 years has brought along a significant change in our family patterns, and it could be said that the family of today is 'emptied of function', since people no longer have a relationship of dependency on each other and also because the welfare state has taken over many of the family's tasks.

Moreover, the very design of the Danish welfare state that we see today has been powerfully influenced by modernism, which has standardized our welfare through effective, functionally-divided buildings, which have, in turn, led to a division of people. Children are in one institution and the elderly are in another. For this very reason, I believe that there is a need for us to rethink the organization and the design of our welfare institutions.

The thesis of this article is that children and older people have a great potential to contribute positively to each other in everyday life. Bringing such a situation forth would signify a change in which the architect can take part, through a rethinking of our welfare institutions' design and organization, so that children and older people would see more of each other. This has been the focal point of my graduation project, 'Eutopia',[2] which the present article is based on, and from which it contains extracts.

## Generations should meet

Many elderly people in Denmark are lonely. A national health profile compiled in 2013 indicates that there are 65,000 people over the age of 65 who feel lonely.[3] Several studies show that this can be a serious problem, because loneliness greatly increases the risk of diminution in functional capabilities and consequently impairs elderly people's health and living conditions.[4] One way of preventing diminution in functional capabilities and of ensuring older people's joie de vivre is to ameliorate these people's social networks. This has been pointed out by ethnologist Christine E. Swane, who writes: '[...] several studies thus indicate that the correlation between the social relationships and health is linked not only to the support that the individual can obtain from his/her social network, but has just as much to do with the support that the individual him/herself can give by being actively involved in other people's lives ... Reciprocity in a relationship – even if it cannot be measured objectively in the sense that 'each person, individually, gives in equal measure', does appear to play a part in warding off a feeling of dependence and in counteracting any loss of dignity.'[5]

A study carried out by DaneAge Association in 2009 bears out that the problem is especially noticeable among the older people who are living in nursing homes, seeing as 38% of the residents in these institutions often feel lonely or alone. If we look at this in the light of sociologist Erving Goffman's theory from the 1960s about human behaviour, the large quantum of loneliness among elderly nursing home residents might very well have arisen as a consequence of the nursing home's character of 'tution'. According to Goffman's theory, the 'total institution' is characterized as a place where all chores and expressions of life transpire under the same roof, in connection with the same people. The total institution undermines the person's identity and the person's possibilities for establishing a social network since all of life's actions and interactions transpire at one and the same place.[6] To disolve the nursing home as total instituion, it may have an effect to integrate it with a childcare institution, and it will also contribute positively to some older people´s lives. It would open up the institution and offer the residents enhanced opportunities to enter into different contexts and create more different kinds of relationships. Furthermore, I believe that meetings between the elderly and children have a great potential for bringing about mutual relationships, since the older person would then have the opportunity to be meaningful and to enter into a relationship in which he/she becomes 'something to somebody'.

Many Danish children attend day-care institutions. As a matter of fact, when weighed against the other Nordic countries, Denmark is the country where children start at the earliest age to spend their days at such institutions.[7] In addition, there are several studies that show that the children are getting less and less contact with adults while they are at the institution, because cutbacks are being imposed and because more and more time is being spent on administration. For example, Bureau 2000 assesses that nursery school teachers working today are, when all is said and done, actually spending 36% less time together with children than they did in 1986.[8] A large part of the child's socialization development occurs during the period that the child is attending such an institution. For this reason, it is crucial that the child has contact with adults and experiences many different types of activities.

Psychology research[9] bears out that institutions offering less than 3 m$^2$ per child experience a decline in group playing and an increase in children with aggressive behaviour. Conversely, more space in the day-care institution results in a lesser need for planning, less noise and better opportunities for the children to take initiative and be active.[10] Furthermore, it can have a very positive effect on the children when the institution has 'activity areas' – places that are spatially defined and which offer specific use options.

I believe that an organization with, for example, an assisted living – or nursing home – complex,

Fig. 1
Example of three-dimensional tool, H.J. Schøbel, Eutopia (2015), p. 68.

would lead to better day-care institutions, insofar as access to more floorage and space, along with the possibility of more use-specific spots, would lead to fewer conflicts, while at the same time children would have more contact with adults, by being together with the elderly. The elderly people would also be able to contribute with more presence and attention in their everyday lives – and this, in turn, would offer them chances to engage in other types of activities with the children.

## Inter-generational meetings today

There is not a whole lot of literature – and almost no research – that focuses specifically on meetings between generations, and whatever can be found focuses often on family relationships and ties. But despite the lack of attention to this question in the research community, what can be seen is that many institutions are actually working to create meetings between children and elderly people, and that these projects are generating many positive experiences. For example, in the municipality of Tønder, there is a 'Reading Friendships' project where, once a month, pupils in a 5th grade read aloud to residents at the local nursing home. The experience that has been harvested from this project is that the children become better at reading and gain a more conscious appreciation of literature, while at the same time, new relationships and friendships are being created across generations.[11]

Seeing as it was not possible to find research that deals directly with meetings of non-familial character between generations, I set myself to conduct fieldwork connected to two existing projects in Denmark and one in France. Through observations and interviews,[12] I have trained my focus on the impact of the meetings as well as on the attention being paid to the physical framework as generator for the meetings. In order to concretize the users' needs and opportunities in the specific

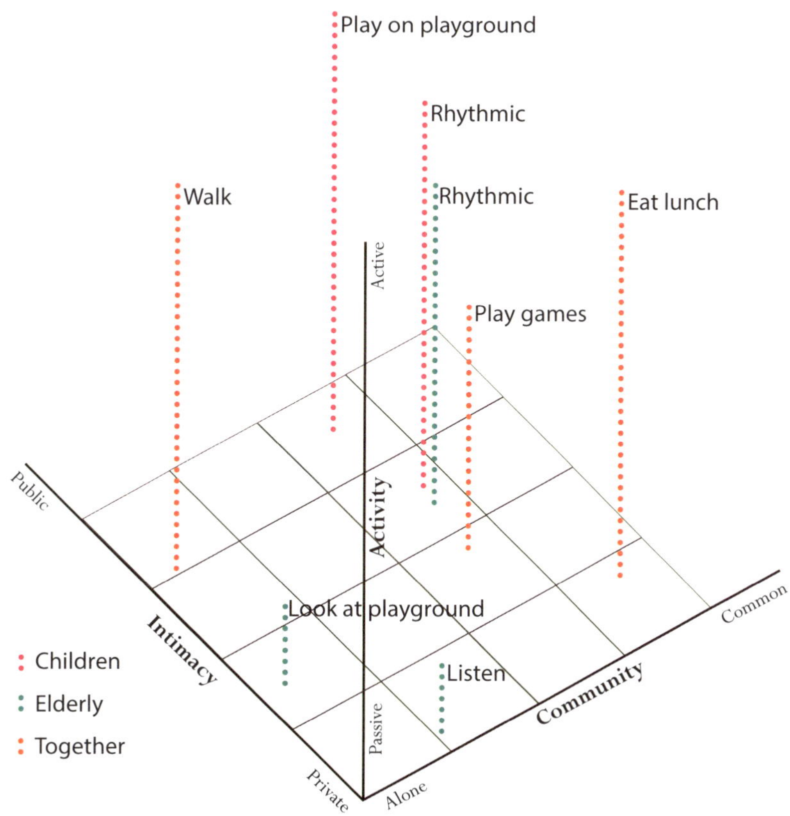

meeting and to accordingly understand the differences from one meeting to another, I have developed a diagram, a three-dimensional tool for analysis (figure 1). This tool can primarily be used to analyse existing meetings between children and elderly people. However, it can also be used as an implement in the programming of a building, so as to visualize and clarify what types of meetings there is an intention to create, for purposes of ensuring a concrete adaptation for the users. Therefore, the tool is also valuable in interdisciplinary collaborations, where the architect, with the aid of the diagram, can promote an understanding of the physical framework's influence on the social life that is being created and encouraged.

The first dimension of the diagram is active-passive. This dimension has to do especially with the physical exertion involved in the meeting in question: whether it is present, and to what extent. The position on the scale indicates how high a level of activity there is in the action in question. The second dimension has to do with the public-private relationship, and thus involves a specification of the space's *intimacy* level, which can have an impact to bear on the psychological resources. The third dimension, 'common-alone', has to do with how many people are present during the meeting and with the size of the community.

As can be seen on figure 1, these three dimensions can be inserted into a diagram, within which the meetings can be positioned according to the level in question. In this manner, the meeting's factors are elucidated. Moreover, what is elucidated here is (a) what activities the children are doing (pink), (b) what the elderly are doing (green), and (c) what they are doing together (orange). I have made use of this tool in connection

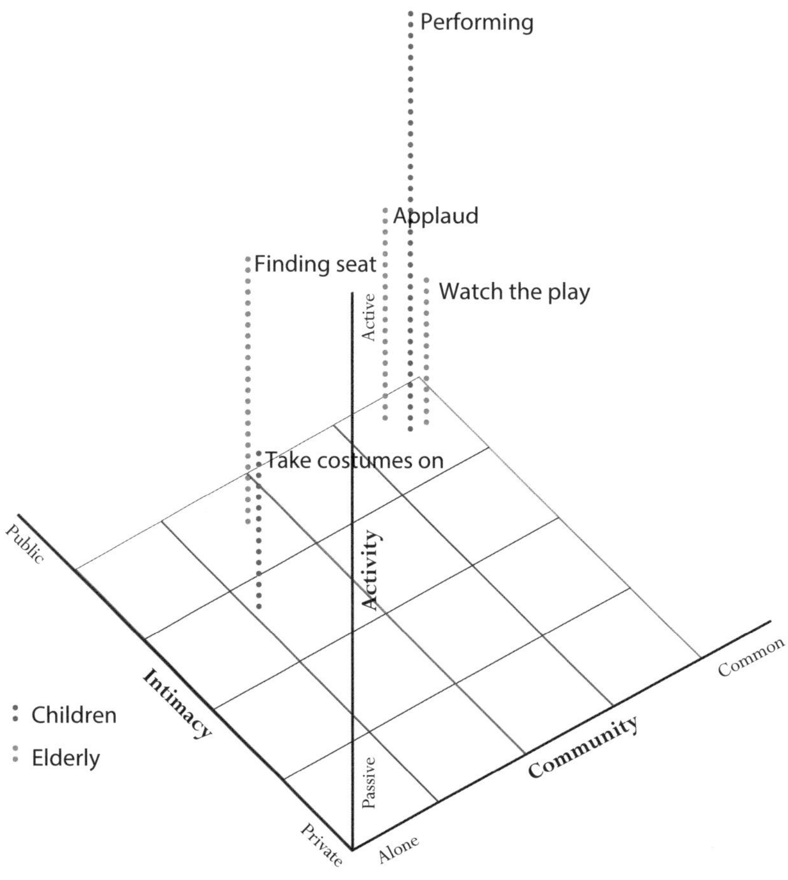


Fig. 2
**Children meeting older people**
Betaniahjemmet retirement home – three-dimensional tool, H.J. Schøbel, Eutopia (2015), p. 78.

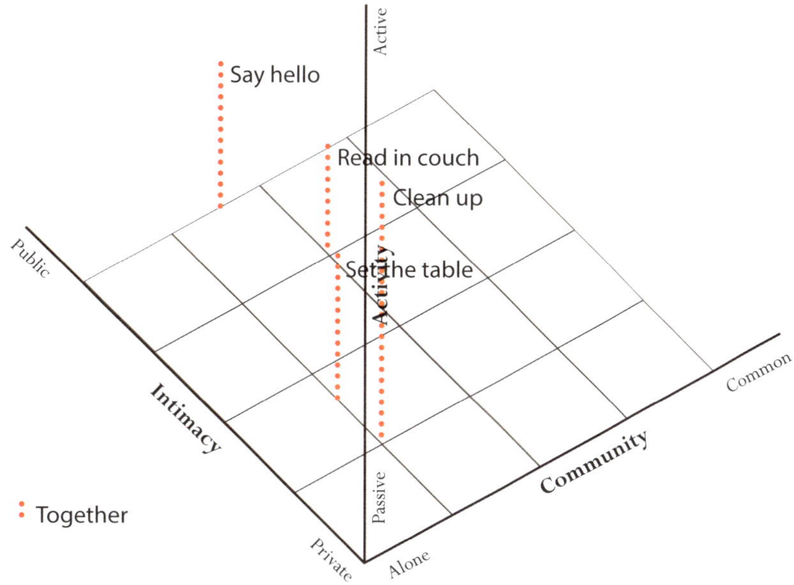


Fig. 3
**Elderly people meeting children**
Højgården nursery school – three-dimensional tool, H.J. Schøbel, Eutopia (2015), p. 72.

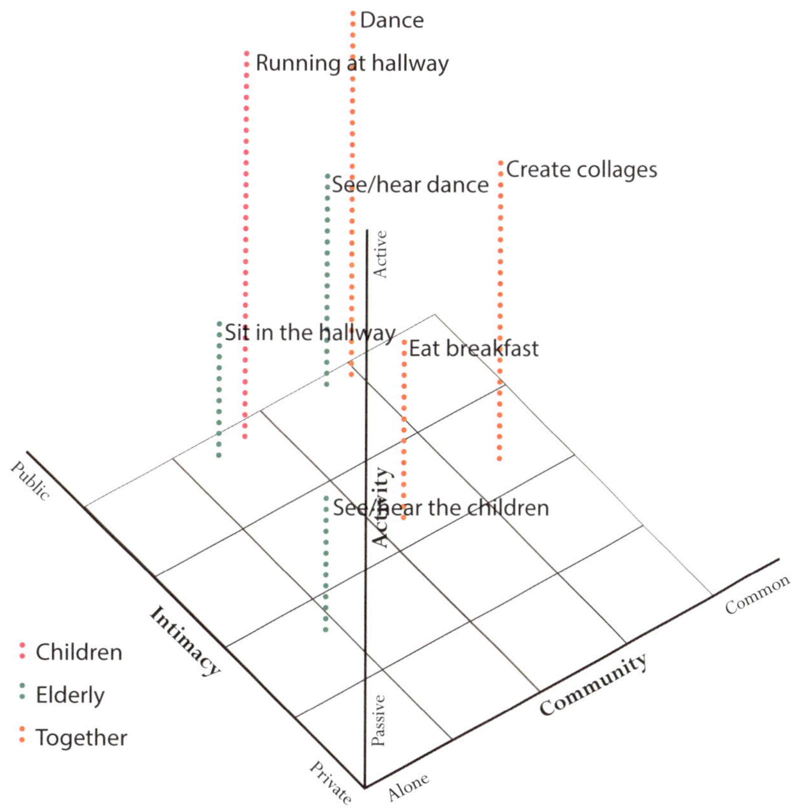


Fig. 4
**Children and elderly people meeting**
Résidence de l'Abbaye – three-dimensional tool, H.J. Schøbel, Eutopia (2015), p. 83.

with my fieldwork, so as to visualize some of the factors that are important to the meeting, factors which are thus important to keep in mind when one is busy planning the institution as a social generator for meetings between children and the elderly.

## When children and elderly people meet each other

I have been conducting fieldwork on the basis of three different categories of meetings: *children meeting elderly people*; *elderly people meeting children*; and *children and elderly people meeting.* The three categories have been charted out on the basis of who is visiting whom, and on what kind of spatiality constitutes the physical framework around the visit. Accordingly, *children meeting elderly people* is a meeting between generations, where the children are visiting the elderly in their familiar surroundings, while *elderly people meeting children* is, on the contrary, a meeting where elderly people are visiting children in *their* familiar surroundings. Finally, there is the *children and elderly people meeting* category, where children and elderly people *share* the physical framework, in such a way that both user groups have ownership of the physical framework. Following this line of investigation, it has been possible to observe and analyse the differences between visiting each other and 'living' together, and to observe and analyse what importance spatialities, interiors, and a sense of affiliation all have to bear on the meeting. Additionally, I have been focusing on the social aspects, and on what resources meet the demands of each party, as well as on how it is possible to create inter-generational meetings, also, for non-resource-strong children and elderly people.
As can be seen in figure 2, 3 and 4, there is a substantial difference between the acts, subsumed in the activity-, the intimacy- and the community levels, that take place within the three respective categories of meetings.
The Betaniahjemmet retirement & assisted living facility in Frederiksberg stands as an example where children meet elderly people in their everyday surroundings. Here, the local children's choir performed the musical 'Mild Moses'. As can be seen in figure 2, this situation did not call for a particularly high level of physical activity on the part of the elderly, and thus it was also possible for function-diminished and assistance-requiring elderly persons to take part on equal footing with the livelier retirement home dwellers. For the most part, the event took place within the setting of joint participation and in a 'public' space, inasmuch as the play was presented in the nursing home's assembly hall; this helped to regulate behaviour. The physical framework gave the meeting an ambience of ceremony, and gearing down and taking the elderly into consideration evidently came naturally to the children. The meeting was very successful and served to spread joy among both the children and the elderly. However, it did not contribute directly to establishing contact and forging relations between them, and the activities were not shared in the way that children and the elderly take part on an equal footing.
The Højgården nursery school, where Gurli, who is 87 years old, volunteers her time and comes every Friday, stands as an example of older people meeting children face-to-face in *their* usual surroundings. First of all, it was clear that inter-generational meetings like these, which often take place with the same participants, have a potential to give rise to strong bonds and relationships. As can be seen in figure 3, all activities took place in the context of joint participation. Gurli and the children were together for the whole meeting; this gives rise to an extraordinari-

Fig. 5
Diagrammatic drawing – ground floor of Résidence de L'Abbaye, H.J. Schøbel, Eutopia (2015), p. 87.

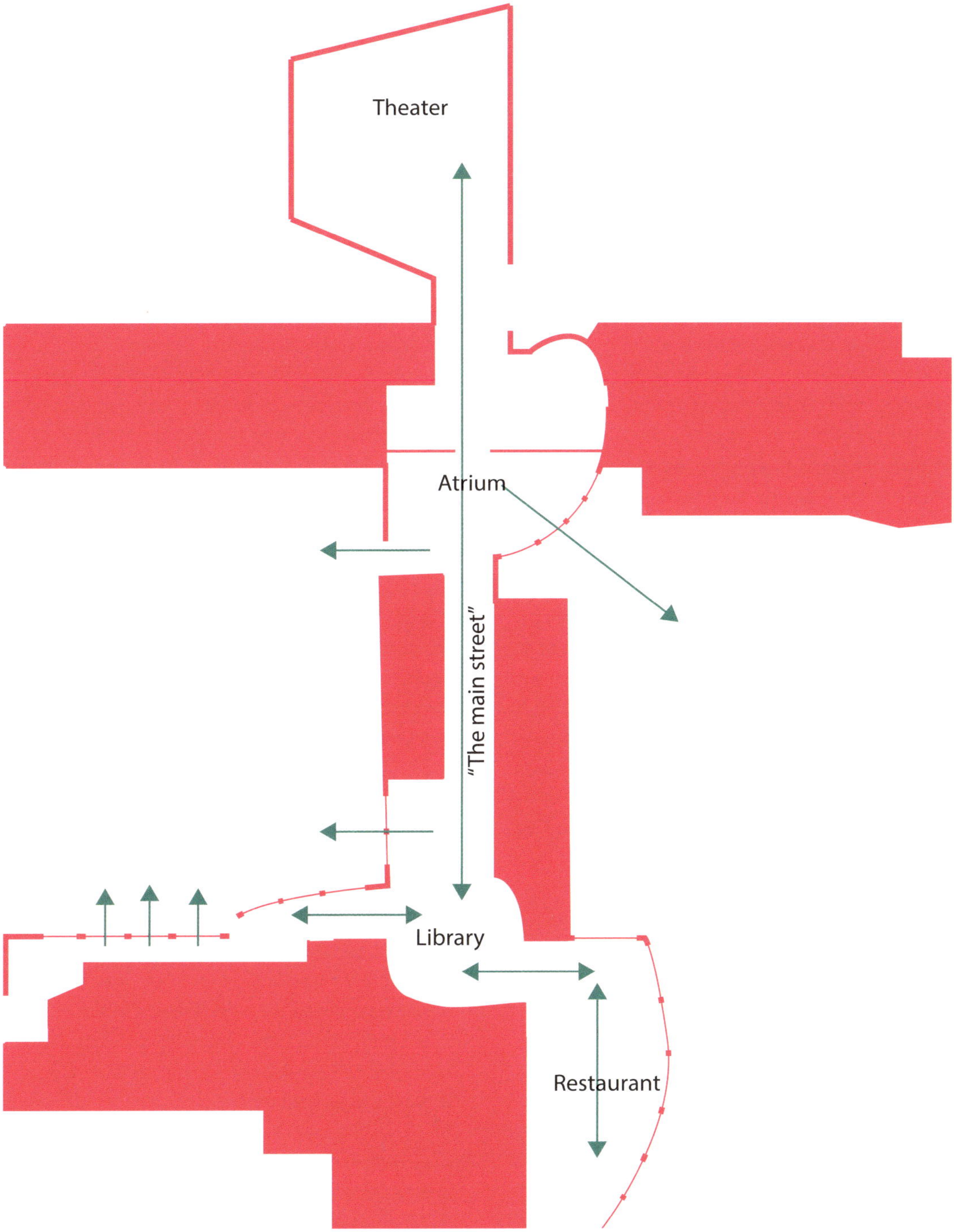
Theater
Atrium
"The main street"
Library
Restaurant

ly direct relationship. What this requires is that the older people are reasonably lively and are able to perform tasks on a somewhat equal footing with the children. It is interesting to note that the meetings worked in both small and large shared settings, and in both private and public spaces. In the course of the day, there was a wide variation in activity-, intimacy- and community levels. The physical framework of the nursery school was closely adapted to the children's needs and was adapted to a lesser degree to the specific needs of elderly people; this, of course, places certain demands on the elderly. These kinds of meetings are therefore only suitable for relatively lively senior citizens.

What is common to all the inter-generational meetings in Denmark that I have observed, read about or heard of, is that they are all planned out and structured in such a way that the one party visits the other. However, if you look beyound Denmark's borders, what you can see, for example, in France are examples where children and elderly people *share* their everyday lives, by virtue of the fact that the day-care (or childcare) centre and the nursing home have been constructed together and share functions and spaces, thus fostering a greater incidence of informal and natural meetings between children and the elderly (figure 4).

## *Intergénérationel* – children and the elderly meet

Résidence de l'Abbaye, located in the Parisian suburb of Saint-Maur-des-Fossés, is a nursing home and a nursery school. The nursing home has 209 residents, who live in individual 'flats', each with 22 m$^2$ of floorage, with access to a wide range of common activity rooms and other facilities. The nursing home has been built together with a nursery school, which functions in everyday life as an important part of the house. The nursery school has 14 children, in all, of ages 1½ to 3 years. The residents and the nursery school children share all the facilities, from the restaurant to the laundry appliances, with the exception of the private flats and one private room that is reserved exclusively for use by the nursery school. The project with the inter-generational work is more than ten years old and is one of four projects in Paris where work is very consciously being done to create an everyday situation where children and the elderly are together.

The building as a physical framework for the meeting between generations was planned out and functions like many other larger assisted living complexes, where the ground floor consists primarily of common functions and the remaining floors consist of private residences and common activity rooms. What is striking here is the building's openness, which buttresses the feeling that it is permissible for the children to move around in the whole building: to illustrate this altogether concretely, virtually all the doors were open, and the common activity rooms typically had several large openings facing the corridors and facing the gardens. The building has, moreover, been designed in its section in such a way that special efforts were also being made with respect to the spatial relationships. In several places, there are double-high rooms and 'balconies' that make it possible to look down on the life going on within the large common rooms. Furthermore, the architect has been working diligently to create views from one room to the next. This effort came to take effect in the form of spatial overlaps of a kind, where functions and spaces were being articulated and were nonetheless overlapping each other, at one and the same time. All this contributed to the results that, for one thing, it came natural to the children to move rather freely around inside the building, and that, for another, the

Fig. 6
Diagram – four types of meetings,
H.J. Schøbel, Eutopia (2015), p. 67.

The planned meeting

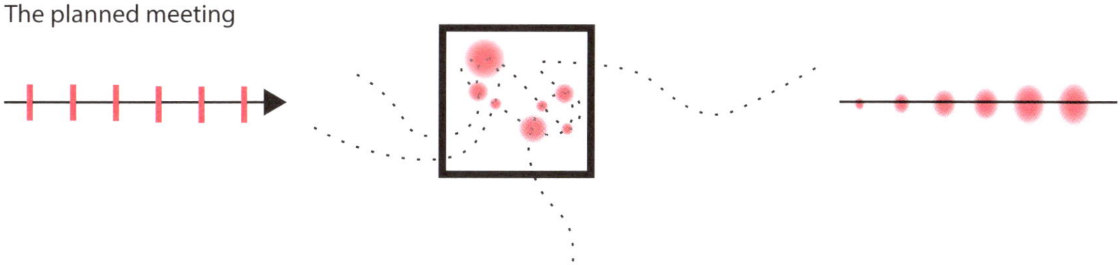

The everyday meeting

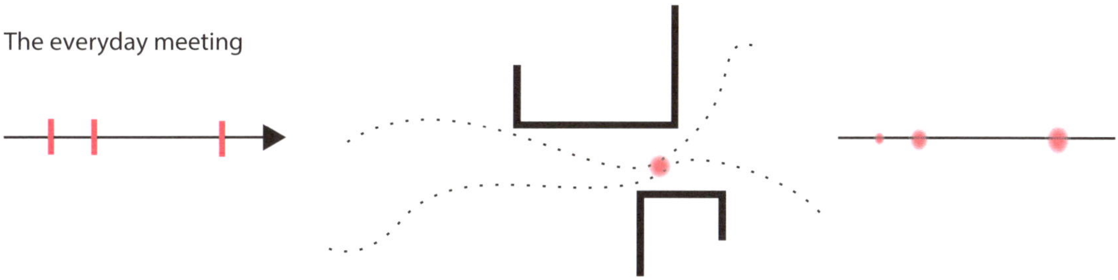

The random meeting

The sensed meeting

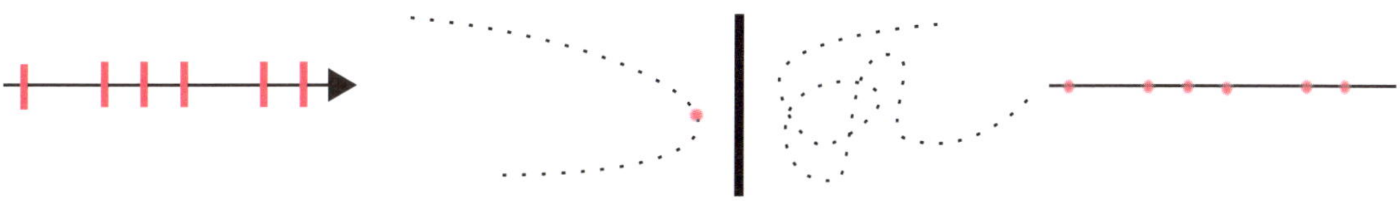

older people could follow along in the activities and perhaps get the urge to participate themselves.

As can be seen in figure 4, what is hereby permitted is that children and the older people 'live' together, and that they have a number of meetings, with different activity-, intimacy- and community levels. Furthermore, the meetings seemed to be altogether natural, and many of them occurred all by themselves: like when a couple of children, with a nursery school teacher in tow, were bent on making collages in a common room on one of the residential floors.

'(...) In the common activity room, they move over to a table where an elderly lady is about to eat her breakfast. 'May we sit here and make collages?' asks the nursery school teacher. The lady, who is obviously impaired and has difficulty eating her food, smiles and nods. The children sit down at the table, and when they see that the lady is about to eat, they also get hungry. Each one of the children gets a sandwich and suddenly all four of them are sitting together and eating.'[13]

At Résidence de l'Abbaye, it was very clear that both the children and the elderly were deriving pleasure, a sense of security and joie de vivre from their shared everyday life. The meetings were supported by the architecture, which promoting a sense of convivial fellowship in various degrees, and the many variations of space and features contributed to fact that many types of meetings could occur. That vivacious children are 'living' side by side with function-diminished older people serves to instil in the children a sense of awareness, a sense of presence and extra contact with adults, while the elderly people are experiencing life and unpredictability in their everyday lives. For a good many years now, the staff, the residents and the children have been harvesting good experiences when it comes to sharing their everyday lives and functions: this is something by which we in Denmark would do well to become inspired.

## The institution as social generator

In order to enable the institutions' proclivity towards being developed into successful social generators for meetings between the children and the elderly, it is fruitful to bear in mind that these two user groups may have different needs. It is therefore important to bring forth different types of meetings that offer different activity-, intimacy- and community levels, within which people can meet. As is being done at Résidence de l'Abbaye, it ought to be possible to enable older people and children to take part on the level that is relevant to – and feasible for – them.

I will therefore propose four types of meetings that individuals working in the municipality, caregivers, nursery school teachers and personnel, and architects can all use when planning out meetings between generations, so that *the planned*, *the sensed*, *the everyday* and *the random* meetings will become natural parts of everyday life (figure 6).

*The planned meeting* is the one where people meet on the basis of an appointment that has been made beforehand. The meeting often revolves around a planned activity like singing, drawing or reading and often has a regular rhythm, in the form of people convening, for example, once a week, once a month or once a year. The planned meeting is, in most cases, continuous and promotes a direct contact between the two generations. The children and the older people will often get to know each other better and better, as time rolls by, and what is brought forth are opportunities for convivial fellowship and presence.

Fig. 7
Diagrammatic sectional view – courtyard,
H.J. Schøbel, Eutopia (2015), p. 121.

*The everyday meeting* is the non-scheduled meeting that arises in daily life when, for example, two people are neighbours or when they make their daily rounds in the same place. Everyday meetings can, for example, take place in front of the building's entranceway, in a shared garden space or on a path that leads to certain functions that both groups make use of. This kind of meeting is promoted through the projecting of buildings' mutual relations, of the building's functions and of the flow of movement: for instance, by planning that one and the same path will lead to the nursery school (or the kindergarten) and the older people's dwellings. The everyday meeting requires that the functions are situated relatively close together, and requires that people are coming there on a regular basis. The everyday meeting does not necessarily bring about direct contact but upon repeated meetings, it can, perhaps in the long run, result in people getting comfortable with each other and maybe even forging some kind of direct contact.

*The random meeting*, as the name suggests, is one where different generations bump into each other by accident; what this means to say is that the chance encounter might have been envisioned by the municipality and the architect, while the children and the older people experience it as a chance encounter. It is often an isolated event, but it can also occur a number of times. For example, it might be the case that a bench which is particularly accommodating to use by senior citizens is set up on a playground: This can then come to take on the significance that children and older people will meet, by chance, more frequently during their everyday doings. Chance meetings are sporadic and unplanned. For this reason, they do not necessarily generate direct convivial contact between the generations, but they can help to

promote an awareness about the other generation and may lead to further convivial contact.
*The sensed meeting* is without any direct physical contact. What this kind of meeting implies is that people, with one or more of their senses, become aware of each other. Maybe it could be some children who are playing in front of an assisted living resident's window, which entails that the elderly person can hear the children's laughter and have the opportunity to observe their activities. The sensed meeting does not give rise to direct contact, but is more rather a subtle reminder about the other party's presence – and thereby also one's own. By becoming aware of others than oneself, about another generation, it can be imagined that a person would have more consideration for other people. And what this can lead to is that the people will start to feel more comfortable and maybe even meet again, perhaps in an even more direct way, some time later on. The sensed meeting is often relatively continuous, since it arises as a consequence of planning out specific functions' mutual relations.

## Architecture can encourage meetings between generations

As examples of how inter-generational meetings can be planned out and supported architecturally, I have set up diagrammatic sectional views for both indoor and outdoor spaces. The situations take their point of departure in the four types of meetings and thus exemplify *planned*, *sensed*, *everyday* and *random* encounters.
In the diagrammatic section (figure 7), there is an example of how a sensed and everyday meeting can be created. By placing dwellings for older people in such a way that they face out towards a yard or an outdoor space where children might be playing, the architect thus gives rise to the possibility that the sound of the children's playing will be drawn into the home. Simply by opening a window, the older person will be able to hear the life surrounding her/him right into her/his room. Additionally, this enables the elderly person to sit out on her/his balcony and watch the children play. Both of these constitute examples of 'sensed meetings', a generation meeting that is suitable for all types of elderly people, even those who are utterly dependent on being cared for. An everyday meeting between children and the elderly would potentially arise if the elderly person were given the chance to move around in amongst the children's games. For this reason, the paths should be relatively wide, so that there will also be room for wheelchair users, and so that there will be a chance for people to pass one another. When envisioning these types of meetings, it is important to remain attentive to thresholds between the private and the public space. For example, the heights of the balconies and the edge zone around the buildings ought to function as thresholds demarcating the resident's private abode and the public space: in this case, the children's playground (figure 7).
By linking a housing unit for elderly people very closely to a group of children in the day-care centre, opportunities for everyday, sensed and planned meetings emerge (figure 8). Setting up a common activity room with access to outdoor areas will contribute to the everyday meetings. Children and the elderly will naturally be using the space, even when they are not together in direct proximity with each other, but they will, for example, tend to meet each other close to the housing unit's entranceway or obtain some form of contact when they happen to be sitting on the same sofa ensemble. Moreover, a shared kitchen and a shared dining area will afford an opportunity for the children and the older people to eat lunch together every day and this most certainly constitutes an example of a planned meeting.

Fig. 8
Diagrammatic sectional view – children and elderly people sharing functions, H.J. Schøbel, Eutopia (2015), p. 123.

One can lend additional support to the sensed meeting by setting up a common room for the elderly, which would be situated adjacent to the large common room that the children and the elderly share. This would offer the opportunity to simply watch or listen to the activities. This sharing of functions will help to create a wide spectrum of different kinds of meetings between generations. There will still be opportunities for activities to transpire separately, but at the same time, what could also arise are meetings that can be characterized as belonging to virtually all levels of activity, intimacy and community. In the design of these spaces, it is important to create different zones and niches so that the opportunity for people to participate on different levels is created.

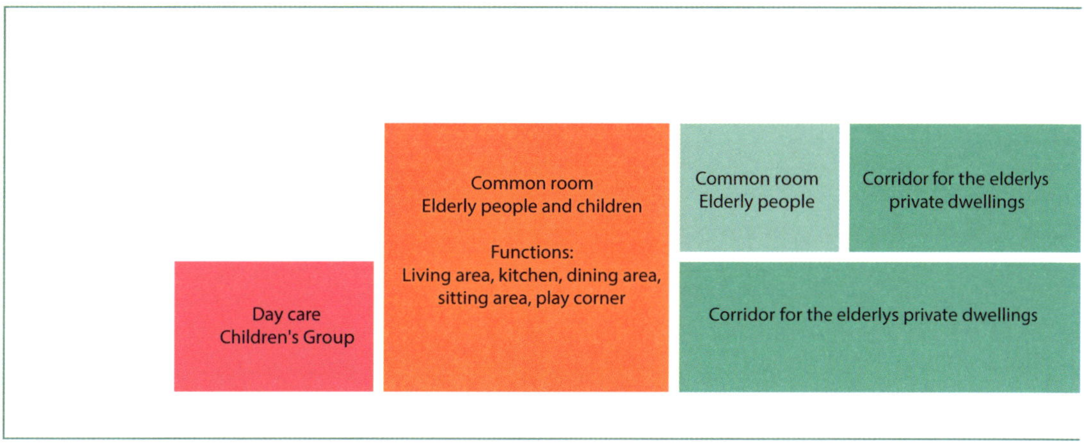

## The architect's role in rethinking welfare institutions

Architecture sets up the framework for the life as it is lived. Via space and interstices, architecture can be both determinating and liberating in its expression – and can thereby promote a specific kind of behaviour among the people who are using it. The architect thus enjoys relatively wide latitude and has a relatively expanded opportunity to ensure development and innovation, both materially and physically, and also in a more political sense. The architect's role in relation to further developing the welfare society is therefore quite significant. When welfare architecture is best, not only is it well thought out in terms of space, materials and technical solutions, but it is *also* innovative in its way of organizing and, once again, it promotes specific kind of behaviour among the people who are using it. It gives something *extra*, is generous when it comes to life, and offers both opportunities and limitations in its physical form.

When making a coordinated planning of institutions for children and the elderly, it is important to have spatial diversity in mind inasmuch as different scales and contexts offer the possibility for people to enter into a fellowship, on various levels, with the result that everybody can participate on the level that they can and want to. The design and elaboration of buildings and spaces, the ambiences that are inherent in the materials etc. can serve to prop up successful meetings between the children and the elderly, and the architect accordingly has an important role in relation to giving form to the physical framework for inter-generational meetings.

Furthermore, the programming phase of the building is also important when it comes to creating meetings between generations. Here, the architect's expertise contributes towards aiming the focus on the functions', the room's and the building-flow's influence on people's surfaces of contact and relationships. The 'Eutopia' project has served as an inspiration for the municipality of Copenhagen's programme for the new Sølund,[14] and therefore stands as a good example that architects have the opportunity to exert their influence on the intent – and on the very early planning – of a construction project.

The architect's efforts to promote meetings between generations can, as we have seen, take place during many phases of the building project. The obvious aspects are seated, of course, in the actual design phase: the sketching, the development and projecting of the buildings. However, as has been discussed, the architect's role is also crucial during the programming phase. And if we may carry this one step further, the architect's role can also be said to be relevant during the pre-programming phase, where the idea becomes conceived, hatched, developed, and cultivated, so that the attentiveness and the client's wishes are clarified and specified more precisely. Via architectural expertise and tools like the three-dimensional diagram, the architect can work with an interdisciplinary approach and can engage in dialogue with other professional groups that revolves around *rethinking the welfare of children and the elderly*. In this way, the architect's role is strengthened so that he/she also operates as a pre-programme developer and can thus make an even more fundamental contribution to a rethinking of the institutions and the welfare society's development. What arises, then, is the possibility of architecture with a clear intention, formulated on behalf of the welfare society. A place where generations will meet.

## Notes

1 G.E. Andersen: presentation at the 'Forming Welfare' conference, KADK, 2013.

2 Graduation project at the Royal Danish Academy of Fine Arts, School of Architcture, June 2015.

3 EGV Foundation.

4 S. Pinker: *The Village Effect* (2014).

5 C.E. Swane: chapter 1, in *Gerontologi – livet som gammel,* 2nd edition, A.L. Blaakilde, C.E. Swane & K. Amstrup (2011), p. 25.

6 E. Goffman: *Anstalt og menneske* (2012).

7 Statistics Denmark: Danish children are the youngest to start attending such an institution.

8 Bureau 2000: *Udviklingen i daginstitutioners bemanding* [the staffing of day-care institutions] 1986-2011 (2000), 2010.

9 P.K. Smith & K.J. Connolly: *The ecology of preschool behaviour* (1980). J. Kampmann: *Barnet og det fysiske rum – et blik ind I barndommens landskab* (1994).

10 I.M. Kirkeby, M.L. Gammelby & S.D. Elle: *Plads til trivsel og udvikling* (2013).

11 Skovsbøl: *Generationsmøder* (2011).

12 Qualitative interviews with participants in meetings between children and older people and participants' observations registered at the meetings. Empirical data has been gathered through sound recordings, photographs and observation notes.

13 Excerpts of observations, Schøbel, 2015.

14 Sølund is an assisted living centre located on the banks of The Lakes in Copenhagen. The present-day Sølund was built in 1976-81. However, because the buildings have recently been assessed as being outmoded, the entire nursing home centre is going to be torn down. The municipality of Copenhagen is currently planning to build a new and more modern assisted living centre.

## Literature


- Andersen, G.E.: presentation at the 'Forming Welfare' conference, KADK, 2013.
- Blaakilde, A.L.: chapter 84, in *Gerontologi – livet som gammel*, 2nd edition, 2011 in Blaakilde, A.L., C.E. Swane & K. Amstrup: Munksgaard, Copenhagen 2011.
- Bureau 2000: *Udviklingen i daginstitutioners bemanding 1986-2011,* 2000, 2010.
- Goffman, E.: *Anstalt og menneske*, Jørgen Paludans Forlag, 12th printing, Hørsholm 2012.
- Kampmann, J.: *Barnet og det fysiske rum – et blik ind i barndommens landskab*, Forlaget Børn & Unge, Copenhagen 1994.
- Kirkeby, I.M., Gammelby, M.L. & Elle, S.D.: *Plads til trivsel og udvikling*, Aalborg University, 2013.
- Pinker, S.: *The Village Effect*, Spiegel & Grau, New York, 2014.
- Schøbel, H.J.: *Eutopia*, 2015.
- Skovsbøl, U.: *Generationsmøder*, Frydenlund, Frederiksberg 2011.
- Smith, P.K. & Connolly, K.J.: *The ecology of preschool behaviour,* Cambridge 1980.
- Swane, C.E.: chapter 1, in *Gerontologi – livet som gammel*, 2nd edition, Blaakilde, A.L., Swane, C.E., & Amstrup, K., Munksgaard, Copenhagen 2011.


## Internet sources


- EGV Foundation, *Hvor mange ældre føler sig ensomme?:* www.egv.dk/faq-alderdom,-ensomhed-og-fattigdom/hvor-mange-aeldre-er-ensomme.aspx (2015, retrieved on March 10, 2015)
- Statistics Denmark, *Danske børn kommer tidligst i institution:* www.dst.dk/da/Statistik/bagtal/2011/2011-11-21-daginstitutioner (2011, retrieved on February 7, 2015)

Svenningsen Kajita

# Use Matters in Architectural Production

**Alongside many other actors, architects contribute to the production of welfare architecture. The architect's role is amongst other to design through various media such as drawing as well as product- and material specification. According to standards and conventions in the current construction industry, architectural drawings and specifications are primarily perceived as a means to communicate what is measurable and what is tangible. However, these media can also embrace the non-measurable and the intangible. This article accordingly presents the potentials for including *use* in architectural production.**

## Welfare in Use

Through the course of history, architecture and urban planning have been used for social restructuring. This is exemplified by the authoritative proposals underlying the post-war era's welfare-architecture and -planning, which can generally be said to aim to ensure equality, freedom and solidarity.[1] There were absolutely benevolent intentions behind the large-scale housing developments of the 1960s and 1970s, but in spite of all the good intentions, the dominant narrative in the flow of breaking news typically put across the idea that these estates manifest an abortive rationality. I challenge this predominant narrative in my PhD project 'Fragile potentialer i de store planer: Rumlige og materielle dimensioner af efterkrigstidens storskala-boligbebyggelser i brug' [Fragile Potentials in the Big Plans: Spatial and Material Dimensions of Post-war Large-scale Housing Estates in Use]. In the thesis, I operate within a feminist methodology that enables the illumination of complex issues by means of presenting several different perspectives. I acknowledge the overriding and predominant criticism of the large-scale housing estates from the 1960s and 1970s, and I also acknowledge that there are technical, social and infrastructural problems on which people are focusing in the current transformation projects.[2] In addition, as supplementary to these problem-oriented analyses and solutions, I point to potentials for quality-ensuring current transformation projects in relation to the adjustments, open spatiality and sensuous materiality that can also be found in these housing estates today. I am thus looking at the housing estates in relation to the changes that have happened to them over time, after they came to be inhabited and since they have been in use.

The term *use/user* is central both in the point of departure for the post-war era's modernist architecture and planning and in the criticism thereof. Here, I use the term *use* in accordance with Henri Lefebvre's notion of 'the right to the city' as the right that includes everything and everybody. Lefebvre describes the city as a collective work where rights are not only rights to specific functions in the city such as rights to housing or other necessities. Use similarly has to do with the right to be engaged in this work and in the processes

through which the city is allocated meaning, enjoyment and care.[3] The critical and creative user,[4] in this perspective, plays a part in redefining meaning and use-values in architecture.
In the present article I focus on how one can incorporate use-value in the architectural representational media. I assume that use is an indispensable aspect of material and spatial aspects of material and spatial description that is not reserved exclusively for participatory processes that have been separated from or delegated out from the architect's core services to a specific work stage. Even though such participatory processes can be meaningful in themselves, it is my contention that use-values first come to take on full significance for architecture when they are integrated into the systems that design processes are subject to. For this reason, I will put forth examples of how use-values can form part of material- and product specification as well as of technical drawings.

## Professional Frameworks

Construction processes were standardized in parallel to the development of the post-war era's functionally divided cities and buildings. One of the most important preconditions for the post-war era's housing developments was that the individual building elements were produced independently of each other and at different locations.[5] The large concrete panel buildings were to be assembled on site without need for adjustments. Time schedules and work plans therefore became necessary. As a consequence of this, both construction processes and the profession at large became increasingly systematized during this period. This product perspective continues to dominate the construction industry today and it continues to systematize the architect's services. The Danish trade associations' professional framework prescribes work stages in a linear progression, leading from the definition of problem and sketch proposal through to the product's completion.[6]
The profession's normative frameworks for use and operations have been the object of heightened attention internationally in recent years, due to sustainability requirements and declining economic welfare. For example, the long-term perspective has exerted a marked influence on the Royal Institute of British Architects' (RIBA) Plan of Work from 2013. Here, it is written:

*While the end of a building's life might be considered at Stage 7 [In Use], it is more likely that Stage 0 [Strategic Definition] of the follow-on project or refurbishment would deal with these aspects as part of strategically defining the future of the building.*[7]

RIBA's introduction of cyclical continuity challenges the linear work stages in the Danish standards. A building is, according to RIBA, always a 'follow-on' project or refurbishment rather than a new beginning. A building is, in other words, conditioned especially by *use*. Thus it is relevant when I propose here that the range of possibilities be broadened so as to include considerations about use in architectural production by examples of specifications and technical drawings. My motivation for these reflections is to contribute to a strengthening of the profession's services and approaches in connection with people's needs and circumstances. Without this focus, the risk may be that projects, in reality, cannot be described in relation to the fundamental social and political levels upon which they are adopted.

## The Eye of the Architect

The proposal being put forth in the present article is to expand the conventions for architectural

A window in Drottninghög, Helsingborg, adapted by the flat's inhabitant (2011). She recounted: 'The windows, they're sitting up high ... the children, you know, always had to stand on a chair, if they wanted to look outside. And then there weren't any windowsills, either. So, I've put them there myself. So that there could be a few flowers.' Photo by the author.

drawings and specifications. The suggestion is to set this expansion into motion through the prominent scholar Donna Haraway's concept of 'Situated Knowledges,' which she elaborates in the article 'Situated Knowledges: The Science Question in Feminism and the Privilege of Partial Perspectives' (1988).[8] In contrast to the post-war era's rationalizing perspectives, which structure from the top down, the feminist empiricist knowledge production has to do with assimilating and absorbing the intimate and action-based.[9] This is accordingly relevant to the question of how to include use in architectural representations.

Looking for knowledge from the 'other' position is not an innocent position but, as Haraway writes, it is: 'least likely to allow denial of the critical and interpretive core of all knowledge.'[10] Haraway subscribes to a feminist strategy of rendering visible that the production of knowledge cannot be value-neutral because both the researcher and the person being researched have to be considered actors. She nuances the discussion about empirical knowledge by pointing out that it is problematic when somebody who is operating within relativistic positions, say in standpoint theory or radical relativism, fails to acknowledge structural relations. The problem is seated, according to Haraway, in that, failing to acknowledge the structural relations, one cannot act critically in relation to the dominance of these. For this reason, she argues instead for a feminist version of objectivity, through localized, partial and embodied knowledge. Here, the objectivity revolves around partial perspectives, which do not split the object from the subject because the objectivity is localized in the knowing subject's body. Knowledge is, in other words, linked to a personal and embodied experience. Situated accounts include multiple perspectives on both structural relations as well as on the intimate and action-based relations. The various perspectives can be refuted or they can be developed, but

within a given framework, they have to be consistent. The objectivity's guarantee is that the reader understands the partiality that arises in the knower. In relation to my enterprise, which is to include knowledge about use in architectural production, Haraway's frame accordingly exposes a need to clarify this partiality.

In my PhD thesis, I demonstrate a situated drawing- and specification method with examples from studies of three large-scale housing estates: Albertslund Syd in Albertslund, Drottninghög in Helsingborg and Lindängen in Malmö. The argument and the illustrations shown in the present article refer to this publication.[11] In this way, I wish to show that it through architectural specification and drawings is possible to obtain knowledge about the formal, spatial and visual dimensions as well as about the life being lived, which, according to architectural theorist Robin Evans, 'do not entail the destruction or domination of the one by the other',[12] as he writes in the essay 'The Developed Surface: An Enquiry into the Brief Life of an Eighteenth-Century Drawing Technique'.

In her description of situated knowledge, Haraway makes use of the faculty of *sight* as a metaphor. With our sense-faculty of sight, we manage both to see and not to see. To represent while, at the same time, not to represent. The eye can give the knowing subject a distance from everything and everybody, in order to attain power. A position that Haraway denotes as a *God trick*.[13] She suggests, alternatively:

*a feminist way through all the visualising tricks and powers of modern sciences. Learn in our bodies to attach the objective to theory and political scanners. In order to name where we are and are not.*[14]

Knowledge is hereby not some abstract and generalizing thesis, because what we see is conditioned by how we see. Our eyes, writes Haraway, are active perceptual systems that build on translations and on specific ways of seeing.

Within the realms of architecture and planning, there are particular conventions for seeing. Here, the eye's systems are conditioned by experiences, formulas, traditions and techniques, such as orthographic projection and material- and product specification. For the architect, the challenge in absorbing everyday perspectives and lived life lies in that which could be called 'the profession's eye', which has been defined and trained to view static abstract visions based on overview, certainty and scale. This could look something like a *God trick,* which cannot assimilate knowledge from below, however also 'the profession's eye' is conditioned by different perspectives. The certainty with which the architect draws and describes can also be seen as partial, as a limited part of a larger complex. My suggestion is, therefore, that use can be assimilated in the architectural sight and site (cf. Haraway) in, for example, drawings and specifications, although this demands that these become linked up with the architect's theoretical and political positions.

I regard the architectural and planning profession's ways of positioning their respective fields of vision and their ways of seeing as part and parcel of the profession's critical contribution to the debates around welfare. In architecture, situated knowledge can have particular relevance if we are going to be able to circumvent having to quantify that which is not quantifiable, namely people's comfort and sense of well-being, which must be said to be the ultimate aim to which architecture can modestly contribute. The intention is, accordingly, not that the architectural media have to provide unequivocal answers about architecture in use, but rather that they can help to establish an objectivity and critique that can promote better, albeit not ideal, solutions.

Six courtyard spaces in the three housing estates. From top to bottom: Albertslund Syd, A1 and A2, Drottninghög, D1 and D2, and Lindängen, L1 and L2. Drawings by the author.

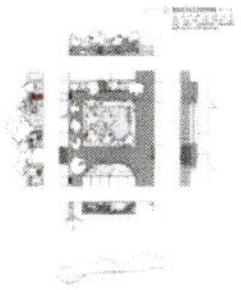

Tegning A1, Adams Place

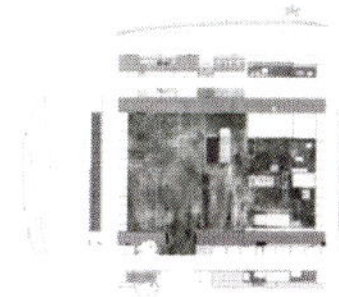

Tegning A2, Genbrugsstation

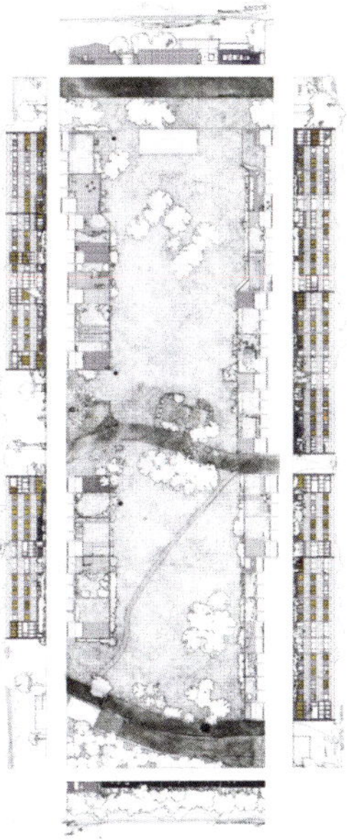

Tegning D1, Beboelsesgård

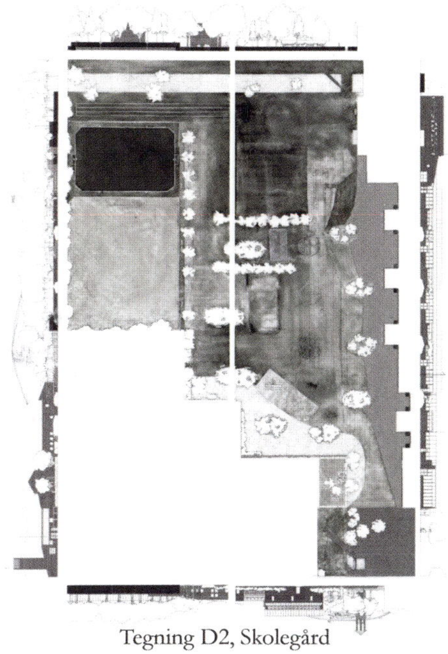

Tegning D2, Skolegård

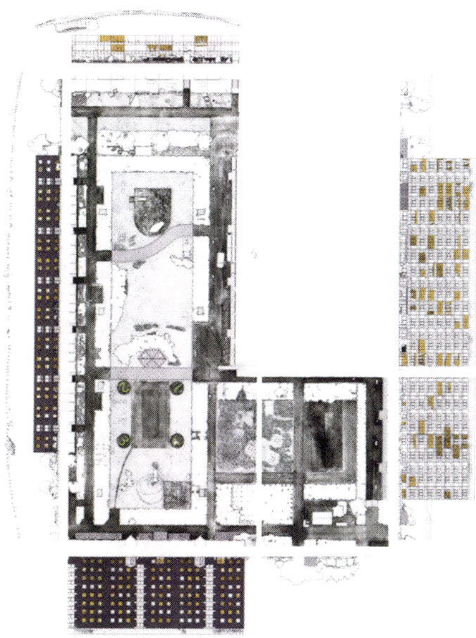

Tegning L1, Stena beboelsesgård

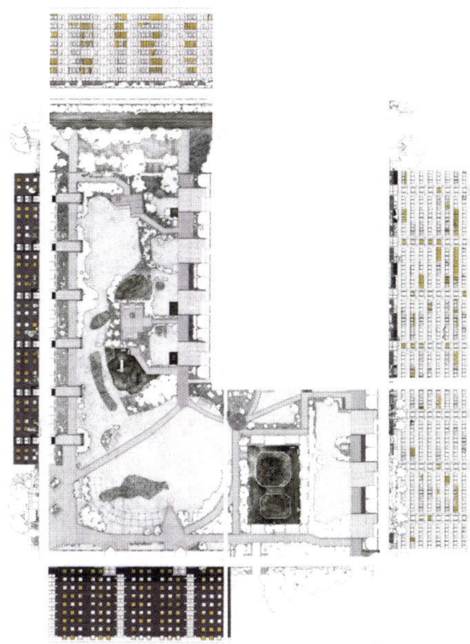

Tegning L2 Wilhem beboelsesgård

## Architectural Specification and Use

The material- and product specification is a written document that describes, in detail, the architecture's materials and construction methods, as well as the construction process's statutory norms and standards. The architectural specification has taken on many forms, for different purposes through the course of centuries. Herein, processes, performance, visual intentions, products and types are specified, with reference to drawings and models.

The architectural historian Katie Lloyd Thomas's research into the specification poses a challenge to the understanding of materials that binds matter to form, an understanding which assigns a lower priority to external processes and conditions. She considers, instead, material as a system related to extra-physical conditions. Materials and products are thus related to potentials in, for example: industry's techniques; the condition of being anchored in societal regulations and principles for work; and, also, principles about the worker's enjoyment. Thomas calls attention to an example from a performance clause. Instead of describing a door's dimensions and type, this proviso stipulates that the door has to withstand being slammed repeatedly. The door's materiality is accordingly being defined by its resilience in use. She writes: 'in the performance clause, use no longer seems to belong to a different realm to the material – 'that of the human being in action.' Instead it seems to have become internal to the material.'[15] The specification can thus, according to Thomas, also include use-values.

In the example from Drottninghög, cited in illustration p. 311, the resident, as in Thomas's example, does not describe specific dimensions and type. Instead, the resident is describing the possibility of putting plants on the windowsill, along with the chance for the children to be able to look out through the window. With the adjustment, she contorts expectations related both to lifestyle and to the universal human body according to which the window has been proportioned.

In my PhD project, I have carried out a comprehensive fieldwork, with qualitative interviews conducted with residents in the three housing developments. Quotations from these interviews have been introduced in the document *Arbejdsbeskrivelse af de store planer i brug*[16] [Specification of the Big Plans in Use]. Herein, materials, products, capabilities, behaviours, building components, concepts, urban components, spatial- and organizational components like right of disposal, workmanship, operations, maintenance and control, and facilities etc. are denominated. These have been singled out on the basis of the residents' descriptions of enjoyment in and care for the architecture. In the document, use categories replace categories like masonry and steel workmanship, which today structure the Danish specification standards, 'Bips'.[17] The relatively

The document, *Arbejdsbeskrivelse af de store planer i brug* [Specification of the Big Plans in Use] describes both material and immaterial, i.e. tangible and intangible, materials and spaces.

→

Quotes from *Arbejdsbeskrivelse af de store planer i brug* [Specification of the Big Plans in Use], dealing with the sorting of waste and recycling.

large volume of text in the transcriptions of the interviews has been abridged in this fragmented form for purposes of linking interpretations to the architectural drawing. The resident's description of the window in Drottninghög supplements, for example, the criteria for windows, which are given by the drawing's space- and proportioning study. The registrations in the specification document and the drawings, which (also) contain use-values, generate new conditions for democratic and participatory approaches and for appreciating the welfare society's architecture.

I am making use of the specification along with drawings, in an analysis across six courtyard spaces in the three estates. Initially, I gather together value-laden descriptions, experiences, criticisms, actions, and so on, from specific situations. Hereafter, I render visible the possibilities in the specific situations' convergence with other situations. For example, I test out the doctrine of recycling and the sorting of waste from one courtyard space in the other courtyard spaces. This serial interpretation is to be regarded both as a chance to spot potential and as a chance to test potentials. *The Specification of the Big Plans in Use* can therefore be regarded as taxonomy, archive or list, but the document has also inventions as its purpose. For example, a recycling container

**4.2 BODILY ENGAGEMENT**

**A**

Catalogue no. A.2.1 – WASTE SORTING AND RE-USE (A2, D1, L1)

Mr & Mrs Z – It is not just a way of teaching people to dispose of their waste the right places [...] it is also much more. It is about socialising. People sometimes come here, without anything, just to talk...

**4.3 PHYSICAL ENGAGEMENT**

**A**

Catalogue no. A.3.1 – WASTE SORTING (see re-use for more) (A2, D1, L1)

Mr & Mrs Z – [The waste sorting] is probably some of the best we have done for our small section [of the housing association]. It has been one factor preventing a rent increase, and we are very pleased about this.
[...] People use to throw it over that fence in there, we only had a timber fence, and they threw it in there. It was in a big pile and cost a great amount of money to sort [...] We are 226 dwelling units, but only nine people. We have a little room to sit in. Then I have made a roster ... then people bring their stuff and we help them to sort it in different sections for iron or flammable material ... then we bought a compactor to throw all flammables in.

Mr L – This is what they call the environment hub, where we throw waste, where you get to sort bottles and such things, but sometimes waste and big metal things and televisions are left. Stena will have to empty this and this service increases the rent [...] When they kept the container here, businesses would come to throw they rubbish, and that fills the container, so there was no room for those who leave here to use. For this reason people [from Stena] minded the container and asked people where they came from. This worked well.

Catalogue no. G.3.2 – RE-USE (see waste sorting for more) (A2)
Mr & Mrs Z – Now, someone came over leaving this whilst the care-takers were here. They open the gate, and then when we have our shifts, we tidy up and throw it where it belongs. [We have] this little space [...] Now, someone brought three chairs. They look good. Maybe one day someone is going to come needing a chair, then we bring this chair [...] That is re-use.

in Albertslund Syd possesses a certain expedient value, but it also contains ambiguous potentials as it occasions meetings among people who would not otherwise have anything to do with each other. This potential is continued further inasmuch as the specification places various descriptions from different situations side by side, and also because the document forms part of the study's broader coherence, with drawings, dialogues with planners and other literature and data. In these contexts, the specification's attribute as collateral is tweaked and re-oriented toward a creative capacity.

## Architectural Drawing and Use

As part of the critique of the modernist city, Lefebvre noted that the architectural drawing, the abstraction, has been drained of lived experience. The drawing is regarded, in Lefebvre's view, as a neutral medium, which plays a part in emptying the lived life from the architect's issues and propositions.[18] On a par with this, the architectural theorist Kathrine Shonfield also problematicizes the drawing's authority, citing examples from technical drawing manuals. About examples from the 1970s, she writes that:

> [...] *variation is restricted and contained to shades of grey. This is compounded by the discipline imposed by a single-line thickness of technical pen. Ink is unable to flow through such pens unless they are used at a consistent vertical angle, giving an 'objective', i.e. non-varying, line.*[19]

All tools and instruments have their limitations. Shonfield argues further that whatever the tool cannot depict is weeded out in mainstream practice. This argument points toward a need to challenge architectural practice that uncritically subjugates itself to systems, including the digital systems with which the profession is operating today.

Robin Evans opens a range of possibilities for such a challenge, as he underlines that drawings are not the same as the buildings that they represent. The drawings are translations, which render the translator's critical positions feasible. In Evans' opinion, the architectural drawing is thus a productively charged medium, within which the parameters outside the architect's immediate control can also be embedded.[20]

The drawing, whether it be digital or analogue, is not connected with some abstract world in contrast to a reality of concrete elements, asphalt and people's doings. I regard both specifications and drawings as material *per se* and as tools to understand something about the reality that is being drawn and described, including that which falls outside the paper or the screen image. I let the specifications and drawings be informed by the material reality, but the knowledge that is obtained is partial and is localized in the professions systems. Items of information are accordingly incorporated into the productive system (knowledge, local development plans, technology, etc.), and here, the items of information can act critically. The drawings, which I have executed, are thus also conditioned by a specific drawing technique.

## "The Developed Surface'

In the essay 'The Developed Surface: An Enquiry into the Brief Life of an Eighteenth-Century Drawing Technique' (2003) Evans concentrates on the architect Robert Adam's practice of the drawing technique that Evans names 'the Developed Surface.' Evans fastens his interest particularly on the special capacity of the technique to conjoin the visual with the social, within the frames of a study of Adam's interiors from the closing of the 18th century and beginning of the 19th century. Adam drew elevations as if folded out from the plan. Evans argues that this special focus on the room's unfolded surfaces is grounded in the overall space planning. In Adam's circuit plans, there is equality between the rooms, which could have resulted in monotony and uniformity, but, by way of countering this, the manner of thinking in the unfolded plan-drawings revolves, instead, around differentiating the rooms through detailing of their surfaces. Spatial and social hierarchies are explored and are defined, in their particularity, in the rooms' form, the rooms' use and the rooms' decoration.

I made use of the technique in drawings at a scale 1:100. The large drawings of parts of Drottninghög and Lindängen measure approximately 180 x 230 cm. The drawings of Albertslund Syd's courtyard spaces measure approximately 90 × 70 cm. At first, they were produced digitally. Thereafter, the prints, on tracing paper, were re-worked and further elaborated with pencil. I have detailed the drawings with my body bent over the paper on large tables. I have moved my chair around the table in synch with executing the detailing on the drawing, from one vantage point at a time. In this fashion, the drawings have been made in fragments. The detailing of material components, curtain patterns, lawns, and paving, etc. engages the draftsperson and the drawing's readers in the intimate. It is time-consuming, both to draw dots representing grass and to decode strokes and dots. Within this passage of time, associations are formed and questions are raised in relation to planning, operations and maintenance, ownership, the building's construction, industrial parameters, and so on and so forth.

I also had the drawings hanging on the wall and could accordingly, from some distance, identify connections, figures, surfaces, enclosed spaces and structures in parallel to carrying out the analytical work of other empirical material and data. The drawings, in this way, also designate situations that run across the respective housing estates and different focus areas. What we have before us, then, are localized, embodied and particular studies, from which something can be posited about general aspects.

My interest in the Developed Surface drawings started to crystallize in response to aspects of experience that the residents living in the three estates were telling me about. The residents were calling attention to how use over time has changed the interfaces between buildings and courtyard spaces. Room for pursuing this discussion is limited here and does not permit more detailed explanation, but nevertheless I have been trying to illustrate, with a few examples, identified relations between architecture and use.

One of the residents, Mr. X, in Albertslund Syd, told me about the area in front of the entrance to his courtyard house. He told me about plants, sculptures, an open window and a bench. He told me about the differences between this specific courtyard and other similar courtyards close by. In Mr. X's descriptions, as is the case in the other interviews with residents, the appreciation for – and the care for – space and materiality are linked to delimited sites that are sometimes connected with each other, and sometimes not. In much the same way as it happens in the drawing- and specification analyses. Sometimes the use-values can be linked to architectural order, form and space, while sometimes they can be described independently of these. Sometimes the residents' way of finding meaning, enjoyment and care are connected with the original intentions in the architecture. At other times, we find creative use and adjustments of the welfare state's housing model.

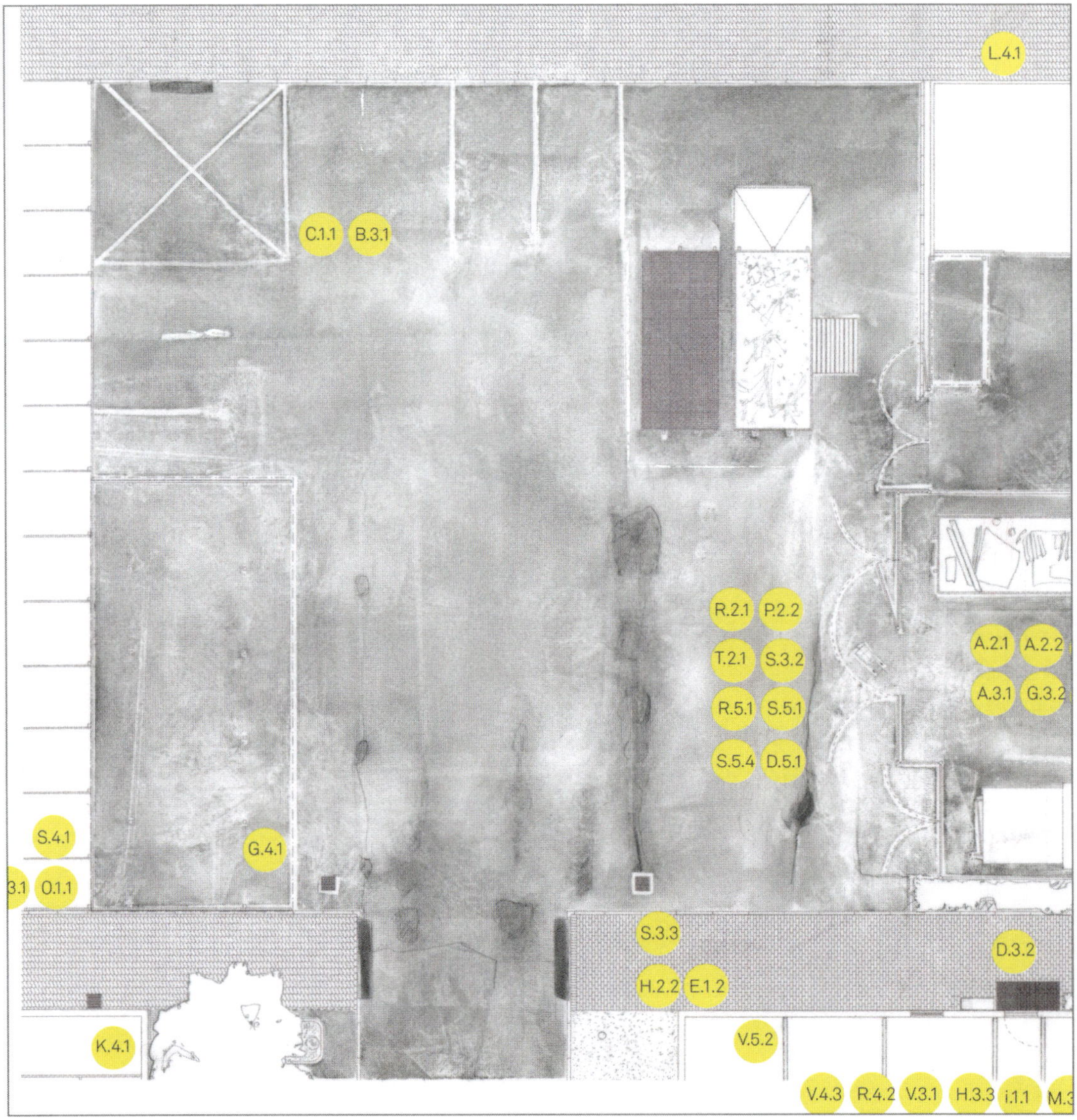
L.4.1
C.1.1
B.3.1
R.2.1
P.2.2
A.2.1
A.2.2
T.2.1
S.3.2
A.3.1
G.3.2
R.5.1
S.5.1
S.5.4
D.5.1
S.4.1
G.4.1
O.1.1
S.3.3
D.3.2
H.2.2
E.1.2
K.4.1
V.5.2
V.4.3
R.4.2
V.3.1
H.3.3
i.1.1

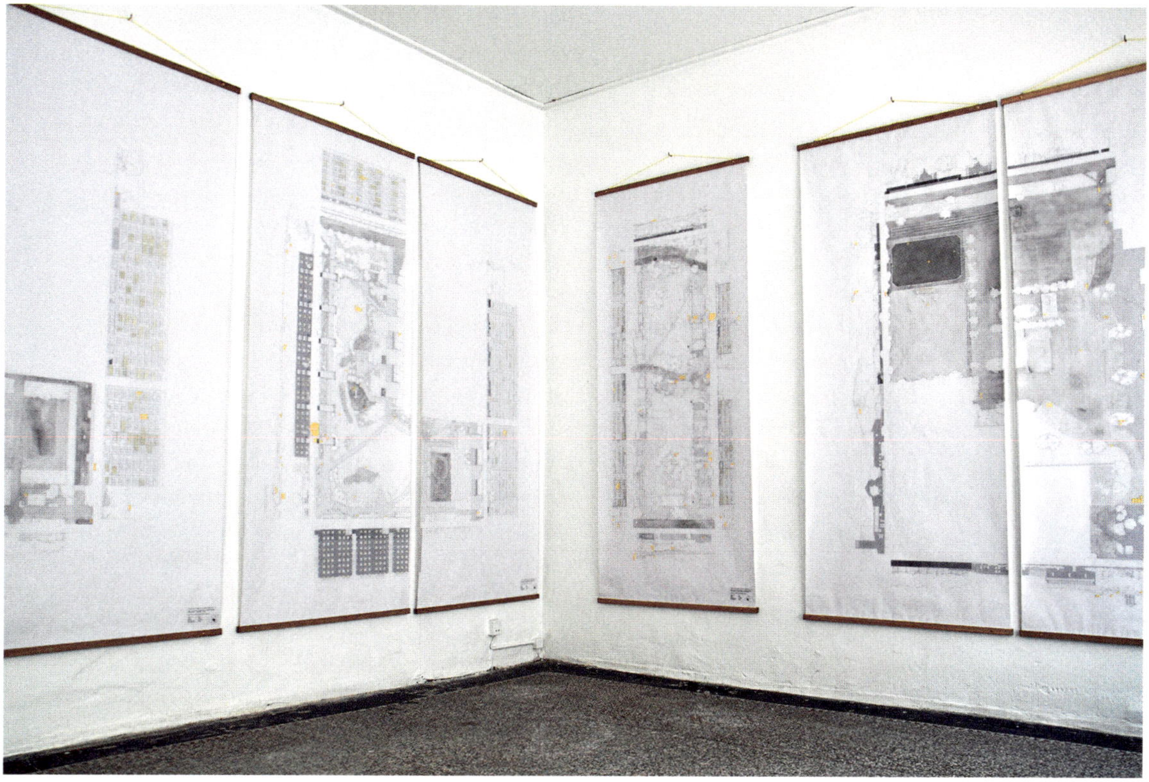

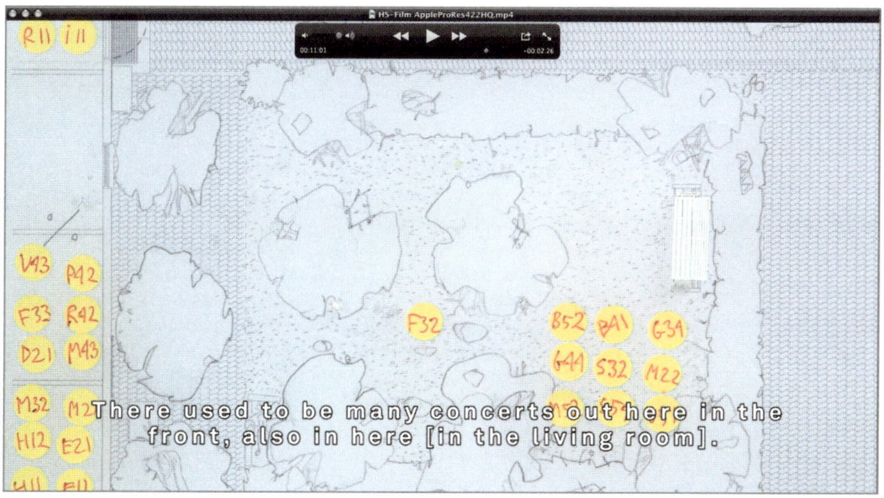


Drawings during exhibition at Leth & Gori gallery, Copenhagen 2014. Photo by the author.

Detail from drawing A1, Adam's Place. The photograph is from the film entitled 'About Appreciation and Care – Architectural Recordings' (2014) by the author.

←

Details from drawings of the three housing estates. Drawings by the author.

## Conclusion

The Big Plans' functional planning is deterministic, under-deterministic and it is anti-deterministic. Use parameters open for complexity and changeability, but both drawings and specifications also provide a static image of here-and-now, which makes it possible to discuss architectural form in use.

As the situation is laid out in the work of both Robin Evans and Katie Lloyd Thomas, representational techniques do not have permanent values. Both the architectural drawing and specification are conditioned by changeable structural issues as well as by interpretations. In the preceding discussion, I have exemplified how the very drawing process in the study of the three estates leads to the drawings being seen close up and far away; this affects the motives that are being discussed. Through the analysis of interviews with residents, the architectural eye is drawn all the way in, close to the home, such as through the Swedish interviewee's description of a windowsill. A moment later, another resident turns his attention to the Big Plans' structural organization and turns his attention thereafter to relations between the neighbours. For this reason, the estates in the study appear both as static forms across different scales, and also as dynamic overlapping situations and hegemonies. In this way, various aspects and experiences of the drawing appear in a variety of readings. The representations are partial, inasmuch as they actually are more or less abstract: this means to say that the situated drawing and specification do not offer a full picture of an architectural project and thus do not prioritize subjects. Drawings and specifications are accordingly linked to the situation within which they happen to be inscribed, which means to say that the drawings, just like matters of the architectural specification, can challenge the power discourses from within which the architect operates. In the present study, it is the residents' descriptions, such as the one about a do-it-yourself windowsill and about the appropriated courtyard that directly challenge the architectural representational media and, by this means, also challenge the frameworks to which the profession, and concomitantly, also, the present study, are subjugated.

Architectural specifications and drawings are most often considered as media that represent the static and measurable. I am showing here that these media, through a double obligation – to both close and intimate use-values, and to the general frameworks – can also contain heterogeneous relations between the social and architectural form. There are potentials suggesting that the profession's conventional media, which have been integrated into architecture's core values and -services, (also) can contribute critically to spatial production, with the aim of changeability.

**Notes**

1 Cf. Article 1 of the Universal Declaration of Human Rights, adopted by the United Nations General Assembly in 1948.

2 Including efforts in building renovation, social and cultural programmes, densification, infrastructure, ecology, employment, and so forth.

3 H. Lefebvre, R. Bononno & N. Smith: *The Urban Revolution* (2003).

4 'The Creative User' is defined by the architectural theorist Jonathan Hill as the user who is the co-producer of architecture. J. Hill: *Actions of Architecture: Architects and Creative Users* (2003).

5 E. Nygaard: *Tag over hovedet: dansk boligbyggeri fra 1945 til 1982* (1984), p. 132

6 The Danish Association of Consultung Engineers's (FRI) and the Danish Association of Architectural Firms's performance descriptions for construction and planning (2012).

7 'RIBA Plan of Work, 2013', p. 27.

8 Haraway: 'Situated Knowledges: The Science Question in Feminism and the Privilege of Partial Perspectives', *Feminist Studies* 14 (3), 1988.

9 M.M. Fonow & J.A. Cook: 'Feminist Methodology: New Applications in the Academy and Public Policy' (2005), pp. 2211-36, S. Harding: *The Science Question in Feminism*

(1986), Harding and Kathryn Norberg: 'New Feminist Approaches to Social Science Methodologies: An Introduction' (2005), pp. 2009-15., Haraway (1988), op.cit., and C. Ramazanoglu & J. Holland: *Feminist Methodology: Challenges and Choices* (2002).

**10** Haraway (1988), op.cit., p. 584.

**11** H.S. Kajita: *Fragile potentialer i de store planer – rumlige og materielle dimensioner af efterkrigstidens storskala boligbebyggelser i brug* (2016).

**12** R. Evans: *Translations From Drawing to Building and Other Essays* (2003), p. 198.

**13** Haraway (1988), op.cit.

**14** Haraway (1988), op.cit., p. 583.

**15** K.L. Thomas: 'Building Materials: Conceptualising Materials via the Architectural Specification' (2010), p. 133.

**16** H.S. Kajita (2016), op.cit. I conducted in-depth qualitative interviews with 19 residents across the three respective estates between June 2011 and July 2012.

**17** Bips B1.000, Beskrivelsesanvisning – struktur/september 2008'.

**18** H. Lefebvre: *The Production of Space* (2012), pp. 361-62.

**19** K. Shonfield: *Walls Have Feelings: Architecture, Film, and the City* (2000), p. 21.

**20** R. Evans (2003), op.cit.

### Literature


- 'Arkitekters virke', section 3, Danish Association of Architects, http://arkitektforeningen.dk/arkitektforeningen/organisationen/love-vedtaegter/arkitekters-virke. Retrieved in September 2014.
- Bips B1.000, 'Beskrivelsesanvisning – struktur/september 2008', http:/bips.dk. Retrieved in April 2013.
- Evans, R.: *Translations From Drawing to Building and Other Essays*, Architectural Association, London 2003.
- 'Etiske retningslinjer', from www.danskeark.dk/Om-DANSKE-ARK/Regler-og-vedtaegter/~/media/Dark/Om-DANSKE-ARK/Etiske_retningslinjer_DANSKE-ARK.ashx. Retrieved in November 2014.
- Fonow, M.M., & Cook, J.A.: 'Feminist Methodology: New Applications in the Academy and Public Policy', *Signs: Journal of Women in Culture and Society* 30 (4), 2005, pp. 2211-36.
- The Danish Association of Consultung Engineers's (FRI) and the Danish Association of Architectural Firms's performance descriptions for construction and planning (2012). www.danskeark.dk. Retrieved in January 2016.
- Forty, A.: *Words and Buildings: A Vocabulary of Modern Architecture*, Thames & Hudson, London 2012.
- Harding, S.: *The Science Question in Feminism.* Cornell University Press, Ithaca 1986.
- Harding, S., & Norberg, K.: 'New Feminist Approaches to Social Science Methodologies: An Introduction', *Signs* 30 (4), 2005, pp. 2009-15.
- Haraway, D.: 'Situated Knowledges: The Science Question in Feminism and the Privilege of Partial Perspectives', *Feminist Studies* 14 (3), 1988, pp. 575-99.
- Hill, J.: *Actions of Architecture: Architects and Creative Users*, Routledge, London 2003.
- Kajita, H.S.: *Fragile potentialer i de store planer – rumlige og materielle dimensioner af efterkrigstidens storskala boligbebyggelser i brug,* PhD thesis, KADK, Copenhagen 2016.
- Lefebvre, H.: *The Production of Space*, Blackwell Publishing, Malden, MA, 2012.
- Lefebvre, H., Kofman, E., & Lebas, E.: *Writing on Cities*, Blackwell Publishers, Oxford 1999.
- Lefebvre, H., Bononno, R., & Smith, N.: *The Urban Revolution*, University of Minnesota Press, Minneapolis, Minn, 2003.
- Lehtovuori, P.: *Experience and Conflict: The Production of Urban Space*, Ashgate, Farnham 2010.
- Nygaard, E.: *Tag over hovedet: dansk boligbyggeri fra 1945 til 1982*, The Danish Architectural Press, Copenhagen 1984.
- Pallasmaa, J.: 'Hapticity and Time: Notes on Fragile Architecture', *The Architectural Review* 1239, 2000, pp. 78-84.
- 'RIBA Plan of Work, 2013' www.architecture.com/Files/RIBAProfessionalServices/Practice/RIBAPlanofWork2013Overview.pdf. Retrieved in September 2014.
- Ramazanoglu, C., & Holland, J.: *Feminist Methodology: Challenges and Choices*, Sage, London [etc.] 2002.
- Shonfield, K.: *Walls Have Feelings: Architecture, Film, and the City*, Routledge, London 2000.
- Solà-Morales, I.: *Differences: Topographies of Contemporary Architecture*, Sarah Whiting (ed.), MIT Press, Cambridge, MA, 1997.
- Thomas, K.L.: 'Specifications: Writing Materials in Architecture and Philosophy', *Architectural Research Quarterly* 8 (3-4), 2004, pp. 277-83.
- Thomas, K.L.: *Material Matters: Architecture and Material Practice*, Routledge, London 2007.
- Thomas, K.L.: 'Building Materials: Conceptualising Materials via the Architectural Specification', PhD thesis, Middlesex University, 2010.

Jannie Rosenberg Bendsen

# A Tale of Danish Architecture

## Nils-Ole Lund's Interpretation of Danish Architecture

All illustrations are from
Nils-Ole Lund,
*Nordic Architecture* (1991).
The Danish Architectural Press.

Danish architecture is often portrayed as being in possession of certain special features that render it possible to speak about a Danish architectural tradition, where a humanistic approach to architecture, paired with a strong link to the development of the welfare society, stands in a central position. On this way of understanding, Danish architecture historiography has made a momentous impact. In this article, light will be shed on how a Danish architectural historian has played a role in bringing about a sharply delineated self-understanding and a sense of professional cohesion among Danish architects.

Among a large number of Danish architects, there seems to be consensus around the notion that Danish architecture builds on certain special values.[1] This implies that Danish buildings are in possession of certain special features that distinguish them from other countries' architecture, and also appears to entail that one can speak about a 'Danish architectural tradition'. One of the most central underlying assumptions about Danish architecture, particularly that of the 20th century, is that it is *humanistic*, that is to say that it has been designed with point of departure in the human being, and not only because many of the buildings are what could be called 'welfare architecture', but just as much because of the way in which the architects have conceived and envisioned the architecture. The notion that there is something especially 'Danish' that exists in Danish architecture comes to be manifested, to a significant degree, in the written narratives about Danish architecture: in the historiography.

In his article, 'Arkitekturhistorien og de aktuelle udfordringer' [Architecture history and current challenges], architect and professor Royston Landau writes that historiography can be regarded in the manner of selective sectional views that come to light whenever an author, furnished with his/her own method and professional angle, writes his/her version of history. These selective sectional views will bring forth tales that have the potential to render visible, to underscore or to generate certain conceptions about the described theme, and in some cases, such a sectional view will come to gain widespread acceptance and might even attain, in generations to come, the status of a shared cultural understanding.[2] This can be said about the historical writing about architecture. Internationally, there has, in recent decades, been a rising interest in relating to architecture-historical texts, as such, rather than focusing only on architecture that has actually been constructed. The interest in the history of architecture as an object of autonomous inquiry comes into manifestation especially distinctly in quite a few analyses of architecture-historical texts about modernism.[3] Modernism's architectural historians like Nikolas Pevsner, Sigfried Giedion and Bruno Zevi are often accused of having concocted stories about modernism's architecture, stories that people today feel neither correspond to reality nor provide a complete picture of modernism's architecture. In addition, modernism's architectural historians have participated in playing decisive roles in formulating the definition and even more especially in framing the general understanding of modernism's architecture. In his book *Histories of the Immediate Present* (2008), Anthony Vidler describes the situation in this way: '[...] histories of modernism themselves were constructed as more or less overt programs for the theory and practice of design in their contemporary context.'[4] And as the book's subtitle, *Inventing Architectural Modernism,* similarly foreshadows, Vidler maintains that the architectural histories about modernism's architecture can be understood as independent programmes, each of which has constructed its own respective histories and theories about modernism's architecture. In such an interpretation, it is accordingly not only the built architecture that plays a part in defining how modernism's architecture can be characterized. Architectural historians, with their narratives and interpretations, are also creating their own way of understanding things, which, on a par with the built architecture, helps to shape posterity's interpretation of and understanding about the architecture. How the author chooses to write his/her architecture history therefore has a decisive influence to bear on how the buildings subsequently will be understood and interpreted by the reader.

In the present article, I will be examining how a Danish architect and architectural historian has played a part in creating a tale where Danish architecture, from the second half of the 20th century, has a close relationship to the development of the welfare state. The article takes its point of departure in a reading of Nils-Ole Lund's (born in 1930) book *Nordisk arkitektur/Nordic architecture* (1991, 1993, 2008), and I will be examining how Lund has composed and written his history of architecture, in order to elucidate which tale about Danish architecture he is shaping.

## About Nils-Ole Lund

Nils-Ole Lund graduated from the Royal Danish Academy of Fine Arts' School of Architecture in 1953. After graduating, he worked in both Norway and Sweden, and from 1965 until 1973, he had his own studio in Norway. In the course of his academic career, he has served as professor at Aarhus School of Architecture, where he was also the rector in the period 1972-85.[5] As an author, Lund has a multi-faceted oeuvre behind him, and mentioning all of the articles, books, and so on, in the present framework would take up far too much space.[6]

What is characteristic of Lund's authorship is that his many years of work as a practising and teaching architect in the Nordic countries are clearly reflected in his body of work. In terms of content, his writing focuses on themes like architectural history, criticism and theory, with a special focus on Nordic architecture from the second half of the 20th century and on what he apprehends as the 'Danish architectural tradition'. In quite a few of his articles and books, he attempts both to define the Danish architectural tradition and to zoom in on how one can speak about commonalities within Nordic architecture without necessarily having to define Nordic architecture, although in several places, he does speak about a 'Nordic architectural tradition'. This is especially apparent in the aforementioned book, *Nordisk arkitektur* (1991).

Nils-Ole Lund's book *Nordisk arkitektur* is, as the title clearly indicates, about Nordic architecture, wherein he aims a special focus on buildings from the latter half of the 20th century. In this present framework, I will not be looking any more closely at his view of Nordic architecture: doing so in the present context would require all too much discussion.[7] Suffice it to say that Lund's view of Nordic architecture is closely connected with how he perceives and characterizes Danish architecture. In what follows, I will, however, be taking a look at how he has composed his architectural history.

## About the book *Nordisk arkitektur*

The book *Nordisk arkitektur/Nordic Architecture* consists of 11 chapters, which are very different from one another, seeing as they treat of various themes, of various national traditions, of various typologies and of architectural theory. The chapters' lengths do not vary all that much, so there is accordingly no explicit weighting of themes or issues.[8] In addition to what he has brought forth in his articles about architecture, Nils-Ole Lund is renowned for his collages, and this book therefore bears the stamp of these, insofar as the images of the architecture being described are typically put together in fine, informative series, which makes it easy to cross-compare developments in the various Nordic countries. The book is copiously illustrated, and in the 2008 edition, the buildings come into their own all the more so with the appearance of new photographs that show the buildings in their very best light. There are more images in colour and, moreover, the pictures are larger than they are in the book's first edition.

NATIONALROMANTIKKEN

*Fra venstre til højre:*
*Edwin Lutyens: Deanery Garden, i Berkshire. 1900–01.*
*Povl Baumann: Raagegaarden, Rågeleje. 1915.*
*F. Konow Lund: Hus ved Godøysund. 1923.*
*F. Boberg: Bergsgården, Stockholm. 1905–06.*
*Gesellius, Lindgren og Saarinen: Hvitträsk, sydfløjen. 1901.*

VERDEN

DANM

NYKLASSICISMEN

*Fra venstre til højre:*
*H. Tessenow: Skitse til rækkehus. 1916.*
*Poul Holsøe: Alderdomsstiftelse for Helsingør kommune. 1918–21.*
*Boligdirektørens kontor v/ Harald Hals: Hegermanns Plass, Oslo, 1919.*
*Wallander og Westholm: Boligbebyggelse, Nybrogatan, Stockholm. 1926–28.*
*Stadsarkitekt Gunnar Taucher: Boligbebyggelse, Mäkelänkatu, Helsinki. 1926.*

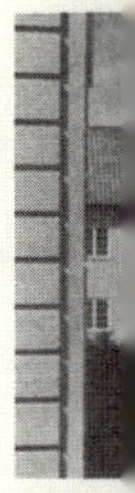

1930'RNE

*Fra venstre til højre:*
*Mies van der Rohe: Boligblok i »Weissenhof-Siedlung«, Stuttgart, 1927*
*Stadsarkitekt Poul Holsøe: Kødbyen, København 1932–34.*
*F. Reppen: Boligbyggeri, Prof. Dahls gate 31–33, Oslo, 1932.*
*N. O. Ahrbom og H. Zimdahl: Högre allmänt läroverk för flickor, Stockholm, 1937.*
*Alvar Aalto: Tuberkulose-sanatorium, 1929–33.*

1940'RNE

*Fra venstre til højre:*
*De Renzi og Muratori: Boligbyggeri, Valco San Paolo, Rom. 1950.*
*Kooperative Arkitekter v/Edv. Heiberg, Ole Buhl, Harald Petersen: Boligbyggeri, Bispeparken, blok V, København. 1940–41.*
*Frode Rinnan, Olav Tveten m. fl. : Lambertseter Sør, Oslo. 1951–62.*
*Backström og Reinius: Boligbyggeri, Gröndal, Stockholm. 1944–46.*
*Yrjö Lindegren: »Slangehuset«, Helsingfors. 1951.*

1950'ERNE

*Fra venstre til højre:*
*Frank Lloyd Wright: Taliesin East, Spring Green, Wisconsin. 1911–41.*
*Jørn Utzon: Enfamiliehus ved Furesøen, Holte. 1953.*
*Knut Knutsen: Sommerhus, Portør. 1948.*
*Ralph Erskine: Skihotel i Borgafjäll. 1948–50.*
*Alvar Aalto: Rådhus i Säynätsalo. 1950–52.*

*NORGE* | *SVERIGE* | *FINLAND*

The book leads off with a general chapter, 'Om det nordiske' [The Nordic]. In addition to this one, there are four chapters, which build upon a theme. These have been chosen to cover the gamut of Lund's perceptions of what the most important architectural ideas and discussions have been in the latter half of the 20th century. In his 1992 article 'Nordisk arkitektur. Refleksioner over bogens sigte og metodeanvendelse' ['Nordic Architecture'. Reflections on the book's aims and methodology], Lund writes that his original intention was that the themes would be selected in such way that each of them would open up for a description running across the national borders.[9] As things would have it, Lund was not able to bring into effect such a consistency in the choice of themes, and he even takes the trouble to point out that there were problems with delving deeply into the respective countries' architecture. Lund was able to solve this quandary by employing a less consistent construction, where he has two chapters on, respectively, 'The Swedish Tradition' and 'The Danish Tradition', one chapter about the Finnish architect Alvar Aalto, one about 'Nordic Housing' and one more that is entitled 'The Architectural Theories of the Period, with Christian Norberg-Schulz as an Example'. Lund's structuring of primary themes entails that a number of repetitions appear in the presentation, as well as a number of overlappings.

The book is most decidedly not a style-historical review of the Nordic countries' architecture. This does not mean to say, however, that Lund refrains entirely from setting the buildings into style-historical categories. He continuously makes use of various *isms* and speaks, for example, about modernism, classicism, Nordic pragmatism (new empiricism) and postmodernism. It seems, however, that the focus is more on analyzing architecture based on formal architectural elements like form, colour, proportioning, scale, ground plan and site plan than it is concerned with style-historical features. Nor do we have before us complete analyses of the buildings: Lund emphasizes only those architectural features of the buildings that have the most significance to bear in relation to the issue being described or to the ideological context within which the building is being situated.

## History of architecture or history of ideas?

An interesting feature about the book is that Nils-Ole Lund does not characterize his own book as a history of architecture but, instead, as a history of ideas.[10] This means to say, according to Lund, that he has not been harbouring any intention to describe and enumerate all the most important buildings in the Nordic region, but has rather had the aim of illuminating the ideas underlying them and the contexts within which they were conceived. Lund touches upon this very aspect and makes the reader aware that going about things in this fashion can potentially result in a glaring lack when it comes to the omission of certain architects and certain buildings. But, once again, his intention has not been to bring forth a fully elaborate presentation of architectural history but rather to examine whatever he finds wide-ranging and exemplary. Lund's architecture history thus does not possess a wide breadth in relation to the presentation of the individual nations' architecture, but it does possess, by way of compensation, a reasonable breadth in relation to the presentation of the Nordic region's architecture. Lund is thus dealing with the period's most important ideas and issues as they manifest themselves in architecture. Buildings and architects are therefore selected not on the basis of a certain criterion about the building being good architecture or on the basis of a certain criterion about the architect being a great artist, but rather by virtue of their capacity to stand forth as *examples* of specific ways of understanding architecture or as architectural illustrations of an ideology. Seeing as Lund clearly points out that he regards his own narrative as a 'history of ideas', the reader can consequently not expect to encounter a chronological or style-historical review of the Nordic region's architecture; this is already expressed very clearly in the table of contents. Lund's own description of his architecture history as a history of ideas is, in some ways, very telling, inasmuch as, in his book, the architecture is set in relation to the contemporaneous architecture-theoretical developments. Lund attempts to find his way towards the underlying idea of a period, a building or a tendency within architecture: In doing so, he offers his reflections on what manner of thinking lies behind the particular building. These ruminations are unfurled especially articulately when Lund sets specific building types in relation to societal discussions and issues. In this vein, I am thinking especially about his treatment of housing, which, according to Lund's line of thought, occupies a very special status in Nordic construction, and especially in the period after the Second World War, when many new homes were built. In his optics, housing should be regarded not only in an aesthetic and architectural context: quite the contrary, he links this residential construction with the Nordic countries' welfare states and consequently with the political developments in the Nordic countries. One example of this is the introduction to the chapter 'Nordic Housing', where Lund writes:

*In the Nordic welfare states housing is a political domain. This means that an attempt is made at political control of the conditions in which the housing project arises. Since World War II housing construction has therefore in many ways been a reflection of the political and economic conditions in the post-war period in the Nordic countries. The differences among the Nordic countries can be explained as variations in the political attempts to control development and differences in the economic preconditions.*[11]

Lund's primary focus is not to explain why residential construction manifests itself aesthetically as it does in the Nordic countries; what he is trying to do, instead, is to explain what influence societal aspects like political initiatives and economic conditions have had to bear on the architectural expressions. On the one hand, he believes that society's development does have a significance to bear on architecture. But then again, the architects have conversely exerted an impact on the welfare state's evolution. This manifests itself quite distinctly in both the architectural expression and the spatial design of the homes. Lund's employment of the historical context implies that architecture, in his reading, is not to be regarded solely as a consequence of architectural discourses but rather as a consequence of societal circumstances and conditions. Architecture is not only aesthetics, it is also ethics.[12]
The problem with Lund's text in this connection is, however, that there are very few clarifying accounts concerning these historic events or conditions, which are not directly a part of architectural discourses. Historic events are often cited: such as the economic crisis that befell the Nordic countries at the end of the 1980s and in the early 1990s, which led to bank failures, unemployment and a downturn in the construction industry. But *how* this event came, in a concrete sense, to make an impact on construction is not explained any further.[13] This simultaneously looms up as a problem when it comes to the references Lund makes to the connections between the societal development in the 1930s and Nordic architecture, where Lund goes so far as to declare that 'the marriage

*1. Axel Dokeberg, Stockholms fastighetsdirektør 1933–45, som sædemand. Karikatur af Nils Melander i Sv. Dagbladet, 1939.*
*2. Bostadsutredningen 1945: Tilberedelse af frikadeller i prøvekøkken i Folkhälsans lokaler, Sverige. Foto: Atelje Wahlberg, Nordiska Museet.*
*3. »Köket«, 1940. Svensk undersøgelse med dårlig og god indretning.*
*4. Bostadsutredningen 1945: Sammenhæng mellem forskellige arbejdspladser i køkkenet.*

1

2

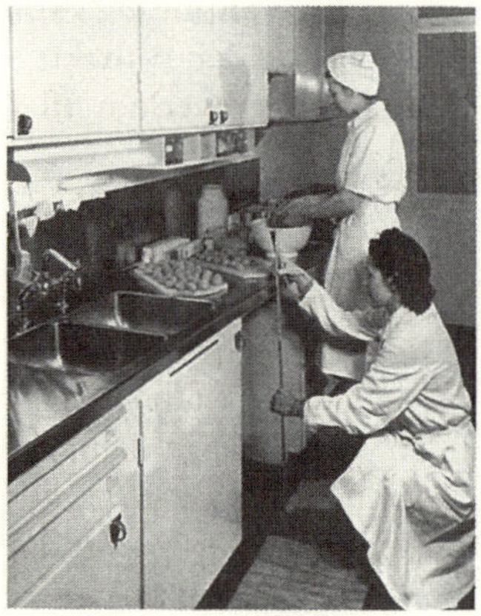

3

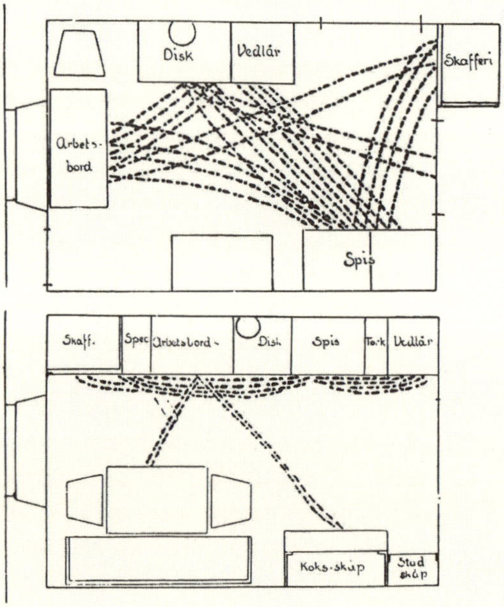


4

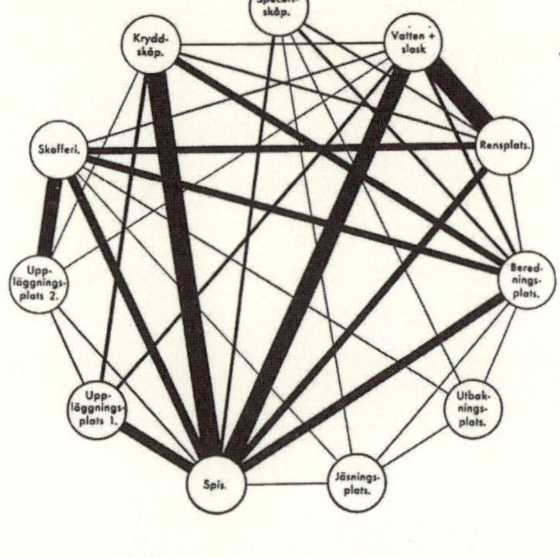

5

Kære Kvinde:
VI VED GODT AT ET SKUR
MED FOR LIDT PLADS
KAN DANNE RAMMEN OM
LYKKE OG HARMONI
MEN
EN GOD BOLIG
LAV ELLER HØJ
ER EN BEDRE RAMME
OM
SÆRLIG HVIS
BOLIG-BEHOVET
FOR
HJEMMEKVINDE OG
UDEKVINDE
DÆKKES
EFTER BEGGES
VILKÅR

I GAMLE DAGE HAVDE
KVINDEN HJÆLP
INDENFOR
FAMILIEN
BEDSTEMØDRE MØDRE
TANTER · KUSINER · DØTRE
HUN SKULLE
OG DET HAVDE HUN
PLADS OG HJÆLP
TIL I SIN BOLIG
HUN HAVDE DOG TID
HENDES BOLIG SVAREDE
TIL HENDES LEVEVIS

6

DU Kære Kvinde
HAR INGEN HJÆLP
HUSASSISTENTER ER
DYRE ELLER FINDES IKKE
DINE DØTRE
GÅR I SKOLE
DINE TANTER LEVER
DERES EGET LIV
OG YDERLIGERE
ER DU SELV · I ET VIST
OMFANG .... BLEVET
U D E KVINDE
PRIVAT
DAB
MEN! Kære Kvinde
DU BOR STADIG · STORT
SET SOM DINE
DET GÅR IKKE

VI SKAL BYGGE
OG DU · Kære Kvinde
MÅ VÆLGE DIN BOLIG
EFTER DIT LEVESÆT

FOR
Hjemmekvinden
F. EKS.
SØGÅRDEN
SORGENFRI VANG
FOR
Udekvinden.
DAB
F. EKS.
SØNDERGÅRDS PARK
HØJE SØBORG

between social commitment and a professional awareness of quality is, I dare say, the most important [aspect] in the Nordic tradition.'[14] His discussion of the societal aspects that have an import to bear on the architectural development is relatively superficial, and where it is exactly that any direct connections can be found is something that Lund fails to specify. For example, he writes: 'In the course of the 1930s, a type of society was built up in the Nordic countries where the government intervened and regulated. [...] The Nordic region had demonstrated that it was possible to transform society, step by step, and that a revolution was not necessary.'[15] Here, Lund could have gone further into *how* the government intervened, and could have delved deeper into what significance – in a more concrete sense – this came to take on for the architecture – and especially with respect to residential construction.[16] The reason that I am of the opinion that it is important to have these items of information included is that we are left to face a situation where the reader either has to possess extensive knowledge about the political developments in the Nordic countries during the period in question or simply has to accept Lund's view of history and architecture at face value. Therefore, it seems paradoxical that Lund actually underscores the societal developments which transpired in the 20th century, along with their influence on architecture in the Nordic countries, while, for his own part, it is only seldom that he explains any further – and seldom that he even tries to explain – the events or the political initiatives' concrete import. I do not mean to say that Lund is out of bounds here. But generally, it can be said that when he links the architecture to the societal development, the discussion remains on what is merely a superficial level, and what is called for, then, is either extensive background knowledge on the part of the reader or the reader's blind faith in the writer, a faith that what Lund is writing is correct. Accordingly, Lund's historiography is, at first glance, characterized by a sense that the author is trying to find his way forward to the underlying idea behind the carefully chosen buildings. In this fashion, he offers his reflections on what manner of thinking lies beneath the building in question. Above and beyond this, he claims that architecture, and especially housing, must not be regarded only as an upshot of the development within architecture's world but rather that architecture is inextricably linked to society and to its development; this is something, however, that he fails to clarify more directly in his text.

## On throwing a specific narrative into relief

One way of getting closer to understanding Lund's historiography and understanding what he writes about Danish architecture is to turn our gaze towards one of the 20th century's great architectural historians, the Italian architect Manfredo Tafuri. In his book *Theories and History of Architecture* (1980) he presents his concept 'Operative Criticism', of which he avails himself in order to criticize several of – chiefly – the 20th century's architectural historians. Tafuri holds that many of modernism's architectural historians, in their history narratives, were shaping the past in a certain way, either by neglecting entirely to write about a certain tendency or by over-emphasizing the use of a specific architectural element. Tafuri's notion of an 'Operative Criticism' thus zooms in and describes a situation where the architectural historian, by throwing certain values and architectural expressions into relief, comes to tell a story that has major flaws. In this way, Tafuri maintains that an author, by constantly insisting that a particular architectural element is continuously turning up in different periods, is telling us that this particular element has a special importance, which is worth working out from in the creation of new architecture. This gives rise to the consequence, however, that the architectural historian ascribes to history and to architecture a specific ideology, an ideology that points in a certain direction. According to Tafuri, the architect's chances to develop a new architecture that can address the issues of the present day are thus being diminished.[17]

If we make use of Tafuri's concept to look more closely at how and what Nils-Ole Lund writes about Danish architecture, we would see that the 'operative' element in Lund's historiography is not that he neglects to mention a good number of Danish buildings that one might reasonably expect would be named. One is almost tempted to write that the author simply has to do this, because the book, as its chief enterprise, is offering a description of Nordic architecture, one where Danish architecture is only one part of the aggregate pool of buildings. Lund also makes the reader aware that it is inevitable that certain buildings are going to missing. Conversely, one, as a reader, needs to address him/herself to the fact that an essential part of the book's content is Lund's narrative about 'the Danish architectural tradition'. And it is precisely in the description of this that one finds something which calls an 'operative element' to mind.

As one example of how Lund describes Danish architecture, the following quote is very telling:

[...] *Danish architecture is best explained as an institution with a given tradition. More than in most other countries, Danish architecture is influenced by a particular set of values. The members of an institution share certain values and give more consideration to internal opinions than to the views that come from the outside. The institution is not a closed or fossilized community. Others parties to the construction influence the institution, and it is constantly in flux, not least because developments force it to adapt. The values that keep the institution together change only slowly in a dialogue between the parties. The result is that the members of the institution are more or less in agreement on what is beautiful and what is ugly, what is right and what is wrong, what is important and what is less important.*

*If new impulses come from the outside, impulses that threaten to change the shared values, the institution acts as a moderator. The new is trimmed and polished so it can be accepted. One could also liken the institution to a filter that sieves the foreign bodies out.*[18]

According to Lund, Danish architecture is characterized, in the first instance, by a particular set of values, and secondly, this set of values elicits the effect that new impulses are translated and reworked so that they can be adapted to Danish conditions. As Lund expounds it in his architectural history, the presence of this set of values has exerted a decisive influence on how Danish architecture appears. And this elicits the consequence that Danish architecture in the 20th century can be split into different styles or movements: like neoclassicism, national romanticism, and functionalism. But it is only on the surface – in the architectural expression – that the changes are occurring: fundamentally, the values underlying the various buildings are the same. Here, it is important to underscore that Lund's set of values does not directly have anything to do with architectural motifs and expression. The values that he is talking about rather have something to do with a specific way of working and thinking: the architects' approach to creating architecture.

In this context, it is interesting to examine how Lund manages to put more words on this specifi-

1

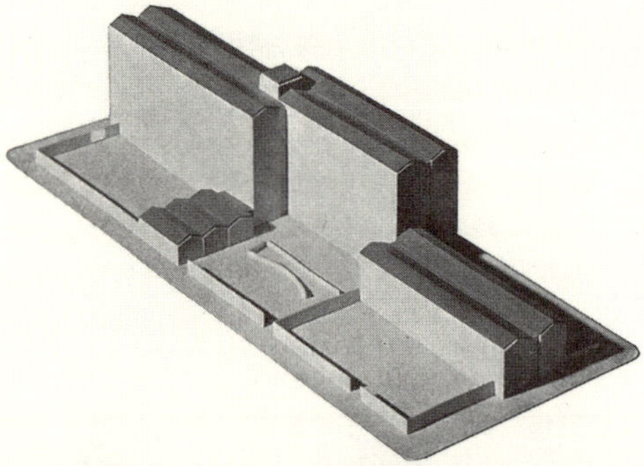

*Kay Fisker: Den danske pavillon, Verdensudstillingen i Paris. 1925.*

2

3

4

5

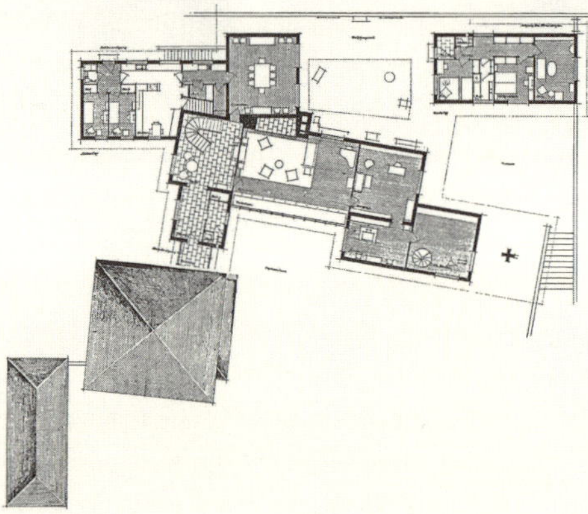

*1, 2. Kay Fisker: Mødrehjælpens bygning, Østerbro, København. 1953–54. Model og facade mod Strandboulevarden.*
*3. Kay Fisker: Voldparkens skole, Husum, København. 1952–56.*
*4. Kay Fisker: Boligbebyggelse, Hansaviertel, Berlin. 1957–58. Opført i forbindelse med den internationale byggeudstilling Interbau.*
*5, 6. Kay Fisker: Om- og tilbygning til Højstrup, Strandvejen, København. 1946. Projekt.*

6

cally Danish ethos. Doing this, he holds, is something that can be done by analyzing what he calls 'the value judgments' that are pronounced upon the Danish buildings. In his article 'Nordisk Arkitektur. Refleksioner over bogens sigte og metodeanvendelse' [Nordic Architecture. Reflections on the book's aims and methodology], Lund writes:

*'I have therefore noticed that the terms used in the specialized literature, whenever a building is to be lauded or condemned, seem to be unaffected by the period or by current-day usage. In Danish architecture, words like 'straightforward', 'simple', 'moderate', 'orderly', 'logical', 'rational', 'genuine', 'clear', 'precise' and 'harmonious' signal virtues that are not specifically targeted towards the architectural world of form but that rather serve to characterize the architectural attitude, the ethics.'*[19]

There are very few spots in *Nordisk arkitektur* where Lund actually establishes any direct links to what he believes characterizes Danish architecture. Instead, Lund makes use of other strategies in order to encircle what he apprehends about the set of values underlying Danish architecture. Initially, he makes use of other people's understanding of Danish architecture. Among other things, he takes a closer look at foreign reviews of architecture exhibitions featuring Danish architecture, which he takes for granted without placing any question marks beside their interpretations of Danish architecture. Moreover, he avails himself of what other Danish architects have written.

Altogether crucial, in this connection, is the Danish architect Kay Fisker, who plays a central role in Lund's way of identify and subsequently characterizing the Danish set of values. There are especially two articles by Fisker that are used in this connection: 'Den funktionelle tradition. Spredte indtryk af amerikansk arkitektur' [The functional tradition. Scattered impressions of American architecture] (1950) and 'Persondyrkelse eller anonymitet' [Person cult or anonymity] (1964). Lund's grip here is altogether elegant: rather than actually analyzing a number of Danish buildings and then, on this basis, describing and demonstrating the different values that characterize them, he allows, first and foremost, foreign architecture critics and other Danish architects to be those who put words on the Danish values, even if one must not be blind to the fact that Lund, as the author, has ultimately selected the comments that are being used as arguments, and which he then reproduces. Above and beyond this, the attached comments are linked with the selected buildings, which constitute only one specific and carefully selected assortment of Danish architecture. His own motivation for this approach is that he does not want to indulge in self-overvaluation or self-glorification, or to take recourse in a national pathos, which there would always be a tendency to do whenever one goes about identifying the 'typically Danish', as he calls it: but in reality, Lund does not manage entirely to avoid this, either, precisely on account of the selection process that he has carried out.[20]

What I mean to say with all this is that one can characterize Lund's architecture historiography by an 'operative' element, since he speaks about Danish architecture against a backdrop of an entire series of concepts that he discovers by looking more closely at what a chosen troupe of foreign critics and Danish architects has written about Danish architecture. This results in a cogent tale about Danish architecture, which still plays a crucial role in how Danish architecture is spoken about and how Danish architecture is written about.

## Closing reflections on Lund's tale of Danish architecture

As we saw above, in Lund's narrative about Danish architecture, there are two central factors that come into play when he goes about determining what it is that characterizes Danish architecture.

Lund claims that there is a set of values that has its roots in a Danish culture. The set of values is, for one thing, formed by the particular geographical conditions that characterize the Danish landscape, and for another, formed by continual changes in the history of the Danes' mentality, which might be of political, economic or ideological character. Moreover, the set of values, in Lund's optics, is characterized as running *pari passu* with history and reveals more about architecture's ethics than it does about its aesthetics. The similarities among Danish buildings from different periods therefore do not manifest themselves in the manner of some uniform kind of architectural idiom. On the contrary, architecture, on the surface, can appear in a particularly varied way, depending on, for example, the prevailing style. The similarities are therefore to be found, instead, in the values underlying the architecture. The values tell us something about how Danish architects work, think and practise architecture. What this means to say is that there is a strong correlation between Danish architecture and the more general developments in society. Lund claims that it is possible to spot a connection between the development of the welfare state and the architectural manifestations of the 20th century. He accordingly establishes a narrative that Danish architecture develops in parallel with the welfare state. What is characteristic of Danish architectural history is that its 20th-century architectural history can largely be written on the basis of the ordinary housing, and Lund delineates a picture of a Danish architectural tradition wherein he states, again and again, that Danish architecture has more to do with ethics than it does with aesthetics. Architecture is thus not merely a consequence of architectural discourses but also a consequence of societal conditions and circumstances.

The second essential factor in Lund's assessment is that Danish architecture cannot be seen as a special, demarcated institution, but must rather be apprehended as a result of an interaction between specifically Danish factors and whatever is happening on an international level: it is especially European and American architecture that have given Danish architects impulses to work with. These impulses from abroad are not received in an unconditional or uncritical way, but become reworked and adapted to Danish conditions. The critical attitude and use of foreign impulses is rooted, in Lund's optics, in the existence of the Danish set of values and fosters an architecture that can be exported to countries abroad as something specifically 'Danish'. In Lund's interpretation, the element of originality in Danish architecture consists, quite precisely, in this translation process.

In his architectural history, Lund delineates a picture of a Danish architectural tradition, which has been influenced to a great extent by a particular set of values. Especially in the 20th century, but also in the 21st century, this set of values has borne a great deal of importance for the Danish architects, and I would argue that it has played a role in giving rise to a strong self-understanding among Danish architects and to a notion of professional solidarity.[21] Similarly, one can argue that Lund's narrative about Danish architecture has fashioned a background for practising architects, for better or for worse,[22] even if this has not necessarily transpired consciously, but has more likely made its effect unconsciously. I would not claim that Lund's description of Danish architecture is incorrect or presumably misleading. On the contrary. The architecture histories that have been written about Danish architecture have exerted a major influence on their readers' and thereby also on the architect trade's own understanding about Danish architecture. I could cite many examples of the re-telling of Lund's tale,[23] but here and now, I would like to throw into relief the Danish contribution to the Venice Biennale in 2016, where the curators were trying to come up with what they call 'a snapshot of a new humanism in Danish architecture'. They claim that it is, quite precisely, a humanistic approach to architecture that is a core concept in Danish architecture, where the architects are working to renew the Danish tradition of thinking and building societies and societal institutions that focus on human beings.[24]

1

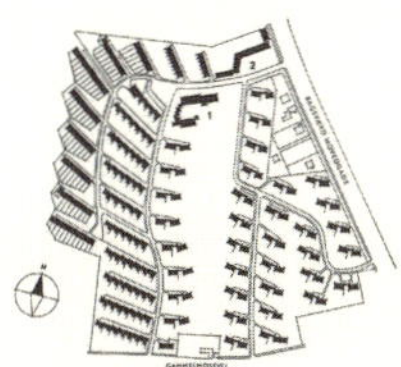

2

3

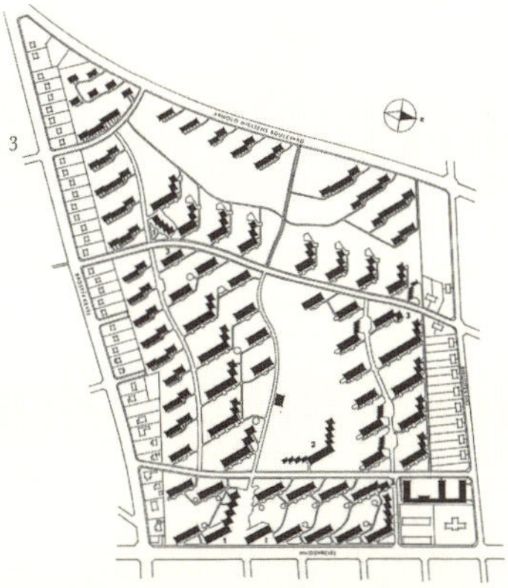

4

5

6

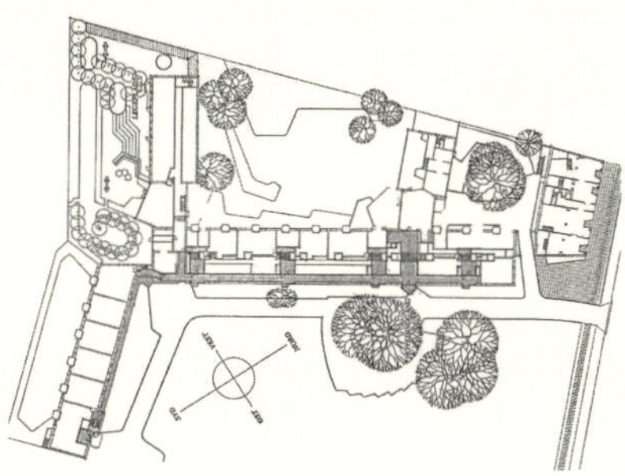

*1, 2. Hoff og Windinge: Søndergård Park, Gladsaxe, København. 1949–50. Plan 1:10.000, børneinstitutioner (1) og butikker (2). Foto: Strüwing.*
*3, 4. Eske Kristensen: Bredalsparken, Hvidovre, København. 1949–54. Plan 1:10.000, butikker (1), børneinstitutioner (2) og varmecentral (3). Foto: Strüwing.*
*5, 6. Hoff og Windinge: Kollektivhus i Høje Søborg, Gladsaxe, København. 1951. Stueplan 1:1800. Foto: Strüwing. Fælleslokalerne lå i en enetagers sidebygning, boligerne i en 5 etagers ejendom.*

In his review of the exhibition, the architecture critic Karsten Ifversen wrote the following:

*The* [exhibition] *shows that under all of the different turns and twists when it comes to style and methodology in Danish architecture, there is an undercurrent of consensus, which rests on social equity, openness and community. It is the welfare state, which has saturated the DNA at all Danish drafting offices, and which recurs when Schmidt Hammer Lassen design libraries and public spaces in China, and when BIG design coastal protection in New York as a park area full of public recreational opportunities.*[25]

The presentations of Danish architecture in the architecture histories have thus played a part in shaping posterity's perception of Danish architecture, and one must not be blind to the fact that architectural historiography can exert a crucial influence on the reader's understanding of Danish architecture. What I am thinking about here is that the compelling history of Danish architecture has actually given rise to the upshot that certain Danish architects and certain currents of activity have not been afforded a particularly prominent place in the historiography and subsequently in our consciousness. And perhaps an awareness and a knowledge about these architects, and/or about these currents of activity, might have been able to play a part in furthering Danish architecture in several directions, or, in any case, they might very well have been able to play a role in widening our gaze on Danish architecture.

**Notes**

1 The concept, 'Danish architecture', turns up in many different contexts and can have different meanings: ranging from covering everything that is built in Denmark, that is to say, a descriptive, geographical designation, to characterizing architecture and certain buildings as manifestations of something especially or typical 'Danish'.

2 R. Landau, 'Arkitekturhistorien og de aktuelle udfordringer' in K. Dirckinck-Holmfeld, E. Nygaard and J.H. Christiansen (eds.): *At fortælle arkitektur. Et festskrift til Nils-Ole Lund* (2000), p. 100. See also my article: 'En fortælling om enkelhed. Om Tobias Fabers arkitekturhistorieskrivning', 2016 KADK.

3 The present article builds on my PhD thesis, *Enkelhed, mådehold og funktionalitet – en analyse af fremtrædende danske arkitekters udlægninger af dansk arkitektur* (2009), University of Copenhagen, which is based on close readings of important Danish texts about Danish architecture. For examples of the interest taken in architectural historiography, see the thesis, pp. 7-12.

4 A. Vidler: *Histories of the Immediate Present* (2008), p. 1.

5 S. Hartmann (ed.): *Weilbach, Dansk Kunstnerleksikon, femte bind Hans W. Larsen – C.F. Møller* (1995), p. 182.

6 For a more complete overview of Lund's authorship up until 1998, see K. Dirckinck-Holmfeld, E. Nygaard & J.H. Christiansen (editors): *At fortælle arkitektur. Et festskrift til Nils-Ole Lund* (2000), p. 260.

7 See, instead, the aforementioned thesis, pp. 138-88.

8 Most of the chapters have a length of around 30 pages.

9 N.-O. Lund: 'Nordisk arkitektur. Refleksioner over bogens sigte og metodeanvendelse' (1992), p. 51.

10 Whether or not this is the correct designation for the book, I will choose to leave unanswered in the present context. However, I would mention, in any case, that this calls for a longer discussion about what a history of architecture ought to be.

11 N.-O. Lund: *Nordisk arkitektur* (1991), English edition: *Nordic Architecture* (2008), translation James Manley, p. 245.

12 At the conference, 'Architectural History: Between History and Archaeology?', one of the central themes was that, notwithstanding the fact that architecture is the cultural object that is most directly linked with political and social history, there is seldom any research into architecture history outside of the aesthetic profession. What this entails is that architecture history is most often viewed as an aesthetic field where the societal implications are overlooked or underplayed. Lund's way of calling attention to the societal circumstances' impact on the architectural development and, on the whole, to the coupling between these comes, in such a context, to take shape as an incredibly important contribution in the attempt to write

architecture history from a different vantage point than the purely aesthetic. D. Arnold, et al. (eds.): *Rethinking Architectural Historiography* (2006), p. xvii.

**13** Lund (1991/2008), op.cit., p. 276.

**14** Ibid., p. 17.

**15** Ibid., p. 22.

**16** For example, after the Second World War, people in Denmark concentrated on three areas that were oriented around a genuinely inclusive construction and housing policy: regulation of rental costs; more efficient use of the existing housing stock and housing-subsidy benefits. It is especially the latter-named point in the legislation that is often assessed as having made a particular impact. This point involves governmental loans to residential construction that were extended at favourable interest rates. In addition to the low interest rates, the building owners could receive out-and-out governmental subsidies corresponding to somewhere between 10 and 24% of the construction's total costs. M.L. Larsen & T.R. Larsen: *I medgang og modgang. Dansk byggeri og den danske velfærdsstat 1945-2007* (2007), pp. 13-14.

**17** M. Tafuri: *Theories and History of Architecture* (1980), pp. 141-153.

**18** Lund (1991/2008), p. 85.

**19** N.-O. Lund: 'Nordisk arkitektur. Refleksioner over bogens sigte og metodeanvendelse' (1992), p. 48.

**20** N.-O. Lund: 'Den danske egenart' (1986), p. 64.

**21** Some critics would argue, however, that this sense of solidarity and shared conceptions helped to weaken Danish architecture in the latter part of the 20th century. Conversely, the contrary can also be claimed.

**22** Along with a number of other prominent Danish architects, who also made contributions to the ongoing narrative of Danish architecture, I am thinking here especially of Tobias Faber, Kay Fisker and Steen Eiler Rasmussen. I have accordingly addressed myself to focusing on these architects in the aforementioned thesis.

**23** See also my PhD thesis.

**24** www.arkitektforeningen.dk/artikel/nyheder/130-danske-projekter-valgt-til-venedigbiennalen-2016 and www.dac.dk/da/dac-life/udstillinger/2016/biennale2016/.

**25** K. Ifversen: 'En fælles bund af humanisme i den danske pavillon', *Politiken,* May 28, 2016.

**Literature**


- Bendsen, J.R.: *Enkelhed, mådehold og funktionalitet – en analyse af fremtrædende danske arkitekters udlægninger af dansk arkitektur*, University of Copenhagen 2009.
- Bendsen, J.R.: 'En fortælling om enkelhed. Om Tobias Fabers arkitekturhistorieskrivning', article based on a discussion paper presented at the seminar 'Mellem huse og ord' at KADK in March 2015, published 2017.
- Fisker, K.: 'Den funktionelle tradition – Spredte indtryk af amerikansk arkitektur' in *Arkitekten Månedshæfte* nos. 5-6, 1950, pp. 69-100.
- Fisker, K.: 'Persondyrkelse eller anonymitet'. *Arkitekten,* no. 26, 1964, pp. 522-526.
- Hartmann, S. (ed.): *Weilbach. Dansk Kunstnerleksikon. Femte bind. Hans W. Larsen – C.F. Møller.* Munksgaard. Rosinante, Copenhagen 1995, pp. 182-83.
- Ifversen, K.: 'En fælles bund af humanisme i den danske pavillon', *Politiken* May 28, 2016. Retrieved August 20, 2016.
- Landau, R.: 'Arkitekturhistorien og de aktuelle udfordringer'. K. Dirckinck-Holmfeld, E. Nygaard and J.H. Christiansen (eds.): *At fortælle arkitektur. Et festskrift til Nils-Ole Lund.* The Danish Architectural Press, Copenhagen 2000, pp. 100-11.
- Larsen, M.L. and Larsen, T.R.: *I medgang og modgang. Dansk byggeri og den danske velfærdsstat 1945-2007.* Byggecentrum, Copenhagen 2007.
- Lund, N.-O.: 'Den danske tradition – et forsøg på en definition' i *Arkitektur DK*, nos. 1-2, 1985, pp. 3-85.
- Lund, N.-O.: *Den danske egenart*. Exhibition catalogue, Danish Architecture Centre, Gammel Dok, Copenhagen 1986, pp. 64-70.
- Lund, N.-O.: *Nordisk arkitektur.* The Danish Architectural Press, Copenhagen 1991 (1993, 2008).
- Lund, N.-O.: 'Nordisk arkitektur. Refleksioner over bogens sigte og metodeanvendelse' in *Nordisk arkitekturforskning,* 1992:2, pp. 47-52.
- Tafuri, M.: *Theories and History of Architecture.* Granada Publishing Limited, London 1980 (translated from Italian: *Teorie e storia dell'architettura.* Laterza, Rome 1968).
- Vidler, A.: *Histories of the Immediate Present. Inventing Architectural Modernism.* MIT Press, Cambridge, MA, London, England 2008.
- Watkin, D.: *The Rise of Architectural History.* The Architectural Press, London 1980.
- www.arkitektforeningen.dk/artikel/nyheder/130-danske-projekter-valgt-til-venedigbiennalen-2016. Retrieved/Visited on August 21, 2016.
- www.dac.dk/da/dac-life/udstillinger/2016/biennale2016/. Retrieved/Visited on August 21, 2016.

## Authors

**Katrine Lotz** (b. 1964) is an architect, PhD and currently associate professor and head of Institute for Architecture, Urbanism and Landscape at the Royal Danish Academy of Fine Arts, School of Architecture. Her research takes a broad look at how the specific skills of architects are deployed. Since 2010, she has primarily focused on the relationship between architecture, architects and the development of the Scandinavian welfare societies. Katrine co-initiated the project 'Forming Welfare', the conference by the same name and the associated inter-Scandinavian Network for Architecture and Welfare. She is also part of the trans-disciplinary research project 'Spaces of Danish Welfare', which received support from the Danish Council for Independent Research in 2016.

**Jesper Pagh** (b. 1977), who qualified as an architect from the Royal Danish Academy of Fine Arts, School of Architecture in 2002, is CEO of the Danish Association of Architects. His research focuses on architects' contribution to the development of the welfare state, from the post-war period to the present. His main interest is the development of the framework conditions for architecture, seen in conjunction with the way that architecture affects our social relations, and how this can be understood in a historical context.

**Ellen Marie Braae** (b. 1965) is an architect and landscape architect with a PhD in urbanism and heritage issues. She is also a professor of landscape architectural theory and methodology at the University of Copenhagen, where she researches the preservation and development of urban landscapes.

**Rosalina Wenningsted-Torgard** (b. 1979) is a qualified architect from the Royal Danish Academy of Fine Arts, School of Architecture. She is currently a PhD fellow at the University of Copenhagen, Department of Geosciences and Natural Resource Management, Landscape Architecture and Planning. Her area of research is landscape architecture and urbanism and climate adaptation of cities.

**Tomas Wikström** (b. 1949) is an architect and researcher, a former professor at the School of Architecture, Lund University and since July 2010 adjunct professor at the Department of Urban Studies at Malmö University. In the broadest sense, his research concerns people's opportunities to animate and shape the spaces that constitute their lifeworld. His understanding of human space is influenced by continental phenomenology: Space is continuously (re)created by means of daily human activity. More concretely, his research deals with the intermediate zones of suburbs, where the user's contribution is evident; the mobile phone as a tool for daily coordination in fragmented urban landscapes.

**Kirsten Birk Hansen** (b. 1940) is an architect and former assistant/associate professor at the Aarhus School of Architecture. For a period in the late 60s, she worked as an architect in Greenland. She has also designed minor projects such as Red Cross kindergartens, communal houses etc. for Architect Leif Damgaard. On top of that, she has been employed at Karen and Ebbe Clemmensen's and Henning Larsen's offices, respectively. A former research fellow on criticisms of functionalism, she has since elaborated that topic in several articles. She has moreover contributed to and co-edited the journals *BLØD BY* and *SKALA*, focusing on subjects such as women in architecture and sustainability.

**Jens Kvorning** (b. 1946) is professor of urbanism at the Royal Danish Academy of Fine Arts, School of Architecture. For a number of years, he has been head of the school's urban planning programme as well as the related research at Centre for Urban Planning. Since the restructuring, Jens Kvorning has also been responsible for the school's master programme in Strategic Urban Planning. His own research focuses on urban regeneration, i.e. the processes that impact and transform the cities, as well as the strategies and plans which cities rely on to accommodate the change in circumstances. As part of this, studies have been made of regeneration efforts in European cities and localities within the Danish capital region. The past few years, he have taken a special interest in suburbia and associated issues and problematics.

**Jørgen Møller** (1949-2017) was trained at the Aarhus School of Architecture, Department of Physical and Economic Planning. Since 1986, he worked as a lecturer in municipal planning at Aalborg University. Jørgen Møller taught and researched planning systems, planning history, planning legislation and urban history. The past 10-12 years saw him specialize in rural marginalization, with particular emphasis on 'turn around planning', Decline Management and village clusters. Jørgen was moreover a keen debater on the challenges of peripheral Denmark.

**Deane Simpson** (b. 1971) was educated as an architect and urbanist at Columbia University in New York and ETH Zurich. He is now an associate professor at KADK and co-head of the programme Urbanism and Societal Change. His research addresses contemporary architectural and urban issues of fields such as demographic change, securitization, liveability, sustainability and welfare. He is the author of *Young-Old*, and co-editor of *The City between Freedom and Security.*

**Kirsten Marie Raahauge** (b. 1962) has an MSc and a PhD in anthropology and is currently an associate professor at the Royal Danish Academy of Fine Arts, Schools of Architecture and Design. She is interested in the relationship between people and their spatial surroundings. Her research concerns Inca spatial perception, Danish cities, squares and neighbourhoods, homes in Denmark and haunted houses in Denmark. Her next research venture, under the project 'Spaces of Danish Welfare', concerns the spaces of welfare and peripheral Denmark, with fieldwork in Tønder.

**Peter Thule Kristensen** (b. 1966) is an architect, Dphil, PhD and head of Institute of Architecture and Culture at the Royal Danish Academy of Fine Arts, School of Architecture. His research revolves around the field of architectural history, which he often places within a political context. He is the author/editor of several articles and books, notably the monograph and doctoral thesis *Gottlieb Bindesbøll – Denmark's First Modern Architect* from 2013. He is currently writing a monograph on the architect Svenn Eske Kristensen (1905-2000), who contributed significantly to the development of the Danish welfare state.

**Loa Kristine Teglgaard Christensen** (b. 1982) is an anthropologist and PhD fellow at the Department of Anthropology and Center for Healthy Aging at the University of Copenhagen. She studies cultural understandings of aging, and in her present research project she focuses on the rehabilitation of the municipal eldercare in Denmark.

**Camilla Hedegaard Møller** (b. 1974), is an architect MAA, MDL, a PhD and is working as a postdoctoral fellow at the Royal Danish Academy of Fine Arts, School of Architecture where she researches into architectural practices, method development and urban landscape architecture.

**Kjeld Vindum** (b. 1950) is an architect and associate professor at the Royal Danish Academy of Fine Arts, School of Architecture. Together with Mette Jerl Jensen, he is responsible for the school's bachelor programme. Kjeld's field of research is architectural history, criticism and theory. He is the author of the books *Arne Jacobsen* (with Carsten Thau) from 1998 (English edition 2001, German edition 2002) and *The New Wave in Danish Architecture* (with Kristoffer L. Weiss) from 2012.

**Mette Jerl Jensen** (b. 1963) is an architect, PhD and associate professor at the Royal Danish Academy of Fine Arts, School of Architecture. Together with Kjeld Vindum, she is responsible for the school's bachelor programme. Mette's research focuses on architectural materials and their processes. She is the author of several books, among them *Revitalization of the Masonry Wall* (KADK, 2012) and *Mur Sten* (KADK, 2008).

**Maja de Neergaard** (b. 1978) is an assistant professor at the Department of People and Technology at Roskilde University, Denmark. Her research interests are theories of practice, the interstices between human and non-human, nature, materiality and architecture, ethnographic writing and philosophy of geography. Maja is currently engaged in the project 'Paradoxical Spaces: Encountering the Other in public space', which explores cross-cultural encounters in Copenhagen.

**Marie Stender** (b. 1978) is an anthropologist and researcher at the Danish Building Research Institute. Her main field of research is the relationship between architecture and everyday life, and how the built environment interacts with social and cultural dynamics. She has also focused on the demarcations between public and private space, the community, identity and branding in new residential areas, as well as the segmentation of city enclaves and change processes in disadvantaged areas.

**Masashi Kajita** (b. 1974) is an MA with a PhD in Architecture. He is currently an assistant professor at the Royal Danish Academy of Fine Arts, School of Architecture. He is also co-founder of Bureaus, a platform for spatial research, design and strategies. He researches, teaches, designs and consults with the aim of promoting the realization of inclusive environments and an architecture of enjoyment. A current and related series of design research projects revolves around environmental accessibility and spatial inclusiveness through discourse on body, material environment and architectural space.

**Heidi Jacobsgaard Schøbel** (b. 1986) qualified as an architect from the Royal Danish Academy of Fine Arts, School of Architecture with 'Eutopia' – a project that rethinks the welfare institutions' design and organization in order to promote meetings between generations. Heidi works at KHR Architecture where she specializes in architectural and strategic development, focusing on architecture driven by visions.

**Heidi Svenningsen Kajita** (b. 1975) has a diploma in Architecture (Dist.) from 2001 and a PhD in architecture from 2016. She is currently a teaching associate professor at the Royal Danish Academy of Fine Arts, School of Architecture and a lecturer at Umeå School of Architecture. She is also co-founder of *Bureaus*, a platform for spatial research, design and strategies. Her research focuses on architecture and the everyday and use/the user within architectural practice and -concepts explored in the contexts of the public realm and large-scale housing studies.

**Jannie Rosenberg Bendsen** (b. 1976) has an MA in Modern Culture and Cultural Communication. She is also a PhD from University of Copenhagen's Department of Art and Culture Studies with a thesis on Danish architectural historiography. Jannie has been employed at the Agency for Culture and Palaces but is now attached to the Aarhus School of Architecture. Her main research interest is architectural history, a topic on which she has written several books and articles, with emphasis on 20th-century Danish architecture.

# Index

**Forming Welfare**

Edited by Jannie Rosenberg Bendsen,
Mette Jerl Jensen, Katrine Lotz,
Kirsten Marie Raahauge, Deane Alan Simpson
and Kjeld Vindum
Production management: Jannie Rosenberg Bendsen
Graphic design: Michael Jensen
Translated from Danish by Dan Marmorstein
except the articles by Katrine Lotz
and Tomas Wikström which were translated
by Cornelius Holck Colding
The articles by Deane Alan Simpson
and Masashi Kajita were written in English
Print: Narayana Press, Gylling

Published by The Danish Architectural Press
1. edition
Printed in Denmark 2017
ISBN 978-87-7407-434-2

Published with support from:
Realdania & KADK